The Great Repair

Practices of Interstitial Change

Praktiken des interstitiellen Wandels

DE

The Great Repair ist ein Oxymoron. Im Titel treffen zwei scheinbar gegensätzliche Prinzipien aufeinander: Die revolutionäre Ambition des radikalen Systemwechsels, ein Wesensmerkmal großer Lösungen, kollidiert mit dem evolutionären Akt der Reparatur. Denn trotz aller berechtigter (postmoderner) Skepsis gegenüber der Revolution als Denkfigur des Bruches dürfen wir den Anspruch auf tiefgreifende Veränderungen nicht aufgeben. Ähnlich formuliert es die Philosophin Eva von Redecker in dieser Ausgabe:

> Wir stehen gegenwärtig vor einem so immensen Transformationsbedarf, dass es geradezu absurd wäre, den Maximalbegriff für Wandel auszuklammern, den wir in unserem politischen Vokabular haben. Dann ist die Frage, wie man ihn füllt. Ich verstehe Revolution tatsächlich viel weniger als Bruch und mehr als interstitiellen Wandel, also als Wandel, der über die und aus den Zwischenräumen des Alten heraus das Neue schafft.[1]

An diesen brüchigen Zwischenräumen im Bestehenden kann die Reparatur beginnen. Mit diesem Verständnis von Revolution als „Prozesse des sukzessiven Austauschs“ von „Ankerpraktiken“[2] bietet Eva von Redecker zudem einen praxisorientierten Ansatz für Wandel an.

Aus dieser Perspektive geht es bei gesellschaftlichen Transformationen nicht in erster Linie um die Abschaffung einer sozialen Ordnung, sondern auch und vor allem um den Austausch ihrer sozialen Praktiken. Der Umbau einer Gesellschaft kann so nur im Wechselverhältnis der Veränderungen ihrer Politiken und Praktiken begriffen werden.[3] Denn soziale Ordnungen sind keine abstrakten Setzungen. Sie müssen fortwährend in der Praxis hervorgebracht und reproduziert werden. Diesen Nexus bringen die beiden sich ergänzenden Ausgaben *The Great Repair – Politiken der Reparaturgesellschaft* und *The Great Repair – Praktiken der Reparatur* zum Ausdruck. Sie sind explizit nicht als Trennung von Theorie und Praxis zu verstehen. So wie Praktiken den Kontext von sozialen Ordnungen und soziale Ordnungen den Kontext von Praktiken bilden,[4] spiegeln die beiden Ausgaben den „Kontext“ des jeweils anderen Feldes wider.

Doch nicht nur soziale Ordnungen und Praktiken sind untrennbar verbunden, auch die Praktiken selbst existieren nicht isoliert, sondern sind stets mit anderen verknüpft. In diesem Sinne haben wir auch die vorliegende Ausgabe, die als Katalog zur gleichnamigen Ausstellung in der Akademie der Künste in Berlin dient, nach sich gegenseitig bedingenden Praktiken organisiert. Die Grundfrage lautete, um mit Eva von Redecker zu sprechen, welche „Ankerpraktiken“ ausgetauscht werden müssten, damit wir nicht nur einen Missstand fixen, sondern das System reparieren können.

Das vorherrschende Narrativ einer grünen, wachstumsorientierten Transformation verspricht, die Klima- und Ressourcenkrise allein mithilfe technologischer Innovation in den Griff zu bekommen. Solche Visionen mit ihrem Effizienz- und Konsistenzversprechen sind im Grunde Technofixes, die das extraktive Paradigma nicht überwinden. Es sei denn, das produktive System ist in der Lage, alle Material- und Energiekreisläufe zu schließen, was unter den heutigen technologischen Bedingungen undenkbar ist. Es hat sich nämlich gezeigt, dass die verschiedenen „smarten“ Lösungen oft gut mit unterschiedlichen Formen des staatlichen und

EN

“The Great Repair” is an oxymoron. The title captures the convergence of two seemingly contradictory principles: the revolutionary ambition for systemic change and the evolutionary act of repair. Despite the justified (postmodern) skepticism toward revolution as a concept of rupture, we must not abandon our aspiration to bring about profound transformation. The philosopher Eva von Redecker formulates this thought along similar lines in this issue:

> We face such an enormous need for transformation that it would be downright absurd to disregard the most radical term for change that we have in our political vocabulary. The question is how to fill it with meaning. I understand revolution less as a break and more as an interstitial change, a change that creates the new *through and out of* the in-between spaces of the old.[1]

At such interstices in the existing fabric—this is where repair can begin. Moreover, understanding revolution in this way, as “processes of successive replacement” of “anchor practices,” Eva von Redecker offers an approach to change that is oriented toward practice.[2]

From this perspective, societal transformation is not primarily about the abolition of a social order, but also—and above anything else—the replacement of its social practices. The transformation of a society can thus only be understood in the interrelationship of changes made to its politics and practices.[3] This is because social orders are far from abstract formations. They must continually be produced and reproduced through practice. This nexus is expressed in the two complementary *ARCH+* issues *The Great Repair: Politics for the Repair Society* and *The Great Repair: A Catalog of Practices*. This complementarity should not be understood as an attempt to separate theory from practice. Just as practices create the context for social orders, and social orders create the context for practices, each of these two issues reflects the “context” of the corresponding field.[4]

While social orders and practices are inextricably linked, it is important to note that practices themselves do not exist in isolation; they are always bound up with other practices. With this in mind, we have organized this issue, which also serves as a catalog for an exhibition of the same name at the Akademie der Künste in Berlin, according to mutually dependent practices. Our fundamental question is, to paraphrase Eva von Redecker, which “anchor practices” need to be replaced, not just to fix specific deficits, but to repair the entire system?

The prevailing narrative of a green, growth-oriented process of transformation promises to solve our climate and resource crises exclusively through technological innovation. However, visions of this sort, despite their claims of consistency and efficiency, amount to little more than “techno-fixes” that fail to move beyond the extractive paradigm—unless the productive system can completely close all existing material and energy loops, which seems unfeasible given today’s technological constraints. In fact, many of the various “smart” solutions have proven to be very compatible with various forms of state and corporate conservatism. Within architecture, in any case, the techno-fix narrative entails tearing down existing buildings and replacing them with new ones that are only ostensibly sustainable. In the process, enormous amounts of gray energy (to say nothing of cultural energy and social resources) are wiped out. Techno-fixes do not alter the anchor practices of contemporary building, which are responsible for around 38 percent

unternehmerischen Konservatismus kompatibel sind. In der Architektur jedenfalls impliziert die Technofixerzählung den Abriss von Gebäuden und deren Ersatz durch nur scheinbar nachhaltige Neubauten. Dadurch wird viel graue Energie vernichtet (von der kulturellen Energie und den gemeinschaftlichen Ressourcen ganz zu schweigen). Technofixes verändern nicht die Ankerpraktik des Bauens, die für rund 38 Prozent der weltweiten Treibhausgase, für Versiegelung, Ressourcen- und Artenschwund verantwortlich ist. Ein reparativer Ansatz wäre hingegen, nicht abzureißen und „effizienter" neu zu bauen, sondern um- und weiterzubauen. Mit dem zu arbeiten, was bereits da ist, sowohl auf materieller Ebene als auch hinsichtlich der Akteur*innen.

Mit dem Bestand arbeiten[5]

Mit dem Bestand arbeiten heißt – im buchstäblichen wie übertragenen Sinne – nicht Denkmalpflege, sondern Substanzpflege. Dabei werden die vorhandenen materiellen Artefakte und das ökologische und soziale Gefüge als Ausgangspunkt akzeptiert, ohne eine rückwärtsgewandte Restauration oder unkritische Übernahme zu verfechten. Reparatur basiert auf einem potenziellen Nutzwert; sie ist grundsätzlich nicht konsumorientiert. Reparieren heißt daher, etwas wieder parat zu machen, also bereit zu machen für die Weiterverwendung.[6] Der Akt des Reparierens lebt von dem Bewusstsein, dass etwas beschädigt, kaputt ist. Dieses Bewusstsein für den Schaden kann dazu beitragen, die Produktionsbedingungen und den Gebrauch kritisch zu hinterfragen – und zu verändern. Auf diesem Veränderungswillen fußt das Projekt *The Great Repair*, das jedoch nicht im üblichen Sinne von modellhafter nachhaltiger Architektur handelt. Denn der Erhalt und die Umnutzung von Bestandsbauten und Infrastrukturen – von denen viele, wie etwa Straßen- oder Stromnetze, planetarische Ausmaße haben – ist nicht nur eine ökologische, sondern auch eine soziale Zukunftsaufgabe.

„Behutsamkeit als raumpolitisches Prinzip" nannte Andrej Holm diesen Ansatz in Bezug auf die Praxis der Instandbesetzung und das Konzept der behutsamen Stadterneuerung Berlins von Hardt-Waltherr Hämer in ARCH+ 252 *Open for Maintenance – Wegen Umbau geöffnet.*[7] Die Pflege und Instandhaltung der Bausubstanz im Alltag gewinnt dadurch einen neuen Stellenwert: Die regelmäßige Reinigung von Oberflächen, die Wartungsarbeiten und Reparaturen von Infrastrukturen verlängern den Lebenszyklus der gebauten Umwelt. Aus diesem Blickwinkel wird deutlich, welchen Anteil auch Reinigungskräfte und Handwerker*innen neben Planer*innen und Ingenieur*innen an der nachhaltigen Bestandspflege haben. Doch ihre Rolle wird häufig nicht wahrgenommen, ihre materiellen Kenntnisse der gebauten Umwelt werden nicht wertgeschätzt. Um dieses Wissen ins Bewusstsein zu rufen, macht *The Great Repair* den Umgang mit dem Gebäude der Akademie der Künste am Hanseatenweg, seiner Geschichte der Instandsetzung und seiner alltäglichen Pflege zum Thema.

Mit dem Alltag beginnen

Die Auseinandersetzung mit dem materiellen Erbe beinhaltet damit auch eine konzeptuelle Kritik an der Disziplin – an einer Architekturvorstellung, die die Räume der Repräsentation gegenüber den Räumen der Reproduktion vorrangig behandelt. *The Great Repair* kehrt dazu den gewohnten Rundgang in der Akademie der Künste am Hanseatenweg um und erschließt die Ausstellungshallen über den Servicebereich und ein Nebentreppenhaus.

Die räumlichen Eingriffe machen die reproduktive Arbeit der Institution öffentlich. Dies geschieht auch durch die Beteiligung der Reinigungskräfte der Akademie der Künste an dem Projekt. Zum einen werden ihre Utensilien und Arbeitsbedingungen aus dem Verborgenen geholt und als Teil der Ausstellung installiert. Zum anderen dokumentierte die Fotokünstlerin Zara Pfeifer die alltäglichen Reinigungsarbeiten, die normalerweise unsichtbar gemacht werden. In ihren Fotografien wird die handwerkliche Expertise der Sorgearbeiter*innen als eine Form des verkörperten

of global greenhouse emissions alongside soil sealing, resource depletion, and species extinction. A reparative approach, in contrast, would not seek to tear down and rebuild more "efficiently," but rather to convert and build on existing structures. To work with what is already there, respecting both the materials and actors involved.

Work with the existing[5]

Working with the existing—in a literal and figurative sense—does not mean heritage preservation, but responsible care of the built fabric. What matters is recognizing the available material artifacts and their ecological and social contexts as a starting point, rather than endorsing a return to the past or embracing them without critical examination. Repair is firmly rooted in an object's potential use value; it is fundamentally distinct from a mindset of consumption. Repair means returning something to working order, preparing it for further use.[6] The act of repair arises from the awareness that something has been damaged or broken. This awareness of damage can foster a critical examination of the circumstances surrounding the object's production, past usage—and ultimately lead to change. *The Great Repair* is grounded in this desire for change, yet it diverges from conventional notions of exemplary sustainable architecture.

This is because the preservation and conversion of existing buildings and infrastructures—many of which exist at a planetary scale, including street networks and energy grids—is not only an ecological task, but above all a social one. In the *ARCH+* issue *Open for Maintenance*, the sociologist Andrej Holm termed this approach "Cautiousness as a Spatio-Political Principle," invoking the concept of "cautious urban regeneration" advocated by the urban planner Hardt-Waltherr Hämer and the practice of *Instandbesetzung* adopted by Berlin's housing activists in the 1980s (a portmanteau of *Instandsetzung*, i.e., maintenance, and *Besetzung*, i.e., squatting).[7] This approach imparts a new significance to the everyday care and maintenance of building fabric. Routine cleaning of surfaces, ongoing upkeep efforts, and infrastructure repairs all prolong the life cycle of the built environment. From this perspective, it becomes clear that cleaning personnel and craftspeople play a critical part, alongside planners and engineers, in the sustainable care of existing building stock. Yet their role often goes unrecognized and their material knowledge about the built environment is underappreciated. To direct more attention to this knowledge, *The Great Repair* addresses the Akademie der Künste building on Hanseatenweg, making its maintenance history and everyday upkeep a subject of the exhibition.

Start with the everyday

Engaging with our material legacy also involves a conceptual critique of the discipline—of a conception of architecture that prioritizes spaces of representation over spaces of reproduction. This is why *The Great Repair* exhibition inverts the traditional circulation route at the Akademie der Künste on Hanseatenweg; the exhibition halls are now reached by passing through the service area and a side stairwell.

This spatial intervention renders the institution's reproductive work public. This is also achieved by involving the cleaning personnel of the Akademie der Künste in the project. Their tools and working conditions are brought out of hiding and displayed within the exhibition. Additionally, the photographer Zara Pfeifer has documented their everyday cleaning work, which is normally hidden from sight. Her photographs reveal and pay tribute to the manual expertise of care workers as a form of embodied knowledge, while respecting the privacy of the individuals involved.

This approach illustrates how practices are always embodied and materially grounded. They involve not only people but also encompass artifacts and nonhuman entities. These too, according to the sociologist Andreas Reckwitz, are "bearers" of social practices.[8]

Wissens offengelegt und gewürdigt – ohne die Menschen dahinter bloß- oder auszustellen.

Dieser Ansatz veranschaulicht, dass Praktiken immer auch inkorporiert, körperlich verankert sind. Sie umfassen neben den Menschen auch Artefakte und nicht-menschliche Akteure, die, so der Soziologe Andreas Reckwitz, ebenso „Träger" sozialer Praktiken sind.[8] *The Great Repair* weist damit auf die häufig übersehene Materialität sozialer Praktiken und ihren Stellenwert als Teil der kulturellen und sozialen (Re)Produktion hin.

Praxis reparieren / Reparatur praktizieren

Die geringe Anerkennung körperlicher und reproduktiver Arbeit führt in vielen Bereichen zunehmend zum Verlust handwerklichen Wissens. Im Bauen setzte dieser Prozess bereits in der Neuzeit mit der Trennung von Architektur als entwerfender Disziplin und ausführendem Handwerk ein. Die Herausbildung der Architekturtheorie in der Renaissance diente nicht zuletzt der Abgrenzung und damit der Privilegierung der geistigen gegenüber der körperlichen Arbeit, der immateriellen gegenüber der materiellen, des „kreativen" Anteils der Disziplin gegenüber den anderen Gewerken.[9]

Wenn wir die Architekturpraxis mit ihren inhärenten sozialen Ungleichheiten „reparieren" wollen, müssen wir eine Selbstreparatur der Disziplin angehen. Wir müssen dafür die Arbeitsbedingungen, die Architekturausbildung, die Hierarchien und veralteten Selbstbilder grundlegend infrage stellen. Letztlich auch das Selbstverständnis von Architekt*innen, immer mehr Häuser bauen zu müssen. Für Eva von Redecker stellt das viel diskutierte Neubau-Moratorium von Charlotte Malterre-Barthes den radikalsten Ausdruck der Selbstreparatur dar. Selbst wenn es nur als Provokation tauge, biete es eine produktive Vision:

> Eine andere Art, das Neubaumoratorium auf den Punkt zu bringen, wäre, es als Vision für eine No-dig-Baubranche zu beschreiben. Die Chiffre *no dig* ist so konkret, dass es erstaunt, wie übertragbar sie dennoch ist. Dieser Imperativ lässt sich auf die fossile Energieversorgung übertragen, als Forderung nach einem Ende des Extraktivismus unter dem Slogan *Leave it in the ground*.

Dinge auch mal sein zu lassen, sie nicht zu tun, kann man in die Raumproduktion auch so übersetzen, dass wir Dinge nicht um des Neuen willen „neu gestalten", d. h. das Bestehende zerstören, sondern die knappen Ressourcen für dessen Pflege aufwenden. Diesen Ansatz haben Lacaton & Vassal bei ihrem wegweisenden Projekt Place Léon Aucoc in Bordeaux verfolgt, als sie es ablehnten, den funktionierenden Platz neu zu entwerfen, und stattdessen das Budget für dessen Instandhaltung einsetzten (S. 152–155).

Wissenswelten dekolonisieren

Dies käme einer tatsächlichen Reparatur der Ankerpraktik Bauen gleich, nicht zuletzt, weil beim Bauen über zwei Drittel der CO_2-Emissionen durch Arbeiten im Untergrund verursacht werden, etwa für die Fundamentierung und für unterirdische Geschosse. Obwohl diese Fakten bekannt sind, verändert sich die Praxis nur langsam. Dies liegt zum Teil daran, dass für eine grundlegende Praxisreparatur neben wissenschaftlicher Expertise auch solche Nicht-Expert*innen-Kompetenzen und Wissensformen erforderlich sind, die vielfach durch technokratische, profitorientierte und koloniale Verhältnisse verdrängt, marginalisiert und zerstört wurden. Dieser Verlust umfasst auch Wissen über regenerative Landnutzung, Materialgewinnung und Bautechniken. Dazu gehören indigene pluriversale Epistemologien, wie die Arbeiten der Inga-Gemeinschaft in Kolumbien in Zusammenarbeit mit Santiago del Hierro, Marjetica Portč und anderen Künstler*innen zeigen, aber auch alle anderen praxisbasierten, situierten und sozialisierten Formen des Wissens außerhalb des technowissenschaftlichen Paradigmas. Das Projekt einer *großen Reparatur* muss in diesem Sinne unsere Wissenswelten dekolonisieren, d. h.

Keeping this in mind, *The Great Repair* explores the oft-overlooked materiality of social practices as well as their status as part of cultural and social (re)production.

Repair the practice / Practice repair

In many industries, physical and reproductive labor go underrecognized, resulting in the gradual decline of manual skills and craft expertise. In the building sector, this process began as far back as the early modern period, when a division was established between architecture as a design discipline and the crafts that only execute what the architect has designed. A key aspect in the development of architecture theory during the Renaissance was the differentiation, and consequent privileging, of mental labor over physical labor, the immaterial over the material, and the "creative" side of the discipline over other skills.[9]

If we want to "repair" architectural practice with its inherent social inequalities, we need to begin with the discipline's self-repair. To accomplish this, we must fundamentally reevaluate its working conditions, educational models, hierarchies, and outdated self-understanding—especially the notion that architects should design more and more new buildings. For Eva von Redecker, the much-discussed moratorium on new construction proposed by Charlotte Malterre-Barthes represents a radical expression of self-repair. Even if only intended as a provocation, it offers a productive vision:

> Another way to characterize a moratorium on new construction would be to describe it as a vision of a "no-dig" construction industry. The term "no dig" is so concrete, yet it's astonishingly transferrable. The imperative can also be applied to the fossil fuel industry, as a demand for an end to extractivism with the slogan "leave it in the ground."

Letting things be, not doing things: this can be translated into the realm of spatial production by arguing that we should not "redesign" things for the sake of the new—in other words, destroy them—but that we should instead use our scarce resources to maintain what already exists. This is the approach taken by Lacaton & Vassal in their trailblazing project for the Place Léon Aucoc in Bordeaux. The architects turned down an opportunity to redesign the well-functioning square, instead using their budget on the square's maintenance (see pages 152–155).

Decolonize knowledge worlds

Such an approach would be tantamount to repairing the anchor practices of building, in no small part because over two-thirds of the carbon emissions caused by construction occur in underground work, for example in laying foundations or building basement levels. Although these factors are well-known, practice has been slow to adapt. This is partly because the fundamental repair of architectural practice requires the competencies of people who are not usually regarded as experts, as well as types of knowledge that are suppressed, marginalized, and eroded by technocratic, profit-oriented, colonialist dynamics. What is lost as a result encompasses knowledge about regenerative land use, material extraction, and building techniques. It also encompasses pluriversal Indigenous epistemologies—as demonstrated by the work of the Inga People of Colombia in collaboration with Santiago del Hierro, Marjetica Portč, and other artists—as well as all other forms of practice-based, situated, and socialized knowledge that exist outside the techno-scientific knowledge paradigm. The project of a Great Repair must therefore also decolonize knowledge worlds; that is to say, it must diversify stakeholder networks while interweaving different specialties, skillsets, and knowledge bases.

Tools to the people

With these talents, techniques, and traditions of expertise, we can redesign our relationships within the social and natural environment. We can reconcile production and reproduction. When we

das Akteursnetzwerk pluralisieren und unterschiedliche Expertisen, Kompetenzen und Wissensbestände verweben.

Werkzeuge für alle

Mit diesen Fertigkeiten, Techniken und Kenntnissen können wir unsere Beziehungen innerhalb der sozialen und natürlichen Umwelt neugestalten und die Produktion wieder in die für ihre Reproduktion erforderlichen Zusammenhänge einbetten. Denn der Mangel an Wissen darüber, wie die Dinge, die wir benutzen, konstruiert, instandgehalten und repariert werden, führt zu immer neuen austauschbaren Waren, die ihrem Wesen nach dazu bestimmt sind, verbraucht, vernutzt und entsorgt zu werden. Um den daraus resultierenden ökologischen und sozialen Zerstörungen entgegenzuwirken, müssen wir uns die Werkzeuge der Reparatur wieder aneignen. In den Worten des Architekten Yoshiharu Tsukamoto von Atelier Bow-Wow: „Tools to the People!" Werkzeuge für alle!

Der Begriff des Werkzeugs geht jedoch über Gerätschaften hinaus und umfasst auch Werkzeuge der demokratischen Governance. In den industrialisierten Systemen der Raumproduktion, die vom Staat und den Unternehmen gesteuert werden, haben wir oft nicht die Macht, unsere eigene Umwelt und unsere Beziehungen zu reparieren. Daher sind die Vergesellschaftung der Produktionsmittel und die Demokratisierung der Regierungsführung auf verschiedenen Ebenen entscheidende Voraussetzungen für die Ermöglichung umfassenderer sozialer Praktiken der Reparatur. Wie das Projekt des Lehrstuhls Architecture of Territory nahelegt, ist „Tools to the People" gleichbedeutend mit „Power to the People".

Die Narben sichtbar lassen

Der Akt der Reparatur legt allerdings immer auch offen, was nicht repariert werden kann. Insofern beginnt Reparatur damit, das Irreparable, die Unumkehrbarkeit der Zerstörung anzuerkennen. Wir müssen wiederaufbauen, ausbessern, heilen und instandsetzen, aber wir müssen gleichzeitig zugeben, dass unsere Reparaturbemühungen die materiellen oder immateriellen Verletzungen nicht überdecken können. Die Narben sichtbar und das Gedenken lebendig zu halten gehört daher zur *großen Reparatur* dazu. Es geht dabei jedoch nicht nur um ein folgenloses Mea culpa, sondern um die Anerkennung der ungleich verteilten Verantwortung für Klimakrise und Artensterben entlang historisch ausgebildeter kolonialer Linien. Reparatur bekommt in dieser Lesart die aktive Bedeutung der (Klima-)Reparation. Erst wenn wir Fragen der sozialen und ökologischen Gerechtigkeit als Teil der „Praktiken des interstitiellen Wandels" mitdenken, können wir Reparatur als gemeinsame Aufgabe angehen und wiederaufbauen, was zerstört wurde, und in dem, was repariert wurde, neue Bedeutungen finden.

lack knowledge about how to build, maintain, and repair the things we use, they become fungible commodities, destined by their very nature to be consumed, depleted, and discarded. To counteract the resulting ecological and social harm, we must reclaim the tools of repair for our own purposes. In the words of architect Yoshiharu Tsukamoto from Atelier Bow-Wow: "Tools to the people!"

The concept of the tool, however, extends beyond mere devices. It also encompasses tools of democratic governance. In the industrialized system of spatial production controlled by states and corporations, we often lack the power to repair our own environment or relationships. For this reason, socializing the means of production and democratizing governance at various levels of scale are essential for enabling more comprehensive social practices of repair. As the project by the Architecture of Territory design studio at ETH Zürich shows, "tools to the people" ultimately means "power to the people."

Keep the scars visible

Something else the act of repair always reveals, however, is what cannot be repaired. In this respect, repair begins first with a recognition of what is irreparable due to the irreversible nature of the damage. We must rebuild, mend, heal, and maintain, but at the same time we must acknowledge that our repair efforts cannot fully erase the material and immaterial harm. Preserving visible scars and our collective memory are therefore integral aspects of the Great Repair. However, this is not about offering empty apologies; it is about recognizing the unequal distribution of responsibility for species extinction and climate crisis, often along historical colonialist lines. Repair, in this sense, entails a more proactive approach to (climate) reparation. Only when we reframe issues of social and ecological justice as components of "practices of interstitial change" can we truly approach repair as a collaborative endeavor. Only then can we begin rebuilding what has been destroyed, and find new meanings in what has been repaired.

Text:
Florian Hertweck, Christian Hiller, Felix Hofmann, Markus Krieger, Marija Marić, Alex Nehmer, Anh-Linh Ngo, Milica Topalović, Nazlı Tümerdem

1 Eva von Redecker im Gespräch in dieser Ausgabe
2 Ebd.
3 Vgl. Theodore Schatzki: *The Site of the Social*, University Park 2002, xi
4 Ebd., S. 59
5 Dieser und die nachfolgenden Zwischentitel sind Slogans, die in der Ausstellung präsentiert werden.
6 Wilfried Lipp spricht von Reparatur als „Prä-paratur des Künftigen". Siehe Wilfried Lipp et al.: „Reparatur als Präparatur", in: ARCH+ 250 *The Great Repair – Politiken der Reparaturgesellschaft* (Dezember 2022), S. 50–53
7 Andrej Holm: „Behutsamkeit als raumpolitisches Prinzip", in: *ARCH+* 252 *Open for Maintenance – Wegen Umbau geöffnet* (Mai 2023), S. 180–187
8 Andreas Reckwitz: *Unscharfe Grenzen – Perspektiven einer Kultursoziologie*, Bielefeld 2008, S. 153
9 Vgl. Douglas Spencer: „Arbeit, Produktion und der Zweck der Architektur", in: *ARCH+* 251 *Unternehmen Architektur* (März 2023), S. 31

1 Eva von Redecker, interviewed in this issue.
2 Ibid.
3 See Theodore Schatzki, *The Site of the Social* (University Park, PA: Penn State University Press, 2002), xi.
4 Ibid., 59.
5 This and the following heading are slogans presented in the exhibition.
6 Wilfried Lipp describes repair as a "Prä-paratur des Künftigen"—in English a "pre-paration for the future." See Lipp et al., "Repairing as Preparing," *ARCH+* 250, *The Great Repair: Politics for the Repair Society* (2023): 46–49.
7 Andrej Holm, "Cautiousness as a Spatio-Political Principle," *ARCH+* 252, *Open for Maintenance – Wegen Umbau geöffnet* (May 2023): 180–87.
8 Andreas Reckwitz, *Unscharfe Grenzen: Perspektiven einer Kultursoziologie* (Bielefeld: transcript Verlag, 2008), 153.
9 See Douglas Spencer, "Arbeit, Produktion und der Zweck der Architektur," *ARCH+* 251, *Unternehmen Architektur* (March 2023): 31.

S./p. 76

S./p. 59

S. / p. 63

Diese Publikation erscheint anlässlich der Ausstellung *The Great Repair* (14.10.2023 – 14.1.2024) in der Akademie der Künste, Berlin / This publication is released on the occasion of the exhibition *The Great Repair* (Oct. 14, 2023 – Jan. 14, 2024) at Akademie der Künste, Berlin.

Cover:
Bas Princen
Aus der Serie / From the series:
Giotto's Fragments
2023

ARCH+ Team dieser Ausgabe
ARCH+ team for this issue
Nora Dünser (CvD / Managing editor), Mirko Gatti, Christian Hiller, Felix Hofmann, Markus Krieger, Daniel Kuhnert, Alex Nehmer (Projektleitung / Project lead), Anh-Linh Ngo (Redaktionsleitung / Editor-in-chief), Mona Rauch, Lea Scherer, Finn Steffens

Gastredaktion
Guest editorial team
Universität Luxemburg
University of Luxembourg: Florian Hertweck, Marija Marić
ETH Zürich: Milica Topalović, Santiago del Hierro, Nazlı Tümerdem

SSS SIEDLE
Siedle Axiom
Intelligent Interior.
Sicher die Tür im Blick, per Fingertipp die Lichtstimmung wählen, mit oder ohne Hörer telefonieren. Die Zukunft der Gebäudekommunikation in ihrer schönsten Form.
axiom.siedle.de
iF DESIGN AWARD 2019
GERMAN DESIGN AWARD GOLD 2019
Focus Open 2018 Silver
reddot award 2018 winner

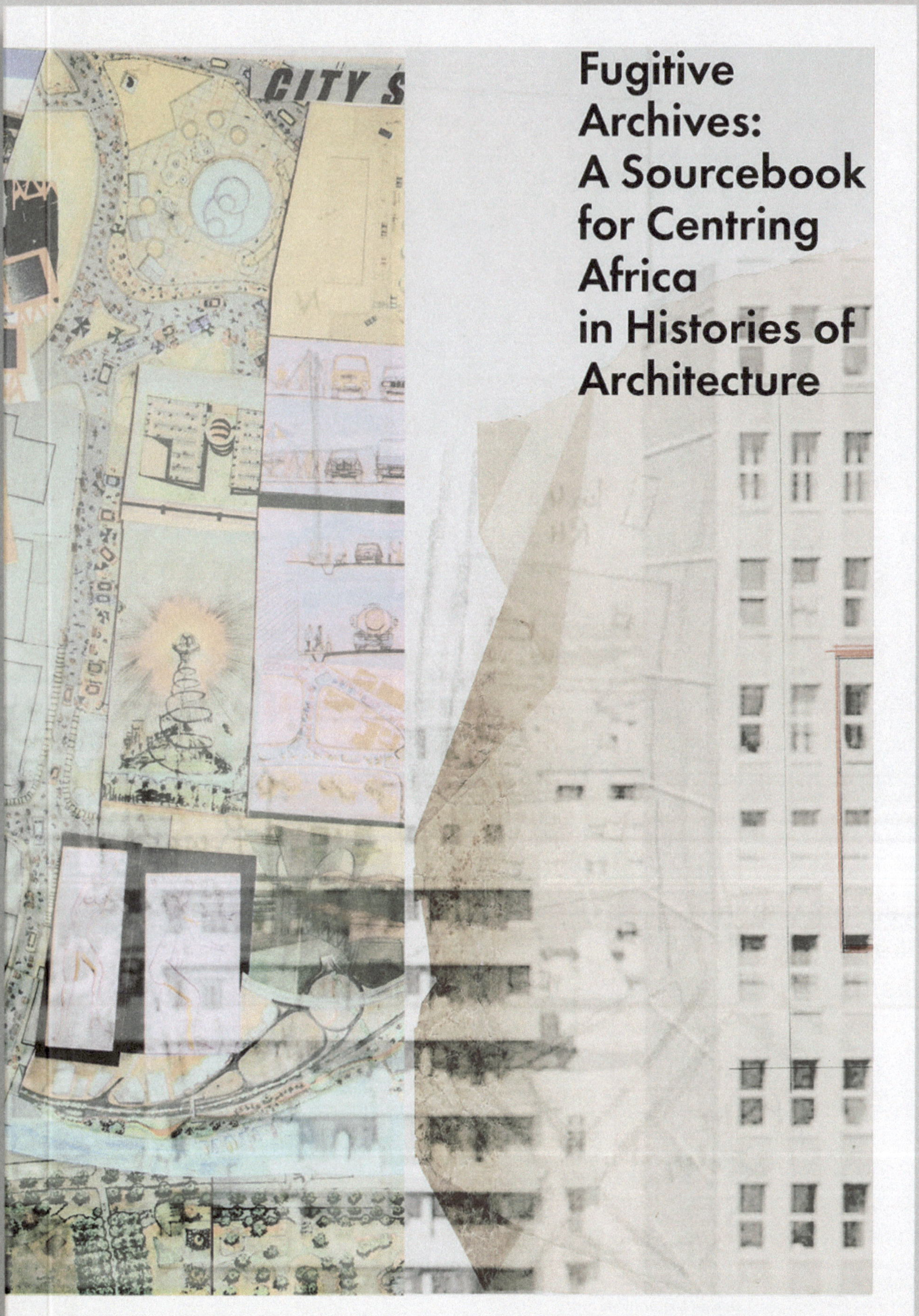

A collection of primary sources chosen by the research fellows of Centring Africa: Postcolonial Perspectives on Architecture.

Doreen Adengo

Dele Adeyemo

Warebi Gabriel Brisibe and Ramota Obagah-Stephen

Rachel Lee and Monika Motylinska

Ikem Stanley Okoye

Cole Roskam

Łukasz Stanek

Huda Tayob

Edited by Claire Lubell and Rafico Ruiz

Published by Canadian Centre for Architecture Jap Sam Books

cca.qc.ca

Genau das Richtige für alles
Area Pro ist das neue Objektfliesen-Programm von Agrob Buchtal, dem führenden Anbieter von Architekturkeramik. Zeitlos im Design, beispiellos vielfältig und durchdacht bis ins Detail. Die große Auswahl an Farben, Formaten, rutschhemmenden Oberflächen und zahlreichen keramischen Spezialprodukten macht diese Kollektion zu einem perfekten Allrounder für jeden Einsatzbereich.
#areapro
www.agrob-buchtal.de
AREA PRO
DEUTSCHE STEINZEUG AGROB BUCHTAL

A VOICE OF ART IN SOCIETY
AKADEMIE DER KÜNSTE
AKADEMIE DER KÜNSTE
Founded in 1696, the Akademie der Künste in Berlin is a community of artists and one of the oldest cultural institutes in Europe. In its two permanent locations in the heart of Berlin – Pariser Platz in the Mitte district and the modernist Hansaviertel in Tiergarten – it is a venue for exhibitions and events, a meeting place for artists and art lovers, hosting public debate on art and cultural policy.
The Academy's archives are considered the most important interdisciplinary archives for modernist art and culture in German-speaking countries, and together with the Brecht-Weigel Museum and the Anna Seghers Museum, the Academy is dedicated to the presentation of contemporary artistic positions and the preservation of cultural heritage. We look forward to welcoming you to one of our many events throughout the year.
adk.de
Funded by
Minister of State for Culture and the Media
AKADEMIE DER KÜNSTE

Stiftung Kunst und Natur
Sand
Ressource
Leben
Sehnsucht
24.9.2023 – 11.2.2024
Museum Sinclair-Haus
museum-sinclair-haus.de
kunst-und-natur.de
hr2.kultur partner
FRIZZ
Ferhat Bouda, Ein Kind spielt in einer Siedlung nahe der Stadt Chinguetti, Mauretanien, 2018
© Ferhat Bouda, Agence VU, 2023

Brenne Architekten

Renovation Akademie der Künste Hanseatenweg

DE

2009 übernahm das Berliner Büro Brenne Architekten den Auftrag zur Sanierung der seit 1995 unter Denkmalschutz stehenden Gebäude der Akademie der Künste im Berliner Hansaviertel. Das von Werner Düttmann und Sabine Schumann 1960 entworfene, aus drei Gebäudeteilen bestehende Ensemble ist im Nachgang der Internationalen Bauausstellung von 1957 entstanden. Es fügt sich in die städtebauliche Gesamtkomposition, die die *Interbau* entsprechend den Vorstellungen der westlichen Moderne für das im Krieg fast vollständig zerstörte Wohnviertel am Rande des Tiergartens konzipieren ließ.

Der Sanierung stellten Brenne Architekten eine detaillierte Aufarbeitung der Nutzungsgeschichte und des Bauzustands der Gebäude voran. Oberste Prämisse war der Erhalt der Originalsubstanz, an der seit der Eröffnung keine größeren Veränderungen vorgenommen worden waren. Die Eingriffe in den Bestand sollten sich auf das absolut Notwendige beschränken. So machten partielle Nutzungsänderungen und energetische wie sicherheitstechnische Modernisierungen bauliche Maßnahmen erforderlich. Um neue technische Standards in die 50 Jahre alte Architektur zu integrieren, galt es, kreative handwerkliche und technische Lösungen zu finden. In Teilbereichen, wie etwa bei der Farbgebung, wurde der Ursprungszustand wiederhergestellt, an anderen Stellen wurden Spuren des Gebrauchs bewusst nicht beseitigt, um Zeitgeschichte und Originalmaterialien sichtbar zu lassen.

Brenne Architekten verstehen unter Denkmalpflege jedoch nicht das „Konservieren in der Zeit“, vielmehr geht es darum, das Gebäude „in die Gegenwart zu überführen, indem wir das Vorhandene lesen, uns respektvoll auf seine Geschichte einlassen und seine Möglichkeiten für die Zukunft erkennen“.[1] Die Zukunftsoffenheit von Architektur liegt in ihrer Fähigkeit, neue Zeitschichten zu akkumulieren, sich zu wandeln. Eine strukturelle Robustheit ist Grundlage dieser Wandlungsfähigkeit. In der Wahl robuster Materialien wie Backstein und Schiefer und deren oft rohem Einsatz hatten Düttmann und Schumann die Langlebigkeit des Akademie-Gebäudes bereits mitgedacht. Die Sanierungsmaßnahmen werden seine zukünftige Wartungs- und Reparaturfähigkeit noch weiter verbessern.

2009–2012
Auftraggeber
Client
Akademie der Künste, Berlin

EN

In 2009, the Berlin-based firm Brenne Architekten was tasked with renovating the Akademie der Künste (Academy of Arts) building in Berlin's Hansaviertel district. Designed in 1960 by Werner Düttmann and Sabine Schumann in the wake of the 1957 International Building Exhibition ("Interbau") and awarded landmark status in 1995, the building is an ensemble comprising three distinct sections. It blends into the broader urban composition that the Interbau, adhering to the concepts of Western modernism, conceived for the residential district on the edge of Tiergarten, which had been heavily damaged during the Second World War.

Before starting their renovation, Brenne Architekten conducted a detailed analysis of the building's use history and condition. Interventions were limited to the absolutely necessary, prioritizing the preservation of its original

substance, which had remained largely unchanged since opening. However, changes to the building's use and upgraded energy and security standards required some structural measures. Integrating modern technical standards into the fifty-year-old architecture called for creative technical solutions. The architects restored the building's original condition in certain aspects, such as the color scheme, and intentionally retained traces of the building's earlier use, highlighting its history and original materials.

Rather than viewing landmark conservation as merely "preserving a building in time," Brenne Architekten consider it a process of "adapting [a building] to the present by reading what already exists, engaging respectfully with its history, and recognizing its possibilities for the future."[1] Architecture's openness to the future lies in its ability to accumulate new layers in time through transformation; structural robustness is the basis of this mutability. Düttmann and Schumann, in fact, had already designed the Akademie building for longevity, using robust materials such as brick and slate, often in their raw, natural state. This renovation further enhances the building's ability to be maintained and repaired for many years to come.

Text:
Mona Rauch

1
Brenne Architekten: „Profil", www.brenne-architekten.de/profil (Stand: 14.7.2023)
Brenne Architekten, "Profil," www.brenne-architekten.de/profil [accessed July 14, 2023].

Die gerade fertiggestellte Akademie der Künste von Werner Düttmann und Sabine Schumann in einer Aufnahme von Horst Siegmann aus dem Jahr 1960
Werner Düttmann and Sabine Schumann's newly built Akademie der Künste, in a photograph by Horst Siegmann from 1960

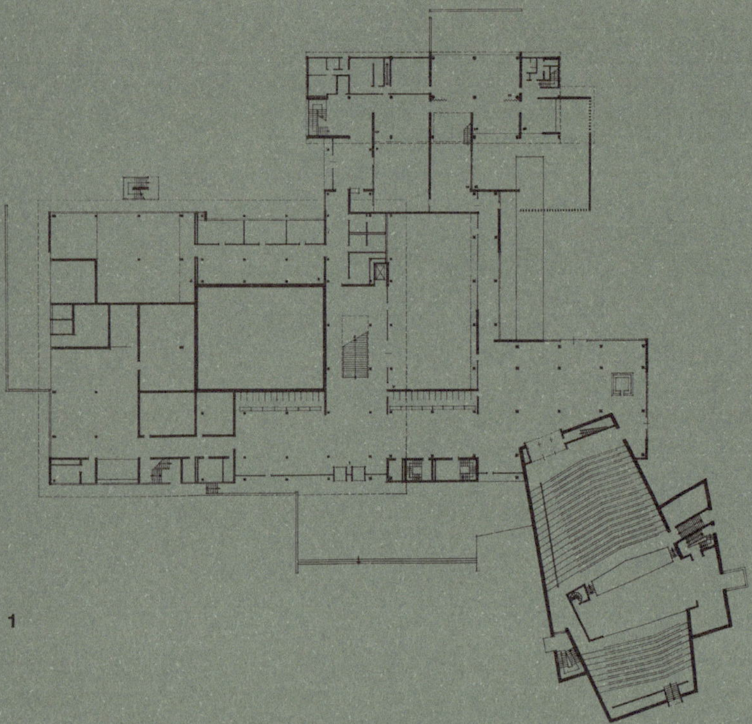

1

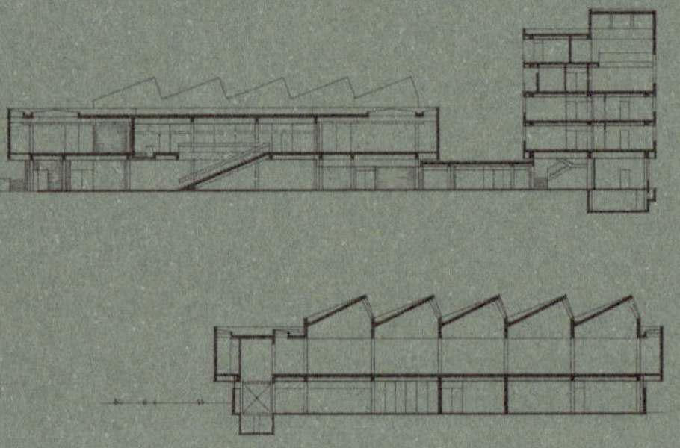

2

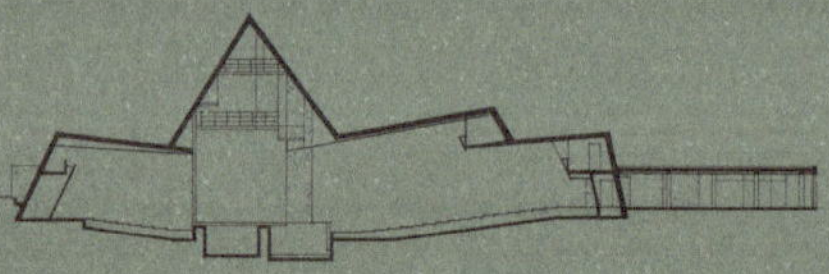

3

1
Grundriss Erdgeschoss
Ground floor
2
Schnitte durch die Ausstellungshallen, die Haupttreppe und das Verwaltungsgebäude
Sections showing the exhibition halls, main staircase, and administration building
3
Schnitt durch das Auditorium
Section of the auditorium
4
Die Haupttreppe, die zu den Ausstellungshallen führt, vor Abschluss der Renovierungsarbeiten unter der Leitung von Brenne Architekten. Foto: Holger Herschel
The main staircase leading to the exhibition halls, pictured here before the completion of renovations overseen by Brenne Architekten. Photo: Holger Herschel

4

DE

Das Alltägliche wird oft als unabänderlich betrachtet, dabei ist es in Wirklichkeit ein Ort der fortwährenden Neuverhandlung und damit des Widerstands und der Transformation. Diese Prozesse mögen sich im Kleinen abspielen, doch in ihnen manifestieren sich globale Phänomene lokal, ganz gleich, ob wir von Geschlechterbeziehungen, der kapitalistischen Produktionsweise oder der Klimakrise sprechen. Denn es ist dieser Lebensalltag selbst, in dem Gesellschaften (re)produziert werden, weshalb dies auch der Ausgangspunkt für Veränderungen sein muss. Um das Prinzip der Obsoleszenz als Triebfeder unserer unnachhaltigen Produktions- und Konsumtionsweise zu überwinden, müssen wir in einem ersten Schritt die Care-Arbeit anerkennen, die bereits überall um uns herum geleistet wird. Oft im Verborgenen, manchmal direkt vor unseren Augen und doch allzu oft übersehen, wird diese unverzichtbare Arbeit in unserem gegenwärtigen Wertsystem unsichtbar gemacht. Doch findet in unserer Welt jeden Tag in ganz alltäglichen und wenig spektakulären Bereichen Fürsorge, Reparatur und Erhaltungsarbeit statt.

Text:
Daniel Kuhnert

Mit dem Alltag beginnen

Begin with the Everyday

EN

Often misjudged as set in stone, the everyday is in fact a site of constant renegotiation, and thus resistance and transformation. These processes may take place on a small scale but they are the areas in which global phenomena manifest themselves locally, irrespective of whether we are talking about gender relations, the capitalist mode of production, or the climate crisis. In fact, it is here, in daily life, that societies are (re)produced, and therefore this must be the starting point for action. To overcome the principle of obsolescence as a driving force for our unsustainable mode of production and consumption, we must start by acknowledging the care work that is already being done all around us. Often out of sight, sometimes right in front of our eyes and still overlooked, this indispensable work is rendered invisible by the current valorization system. Yet every day, in mundane and unglamorous areas, our world is being cared for, repaired, and maintained.

Mierle Laderman Ukeles

Manifesto for Maintenance Art, 1969!

Proposal for an Exhibition "CARE"

DE

1969 verfasste Mierle Laderman Ukeles das ***MANIFESTO FOR MAINTENANCE ART, 1969! Proposal for an Exhibition "CARE"***, in dem sie Wartungs- und Sorgearbeit konsequent zur Kunst erklärte: „Ich mache verdammt viel: waschen, putzen, kochen, erneuern, unterstützen, bewahren etc. Außerdem (bis jetzt separat) ‚mache' ich Kunst. Jetzt werde ich einfach diese alltäglichen Dinge der Pflege tun, sie ins Bewusstsein spülen, sie ausstellen, als Kunst."[1] Das vierseitige Dokument kontrastiert die einem radikalen Neubeginn verpflichtete Avantgardekunst mit der Kunst der kontinuierlichen Instandhaltung, die Idee des linearen Fortschritts mit der repetitiven Sorgearbeit, und letztlich auch den Todestrieb mit dem Lebensinstinkt – und unterstreicht gleichzeitig deren untrennbare Zusammengehörigkeit.

Teil dieses visionären Manifests ist ein Konzept für eine performative Ausstellung mit dem Titel *CARE* (die erste explizite Verwendung dieses Wortes in der Kunst), welches viele der Aktionen und Projekte vorwegnimmt, die Ukeles in den kommenden Jahrzehnten zusammen mit zahllosen Arbeiter*innen, Materialien und Infrastrukturen der Wartung und Instandhaltung in New York City und in vielen Städten auf der ganzen Welt durchführen wird.[2] Dabei berücksichtigt Ukeles nicht nur die Pflegearbeit in der häuslichen Sphäre (eine überwiegend feminisierte Form der Arbeit), sondern auch in der Kunstwelt und im weiteren urbanen Raum – wobei sie sich insbesondere dem städtischen Müllstoffwechsel widmet (und den damals zumeist männlichen Arbeitern, die sich um diese Abfallströme kümmern).

Sowohl ihr Manifest als auch ihr späteres Werk beschäftigen sich auch mit der spezifischen Materialität, mit der Care-Worker bei ihrer meist manuellen Arbeit umgehen müssen: die schmutzigen, klebrigen Substanzen, die die meisten Menschen nicht anfassen und einfach nur loswerden wollen. Dementsprechend schlug sie in ihrem Manifest nicht nur vor, die meist unsichtbaren, materiellen Arbeitsprozesse auszustellen, die mit der Sorgearbeit für den Haushalt, das Museum, die Stadt oder die Erde verbunden sind, sondern auch „den Inhalt eines Mülllasters, einen Behälter verpesteter Luft, einen Tank verschmutzten Wassers aus dem Hudson River, eine Ladung verunreinigten Bodens"[3] ins Museum zu bringen.

Wie ich in anderen Texten ausführlicher argumentiere, stehen solche klebrigen (Abfall-)Substanzen oft auch im Mittelpunkt der Sorge-Arbeit – Substanzen, die der festen Form, dem Objekt oder dem Körper entweichen und diese infrage stellen, wie Blut, Kot, Urin, Eiter, Rotz, Schweiß, Schimmel, Abwasser, Sickerwasser, Müll. Während der Begriff der Pflege häufig mit Reinigung und Reinheit verbunden wird, gehe ich davon aus, dass Pflege- und Sorgearbeit vor allem in dieser unbestimmten Zwischenwelt angesiedelt ist. Außerstande, die Verunreinigung zu beseitigen oder das Leck zu flicken, ist sie vielmehr mit den sich wiederholenden Auflösungen der abgeschlossenen Form konfrontiert. Sie kümmert sich um sie, dämmt sie vielleicht temporär ein, pflegt sie, und vor allem: Sie hält sie aus.[4]

1969
Kuratiert für *The Great Repair* von
Curated for *The Great Repair* by
Bettina Knaup
im Zusammenhang mit ihrer eigenen Forschung zu Pflege und Abfall
in conjunction with her own research on care and waste
Courtesy Mierle Laderman Ukeles & Ronald Feldman Gallery, New York

Dies knüpft in gewisser Weise an das an, was Mierle Laderman Ukeles auf so radikale Weise vorschlägt: verkörperte, wiederholte Akte der Sorgearbeit und der Berührung als integralen Bestandteil des künstlerischen Prozesses zu begreifen und nicht (nur) die intentionale Erschaffung einer in sich geschlossenen (skulpturalen) Form. Ihre Arbeit konfrontiert uns mit der schwindelerregenden Unendlichkeit entwerteter, weggeworfener Materialien und Arbeitsprozesse durch eine kontinuierliche künstlerische Praxis des „Handanlegens an das Material“.[5]

EN

In 1969 Mierle Laderman Ukeles wrote the *MANIFESTO FOR MAINTENANCE ART, 1969! Proposal for an Exhibition "CARE,"* in which she rigorously declared maintenance and care work to be art: "I do a hell of a lot of washing, cleaning, cooking, renewing, supporting, preserving etc. Also, (up to now separately) I 'do' Art. Now, I will simply do these maintenance everyday things, and flush them up to consciousness, exhibit them, as Art." The four-page document contrasts avant-garde art committed to innovation with the art of continuous maintenance, the idea of linear development and progress with repetitive care work, and ultimately the death instinct with the life instinct—while insisting on the inseparable link between them.

This visionary manifesto includes a proposal for an exhibition titled *CARE* (the first explicit use of this word in the arts) that anticipates many of the actions Ukeles would undertake in the decades to come, collaborating with countless workers, materials, and infrastructures related to maintenance in New York City and other cities around the world.[2] Notably, she not only considered care work in the domestic sphere (predominantly feminized labor) but also in the art world and within the wider urban and ecological context. She placed a particular emphasis on the city's waste metabolism (and the mostly male laborers attending to those waste flows).

Her manifesto and later work engage with the specific materiality that care workers must process in their primarily manual labor: the dirty, sticky substances that most individuals typically avoid and dispose of. Accordingly, her manifesto proposes not only exhibiting the material labor processes involved in maintaining the home, the museum, the city, or the Earth, but also bringing items such as "the contents of one sanitation truck; a container of polluted air; a container of polluted Hudson River; a container of ravaged land" into the museum setting.

As I have written elsewhere, care work in many domains often revolves around sticky (waste) substances, particularly those that escape and challenge the solid form, object, or body — such as blood, shit, pee, pus, snot, sweat, mold, sewage, refuse, leachate, and garbage. While the notion of care might lend itself to projects of purification, I suggest that care work mainly inhabits an interstitial world, an in-between realm unable to fully repair leaks or clean up messes. Instead, it involves exposure to, attention toward, and engagement with the repetitive dissolution of solid forms.[4]

This connects in some ways to what Ukeles has so radically proposed: to understand repetitive, embodied acts of care and touch as integral part of the art process, rather than only the willful creation of sealed (sculptural) form. Her work confronts us with the dizzying infinity of devalued, discarded matter, materials, and labor processes through an ongoing artistic practice of "laying on of hands onto material."[5]

Text:
Bettina Knaup

1
Übersetzung durch ARCH+

2
Für einen umfassenden Überblick über Ukeles' künstlerisches Werk siehe: Patricia C. Phillips (Hg.): *Mierle Laderman Ukeles: Maintenance Art*, New York 2016; Shannon Jackson: *Social Works – Performing Art, Supporting Publics*, New York 2011

For a comprehensive overview of Ukeles's practice, see *Mierle Laderman Ukeles: Maintenance Art*, ed. Patricia C. Phillips (New York: Queens Museum of Art, DelMonico Books, Prestel, 2016); Shannon Jackson, *Social Works: Performing Art, Supporting Publics* (New York: Routledge, 2011).

3
Übersetzung durch ARCH+

4
Bettina Knaup: *Performing (as) Waste – Sticky Care in Feminist Materialist Performance and Curation*, Dissertation, Department of Drama, Theatre and Performance, University of Roehampton, London 2021

Cf. Bettina Knaup, *Performing (as) Waste: Sticky Care in Feminist Materialist Performance and Curation*, (PhD diss., University of Roehampton, 2021).

5
Etwa in ihrer prozesshaft angelegten, skulpturalen Arbeit *Blizzard of Agitated Materials in Flux* (1993), siehe Mierle Laderman Ukeles: „Untitled letter“, in: *Recycling through Art*, Ausstellungskatalog, The Taejon International Exposition Organizing Committee, Daejeon 1993, S. 67 f., Übersetzung durch ARCH+

For instance in her processual and sculptural work *Blizzard of Agitated Materials in Flux* (1993), see Mierle Laderman Ukeles, "Untitled letter," in *Recycling through Art*, exh. cat., Taejon Expo '93, August 7 to November 7, 1993 (Daejon: Taejon International Exposition Organizing Committee, 1993), 67–68.

MANIFESTO!

MAINTENANCE ART -- Proposal for an Exhibition

"CARE"

©1969
Mierle Laderman Ukeles

I. IDEAS:

A. The Death Instinct and the Life Instinct:

The Death Instinct: separation, individuality, Avant-Garde par excellence; to follow one's own path to death--do your own thing, dynamic change.

The Life Instinct: unification, the eternal return, the perpetuation and MAINTENANCE of the species, survival systems and operations, equilibrium.

B. Two basic systems: Development and Maintenance. The sourball of every revolution: after the revolution, who's going to pick up the garbage on Monday morning?
Development: pure individual creation; the new; change; progress, advance, excitement, flight or fleeing.
Maintenance: keep the dust off the pure individual creation; preserve the new; sustain the change; protect progress; defend and prolong the advance; renew the excitement; repeat the flight.

show your work--show it again
keep the contemporaryartmuseum groovy
keep the home fires burning

Development systems are partial feedback systems with major room for change.
Maintenance systems are direct feedback systems with little room for alteration.

MAINTENANCE ART -2- Mierle Laderman Ukeles

C. Maintenance is a drag; it takes all the fucking time (lit.) The mind boggles and chafes at the boredom. The culture confers lousy status on maintenance jobs= minimum wages, housewives=no pay.

clean your desk, wash the dishes, clean the floor, wash your clothes, wash your toes, change the baby's diaper, finish the report, correct the typos, mend the fence, keep the customer happy, throw out the stinking garbage, watch out don't put things in your nose, what shall I wear, I have no sox, pay your bills, don't litter, save string, wash your hair, change the sheets, go to the store, I'm out of perfume, say it again--he doesn't understand, seal it again--it leaks, go to work, this art is dusty, clear the table, call him again, flush the toilet, stay young.

D. Art:

Everything I say is Art is Art. Everything I do is Art is Art. "We have no Art, we try to do everything well." (Balinese saying).

Avant-garde art, which claims utter development, is infected by strains of maintenance ideas, maintenance activities, and maintenance materials.
--Process art especially claims pure development and change, yet employs almost purely maintenance processes.

E. The exhibition of Maintenance Art, "CARE", would zero in on pure maintenance, exhibit it as contemporary art, and yield, by utter opposition, clarity of issues.

Mierle Laderman Ukeles, ***Manifesto for Maintenance Art, 1969! Proposal for an Exhibition "CARE"***, 1969

MAINTENANCE ART -3- Mierle Laderman Ukeles

II. THE MAINTENANCE ART EXHIBITION: Three parts: personal, general, and Earth Maintenance.

A. Personal Part:

I am an artist. I am a woman. I am a wife. I am a mother (random order).
I do a hell of a lot of washing, cleaning, cooking, renewing, supporting, preserving, etc. Also, (up to now separately) I "do" Art.
Now, I will simply do these maintenance everyday things, and flush them up to consciousness, exhibit them, as Art. I will live in the museum as I customarily do at home with my husband and my baby (right, or if you don't want me around at night I would come in every day) for the duration of the exhibition, and do all these things as public Art activities: I will sweep and wax the floors, dust everything, wash the walls (i.e. "floor paintings, dust works, soap-sculpture, wall-paintings"), cook, invite people to eat, clean up, put away, change light bulbs. I might save and make agglomerations and dispositions of all functional refuse. The exhibition area might look "empty" of art, but it will be maintained in full public view.

My working will be the work.

B. General Part: Everyone does a hell of a lot of noodiling maintenance work. The general part of the exhibition would consist of interviews of two kinds.

1. Previous interviews of, say, 50 different classes and kinds of occupations that run a gamut from "maintenance man", maid, sanitation man, mailman, union man, construction worker, librarian, grocerystore man, nurse, doctor, teacher, museum director, salesman, baseball player, child, criminal, bank president, mayor, movie star, artist, etc., about what they think maintenance is; how they feel about spending whatever parts of their lives on maintenance activities; what is the relationship between maintenance and freedom; what is the relationship between maintenance and life's dreams.

These interviews will be typed and exhibited.

MAINTENANCE ART -4- Mierle Laderman Ukeles

2. Interview Room--for spectators at the Exhibition: A room of desks and chairs where professional (?) interviewers will interview the spactators at the exhibition along same questions as typed interviews (in 1. above). The responses should be personal.

These interviews are taped and replayed throughout the exhibition area.

C. Earth Maintenance:

Everyday, a container of the following kinds of refuse will be delivered to the Museum: 1) the contents of one sanitation truck; 2) a container of polluted air; 3) a container of polluted Hudson River; 4) a container of ravaged land. Once at the exhibition, each container will be serviced: purified, depoluted, rehabilitated, recycled, and conserved by various technical (and/or pseudo-technical) procedures either by myself or scientists.

These servicing procedures are repeated for the duration of the exhibition.

Mierle Laderman Ukeles

Touch Sanitation Performance

DE

Die feministische und multidisziplinär arbeitende Künstlerin Mierle Laderman Ukeles macht seit den 1960er-Jahren in ihrer wegweisenden Praxis die existentielle Notwendigkeit der alltäglichen Wartungs- und Sorgearbeiten deutlich. 1977 wurde sie Artist in Residence bei der städtischen Müllabfuhr von New York City – eine (wenn auch unbezahlte) Position, die sie seit mehreren Jahrzehnten bis heute innehat. Die erste künstlerische Arbeit, die sie in diesem Zusammenhang realisierte, war *Touch Sanitation.* In dieser einjährigen Performance (Juli 1979 – Juni 1980, nach 1,5 Jahren intensiver Recherche) traf sie jeden einzelnen (nicht einige wenige, nicht eine repräsentative Stichprobe) der 8.500 Reinigungs- und Müllentsorgungsarbeiter[1] von New York City, schüttelte jedem die Hand und bedankte sich bei ihnen allen mit den folgenden Worten: „Danke, dass Sie New York City am Leben erhalten." Die Performance wurde in zehn mehrwöchigen, zirkulären Rundfahrten organisiert, bei denen Ukeles alle 59 Bezirke mit ihren Werkstätten, Müllumschlagplätzen, Verbrennungsanlagen und Deponien besuchte, „eine stadtweite, spiralförmige Spur ziehend, von Hand zu Hand".[2]

Dabei stellte sie auch die 8-stündige Arbeitsschicht nach, trat buchstäblich in die Fußstapfen der Arbeiter und lernte und verkörperte ihre Bewegungsmuster und täglichen Choreografien, die dieses öffentliche Care-System ausmachen. Rückblickend beschrieb Ukeles *Touch Sanitation* als „eine Entkartierung der formellen Stadt und eine Neukartierung der gesamten lebendigen Stadt, von ihrer Unterseite aufwärts"[3] oder – anders formuliert – eine Neukartierung, die von den sich bodennah bewegenden Körpern ausgeht und das Getrennte durch singuläre Gesten wieder zusammenzufügen sucht.

Zwei Videos dokumentieren diese epische Performance: *Touch Sanitation: Sanman Speaks* konzentriert sich auf Ukeles' Begegnungen und Gespräche mit den Arbeitern als Experten, während das Video *Touch Sanitation: Waste Flow* dem Weg des Abfalls von der Straße zur Deponie folgt und den Müll selbst als materiellen Hauptakteur in den Vordergrund stellt.

1979–1980

Touch Sanitation: Sanman Speaks
1979–1984
Video
Farbe, Ton
Color, sound
58 min

Touch Sanitation: Waste Flow
1979–1984
Video
Farbe, Ton
Color, sound
58 min

Kuratiert für *The Great Repair* von
Curated for *The Great Repair* by
Bettina Knaup
im Zusammenhang mit ihrer eigenen Forschung zu Pflege und Abfall
in conjunction with her own research on care and waste
Courtesy Mierle Laderman Ukeles & Ronald Feldman Gallery, New York

EN

Since the 1960s, feminist and multidisciplinary artist Mierle Laderman Ukeles has consistently highlighted the essential value of everyday maintenance work through her pioneering practice. In 1977, she joined the New York City Department of Sanitation as an (unsalaried) artist-in-residence—an engagement that has spanned several decades lasting to this day. The first of her works in this context was *Touch Sanitation.* During this year-long performance (July 1979 – June 1980, preceded by 1.5 years of intense research) she met and shook hands with every single one of New York City's 8,500 sanitation workers (not just with a few or a representative sample), personally thanking them with the words, "Thank you for keeping New York City alive." The performance was carried out in ten circular sweeps encompassing visits to all 59 sanitation districts, including their garages, marine transfer stations, incinerators, and landfills, "creating a city-wide spiral tracking form, hand to hand."[2] She also modeled the 8-hour shift and quite literally followed in the footsteps of the workers, learning and embodying the movement patterns and daily choreographies that constitute this public system of care. In a statement written years later, Ukeles described *Touch Sanitation* as a "dis-mapping of the formal city, and a re-mapping of the entire living City from its underbelly up."[3] To put it differently, the artist started with the gravitational moving body and used a singular gesture to connect what was separated.

Two videos document this epic performance: *Touch Sanitation: Sanman Speaks* focuses on the artist's encounters and conversations with the sanitation workers, highlighting their expertise; meanwhile, *Touch Sanitation: Waste Flow* traces the journey of waste from the streets to the landfill, emphasizing the waste material itself as the primary actor.

1
Ich verwende hier das Maskulinum, da es sich damals ausschließlich um männliche Arbeiter handelte.

2
Lucy Lippard: *Issue – Social Strategies by Women Artists*, London 1980, S. 50 f., Übersetzung durch ARCH+
Lucy Lippard, *Issue: Social Strategies by Women Artists* (London: Institute of Contemporary Arts, 1980), 50–51.

3
Mierle Laderman Ukeles: „Looking back from 2010", in: Patricia C. Phillips (Hg.): *Mierle Laderman Ukeles – Maintenance Art*, New York 2016, S. 223, Übersetzung durch ARCH+
Mierle Laderman Ukeles, "Looking back from 2010," in *Mierle Laderman Ukeles: Maintenance Art*, ed. Patricia C. Phillips (New York: Queens Museum of Art, DelMonico Books, Prestel, 2016), 223.

Text:
Bettina Knaup

Mierle Laderman Ukeles
Touch Sanitation Performance
New York City
1979–1980

"TOUCH sanitation" ©1979

A Maintenance Art Work:

Mierle Laderman Ukeles

City-Performance / Video / Exhibition

Public Art with Public Workers in Public Spaces for the Whole Public. It's Time.

for information call: 566 5527

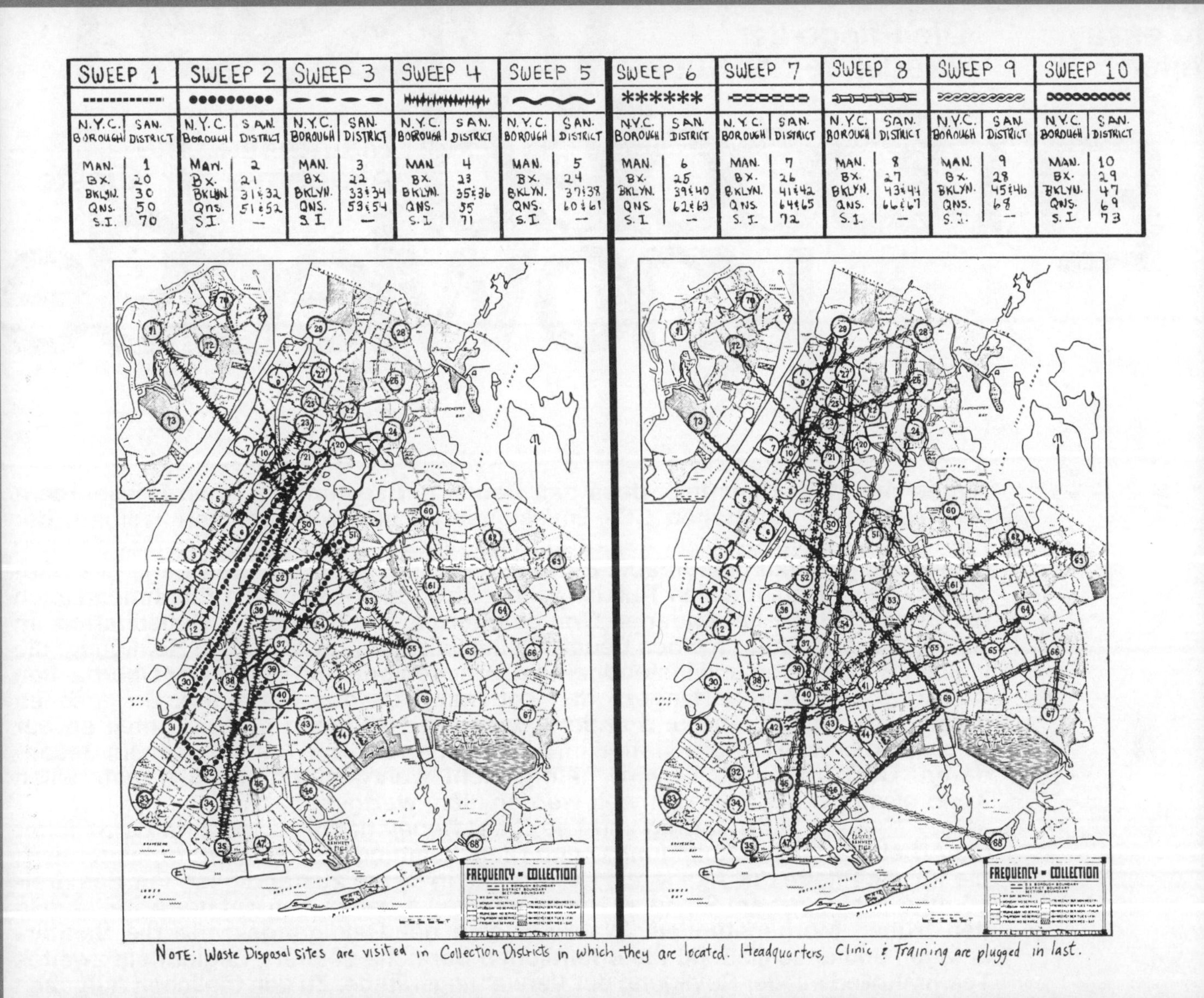

SWEEP 1		SWEEP 2		SWEEP 3		SWEEP 4		SWEEP 5		SWEEP 6		SWEEP 7		SWEEP 8		SWEEP 9		SWEEP 10	
N.Y.C. BOROUGH	SAN. DISTRICT	N.Y.C. BOROUGH	SAN. DISTRICT	N.Y.C. BOROUGH	SAN. DISTRICT	N.Y.C. BOROUGH	SAN. DISTRICT	N.Y.C. BOROUGH	SAN. DISTRICT	N.Y.C. BOROUGH	SAN. DISTRICT	N.Y.C. BOROUGH	SAN. DISTRICT	N.Y.C. BOROUGH	SAN. DISTRICT	N.Y.C. BOROUGH	SAN. DISTRICT	N.Y.C. BOROUGH	SAN. DISTRICT
MAN.	1	MAN.	2	MAN.	3	MAN.	4	MAN.	5	MAN.	6	MAN.	7	MAN.	8	MAN.	9	MAN.	10
BX.	20	BX.	21	BX.	22	BX.	23	BX.	24	BX.	25	BX.	26	BX.	27	BX.	28	BX.	29
BKLYN.	30	BKLYN.	31&32	BKLYN.	33&34	BKLYN.	35&36	BKLYN.	37&38	BKLYN.	39&40	BKLYN.	41&42	BKLYN.	43&44	BKLYN.	45&46	BKLYN.	47
QNS.	50	QNS.	51&52	QNS.	53&54	QNS.	55	QNS.	60&61	QNS.	62&63	QNS.	64&65	QNS.	66&67	QNS.	68	QNS.	69
S.I.	70	S.I.	—	S.I.	—	S.I.	71	S.I.	—	S.I.	—	S.I.	72	S.I.	—	S.I.	—	S.I.	73

1979 wurde eine Broschüre an alle 8.500 Beschäftigten der New Yorker Stadtreinigung verschickt, in der sie zur Teilnahme an der *Touch Sanitation Performance* eingeladen wurden. Die Broschüre enthält einen Brief der Künstlerin und eine Karte mit einer Übersicht über die zehn Rundfahrten, die Ukeles unternahm, um alle 59 Bezirke der städtischen Müllabfuhr von New York City zu erreichen.

In 1979, a brochure was sent to all 8,500 New York City sanitation workers inviting them to participate in the *Touch Sanitation Performance*. The booklet contains a letter from the artist and a map-itinerary of the “10 sweeps” Ukeles made to reach all 59 districts of the New York City Department of Sanitation.

Kleine Reinigungs- und Dienstleistungsgesellschaft, Bildessay
Photo essay
Zara Pfeifer

Verkörpertes Wissen

Die Pflege der Akademie der Künste

Embodied Knowledge

Maintaining the Akademie der Künste

DE

Angesichts der Erkenntnis, dass das Bauen mit seinem enormen Ressourcenverbrauch und den hohen CO_2-Emissionen zu den wesentlichen Treibern der Klimakrise gehört, werden der Erhalt und die Umnutzung von Bestandsbauten eine wichtige Zukunftsaufgabe. Es geht dabei nicht nur um die Pflege des Bauerbes – einen traditionellen Teil der Architekturpraxis –, sondern zunehmend auch um den Erhalt der gebundenen Grauen Energie. Die Pflege der Bausubstanz im Alltag gewinnt dadurch einen neuen Stellenwert: Die regelmäßige Reinigung, die kleinen Reparaturen und Instandhaltungsarbeiten oder die Pflege der Oberflächen und Infrastrukturen verlängern den Lebenszyklus des Gebauten. So gesehen haben Reinigungskräfte und andere Sorgearbeiter*innen großen Anteil an der Reproduktion von Gesellschaften im Allgemeinen und von Institutionen im Besonderen. Doch deren Rolle wird häufig nicht wahrgenommen, ihre materiellen Kenntnisse der gebauten Umwelt werden nicht wertgeschätzt.

Im Auftrag von *The Great Repair* hat die Künstlerin Zara Pfeifer die Arbeit der Kleine Reinigungs- und Dienstleistungsgesellschaft dokumentiert, die für die Pflege der Akademie der Künste in Berlin zuständig ist. Für das dreiköpfige Team, das am Standort Hanseatenweg arbeitet, beginnt der Arbeitstag in den frühen Morgenstunden. Während eine der Reinigungskräfte die Sanitäranlagen und anschließend die öffentlichen Bereiche säubert, beginnt ein zweites Teammitglied mit der Reinigung der Verwaltungsräume. Zu den täglichen Aufgaben gehören das Staubsaugen und Moppen der Böden in einem zweistufigen Verfahren, das Wischen von Oberflächen nach einem farbcodierten System, das Nachfüllen von Hygieneartikeln, das Entsorgen von Abfällen, das Aufschließen von Räumen, das Einschalten der Beleuchtung sowie die Pflege verschiedener Materialien, die jeweils eigene Techniken, Werkzeuge und Pflegemittel erfordern. Hierfür hat das Unternehmen eine Reihe von Zertifikaten erworben, die die Einhaltung verschiedener DIN-Normen bescheinigen, und die geschulten Mitarbeitenden nehmen regelmäßig an Weiterbildungen teil, um neue Reinigungsmethoden oder die Bedienung von Geräten zu erlernen. Neben der täglichen Pflege werden die Ausstellungsräume, Wohnungen und Ateliers in unterschiedlichen Intervallen gereinigt. In größeren Abständen werden Sonderleistungen notwendig, darunter Fenster- und Fassadenreinigung, Denkmalpflege, Reparatur und Sanierung, wie jüngst die Aufarbeitung des historischen Hirnholzparketts im Ausstellungsraum, die über 20 Jahre nicht erfolgt war.

All diese Aufgaben sind erledigt, bevor die ersten Besucher*innen um 10 Uhr eintreffen. Obwohl sich die hochspezialisierten Arbeiter*innen um eine Vielzahl von Gebäuden aus so unterschiedlichen Bereichen wie Bildung, Kultur, Politik, Verwaltung, Medizin, Handwerk und Industrie kümmern – darunter einige der bedeutendsten Wahrzeichen der Stadt wie etwa der Berliner Dom –, wird ihre unverzichtbare Arbeit meist unsichtbar gemacht.

2023
Digitaldruck, 9 Fotografien, jeweils
Digital print, 9 photographs, each
50 × 40 cm
außer ein Foto
except one photograph
40 × 30 cm

EN

Considering that construction, with its enormous consumption of resources and high levels of CO_2 emissions, is one of the main drivers of the climate crisis, preserving and converting the existing building stock becomes a crucial task for the future. Thus, caring for the built heritage, which has traditionally been a part of architectural practice, increasingly includes preserving embodied energy. This gives new importance to the everyday care of building substance: regular cleaning, minor repairs and maintenance work, and care of surfaces and infrastructures extend buildings' life cycles. In this sense, cleaners and other care workers crucially contribute to the reproduction of society in general and institutions in particular. Their role is, however, rarely acknowledged, their material knowledge of the built environment undervalued.

Commissioned by *The Great Repair*, artist Zara Pfeifer has documented the work of the Kleine Reinigungs- und Dienstleistungsgesellschaft, the cleaning and services company responsible for maintaining the Akademie der Künste (Academy of Arts) in Berlin. The three-person team that works in the building on Hanseatenweg begins their day in the early hours of the morning with one of the employees cleaning and maintaining the sanitary infrastructure before moving on to the public areas, while another starts cleaning the administrative areas. Daily duties include vacuuming and mopping floors with a two-tier method, wiping surfaces according to a color-coded system, restocking supplies, disposing of waste, unlocking rooms, switching on lights, and tending to different materials that each require specific detergents, tools, and techniques of maintenance. To this end, the company has acquired a range of certificates attesting their adherence to various DIN standards, and the trained employees regularly take part in vocational training courses to learn new methods of maintenance or how to operate machinery. On top of the daily upkeep, the exhibition area, apartments, and studios are cleaned in different intervals. Special services become necessary at longer intervals, including window and facade cleaning, built heritage conservation, and repair and renovation, such as the recent refurbishment of the historic end-grain parquet in the exhibition halls, which had not been done for over 20 years.

Before the first visitors arrive at 10 a.m., all these tasks are completed. Although the highly specialized workers take care of a multitude of buildings from fields as diverse as education, culture, politics, administration, medicine, crafts, and industry — including some of the city's most notable landmarks, such as the Berlin Cathedral — their indispensable work is routinely rendered invisible.

Text:
Daniel Kuhnert

Strang 3
Strang 1
Strang 2

Edit

Gross Domestic Product (GDP)

DE

Nach seiner Markteinführung Anfang der 1920er-Jahre wurde der Staubsauger als unverzichtbares Haushaltsgerät angepriesen, das Hausfrauen durch seine Effizienz und bequeme Bedienung entlasten würde. Die Mechanisierung der privaten Hausarbeit in Form von massenproduzierten Konsumgütern brachte jedoch nicht nur Erleichterung, sondern verfestigte die Rolle der Hausfrau und beförderte ihre Vereinzelung in den vorstädtischen Siedlungen. Die Vergesellschaftung der häuslichen Arbeit ist daher eine zentrale Forderung von Feminist*innen. Das Kollektiv Edit adressiert das Thema mit einem Staubsauger, der nur funktioniert, wenn er von drei Personen gleichzeitig bedient wird. Statt Sorgearbeiter*innen zu isolieren, wird die Hausarbeit so auf mehrere Schultern einer (Haus-)Gemeinschaft verteilt.

Gross Domestic Product (GDP) ist weniger konkreter Lösungsvorschlag als vielmehr spekulativer Prototyp, der ausgehend vom kleinen Maßstab der Gestaltung von Alltagsgegenständen dazu einlädt, unsere Wachstumsökonomie und den ihr zugrundeliegenden, auf Individualismus und Autonomie basierenden Effizienz- und Leistungsgedanken infrage zu stellen. Die Arbeit ist Teil von Edits fortlaufender Studie *Honey, I'm Home*. Die Serie zielt auf eine Kritik der Spaltung in eine öffentliche und private Sphäre, in Produktion und Reproduktion, in entlohnte Erwerbsarbeit und unsichtbare Haus- und Sorgearbeit, die bis heute unser Alltagsleben wie auch die gebaute Umwelt prägt. Mit seinen Interventionen regt Edit an, gesellschaftliche Verhältnisse neu zu verhandeln und das Potential der Sorgearbeit als kollektiver und politischer Akt zu erkunden.

2019
Installation
Mixed media
65 × 65 × 65 cm

EN

Following its market launch in the beginning of the 1920s, the vacuum cleaner was touted as an essential household appliance designed to offer housewives a convenient and efficient solution for their cleaning needs. However, the mechanization of domestic work in the form of mass-produced household appliances not only brought relief, but also solidified the role of the housewife and promoted her isolation in suburban settlements. Socializing domestic work is therefore a central feminist demand. The collective Edit addresses this issue with a vacuum cleaner that can only be operated when used by three people at the same time. Instead of isolating care workers, it shares the housework among several members of a (household) community.

Gross Domestic Product (GDP) is less a concrete proposal for a solution than a speculative prototype that invites us—starting from the small scale of the design of everyday objects—to question our growth economy and its underlying idea of efficiency and performance based on individualism and autonomy. The three-way vacuum cleaner is part of Edit's ongoing study *Honey, I'm Home*. This series of projects challenges the division between the public and private spheres, production and reproduction, paid employment and unrecognized domestic and care work, which continue to shape society and the built environment. Through its interventions, Edit encourages us to renegotiate social relationships and to explore the inherent potential of care as a collective and political act.

Text:
Franziska Gödicke

Edit, *Gross Domestic Product (GDP)*, 2019
Das feministische Kollektiv Edit hat einen Staubsauger entworfen, der nur funktioniert, wenn drei Personen ihn gleichzeitig benutzen.

The feminist collective Edit designed a vacuum cleaner that functions only if three people operate it at the same time.

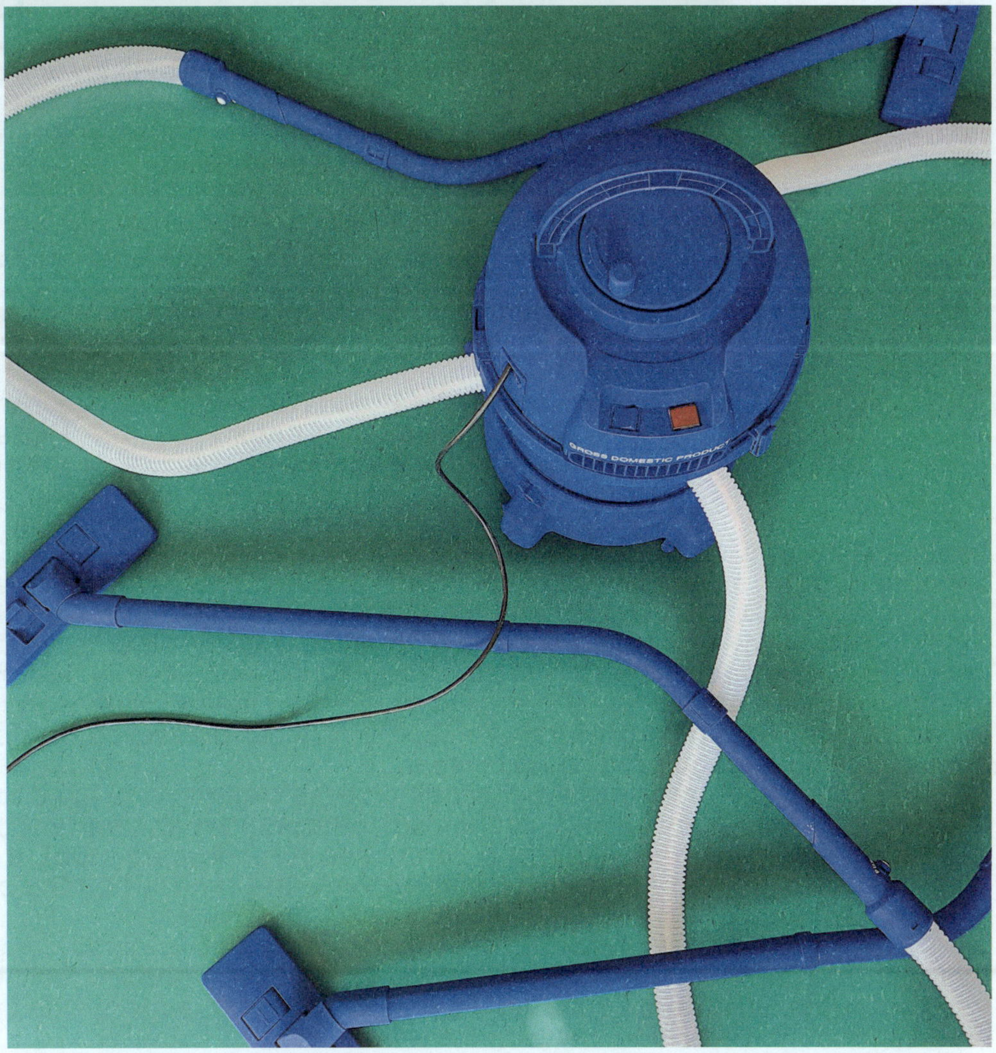

Statt Sorgearbeit Einzelpersonen zu überlassen, zwingt *Gross Domestic Product (GDP)* eine (Haus-)Gemeinschaft aktiv zu werden.

Instead of leaving care work to a sole individual, *Gross Domestic Product (GDP)* forces multiple members of a (household) community to become active.

Silke Langenberg

Repair: Making Things Better

DE

Der Kurs *Reparatur*, den Silke Langenberg 2014 an der Hochschule München und ab 2020 an der ETH Zürich einführte, verbindet grundlegende Konzepte der Denkmalpflege mit neuartigen Methoden der Reparatur- und Fab-Lab-Bewegung. Die Studierenden sind herausgefordert, eigene – häufig industriell gefertigte – Objekte zu reparieren, die aufgrund Alter oder fehlerhafter Konstruktion versagen. Dabei überprüfen sie, ob die Objekte und ihre Teile in Bezug auf ihre Konstruktion, ihre Materialien oder ihr Design verbessert werden können – um sie dauerhafter zu machen, ihren Wert zu steigern und ihre Reparaturfähigkeit zu erhöhen. Oft sind es kleine, aber entscheidende Maßnahmen, die das Objekt erheblich aufwerten und seine Lebensdauer verlängern.

So befestigten die Studierenden beispielsweise die beiden Hälften des defekten Schiebemechanismus zur Größenanpassung eines Kopfhörers mit zwei modifizierten Schlauchschellen. Die Sitzfläche eines handgefertigten dreibeinigen Hockers wurde neu gepolstert und mit einer gestickten Sitzfläche bezogen, die dem Original nachempfunden ist. Die fehlende Rückwand einer aus dem Jahr 1954 stammenden Wanduhr wurde durch 3D-Druck ersetzt.

Häufig wurden die bearbeiteten Objekte nicht dafür gebaut, repariert zu werden oder das entsprechende Know-how und die Handfertigkeit sind längst verloren gegangen. Ihre Reparatur erfordert, etablierte Erhaltungskonzepte neu zu interpretieren und kreativ anzuwenden.

2018–2020
Objekte aus dem Kurs *Reparatur*, Hochschule München und ETH Zürich
Objects from the class *Repair*, Munich University of Applied Sciences and ETH Zürich

EN

Repair, a class introduced by Silke Langenberg at Munich University of Applied Sciences in 2014 and later, in 2020, at ETH Zürich, combines core strategies of monument preservation with innovative repair techniques and principles of the Fab Lab movement. Students were tasked with repairing their own—often industrially manufactured—objects suffering from structural flaws and recurring failures. They explored possibilities for enhancing the construction, materials, and design of the objects and their parts to improve durability and repairability. Often, minor but critical measures can significantly upgrade an object and prolong its lifespan.

For example, two modified hose clamps were used to secure the two sections of a faulty sliding mechanism, enabling the adjustment of the headband on a set of headphones. On a handmade three-legged stool, the seat was reupholstered and adorned with an embroidery pattern based on the original. The missing back cover of a 1954 wall clock was 3D-printed.

In many cases, the objects were not originally designed with their refurbishment in mind, and the knowledge and skills needed for the latter may have been lost over time. Repairing the objects requires reinterpreting established preservation concepts and applying them creatively.

Text:
Silke Langenberg

1

2

3

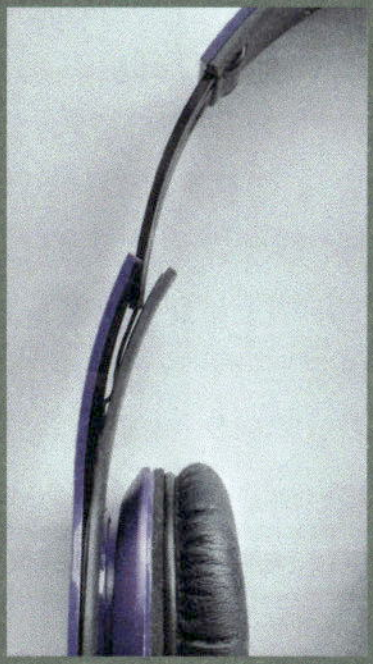
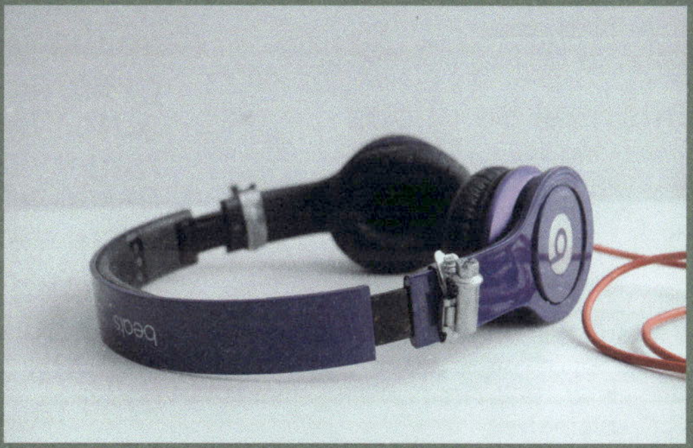

4

5

1
Nils Fischer, 2019–2020
Holz, Metall
Wood, metal
83 × 45 × 50 cm
Das zerrissene Wiener Geflecht des Freischwingers wurde durch ein neu angefertigtes Polster ersetzt, was auch künftige Reparaturen erleichtert.
The torn rattan weave of a cantilever chair was replaced with a custom upholstery, thereby also simplifying future repairs.

2
Helia Jamshidi, 2020
Wolle, Baumwolle
Wool, cotton
95 × 60 cm
Die ausgefransten Ränder des persischen Teppichs wurden in händischer Knüpfarbeit restauriert.
The frayed edges of an old Persian rug were restored by hand knotting.

3
Defne Çetinkaya, 2020
Polstermaterial, Holz
Upholstery, wood
50 × 40 × 40 cm
Das Muster des antiken Hockers wurde digital rekonstruiert und auf einen neuen Bezug gestickt.
The pattern of an antique stool was digitally reconstructed and embroidered onto a new cover.

4
Eloïse Frey, 2020
Plastik, Metall, Schaumstoff
Plastic, metal, foam
Durchmesser
Diameter 20 cm
Der gebrochene Bügel der Kopfhörer wurde mit einer Schlauchschelle repariert.
These headphones' broken headband was repaired with a hose clamp.

5
Nikolaus Berchtold, 2018–2019
3D-Druck mit umweltfreundlichem Polymer und Metall
3D printing with eco-friendly polymer and metal
Durchmesser
Diameter 33 cm
Die fehlende Abdeckung der Wanduhr von 1954 wurde als digitales Modell konstruiert und anschließend im 3D-Druck reproduziert.
The missing back cover of a 1954 wall clock was first recreated as a digital model and then 3D-printed.

Michael Wolf

Bastard Chairs

China 2001–2017
14 skulpturale Objekte
sculptural objects (ready-made)
Mixed media
(Holz, Plastik, Schnur, Weide, Stoff, Metall)
(Wood, plastic, string, wicker, fabric, metal)
Verschiedene Größen
Various sizes
Courtesy Michael Wolf Estate

Informal Solutions

Hongkong 2003–2018
81 Fotografien
photographs
Digitaler C-Print, je
Digital C-print, each
26 × 19 cm
4 skulpturale Objekte
sculptural objects (ready-made)
Verschiedene Größen
Various sizes
Courtesy Michael Wolf Estate

DE

Das Leben in asiatischen Megastädten faszinierte den 2019 verstorbenen Fotografen Michael Wolf zeit seines Schaffens. 24 Jahre wohnte er in Hongkong, wo er unter anderem die bekannte Serie *Architecture of Density* aufnahm. Lag sein Fokus hier auf den endlosen Hochhausfassaden, die in seinen Bildern zu abstrakten Flächen verschwammen, waren es in anderen Arbeiten Details aus der Alltagskultur der Stadt, die Wolfs typologischen Blick auf sich zogen. Auch wenn in diesen Bildern keine Menschen zu sehen sind, erzählen sie doch viel von ihnen. *Informal Solutions* entstand 2003 bis 2017 in den Seitengassen und an den Hinterausgängen Hongkongs und zeigt Gegenstände wie Wischmopps, Handschuhe, Kleiderbügel, Schuhe, Regenschirme und Pflanzentöpfe. Sie lehnen an der Wand, klemmen hinter Rohren, hängen an Nägeln oder sind mit Bändern fixiert. Was gerade verfügbar ist, wird verwendet und für den jeweiligen Zweck nutzbar gemacht. Da die Wohnflächen knapp bemessen sind und auch öffentlicher Raum in der dicht bebauten Stadt rar ist, nahmen sich ihre Bewohner*innen die Freiheit, sich den städtischen Raum anzueignen und für ihre Bedürfnisse zu nutzen. Die Arrangements der Alltagsgegenstände haben geradezu einen skulpturalen Charakter, auch wenn die Autor*innen der improvisierten Installationen – die Menschen, die in den Restaurants, Geschäften und Büros der Vorderhäuser arbeiten – alles andere als Kunst dabei im Sinn hatten. Skulptural wirken auch die Objekte in *Bastard Chairs*, die Wolf auf seinen Reisen durch China sammelte und fotografisch festhielt. Es handelt sich um immer wieder reparierte, aus unterschiedlichen Materialien zusammengeschusterte Stühle ohne offenkundigen gestalterischen Anspruch, die doch gerade aufgrund ihrer Einzigartigkeit von besonderem ästhetischem Wert sind. Wolf fand sie visuell interessant, bewunderte aber auch das Bemühen, mit Material so sparsam wie möglich umzugehen.

EN

Throughout his career, photographer Michael Wolf, who died in 2019, was fascinated by life in Asian megacities. He lived in Hong Kong for 24 years, where he produced, among other things, the renowned photo series *Architecture of Density*. While that series features endless building facades blending into abstract patterns, in other works Wolf's typological gaze zooms in on the details of everyday urban life. Even in the absence of people in the photographs, the objects reveal much about their existence. *Informal Solutions* was created in Hong Kong's alleyways and back exits from 2003 to 2017, depicting objects such as mops, gloves, washcloths, hangers, umbrellas, and planters. They lean on walls, fasten onto pipes, hang from nails, or are fixed with straps. Whatever is available is applied to the task at hand. Since living space is tight and public space is scarce in the densely structured city, residents take the liberty to appropriate urban space and adapt it to their needs. The arrangements of everyday objects reveal an almost sculptural character, even when the authors of such improvised installations—people working in restaurants, shops, or offices on the front side of these buildings—had anything but art in mind. A sculptural quality also radiates from the objects in *Bastard Chairs* that Wolf photographed and collected during his travels across China. This series features repeatedly repaired chairs cobbled together from different materials. Though devoid of design pretension, they are endowed with aesthetic value precisely because of their uniqueness. Wolf was not only captivated by the chairs' appearance but also admired the effort to make the most of available resources.

Text:
Nora Dünser

Michael Wolf
Aus der Serie
From the series
***Bastard Chairs*, 1995–2017**

Michael Wolf
Aus der Serie
From the series
Bastard Chairs, 1995–2017

Michael Wolf
Aus der Serie
From the series
Hong Kong Informal Seating Arrangements, 2013–2015

DE

Der profitgetriebene Kapitalismus hat zu immer schnelleren Zyklen der Verwertung und Vernutzung geführt. Angesichts von Klimakrise und Ressourcenschwund ist dieses auf Verbrauch und Zerstörung von Bestehendem basierende System längst nicht mehr tragfähig. In der Architektur ist es unter dem Primat des Marktes dennoch weiterhin gängige Praxis, Gebäude massenhaft abzureißen und durch Neubauten zu ersetzen. Zugleich besitzt die Disziplin jedoch auch ein spezifisches Reparaturwissen; Strategien der Reparatur sind seit jeher Kernbestandteil des Repertoires der Architektur. Das Arbeiten mit dem Bestand – die Instandsetzung, das Um- und Weiterbauen – kann in dieser Perspektive als Gegenstrategie zur Obsoleszenz begriffen werden, um dazu beizutragen, den unablässigen Kreislauf aus Destruktion und Neuproduktion zu verlangsamen. Das Gebot unserer Zeit ist die Pflege und der behutsame Umgang mit dem, was bereits vorhanden ist.

Text:
Florian Hertweck

Mit dem Bestand arbeiten

Work with the Existing

EN

Profit-driven capitalism has led to ever swifter cycles of consumption and wastage. In light of the climate crisis and fast-dwindling resources, this system, with its insistence on exhaustion and destruction of the existing, has long ceased to be viable. In architecture it is nevertheless still a customary practice under the primacy of the market to simply demolish buildings en masse and build new ones. At the same time, however, the discipline also possesses a specific knowledge of repairing; strategies of repair have always been a core element of architecture's repertoire. In this view, working with existing buildings, overhauling them, converting them, and extending them can be seen as a strategy to counter obsolescence and to contribute to slowing down the incessant cycle of destruction and new production. The order of the day is to nurture what already exists and to treat it with care.

Winfried Brenne

Materialproben-archiv

Brenne Architekten

DE

Das Materialprobenarchiv Brenne Architekten ist eine außergewöhnliche Sammlung, die rund 12.000 Relikte von Bauten der Moderne umfasst. Darunter finden sich die zum UNESCO-Weltkulturerbe zählenden *Siedlungen der Berliner Moderne* und *Das Bauhaus und seine Stätten in Weimar, Dessau, Bernau* sowie 18 denkmalgeschützte Siedlungen, 18 Einzeldenkmäler und 38 ehemals im Besitz der Gemeinnützigen Siedlungs- und Wohnungsbaugesellschaft (GSW) befindliche Wohnanlagen in Berlin.

Seinen Anfang nahm das Archiv 1976/77 mit der von Bruno Taut entworfenen Waldsiedlung Zehlendorf in Berlin, auch bekannt als Onkel Toms Hütte, in deren Nachbarschaft der Architekt Helge Pitz wohnte. Er beobachtete, wie die 1926 bis 1932 entstandenen Häuser über die Jahre ihr ursprüngliches Aussehen durch Sanierungsarbeiten verloren, was er im mangelnden Wissen um die ursprüngliche Bautechnik, Materialität und Farbigkeit begründet sah. Zunächst in Eigeninitiative und dann im Auftrag des Landesdenkmalamts unternahm Pitz gemeinsam mit Winfried Brenne eine erste Bestandsaufnahme der Einfamilienreihenhäuser nördlich der Argentinischen Allee. Daraufhin konnte die Wohnungsgesellschaft GEHAG mit Unterstützung des Landesdenkmalamtes gewonnen werden, für die gesamte Siedlung entsprechende denkmalpflegerische Gutachten als Grundlage für eine sukzessive denkmalgerechte Instandsetzung zu beauftragen. Diese beinhalteten neben einer eingehenden Literatur- und Bauaktenrecherche sowie einer systematischen grafischen Aufzeichnung der noch erhaltenen bauzeitlichen Bauteile Materialprobenentnahmen, um die Farbigkeit der Gebäudeelemente mittels Laboruntersuchungen und Farbwertbestimmung zu analysieren. Denn die Wiederherstellung des originalen Kolorits war der Kern der Instandsetzungsarbeiten. Ausgehend von diesem ersten Bauforschungsprojekt wurde die Architekturwerkstatt Pitz-Brenne und ab 1990 Winfried Brenne Architekten mit weiteren Gutachten zur denkmalgerechten Instandsetzung von Bauwerken der Berliner Moderne, darunter die Siedlungen Britz, Siemensstadt, Weiße Stadt, Gartenstadt Falkenberg und Wohnstadt Carl Legien beauftragt; so wuchs das Materialprobenarchiv konstant an.

Viele der aufbewahrten Materialien sind für die Gestaltung der Gebäudeoberflächen relevant, etwa Holz-, Putz- und Metallfragmente mit Farbfassung oder auch ganze Bauelemente wie Fliesen, Lüftungsgitter, Klinkersteine, Holzfensterbauteile, farbiger Linoleumbodenbelag oder Hauseingangsleuchten. Es gelangten aber auch Materialien wie Torfoleum-Dämmstoff ins Archiv. Der Sammlungsschatz geriet im laufenden Bürobetrieb von Brenne Architekten jedoch mehr und mehr in Vergessenheit und war durch unterschiedliche Archivierungsweisen in einem sehr heterogenen Erhaltungszustand.

Deshalb wurde der Archivbestand durch die Restauratorin Jana Hainbach von 2021 bis 2022 im Rahmen eines Fellowship der Wüstenrot Stiftung inventarisiert. Ziel des Projekts war es, die Materialproben nicht nur als Zeitdokument für die pionierhafte restauratorische Befundsicherung der 1970er- bis 1990er-Jahre, sondern auch als Primärdokumente und Wissensspeicher der herausragenden Objekte und Welterbestätten der Moderne in Berlin, Brandenburg, Niedersachsen und Sachsen-Anhalt zu erhalten und für kommende Forschungen verfügbar zu machen.[1] Im April 2022 wurde das fertig inventarisierte Materialprobenarchiv dem Baukunstarchiv der Akademie der Künste Berlin übergeben, über dessen Archivdatenbank es nun auch öffentlich zugänglich ist.

Durch die Sicherung des historischen Bestands, die Vielzahl von Materialproben und ihre gute Dokumentation ist das Materialprobenarchiv Brenne Architekten eine wichtige Quelle für die historische Bauforschung und Denkmalpflege. Bei vielen der Archivstücke handelt es sich um die einzig erhaltenen originalen Materialien der Gebäude. Darüber hinaus lässt sich mit ihrer Hilfe die

1979–2004
Architekturbüro Brenne Architekten (ehemals/formerly Architekturwerkstatt Pitz-Brenne)
2021–2022 Inventarisierung
Inventory
Jana Hainbach
2022–2023 Übergabe Baukunstarchiv der Akademie der Künste
Transfer to the Architectural Archives at Akademie der Künste
Werner Heegewaldt, Amrei Buchholz, Sibylle Hoiman

Winfried Brenne begann ab 1988 sukzessive mit der Restaurierung des einstigen Wohnhauses von Bruno Taut in Dahlewitz bei Berlin, das der Architekt 1926/27 für sich und seine Familie errichtet hatte. Materialproben – hier vor ihrer Inventarisierung – halfen bei der Bestimmung der originalen Farben, Materialien und Techniken.

In 1988, Winfried Brenne began gradually restoring the house in Dahlewitz that Bruno Taut designed for himself and his family in 1926/27. Material samples, pictured here before being inventoried, helped determine the original colors, materials, and techniques.

Entwicklung von traditioneller handwerklicher Bautechnik, wie Kalkputzmörtel mit Kalkfarbe, hin zu standardisierten, konfektionierten Baustoffen, wie beispielsweise Edelputzen, nachzeichnen.

Die detaillierte Erforschung der ursprünglichen Gestaltung bildet eine der grundlegenden Voraussetzungen für kommende Instandsetzungen. Das Archiv dient bereits jetzt als Vergleichssammlung für den aktuellen Denkmalpflegeplan der Waldsiedlung Zehlendorf. Im Rahmen des DFG-Forschungsprojekts „Die Materialität und Farbigkeit der *Siedlungen der Berliner Moderne* – Eine kritische Revision konservatorisch-restauratorischer und materialkundlicher Untersuchungsmethoden im Lauf der Instandsetzungsgeschichte" von Professor Thomas Danzl (TU München) und Dr. rer. nat. Christoph Herm (HfBK Dresden) werden derzeit archivalische Forschungen betrieben und die Proben aus dem Materialprobenarchiv Brenne Architekten analysiert, um Informationen über die Materialität und Farbigkeit der Siedlungen der Berliner Moderne zu gewinnen.[2] Die Untersuchungsergebnisse werden wichtige Informationen liefern, um bei zukünftigen Reparaturen und Instandsetzungen die richtigen Materialien und Farben auszuwählen und die historische Gestaltung korrekt wiederherzustellen.

EN

Brenne Architekten's Material Samples Archive is an extraordinary collection comprising around 12,000 relics from modernist buildings. These include UNESCO World Heritage Sites such as the Bauhaus in Weimar, Dessau, and Bernau and the Berlin Modernism Housing Estates, as well as 18 other landmark-protected housing estates, 18 individual landmarks, and 38 housing estates in Berlin formerly owned by the Gemeinnützige Siedlungs- und Wohnungsbaugesellschaft (GSW, Association for Cooperative Apartments and Housing Estates).

The archive began in 1976/77 with the Waldsiedlung Zehlendorf in Berlin, also known as Onkel Toms Hütte, designed by Bruno Taut. Living nearby was the architect Helge Pitz, who observed that the buildings of the Zehlendorf housing estate, constructed from 1926 to 1932, had begun to lose their original appearance over the course of various renovations. He blamed this on a lack of knowledge about the original techniques, materials, and colors used in the buildings' construction. At first independently and later commissioned by the Berlin Monument Authority, Pitz teamed with Winfried Brenne to conduct a preliminary survey of the single-family row houses north of Argentinische Allee. Afterward, Pitz and Brenne persuaded the GEHAG housing association, with support from the Monument Authority, to commission an expert assessment of the whole estate as a basis for future restoration adhering to landmark standards. In addition to research into construction files and associated literature, as well as systematic visual documentation of preserved original components, the assessment involved material samples used to analyze the color of the building elements through lab tests and color value examinations. After all, restoring the estate to its original color scheme was central to the restoration. Based on this first research project, Architekturwerkstatt Pitz-Brenne, and, after 1990, Winfried Brenne Architekten, were commissioned to conduct preservation assessments for landmarks of Berlin modernism, including the housing estates of Britz, Siemensstadt, Weiße Stadt, Gartenstadt Falkenberg, and Wohnstadt Carl Legien. In the process, the Material Samples Archive continued to grow.

Many materials stored in the archive are relevant for the design of building surfaces, such as painted wood, plaster, and metal fragments, or even entire construction elements like tiles, ventilation grilles, clinker bricks, timber window components, colored linoleum flooring, and entryway lamps. The archive also contains materials such as Torfoleum insulation made of peat. However, over time at Brenne Architekten, the collection fell into neglect, with the items archived in various ways and exhibiting considerably different preservation conditions.

For this reason, conservator Jana Hainbach received a 2021/22 fellowship from the Wüstenrot Stiftung to inventory the archive. The goal was not only to preserve the material samples as documents of pioneering restoration research undertaken from the 1970s to 1990s, but also to preserve them as primary sources and repositories of knowledge on outstanding buildings and World Heritage Sites in Berlin, Brandenburg, Lower Saxony, and Saxony-Anhalt—while making them available to future researchers.[1] In April 2022, the finalized inventory of the Material Samples Archive was handed over to the Architectural Archives at the Akademie der Künste in Berlin, where it is publicly accessible through the Archives database.

Thanks to the historical building materials it has secured, as well as the sheer number of material samples and their thorough documentation,

Materialprobenarchiv Brenne Architekten

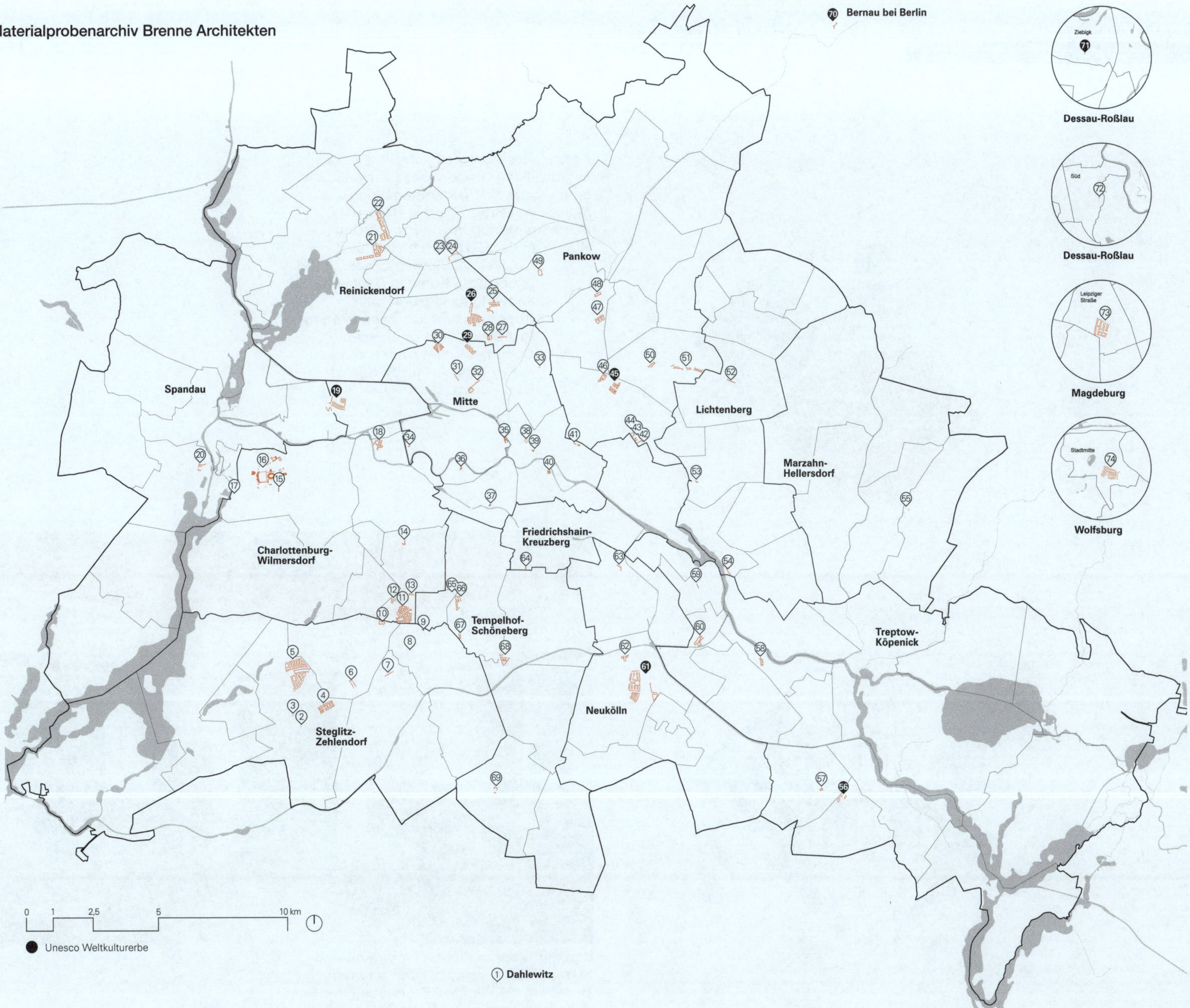

Dahlewitz

① Ehemaliges Wohnhaus Bruno Taut
Bauzeit: 1926-29
Architekt: Taut, Bruno

Berlin, Steglitz-Zehlendorf

② Dörfliches Wohngebäude
Bauzeit: 1800/1850, 1907
Architekt: Bastian & Kabelitz

③ Villa Erdmann
Bauzeit: N/A
Architekt: Erdmann & Spindler

④ Siedlung Am Mühlenberg
Bauzeit: 1931-36
Architekt: Klein, Adolf & Hochhaus, Gustav & Richter, Erich & Paulus und Paulus

⑤ Waldsiedlung Zehlendorf (Onkel Toms Hütte)
Bauzeit: 1911-30
Architekt: Taut, Bruno & Häring, Hugo & Salvisberg, Otto Rudolf
Landschaft: Migge, Leberecht & Willings-Göhre, Martha

⑥ Mietwohnanlage Dahlem II
Bauzeit: 1904-06
Architekt: Köhn, Erich

⑦ Reihenhausanlage Hortensienstraße
Bauzeit: 1924-25
Architekt: Salvisberg, Otto Rudolf

⑧ Schwartzsche Villa
Bauzeit: 1895-96, 1919-20
Architekt: Heidecke, Christian & Noack, Bruno & Antz, Ludwig

⑨ Titaniapalast
Bauzeit: 1927-28
Architekt: Schöffler & Schönbach & Jacobi

⑩ Wohnanlage Lentzeallee & Gregor-Mendel-Straße & Milowstraße & Spilstraße
Bauzeit: 1922-23
Architekt: Preußisches Finanzministerium, Hochbauabteilung

Berlin, Charlottenburg-Wilmersdorf

⑪ Gartenstadt am Südwestkorso mit Künstlerkolonie
Bauzeit: 1927-33, 1938-39, 1950, 1952-53
Architekt: Altmann, Hans & Braun, Josef & Gunzenhauser, Alfred & Bohne, Erich & Iwan, Heinrich & Zamojski, Stephan von & Jessen, Hans & Krämer, Jean & Kraffert, Hans & Roethele, Karl & Rossius-Rhyn, Ernst & Schmidt, Georg & Straumer, Heinrich & Virchow, Hugo, Paulus & Paulus

⑫ Wohnanlage Binger Straße
Bauzeit: 1926-30
Architekt: Gerschel, Alfred & Mebes, Paul, Emmerich, Paul & Bohne, Erich, Stoffregen, Heinz & Pötschke, Georg

⑬ Mietshaus Deidesheimer Straße & Ahrweilerstraße & Homburger Straße & Laubacher Straße
Bauzeit: 1925-26
Architekt: Straumer, Heinrich & Binder, Richard

⑭ Wohnblock Zähringerstraße & Württembergische Straße & Wittelsbacherstraße
Bauzeit: 1925, 1930
Architekt: Stahl-Urach, Carl & Gessner, Albert

⑮ Unité d'Habitation Typ Berlin & Corbusier-Haus
Bauzeit: 1956-58
Architekt: Le Corbusier & Hinssen, Felix

⑯ Olympiagelände & Eh. Reichssportfeld & Eh. Deutsches Sportforum & Eh. Rennbahn Grunewald
Bauzeit: 1906-09, 1912-13, 1926-29, 1933-39
Architekt: March, Otto & March, Werner
Landschaft: Wiepking-Jürgensmann, Heinrich Friedrich

⑰ Wohnhaus am Rupenhorn
Bauzeit: 1930, 1934
Architekt: Luckhardt, Wassili & Luckhardt, Hans & Anker, Alfons

⑱ Wohnanlagen an der Brahestraße „Gerichtsviertel"
Bauzeit: 1925-30
Architekt: Fedler, Franz & Schmidt, H. C. & Leschinsky, Paul & Reinhardt und Süßenguth, Iwan, Heinrich & Zamojski, Stephan von & Engelmann, Ernst

⓳ Großsiedlung und Ringsiedlung Siemensstadt
Bauzeit: 1929-34, 1951
Architekt: Bartning, Otto & Forbát, Fred & Gropius, Walter & Häring, Hugo & Henning, Paul Rudolf & Scharoun, Hans & Mengeringhausen, Max

Berlin, Spandau

⑳ Siedlung Birkenwäldchen
Bauzeit: 1926-28
Architekt: Ermisch, Richard

Berlin, Reinickendorf

㉑ Wohnanlage Tile-Brügge-Weg & Havelmüllerweg & Rohrbrunner Straße
Bauzeit: 1926-27, 1928-30
Architekt: Büning, Wilhelm & Richter, Erich

㉒ Siedlung Freie Scholle
Bauzeit: 1899-1910, 1925-33, 1937
Architekt: Lilienthal, Gustav & Pasdach, Otto & Samter, M. & Anger, Walter & Schabelski und Stephanowitz & Taut, Bruno

㉓ Mietshausgruppe Alt-Wittenau
Bauzeit: 1924
Architekt: Buck, Fritz

㉔ Siedlung Roter Adler
Bauzeit: 1937-38
Architekt: Werner, Wolfgang

㉕ Siedlung Paddenpuhl
Bauzeit: 1927-29, 1936-37
Architekt: Beyer, Fritz & Scherer, Josef & Dieckmann, Erich

26 Weiße Stadt Reinickendorf „Schillerpromenade"
Bauzeit: 1929-31
Architekt: Ahrends, Bruno & Büning, Wilhelm & Salvisberg, Otto Rudolf

㉗ Wohnanlage Letteallee
Bauzeit: 1926-27
Architekt: Grisebach, Hans & Rehmann, Heinz

㉘ Wohnanlage Am Schäfersee
Bauzeit: 1930-31
Architekt: Beyer, Fritz

Berlin, Mitte

29 Siedlung Schillerpark
Bauzeit: 1924-30
Architekt: Taut, Bruno & Hoffmann, Franz

㉚ Wohnanlagen am Nachtigalplatz (Friedrich Ebert Siedlung)
Bauzeit: 1937-39
Architekt: Harting, Werner & Werner, Wolfgang & Taut, Bruno & Mebes, Paul & Emmerich, Paul

㉛ Wohnanlage an der Afrikanischen Straße
Bauzeit: 1926-27
Architekt: Mies van der Rohe, Ludwig

㉜ Wohnanlagen Ostender Straße
Bauzeit: 1927-30
Architekt: Gessner, Albert & Hennings, Friedrich, Möhring, Bruno & Möhring, Rudolf & Seeck, Franz

㉝ Mietshaus Eulerstraße
Bauzeit: 1954-55
Architekt: Hoffmann, Hans

㉞ Wohnanlage Kaiserin-Augusta-Allee
Bauzeit: 1927-28
Architekt: Reinhardt, Heinrich & Süßenguth, Georg

㉟ Hamburger Bahnhof
Bauzeit: 1845-47, 1905, 1910, 1912, 1935 & ab 1989
Architekt: Neuhaus, Georg Ernst Friedrich & Holz, Ferdinand Wilhelm & Schwartz, Ernst

㊱ Akademie der Künste
Bauzeit: 1959-60
Architekt: Düttmann, Werner & Schumann, Sabine

㊲ Ehemaliges Shell-Haus
Bauzeit: 1930-32
Architekt: Fahrenkamp, Emil

㊳ Friedhof I. der Französisch-reformierten Gemeinde
Bauzeit: ab 1780
Architekt: N/A

㊴ Institut für Bauwesen der Akademie der Wissenschaften der DDR, (später Deutsche Bauakademie), Ständige Vertretung der Bundesrepublik Deutschlands
Bauzeit: 1913, 1949,1974-75
Architekt: Scharoun, Hans

㊵ Zeughaus „Deutsches Historisches Museum"
Bauzeit: 1706, 1730, 1950
Architekt: Nering, Johann Arnold & Grünberg, Martin, Schlüter, Andreas & Häsler, Otto

㊶ Wohnanlage Linienstraße & Torstraße
Bauzeit: 1935
Architekt: Ermisch, Richard

Berlin, Pankow

㊷ Wohnanlage Rudi-Arndt-Straße & Conrad Blenkle-Straße
Bauzeit: 1926-27
Architekt: Taut, Bruno

㊸ Wohnanlage Heinz-Bartsch-Straße & Paul-Heyse-Straße
Bauzeit: 1926-27, Wiederaufbau 1951-52
Architekt: Taut, Bruno

㊹ Wohnanlage Erich-Boltze-Straße & Ernst-Fürstenberg-Straße & Heinz-Bartsch-Straße
Bauzeit: 1926-28
Architekt: Taut, Bruno & Mebes, Paul & Emmerich, Paul

45 Wohnstadt Carl Legien
Bauzeit: 1928-30
Architekt: Taut, Bruno & Hillinger, Franz

㊻ Wohnanlage Kuglerstraße & Krügerstraße & Gudvanger Straße
Bauzeit: 1928-29
Architekt: Fedler, Franz & Kraffert, Hans; Braun, Josef & Gunzenhauser, Alfred & Wutzky, Max

㊼ Kissingenviertel
Bauzeit: 1930-31
Architekt: Goettel, Jakobus & Mebes, Paul & Emmerich, Paul

㊽ Wohnanlage Paracelsusstraße II
Bauzeit: 1927-28
Architekt: Tiedemann, Joseph

㊾ Siedlung Friedrich-Engels-Straße & Blumenthalstraße & Lutherstraße & Uhlandstraße
Bauzeit: 1930
Architekt: Krebs, Paul

㊿ Holländerviertel
Bauzeit: 1925-29
Architekt: Tiedemann, Joseph

51 Wohnbebauung Buschallee I & II
Bauzeit: 1928-29, 1925-30, Wiederaufbau 1954-55
Architekt: Schneidereit, Bruno & Taut, Bruno

Berlin, Lichtenberg

52 Wohnanlage Suermondtstraße
Bauzeit: 1926
Architekt: Werner, Max

53 Cecilien-Lyzeum „Haupt- und Realschule Lichtenberg"
Bauzeit: 1908-10
Architekt: Grieme, Wilhelm & Uhlig, Johannes

54 Gaswerksiedlung
Bauzeit: 1925-26
Architekt: Engelmann, Ernst & Fangmeyer, Emil

Berlin, Marzahn-Hellersdorf

55 Streusiedlung Mahlsdorf II
Bauzeit: 1926-31
Architekt: Taut, Bruno

Berlin, Treptow-Köpenick

56 Gartenstadt Falkenberg „Tuschkastensiedlung"
Bauzeit: 1913-16
Architekt: Taut, Bruno & Tessenow, Heinrich
Landschaft: Lesser, Ludwig

57 Kleinhaussiedlung Altglienicke „Preußensiedlung"
Bauzeit: 1910-13
Architekt: Bel, Max, & Clement, Franz & Muthesius, Hermann

58 Spreesiedlung
Bauzeit: 1928-30
Architekt: Mebes, Paul & Emmerich, Paul

59 Siedlung Neue Krugallee
Bauzeit: 1927-28
Architekt: Krebs, Paul & Henning, Paul Rudolf

60 Siedlung Baumschulenstraße (Reichs-Eisenbahnsiedlung)
Bauzeit: 1927-32, 1938-40
Architekt: Kaas, Walter & Poeschla, Arthur

Berlin, Neukölln

61 Großsiedlung Britz „Hufeisensiedlung"
Bauzeit: 1925-31
Architekt: Taut, Bruno & Wagner, Martin
Landschaft: Migge, Leberecht & Wagler, Ottokar

62 Siedlung Ideal
Bauzeit: 1929-30
Architekt: Taut, Bruno
Landschaft: Migge, Leberecht

63 Wohnanlage Ossastraße & Fuldastraße
Bauzeit: 1927-28
Architekt: Taut, Bruno

Berlin, Friedrichshain-Kreuzberg

64 Verbandshaus der Deutschen Buchdrucker
Bauzeit: 1924-26
Architekt: Taut, Max & Bernhard, Karl & Hoffmann, Franz

Berlin, Tempelhof-Schöneberg

65 Wohnanlage Rubensstraße I
Bauzeit: 1926-28
Architekt: Mebes, Paul & Emmerich, Paul

66 Wohnanlage Eisackstraße
Bauzeit: 1924-28
Architekt: Lassen, Heinz

67 Wohnanlage Rubensstraße
Bauzeit: 1928-30
Architekt: Jürgensen, Peter

68 Siedlung Attilahöhe
Bauzeit: 1928-30, 1936-37, Wiederaufbau 1951-1952
Architekt: Hoffmann, Franz & Taut, Bruno & Salvisberg, Otto Rudolf & Zimmerreimer, Paul

69 Gut Marienfelde
Bauzeit: vor 1832,1930
Architekt: N/A

Bernau bei Berlin

70 Bundesschule, Bernau
Bauzeit: 1928-30
Architekt: Meyer, Hannes & Mitarbeit Wittwer, Hans & Waterstradt, Georg

Dessau-Roßlau

71 Meisterhaus Muche-Schlemmer
Bauzeit: 1925-26
Architekt: Gropius, Walter

72 Bauhaussiedlung
Bauzeit: 1926-28
Architekt: Gropius, Walter

Magdeburg

73 Gartenstadt Kolonie Reform
Bauzeit: 1911-38
Architekt: Taut, Bruno & Glimm, August

Wolfsburg

74 Siedlung Steimker Berg
Bauzeit: 1938-40
Architekt: Koller, Peter & Taeschner, Titus

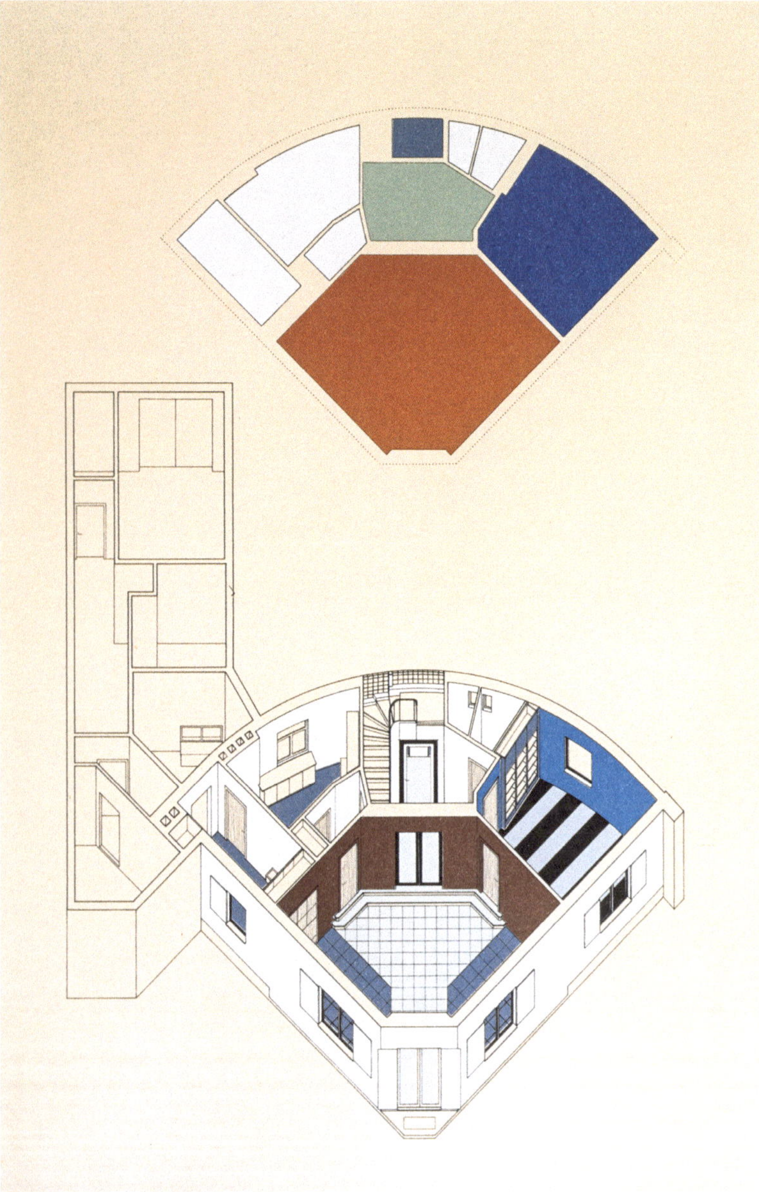

Farbaxonometrie des aufgrund seines eigenwilligen Grundrisses „Tortenstück“ oder „Käseecke“ genannten Wohnhauses von Bruno Taut in Dahlewitz. Seminarunterlagen von Prof. Arthur Rüegg an der ETH Zürich von 1995

Colored axonometric view of the Bruno Taut home in Dahlewitz, showing its idiosyncratic floor plan that has been likened to a slice of pie or cheese. Documentation from a seminar led by Prof. Arthur Rüegg of ETH Zürich, 1995

Von der ursprünglichen Farbigkeit und Materialität des Hauses war kaum noch etwas zu sehen, als Winfried Brenne mit der Restaurierung begann. Die Rot-, Gelb- und Blautöne des Innenraums waren von Taut gezielt gewählt worden, um auf die Lichtwechsel der Tages- und Jahreszeiten zu reagieren und den Landschaftsraum in das Haus zu holen.

Before Winfried Brenne's restauration, the building's color scheme and materials had been significantly altered from Taut's original design. Taut had chosen red, yellow, and blue hues for the interior to respond to the changing light conditions throughout the day and seasons, and to incorporate the landscape into the interior space.

Brenne Architekten's archive is an essential source for historical building research and landmark preservation. Many of the archived materials are the only surviving fragments of the original building. They can also be used to trace the historical development from traditional construction techniques like lime plastering with limewash paint to standardized, readymade construction materials such as high-grade plaster.

Detailed research into a building's original design is a prerequisite for any future restoration. The archive is already being used as a basis for comparison in contemporary conservation plans for the Waldsiedlung Zehlendorf. Similar archival research is currently underway for a research project by the Deutsche Forschungsgemeinschaft (German Research Foundation) led by Professor Thomas Danzl (TUM) und Dr. rer. nat. Christoph Herm (HfBK Dresden) on Berlin modernist housing estate materials and colors to reevaluate conservation methods.[2] The analysis of samples from the Brenne Architekten archive will provide important insights for selecting materials and colors in future restoration efforts aimed at restoring historical designs.

Text:
Jana Hainbach

Die Straßenfassade war bei einer früheren Sanierung mit glänzender Teerfarbe gestrichen worden (links). Winfried Brenne gab ihr bei seiner Instandsetzung ihren mineralischen matten Anstrich wieder zurück (rechts).

The facade facing the road was painted with a glossy tar color during a previous renovation (left). Winfried Brenne restored it to its mineral matt finish during his refurbishment (right).

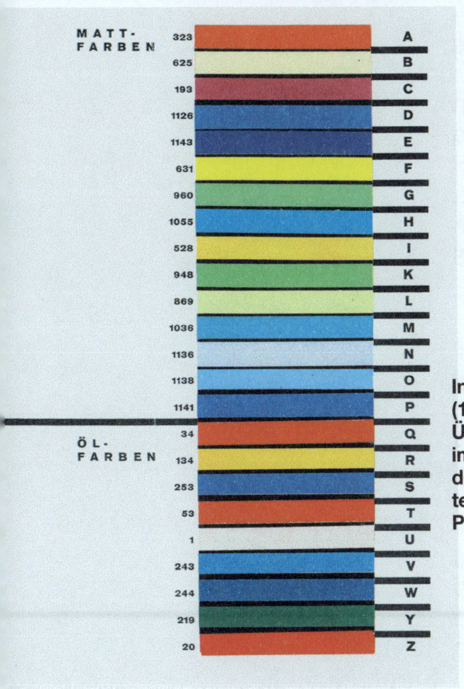

In der Monografie *Ein Wohnhaus* (1927) hielt Bruno Taut seine Überlegungen zum Farbeinsatz im Dahlewitzer Bau fest. Seine dort „hauptsächlich angewendeten Farben" sind einer Baumann-Prase-Farbtonkarte zu entnehmen.

In the monograph *Ein Wohnhaus* (1927), Bruno Taut explains his rationale for using color in the building in Dahlewitz. A Baumann-Prase color tone card documents the main colors he used in the house.

1
Das Forschungsprojekt *Inventarisierung Materialprobenarchiv Brenne Architekten* war an der Technischen Universität München bei Professor Dr. phil. Thomas Danzl angesiedelt, in Kooperation mit der Hochschule für Bildende Künste Dresden, Professor Dr. rer. nat. Christoph Herm und dem Architekturbüro Brenne Architekten.

The research project *Inventory Material Samples Archive Brenne Architekten* was based at the Technical University of Munich (TUM) under Professor Dr. phil. Thomas Danzl, in cooperation with the Dresden University of Fine Arts (HfBK Dresden) under the guidance of Professor Dr. rer. nat. Christoph Herm, and with Brenne Architekten.

2
Das Projekt findet in Zusammenarbeit der Technischen Universität München, Lehrstuhl für Restaurierung, Kunsttechnologie und Konservierungswissenschaft (Professor Thomas Danzl), und der Hochschule für Bildende Künste Dresden, Archäometrie und Naturwissenschaften in der Konservierung/Restaurierung (Professor Christoph Herm) statt. Weitere Kooperationspartner sind die Akademie der Künste Berlin, das Landesdenkmalamt Berlin und das Architekturbüro Brenne Architekten.

The project *The Materiality and Color of Berlin Modernism Housing Estates: A Critical Reevaluation of Conservation, Restoration, and Material Science Research Methods in the History of Restoration* is a collaboration between the Technical University of Munich (TUM), Chair of Conservation-Restoration, Art Technology, and Conservation Science (Professor Thomas Danzl) and Dresden University of Fine Arts (HfBK Dresden), Education and Research Laboratory for Analysis Based on Natural Sciences (Professor Christoph Herm). Additional partners include Akademie der Künste Berlin, the Berlin Monument Authority, and Brenne Architekten.

THEMA (Sarah Nichols, Akshar Gajjar, Marion Moutal), Syn Liu

Concrete: Cosmetic and Care

Installation
Mixed media
Video
Farbe, Ton
Color, sound
3 min

DE

Die Arbeit befasst sich mit einem schwergewichtigen Erbe: den Unmengen von Stahlbeton, mit denen wir den Globus seit dem Bauboom der Nachkriegszeit überzogen haben. Weltweit werden jedes Jahr 30 Milliarden Tonnen Beton verbaut, in weniger als zwei Jahrzehnten wird es auf der Erde mehr Beton als Biomasse geben. Allein die Herstellung von Zement, einem der Hauptbestandteile von Beton, ist für mindestens 8 Prozent der weltweiten Kohlendioxidemissionen verantwortlich. Die ökologische Krise zwingt uns, anders zu bauen und den immensen Bestand an Gebäuden in den Blick zu nehmen, der bereits existiert. Bislang lag der Fokus beim Beton auf dem Erhalt ikonischer brutalistischer Gebäude oder maroder Infrastruktur. Dieser Beitrag hingegen zielt darauf, Strategien für die Pflege und Reparatur des unspektakulären, aber allgegenwärtigen Stahlbetons zu entwickeln.

Wie lernen wir, uns dieses Vermächtnisses anzunehmen und es zu erhalten? Wie pflegen wir ein Material, das wir nicht besonders schätzen? Viele Betonbauten und insbesondere Sichtbetonflächen erleiden Risse, Abplatzungen, Streifenbildung und weisen andere Alterungs- und Zerfallsspuren auf. Auch wenn die Realität uns eines Besseren belehrt, hält sich die hartnäckige Vorstellung, Beton sei kontrollierbar und unveränderlich. Um diesen von Werbung und Materialwissenschaft gepflegten Mythos zu entlarven, geht *Concrete — Cosmetic and Care* dessen Entstehung nach. Den Glauben an die Unveränderlichkeit von Beton entkräften auch Archivdokumente, die kontinuierliche Versuche seiner Instandhaltung über die vergangenen Jahrzehnte belegen. Ein Dokumentarfilm über verschiedene Reparaturverfahren sowie Betonproben und Reparaturwerkzeuge veranschaulicht, welche Zerfallsprozesse das Material durchläuft und welche Möglichkeiten es gibt, es zu reparieren. Das Projekt setzt sich zum Ziel, die fragile Härte von Beton und jene Praktiken zu untersuchen, mit denen wir seiner Verletzlichkeit besser Rechnung tragen können.

EN

This contribution addresses a weighty heritage: the mass of reinforced concrete with which we have covered the globe since the postwar construction boom began. Worldwide, 30 billion tons of concrete are used each year. In under two decades, the mass of concrete on Earth will outweigh all biomass. The manufacturing of cement alone, one of concrete's main ingredients, accounts for at least 8 percent of the world's carbon dioxide emissions. The ecological crisis forces us to build differently and consider the huge pool of buildings that already exist. While the preservation of concrete is often discussed in relation to iconic brutalist structures and crumbling infrastructure, here the aim is to put forward a strategy for the maintenance of unspectacular yet ubiquitous reinforced concrete buildings.

How do we learn to handle this inherited mass and how do we maintain it? How do we care for a material we do not particularly care for? Many concrete structures suffer from cracking, spalling, streaking, and other degradation, particularly when exposed. Yet despite ample evidence to the contrary, we think of concrete as both under control and immutable. To untangle this, *Concrete — Cosmetic and Care* traces the construction of this myth through advertising and materials science. Archival documents show that there have been continuous attempts at concrete repair over the past decades, demystifying the belief in its immutability. A film documenting different repair practices along with physical samples of concrete and tools for repair illustrate how the material degrades and what options there are to repair it. The project also explores concrete's fragile hardness and what practices might take better account of this vulnerability.

Text:
Sarah Nichols

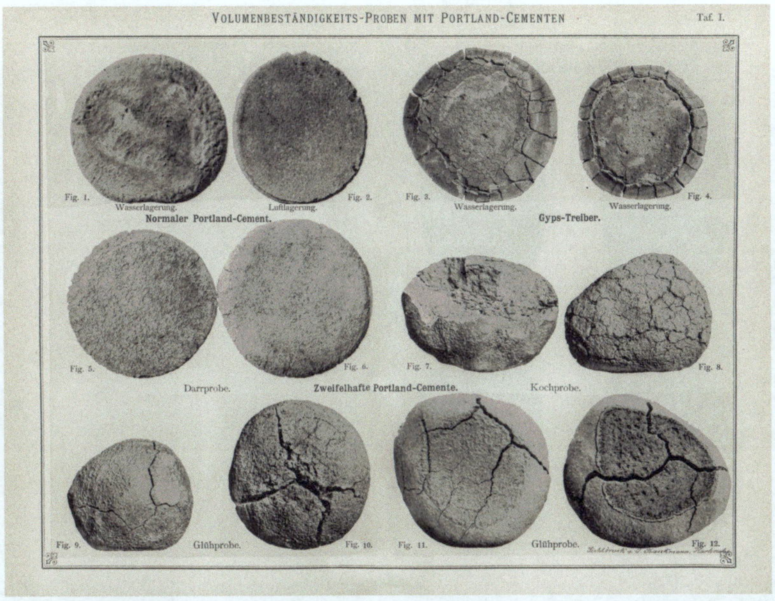

1

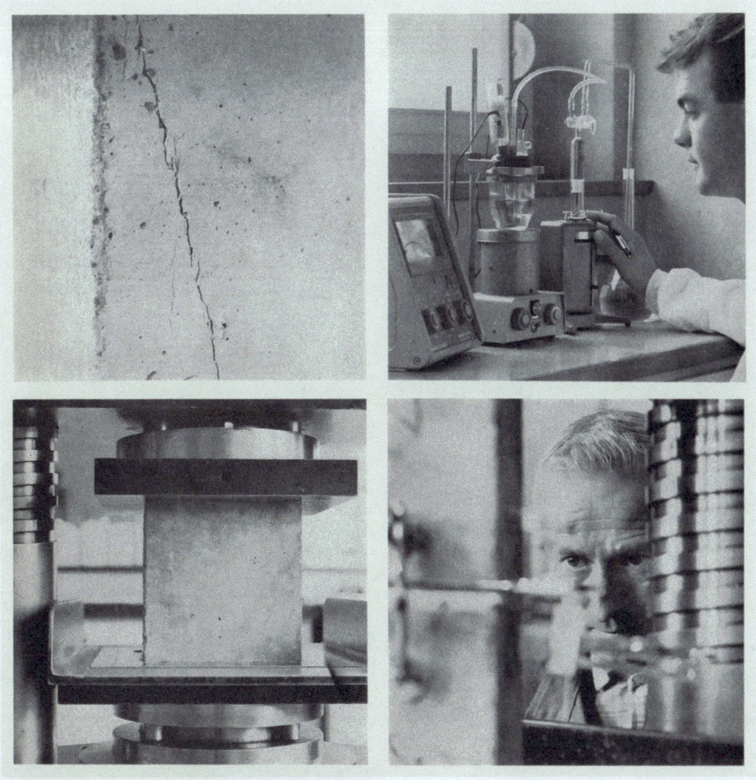

2

3

1
Sammlung von Zementproben aus Volumenbeständigkeitstests, die Ludwig von Tetmajer in *Normen für eine einheitliche Benennung, Klassifikation und Prüfung der hydraulischen Bindemittel* 1893 publizierte.

A collection of cement samples from consistency tests published in Ludwig von Tetmajer's *Normen für eine einheitliche Benennung, Klassifikation und Prüfung der hydraulischen Bindemittel* [Standards for uniform naming, classification, and testing of hydraulic binders], 1893

2
Mit der zunehmenden Popularität von Beton in der ersten Hälfte des 20. Jahrhunderts schuf die Industrie ein neues Narrativ für das Material. In diesen inszenierten Laboraufnahmen in einem Schweizer Fachjournal aus den 1970er-Jahren wurde der Baustoff als beständige, monolithische und wissenschaftlich erforschte Substanz dargestellt – ein Verständnis, das bis heute unser Bild von Beton prägt.

As concrete became increasingly popular in the first half of the 20th century, the industry forged a new conceptual framework for the material. These staged laboratory photos from a 1970s Swiss technical study show how concrete came to be seen as a permanent, monolithic, and scientifically controlled mass—an understanding that continues to shape our perception of the material today.

3
Der im Rahmen der Ausstellung *The Great Repair* gezeigte Film wurde von THEMA (Sarah Nichols, Akshar Gajjar, Marion Moutal) mit Bildern von Syn Liu, Akshar Gajjar und Marion Moutal realisiert. Er handelt von den Auswirkungen der Verwitterung von Beton und den Herausforderungen bei seiner Instandhaltung und Reparatur.

Presented as part of *The Great Repair* exhibition, a film produced by THEMA (Sarah Nichols, Akshar Gajjar, Marion Moutal) and featuring images by Syn Liu, Akshar Gajjar, and Marion Moutal, investigates the effects of weathering on concrete and the challenges of maintaining and repairing it.

4

4
Die 1930 fertiggestellte Salginatobelbrücke von Robert Maillart in Graubünden wurde zwischen 1997 und 1998 umfassend renoviert und in jüngerer Zeit instandgesetzt. Das monolithisch erscheinende Bauwerk ist in Wahrheit ein Flickenteppich aus Materialien verschiedener Epochen.

Completed in 1930, Robert Maillart's Salginatobel Bridge in Graubünden, Switzerland, was extensively renovated between 1997 and 1998, followed by more recent maintenance works. Despite its monolithic appearance, the bridge comprises a fusion of materials from different eras.

5
Balkrishna Doshis 1965 errichtete Fakultät für Architektur der CEPT University in Ahmedabad wurde im Laufe der Jahre mehrfach saniert. In einem der Treppenhäuser sind die Ausbesserungsarbeiten am Beton zu erkennen, die zwischen 2017 und 2022 durchgeführt wurden.

Built in 1965, Balkrishna Doshi's School of Architecture at CEPT University in Ahmedabad has undergone several renovations over the years. Repairs carried out between 2017 and 2022 are still visible in the concrete patching of the staircases.

5

Matthias Brenner,
Silke Langenberg

CLA

Forschungsprojekt am Lehrstuhl für Konstruktionserbe und Denkmalpflege, ETH Zürich (Prof. Dr. Silke Langenberg) in Kollaboration mit dem Lehrstuhl für Neue Fertigungstechnologien ETH Zürich (Prof. Dr. Markus Bambach). Im Rahmen des Dissertationsprojekts *High-Tech for High-Tech: Zum Potential digitaler Fabrikationstechniken für die Instandsetzung architektonischer Innovationen der 1980er Jahre* von Matthias Brenner

Research project at the Chair of Construction Heritage and Preservation, ETH Zürich (Prof. Dr. Silke Langenberg) in collaboration with the Chair of Advanced Manufacturing, ETH Zürich (Prof. Dr. Markus Bambach). As part of the dissertation project *High-Tech for High-Tech: On the Potential of Digital Fabrication for the Repair of Architectural Innovations of the 1980s* by Matthias Brenner

DE

Das Institutsgebäude der ETH Zürich an der Clausiusstrasse (CLA) wurde zwischen 1990 und 1998 in zwei Bauetappen realisiert. Ein original erhaltenes Fassadenmodell zeigt seine offene, vielgliedrige Technikfassade auf der Südwestseite, die zum Teil aus maßgefertigten Sonderbauteilen besteht. Im Rahmen des Dissertationsprojekts *High-Tech for High-Tech* des Architekten Matthias Brenner entstand mithilfe digitaler Fabrikation ein Ersatzbauteil für die Fassade. Der dafür entwickelte Prozess ermöglicht, auf Basis eines einmal erstellten Modells einzelne Ersatzteile der ursprünglich in limitierter Stückzahl seriell gefertigten Fassadenelemente digital nachzuproduzieren. Statt vorzeitig eine ganze Fassade ersetzen zu müssen, wenn einzelne Bauteile versagen, können diese schnell und günstig einzeln ausgetauscht werden.

Der Gebäudeentwurf basiert auf einem Wettbewerbsbeitrag des Büros Fosco Fosco-Oppenheim Vogt von 1986. Der filigrane Brise Soleil der Fassade verhindert die direkte Sonneneinstrahlung und lässt diffuses Licht in die Innenräume. Die flächigen Bauteile sind aus zwei Schichten Verbund-Sicherheitsglas gefertigt, die mit einer weißen PVB-Folie laminiert sind. Sie sind durch eine maßgefertigte Konstruktion aus thermolackierten Stahlsätteln und vertikalen Tragrohren aus Edelstahl verankert. Da die Konstruktionspläne zunächst nicht auffindbar waren, wurde mithilfe von Reverse Engineering ein neues 3D-Modell erstellt. Hierzu wurde die Fassade mit Laser Scan und Fotogrammetrie untersucht, wobei Skizzen des Architekturbüros hinzugezogen wurden. Das so entstandene Modell diente als Grundlage für den 3D-Druck des Ersatzbauteils aus Metall. Der Einsatz von Wire Arc Additive Manufacturing (WAAM) erlaubt es dabei, Material nur an den Stellen aufzutragen, wo es konstruktiv benötigt wird – und so ressourcenschonend zu produzieren.

EN

The ETH departmental building on Clausiusstrasse (CLA) in Zurich was constructed in two stages between 1990 and 1998. An original model shows its open, multipart technical facade with custom-made components on the southwest side. For his dissertation project *High-Tech for High-Tech*, architect Matthias Brenner employed digital fabrication techniques to produce a replacement component for the building's facade. A newly created 3D model allows replicating the components, which originally were serially produced in a limited quantity. This represents a quick and cost-effective alternative to prematurely replacing the entire facade when individual components fail.

The building's design stems from a competition entry by Fosco Fosco-Oppenheim Vogt from 1986. Its slender brise-soleil protects from direct sunlight while providing interior spaces with diffused light. The planar elements of this structure are made of two layers of safety glass laminated with a white PVB film. They are secured to the building by a custom-made construction of thermo-painted steel saddles and vertical stainless steel support tubes. Because the original plans were unavailable, a new 3D model of the construction was reverse-engineered. The process involved analyzing the facade using laser scans and photogrammetry as well as sketches provided by the architecture firm. The resulting model served as the basis for 3D printing the metal replacement component. The use of wire arc additive manufacturing (WAAM), which only uses material where it is structurally required, ensured efficient resource usage.

Text:
Matthias Brenner,
Silke Langenberg

Fassadenmodell des Institutsgebäudes CLA an der Clausiusstrasse der ETH Zürich von Fosco Fosco-Oppenheim Vogt (1986–1998)

Model of the facade of the CLA faculty building at ETH Zürich on Clausiusstrasse, by Fosco Fosco-Oppenheim Vogt (1986–1998)

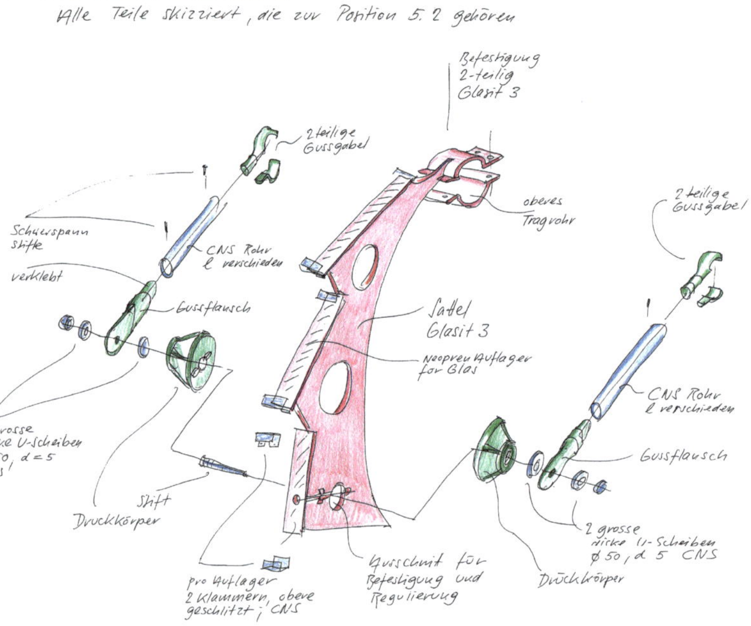

1

2

3

4

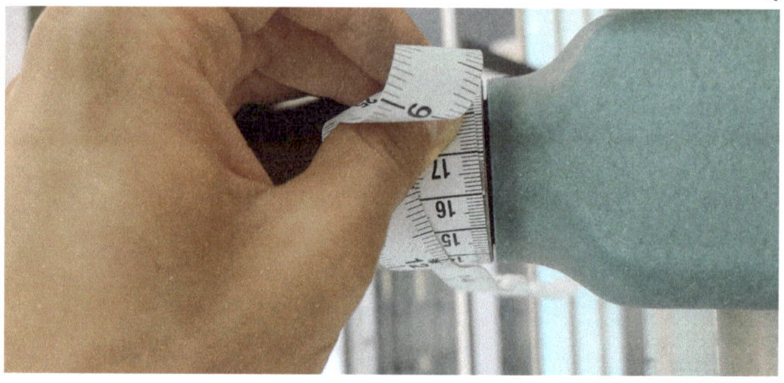

5

1
Schemaskizze der Fassadenkonstruktion des CLA von Fosco Fosco-Oppenheim Vogt, die zum Teil aus maßgefertigten Sonderbauteilen besteht
Sketch of the technical details of the facade elements of the CLA building, partially constructed with custom-made components, by Fosco Fosco-Oppenheim Vogt

2
Axonometrie der Fassadenkonstruktion von Fosco Fosco-Oppenheim Vogt
Axonometric drawing of the structural components of the facade, by Fosco Fosco-Oppenheim Vogt

3
Die Gliederung der Technikfassade auf der Südwestseite des CLA
The technical facade structure on the southwest side of the CLA faculty building

4, 5
Im Rahmen des Dissertationsprojekts von Matthias Brenner entstand ein Ersatzbauteil für die Fassade des CLA. Zunächst wurde dafür die Fassadenkonstruktion genau vermessen und analysiert.
Matthias Brenner's dissertation project involved developing a replacement component for the facade of the CLA building. To achieve this, the facade was meticulously measured and analyzed.

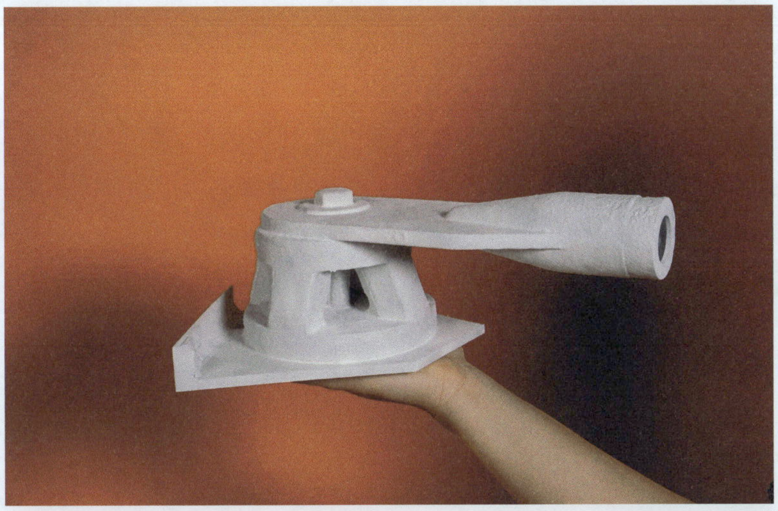
6

7

6, 7
Knotenpunkte des CLA, hergestellt im Maßstab 1:1 im Nylon-3D-Druck

Node elements of the CLA building at a 1:1 scale, created using nylon 3D printing technology

8
Axonometrie der Fassadenkonstruktion, basierend auf Ergebnissen der fotogrammetrischen Untersuchung

Axonometric drawing of the facade construction based on findings from photogrammetric studies

9, 10, 11
Mithilfe von Reverse Engineering entstand ein neues 3D-Modell der Fassade. Dazu wurde eine Punktwolke der Konstruktion fotogrammetrisch erstellt und aufbereitet.

A new 3D model of the facade was created using reverse engineering. To do this, a photogrammetric point cloud of the construction was produced and processed.

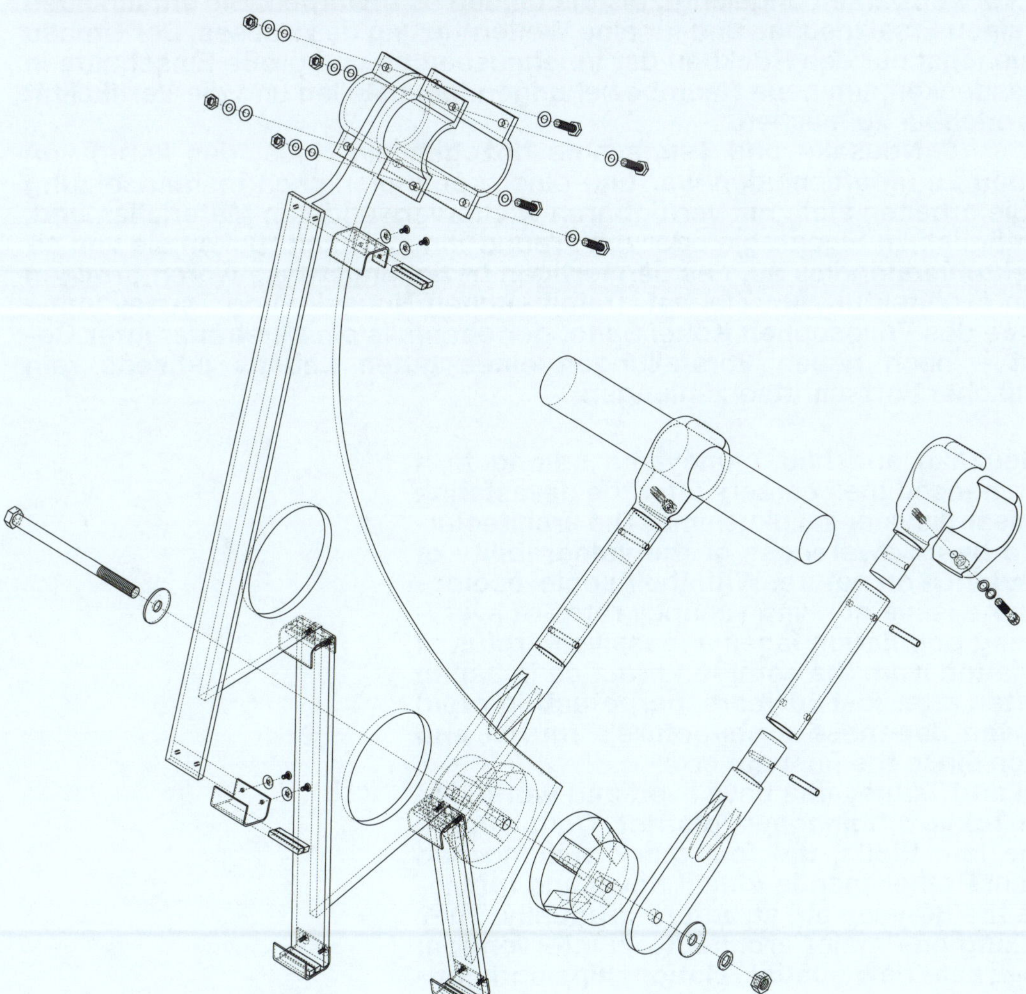
8

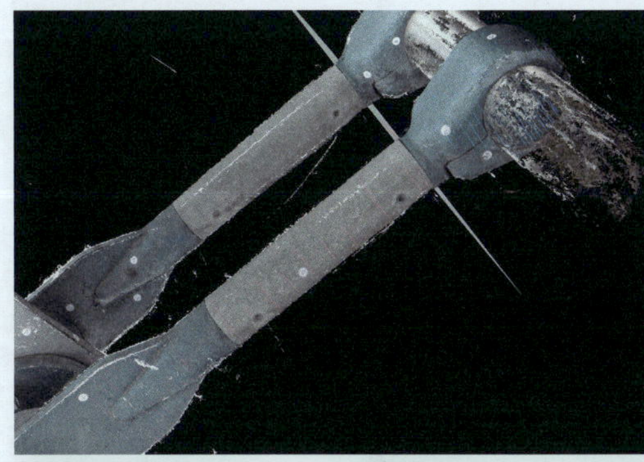
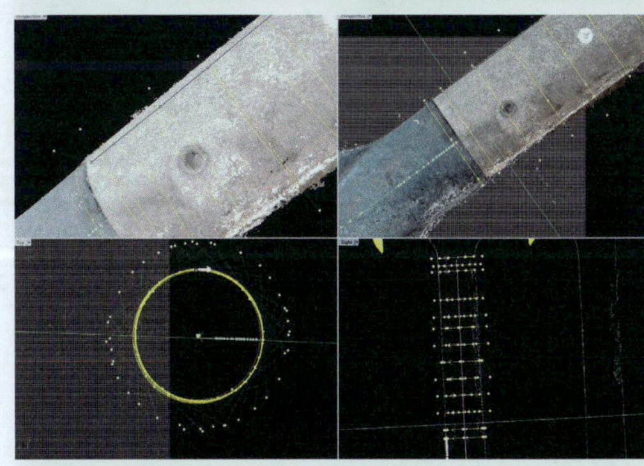

9, 10, 11

Fuminori Nousaku
& Mio Tsuneyama

Holes in the House

DE

Fuminori Nousaku und Mio Tsuneyama gehören einer jungen Generation Architekt*innen an, die nach dem verheerenden Tōhoku-Erdbeben und der darauffolgenden Nuklearkatastrophe in Fukushima in den Beruf einstiegen. Das Bewusstsein für die Fragilität gesellschaftlicher Strukturen und deren natürlicher Grundlagen prägt die Denkweisen dieser Büros. Sie richten ihre Praxis sozialökologisch aus und widmen sich angesichts einer schrumpfenden Bevölkerung dem Umgang mit dem steigenden Leerstand, insbesondere den einfachen und oft baufälligen Bestandsgebäuden. Damit kehren sie von der in Japan verbreiteten Praxis ab, dass Gebäude häufig nach nur 30 Jahren abgerissen und neu gebaut werden. Diese schnellen Obsoleszenz-Zyklen bildeten eine wichtige Grundlage für die formale und programmatische Innovationsfreude der japanischen Architektur seit der Nachkriegszeit.

Seit 2017 wohnen und arbeiten Nousaku und Tsuneyama in einem auf den ersten Blick unscheinbaren Bestandsgebäude im Bezirk Shinagawa in Tokio. Das rund 30 Jahre alte viergeschossige Haus, das während der japanischen Wirtschaftsblase Ende der 1980er-Jahre errichtet worden war, war am Ende seiner ökonomischen Verwertbarkeit angelangt, als die beiden es erwarben. Sie entschieden sich gegen einen Ersatzneubau und für eine Weiternutzung des Hauses. Der Umbau umfasste zunächst nur den Rückbau der Innenausbauten und große Einschnitte in die Geschossdecken, um neue Raumbeziehungen herzustellen und die Vertikalität des Hauses erlebbar zu machen.

Nousaku und Tsuneyama bezogen ein Haus, das kaum von einem Rohbau zu unterscheiden war und einer kontinuierlichen Instandsetzung unterliegt. Sie arbeiten stets mit verfügbaren wiederverwendeten Materialien und, wo immer möglich, in Eigenregie oder mit Freund*innen. Damit rücken sie von einem Architekturverständnis ab, das den fertigen beziehungsweise warenförmigen Zustand von Architektur zum Ziel hat. Damit suchen Nousaku und Tsuneyama – ganz im Sinne des Philosophen Kohei Saito, der ebenfalls ein Mitstreiter ihrer Generation ist – nach neuen Vorstellungen eines guten Lebens jenseits rein produktivistischer Fortschrittserzählungen.

2017–fortlaufend
ongoing
Installation
Recyclingholz, bedrucktes Shoji-Papier
Salvaged wood, printed shoji paper
Modell
Model
1:10, 129 × 93 × 80 cm
Courtesy Fuminori Nosaku Architects, Tokyo

EN

Fuminori Nousaku and Mio Tsuneyama belong to a generation of young architects who commenced their careers after the devastating Tōhoku earthquake and the ensuing nuclear disaster in Fukushima. The architectural approach of these offices is shaped by an awareness of the vulnerability of social structures and humanity's dependence on nature. With their socio-ecological orientation, the architects address the issue of rising vacancy rates of everyday buildings in Japan, where a shrinking population faces a massive surplus of built inventory. This is a deliberate deviation from the common practice in Japan of demolition and new construction, often after just 30 years, perpetuating rapid cycles of obsolescence that have driven Japanese architecture's formal and programmatic enthusiasm for innovation since the postwar era.

Since 2017, Nousaku and Tsuneyama have lived and worked in a seemingly ordinary older building in Tokyo's Shinagawa district. Constructed during Japan's economic boom in the late-1980s, the four-story building had reached the end of its economic lifespan. Rather than tearing it down and replacing it, the architects opted to renovate the 30-year-old structure gradually. They began by gutting the interiors and making one major architectural intervention: cutting openings through the floors to create new spatial relationships and convey a sense of vertical flow.

Reducing the house to a bare-bones structure, Nousaku and Tsuneyama embarked on an ongoing process of repair. They only use recycled materials and, wherever possible, perform the labor themselves or with the help of friends. By doing so, they have rejected the prevailing view of architecture focused solely on completion and commodification. Instead, they have embraced a new concept of the good life beyond productivist narratives of progress, very much in the spirit of philosopher Kohei Saito from their generation.

Text:
Markus Krieger

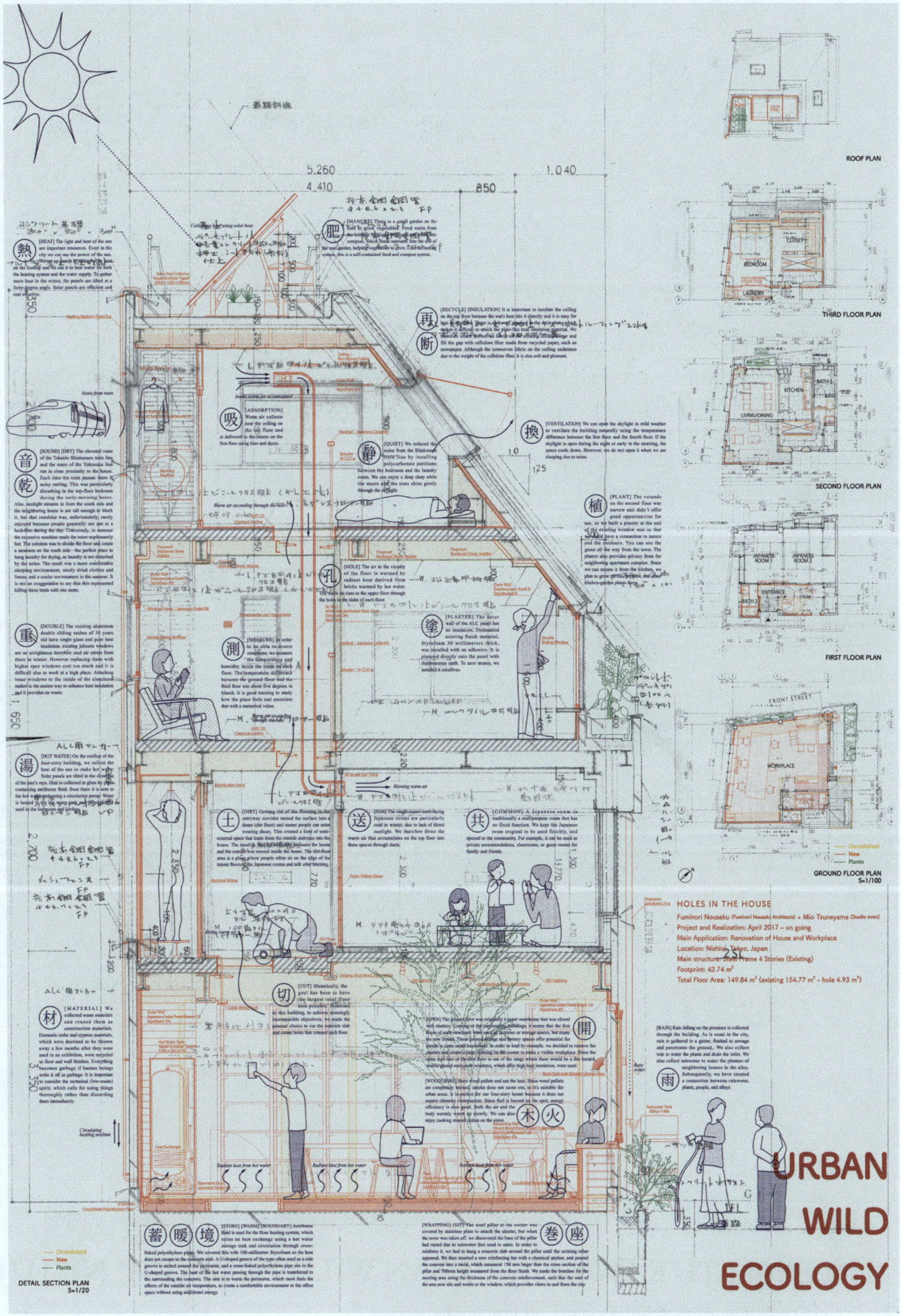

2017 bezogen die Architekt*innen Fuminori Nousaku und Mio Tsuneyama ein Stadthaus aus den 1980er-Jahren im Tokioter Bezirk Shinagawa, das sie seither in einem langsamen und sorgfältigen Prozess der Instandsetzung renovieren.

Architects Fuminori Nousaku and Mio Tsuneyama moved into a 1980s townhouse in Tokyo's Shinagawa district in 2017. They have since been refurbishing the building through a gradual and meticulous process of repair.

Das Projekt besteht aus einer Reihe kleiner programmatischer Interventionen im Haus und seinem Außenraum, die darauf abzielen, eine neue symbiotische Beziehung mit der städtischen Umwelt zu schaffen, ein Ansatz, den Nousaku und Tsuneyama „Urban Wild Ecology“ nennen.

The project involves making small functional modifications both inside and outside the house. The goal is to create a new symbiotic relationship with the urban environment, an approach Nousaku and Tsuneyama call “Urban Wild Ecology.”

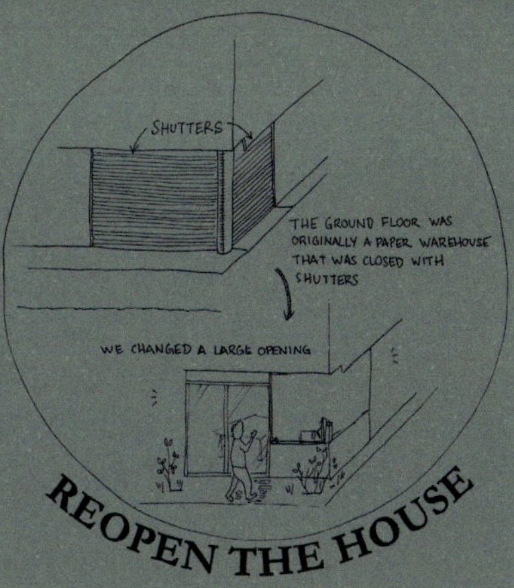

REOPEN THE HOUSE

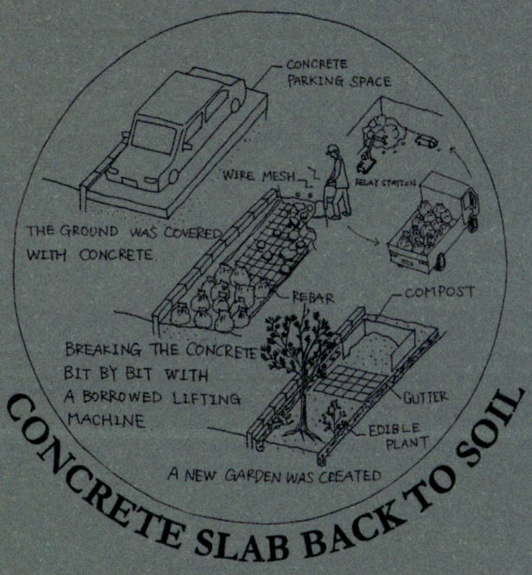

CONCRETE SLAB BACK TO SOIL

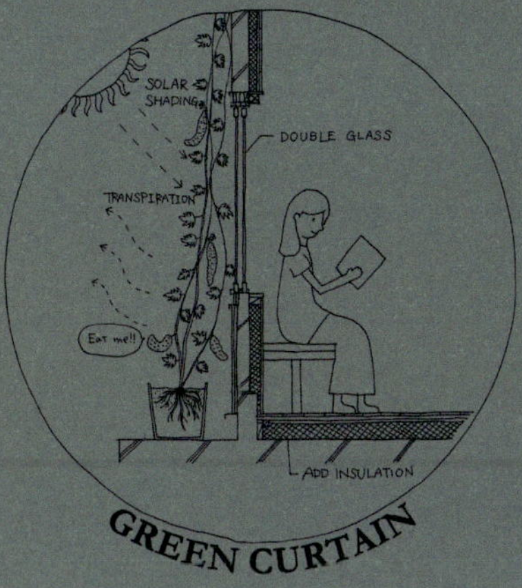

GREEN CURTAIN

BRINGING LIGHT
AIRFLOW
CREATING AIR FLOW THROUGHOUT THE BUILDING
GLANCES, SOUNDS AND SIGNS OF LIFE
HOLES IN THE FLOORS

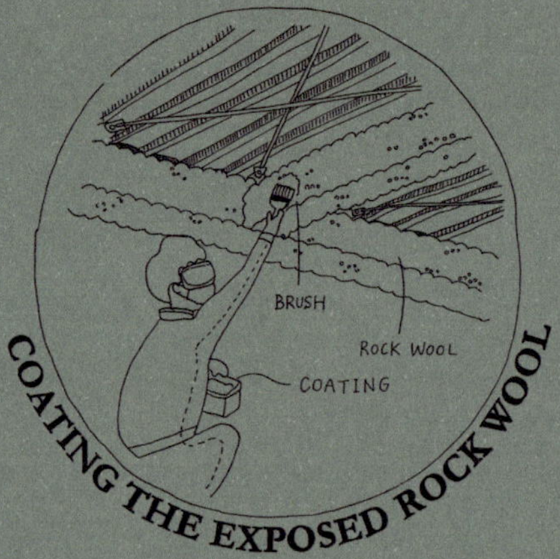
BRUSH
ROCK WOOL
COATING
COATING THE EXPOSED ROCK WOOL

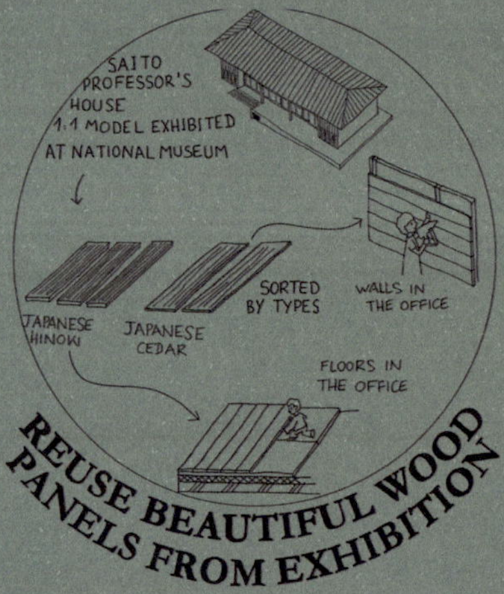
SAITO PROFESSOR'S HOUSE
1:1 MODEL EXHIBITED AT NATIONAL MUSEUM
SORTED BY TYPES
WALLS IN THE OFFICE
JAPANESE HINOKI
JAPANESE CEDAR
FLOORS IN THE OFFICE
REUSE BEAUTIFUL WOOD PANELS FROM EXHIBITION

Nousakus und Tsuneyamas zentrale gestalterische Strategie ist die der Subtraktion; sie begannen damit, alle unnötigen Schichten zu entfernen und eine Reihe von Öffnungen durch die Geschossdecken zu schneiden.

The core design strategy employed by Nousaku and Tsuneyama revolves around subtraction. They started by eliminating all unnecessary layers and cutting a series of holes through the floors.

Von allem Unwesentlichen befreit, wird das Haus zu einem durchgehenden fließenden Raum, vom Büro im Erdgeschoss bis zum Schlafzimmer auf dem Dachboden.

By removing anything non-essential, the house was transformed into a continuous space that unfolds vertically, from the ground floor office to the attic bedroom.

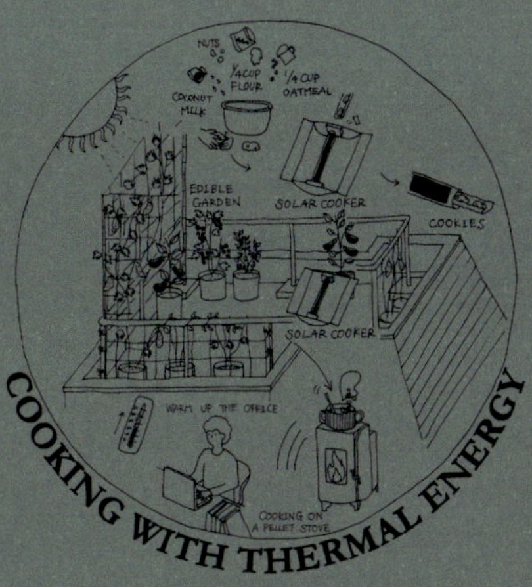
NUTS
1/4 CUP FLOUR
1/4 CUP OATMEAL
COCONUT MILK
EDIBLE GARDEN
SOLAR COOKER
COOKIES
SOLAR COOKER
WARM UP THE OFFICE
COOKING ON A PELLET STOVE
COOKING WITH THERMAL ENERGY

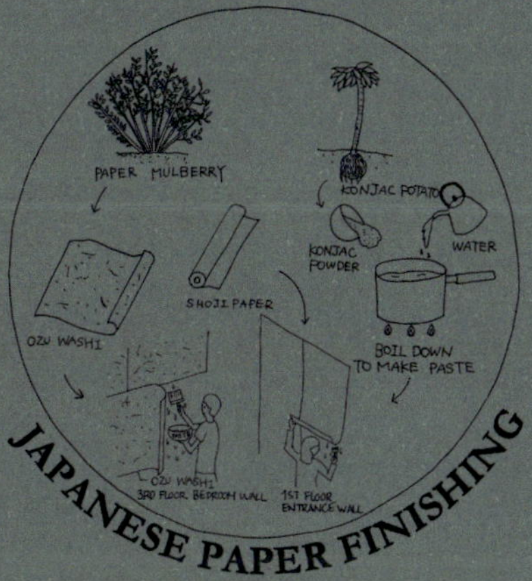
PAPER MULBERRY
KONJAC POTATO
KONJAC POWDER
WATER
SHOJI PAPER
OZU WASHI
BOIL DOWN TO MAKE PASTE
OZU WASHI 3RD FLOOR BEDROOM WALL
1ST FLOOR ENTRANCE WALL
JAPANESE PAPER FINISHING

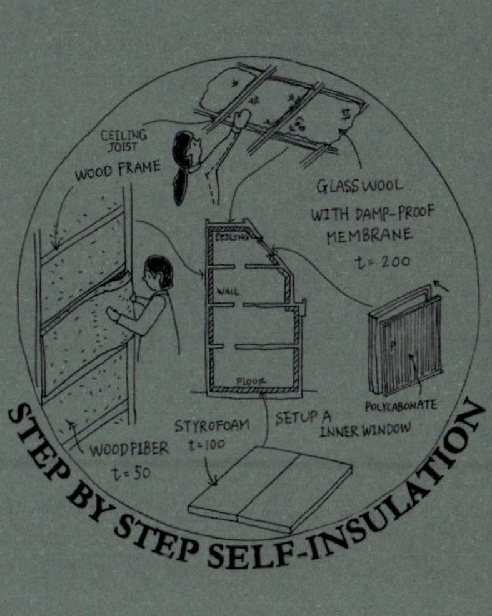
CEILING JOIST
WOOD FRAME
GLASS WOOL WITH DAMP-PROOF MEMBRANE t= 200
CEILING
WALL
FLOOR
POLYCABONATE
STYROFOAM t=100
SETUP A INNER WINDOW
WOODFIBER t=50
STEP BY STEP SELF-INSULATION

DE

Angesichts der multiplen Krisen planetarischen Ausmaßes ist es eine unbestreitbare Tatsache, dass wir unsere Welt reparieren und wiederaufbauen müssen. Allerdings müssen wir nicht eine einzelne „Welt“ instand halten, sondern vielfältige Welten mit ihren materiellen und immateriellen Beziehungen, die in einer komplexen Gleichzeitigkeit existieren. Das Projekt einer *großen Reparatur* erfordert daher vielfältige wissenschaftliche Expertise, Kompetenz und Kenntnisse. Doch durch den Kolonialismus und globalen Kapitalismus wurden unzählige Wissenswelten und Weltzugänge verdrängt, marginalisiert und zerstört. Dieser Verlust betrifft auch Wissen über nachhaltige Landnutzung, Materialgewinnung und Bautechniken. Wenn wir uns die Werkzeuge, die für den Aufbau einer besseren Welt notwendig sind, wieder aneignen wollen, müssen wir den Wissenskanon und die Art und Weise, wie er produziert wird, infrage stellen. Dieser Prozess erfordert zwingend, Institutionen zu dekolonisieren und das Akteursnetzwerk zu pluralisieren.

Text:
Nazlı Tümerdem

Wissens-welten dekolonisieren

Decolonize Knowledge Worlds

EN

In the midst of multiple planetary crises, it is an irrefutable fact that we need to repair and rebuild our world. However, it is not a singular "World" that we will be maintaining, but rather manifold worlds of tangible and intangible relations which exist in a complex simultaneity. A *great repair* endeavor therefore requires a plurality of scholarship, wisdom, and expertise. Yet, through colonialism and the spread of capitalism, a whole raft of knowledge worlds and ways of relating to the world were repressed, marginalized, and lost. This loss includes knowledge about sustainable land use, materials extraction, and building techniques. To reappropriate the tools necessary to build better worlds, we must question canonical knowledge and the modes of its production. This process inherently requires decolonizing institutions and pluralizing the constellation of actors involved.

Kader Attia

Hypo-mnemata

2023
Skulptur, Papiermaché
Sculpture, papier-mâché
1 × 1 × 8 m
3 Collagen auf Karton, je
3 collages on cardboard, each
100 × 80 cm
Recherchematerial
Research material
Courtesy Kader Attia & Galerie Nagel Draxler

DE

Von prähistorischen Knochenschnitzereien bis zu heutigen USB-Sticks – Menschen haben immer Hypomnemata als materielle Externalisierungen benutzt, um ihr neuronales Gedächtnis zu erweitern. Das individuelle, aber auch soziale Gedächtnis lebt somit nicht nur im menschlichen Gehirn, sondern auch außerhalb dessen, in den Artefakten selbst.

In diesem Sinne können auch die Lehmbauten des Tales von M'zab in der algerischen Sahara als Hypomnemata betrachtet werden. Von Hand geformt und perfekt an ihre Umgebung angepasst, überlieferte sich in ihnen über Jahrtausende hinweg Bauwissen von einer Generation an die nächste. Doch im frühen 20. Jahrhundert, unter französischer Kolonialherrschaft, eigneten sich westliche Architekten wie Le Corbusier die Ästhetik und Funktionalität dieser Architekturen an, ohne die vernakulären Ursprünge der modernen Architektur, etwa in den Bauten der Mzabiten, explizit zu machen. Der Kolonialismus hat nicht nur Körper ausgebeutet, sondern auch jahrtausendealtes Wissen geplündert.

Die Spuren dieser kulturellen Aneignung sind noch heute in einer Ästhetik sichtbar, die unsere Konsumlandschaft durchzieht: in Form von Verpackungsmaterial weit verbreiteter Alltagsgüter. Aus Pappmaché geformt, tragen diese Verpackungen unbemerkt die Gestalt der Lehmarchitektur in sich. Ist das Produkt einmal ausgepackt, wird die quasi-architektonische Form, die es umschloss, entsorgt und erneut zu Pappmaché recycelt …

EN

From prehistoric carved bones to present-day USB sticks, humans have always used hypomnemata as material externalizations to expand their neural memory. Memory, both individual and social, thus not only dwells in the human brain but also beyond it—in artifacts themselves.

In this sense, the earthen architectures of the M'zab Valley in the Algerian Sahara are also hypomnemata. Hand-molded and perfectly adapted to their environment, they have been transmitting construction know-how from one generation to the next for millennia. However, in the early 20th century, under French colonial rule, Western architects like Le Corbusier appropriated the aesthetic and functionality of these architectures without naming the vernacular origins of modern architecture, such as the buildings of the M'zabite people. Indeed, colonialism not only exploited bodies but also plundered millennia-old knowledge.

Today, traces of this cultural appropriation are still visible in an aesthetic that haunts our consumerist landscape in the form of packaging materials for everyday goods. Made from papier-mâché, these packaging materials have unconsciously been made to carry the shapes of vernacular earthen architecture. Once the product is unpacked, the quasi-architectural form containing it is discarded and recycled, once again becoming just papier-mâché …

Text:
Kader Attia

Für die Internationale Kolonialausstellung, die 1931 in Paris stattfand, haben die französischen Architekten Germain Olivier und Jacques Georges Lambert das sogenannte Indigene Restaurant entworfen.

French architects Germain Olivier and Jacques Georges Lambert designed the "Indigenous Restaurant" for the International Colonial Exhibition, held in Paris in 1931.

Kader Attia, *Hypomnemata*, 2023
Archivmaterial

Archival material

Unter französischer Kolonialherrschaft eigneten sich westliche Architekten die Ästhetik und Funktionalität vernakulärer Lehmbauten an.

During the era of French colonial rule, Western architects appropriated the aesthetics and functionality of vernacular earthen architectures.

Die sogenannte Indigene Moschee, ebenfalls von Olivier und Lambert gebaut, auf dem Gelände der Internationalen Kolonialausstellung 1931, dem Park Bois de Vincennes in Paris.

The "Indigenous Mosque" was also designed by Olivier and Lambert and built on the International Colonial Exhibition's grounds at the park Bois de Vincennes in Paris.

Kader Attia, *Hypomnemata*, 2023
Filmstill
Film still
Laut Attia zeugt die Ästhetik der Moderne, sei es die Architektur oder auch Alltägliches wie Verpackungsmaterial, von Prozessen kultureller Aneignung.
Attia argues that the aesthetics of modernism, from architecture to everyday objects like packaging materials, reflect processes of cultural appropriation.

Bas Princen

Earth Pillar

DE

Jedes Frühjahr am Tag der *crépissage* wird die Große Moschee von Djenné in Mali einem kollektiven Akt der Instandhaltung unterzogen. Dabei wird das aus Lehmziegeln konstruierte Gebäude mit einem neuen Putz aus Lehmschlamm, Sand und Reishülsen vor der herannahenden Regenzeit geschützt. Diese kollektive Praxis der Reparatur geht bis auf die erste Große Moschee zurück, die schon im 13. Jahrhundert an dieser Stelle stand. Nachdem das Bauwerk im 19. Jahrhundert infolge lokaler Konflikte zur Ruine verfallen war, wurde es 1907 auf den alten Fundamenten rekonstruiert. Bas Princens großformatige Fotografie *Earth Pillar* von 2010 zeigt den Fußpunkt eines der 90 Stützpfeiler der großen Säulenhalle im Inneren der Moschee, die aus dem Erdboden zu wachsen scheinen.

Auch die rund 2.000 Häuser der Altstadt von Djenné sind traditionell aus Lehm gebaut und werden von ihren Bewohner*innen ständig ausgebessert und instandgehalten. Der Lehm stammt vom Ufer des Bani, eines Nebenflusses des Niger, der die Stadt umfließt. Lange war die Stadt an die natürlichen Zyklen des Flusses angepasst. Die Regenzeit macht Djenné zu einer schwer zugänglichen, aber fischreichen Insel. Geht das Wasser zurück, wird auf den Feuchtflächen Reis angebaut. Wenn diese wiederum trockenfallen, werden sie nach und nach als Weideflächen genutzt und schließlich in Gruben für die Herstellung von *banco* umgewandelt, dem Lehm, aus dem Ziegel und Putz gefertigt werden. Dieser natürliche Zyklus ist aufgrund des Klimawandels gestört: Das Nigerdelta trocknet zunehmend aus und Fischerei- und Ernteerträge brechen ein. Auch Lehm als hochwertiger Baustoff wird knapper. Die Stadtbewohner*innen sind darum immer häufiger gezwungen, zur Reparatur der Gebäude auf Baumaterialien wie Beton und gebrannte Tonziegel auszuweichen, die jedoch weit weniger gut für die klimatischen Bedingungen der Region geeignet sind.

2010
C-print, 190 × 153 cm

EN

Each spring, on the day of *crépissage*, the Great Mosque of Djenné in Mali undergoes a collective act of maintenance. To protect it from the upcoming rainy season, a new plaster coat of clay slurry, sand, and rice husks is applied to the exterior of the adobe brick structure. This collective practice of repair can be traced back to the very first Great Mosque that was erected on this spot in the 13th century. After the building had fallen into decay in the 19th century due to local conflicts, it was rebuilt on the original foundations in 1907. Bas Princen's large-format photograph *Earth Pillar* from 2010 shows the base of one of the mosque's 90 supporting pillars inside the large prayer hall, appearing to seamlessly grow out of the ground.

The approximately 2,000 houses comprising the historical Old Town of Djenné are traditionally constructed using the same mud-brick technique. The inhabitants diligently mend and maintain them, collecting mud from the banks of the Bani, a tributary of the Niger River that encircles the city. For a long time, the city was well adapted to the river's natural cycles. During the rainy season, Djenné transforms into an island, which is challenging to access yet brimming with fish. When the water recedes, rice is grown on the wetlands. When the wetlands dry, they gradually transition into grazing fields and are eventually used as pits for the production of banco, the clay used to make bricks and plaster. This natural cycle is disrupted by climate change: Lower water levels in the Niger Delta have caused fish populations and crop yields to decline dramatically, and mud as a high-quality resource has become scarcer. City residents are increasingly compelled to resort to alternative building materials such as concrete and fired clay bricks for repairs—materials that are far less suitable for the region's climatic conditions.

Text:
Markus Krieger,
Alex Nehmer

Bas Princen

Djenné Mosque

1

1

Bas Princens Fotoserie von 2010 zeigt die Moschee von Djenné während einer großangelegten Renovierung durch den Aga Khan Trust for Culture. Um die Konstruktion des Denkmals wieder sicher zu machen, wurden Lehmschichten abgetragen, wodurch aber auch das organische Aussehen des Baus verändert wurde. Der Eingriff und die daraus resultierende mehrjährige Unterbrechung der kollektiven Instandhaltung der lokalen Bevölkerung selbst führten zu Protesten durch Einwohner*innen von Djenné.

Bas Princen's photo series from 2010 shows the Djenné Mosque during a major reconstruction, which was launched by the Aga Khan Trust for Culture. To secure the monument's structure, layers of clay were removed, altering the mosque's organic appearance. The intervention as well as the resulting multiyear interruption of the collective maintenance by the local population itself was protested by citizens of Djenné.

2

Nicht-Muslim*innen ist der Zutritt in die Moschee normalerweise untersagt. Für die Dauer der Renovierung wurden die Gebetsteppiche jedoch entfernt und die Moschee nicht als geheiligter Boden betrachtet. Bas Princen war es so 2010 möglich, das Monument zu betreten. In gewissem Sinne dokumentierte er mit seiner Fotografie *Earth Pillar* (auf der vorherigen Doppelseite) daher nicht die eigentliche Moschee, sondern nur das, was ihm zu sehen erlaubt war.

Non-Muslims are normally prohibited from entering the mosque. However, for the duration of the renovation, the prayer rugs were removed, and the mosque was not considered holy ground, allowing Bas Princen to enter the monument in 2010. In a sense, therefore, his photograph *Earth Pillar* (on the previous double page) did not document the actual mosque, but only what Princen was allowed to see.

2

3
Die erste Große Moschee wurde schon im 13. Jahrhundert an dieser Stelle errichtet. Nachdem das Bauwerk im 19. Jahrhundert verfallen war, wurde es 1907 auf den alten Fundamenten rekonstruiert.

The monument dates back to the very first Great Mosque that was built on this spot in the 13th century. The edifice became dilapidated in the 19th century; in 1907 it was rebuilt on the old foundations.

4
Die Planung der Rekonstruktion wurde später der französischen Kolonialmacht zugeschrieben, Symmetrien und Ordnungshierarchien auf die polytechnische Ausbildung französischer Ingenieure zurückgeführt. Dieses Narrativ ist jedoch nicht unangefochten: Der Architekturhistoriker Jean-Louis Bourgeois argumentiert, dass die Architektur das Werk lokaler Maurer unter dem Zunftleiter Ismaila Traoré sei, unter anderem da sie keine Spuren der Verwendung kolonialer Vermessungstechniken aufweise.

The planning of the reconstructed building was later attributed to the French colonial power, and symmetries and hierarchies of order were projected back onto the polytechnic training the French engineers had enjoyed. This narrative is, however, not uncontroversial: Architectural historian Jean-Louis Bourgeois argues that the architecture is the work of local masons headed by guild leader Ismaila Traoré, as it bears no traces of the use of colonial surveying techniques.

4

Limbo Accra

Into the Void

2021–fortlaufend
ongoing
Installation
Mixed media

DE

Wie können uns moderne Bauruinen dabei helfen, die Zukunft afrikanischer Städte neu zu denken? Vom unvollendeten Airport Tower in Accra, Ghana, bis zu dem spektakulären Hochhaus La Pyramide in Abidjan, Côte d'Ivoire, sind aufgegebene Bauprojekte in ganz Westafrika zu unübersehbaren Zeichen im Stadtbild geworden. Mögen die Gründe für ihr Scheitern auch vielfältig sein, so wurden sie doch alle einmal in der Absicht errichtet, Afrikas verheißungsvolle Zukunftsperspektiven zu demonstrieren. Den umliegenden Vierteln schaden diese unvollendeten Immobilienprojekte heute jedoch meist. Oft entstehen um sie herum urbane Wüsten, denen es an wesentlichen infrastrukturellen Einrichtungen fehlt. Es mag daher naheliegend erscheinen, sie als Symbole von Staatsversagen und Misswirtschaft zu betrachten, aber was wäre, wenn wir sie stattdessen als Träger von Möglichkeiten, Inspiration und Hoffnung begreifen? Was wäre, wenn wir sie in afro-utopische Modelle räumlicher Gerechtigkeit und Orte gemeinschaftlichen Engagements verwandelten?

Limbo Accra dokumentiert solche unvollendeten Gebäude mithilfe von Fotografie und Fotogrammetrie, um ein interaktives digitales Archiv dieser Bauwerke auf dem afrikanischen Kontinent zu schaffen. In Ghana, Nigeria, Senegal und Sierra Leone wurde damit bereits begonnen; in Zukunft soll durch das Einbeziehen weiterer Akteur*innen die Arbeit auf Ost-, Süd- und Nordafrika ausgedehnt werden, um das Archiv zu erweitern. Ziel des Archivs ist es, diese Bauten wieder mit Leben zu füllen und das ihnen innewohnende Potential sichtbar zu machen, insbesondere angesichts des Mangels an öffentlichen Räumen in vielen afrikanischen Städten. Statt Top-down-Entscheidungen zu fällen, wie diese leerstehenden Räume genutzt werden sollen, verfolgt Limbo Accra die Vision einer nachhaltigen, redistributiven und gemeinschaftsgetragenen Planung. Seit 2018 hat das Studio mit einer Reihe von öffentlichen Veranstaltungen und Installationen in solchen Bauten in ganz Accra erste Schritte unternommen, diese aufgegebenen Architekturen wiederanzueignen, um sie in den Dienst der Gesellschaft zu stellen.

EN

How can ruins help us rethink the future of African cities? From the incomplete Airport Tower in Accra, Ghana, to the deserted highrise La Pyramide in Abidjan, Côte d'Ivoire, abandoned property developments have become unmissable icons within cityscapes across West Africa. There is a variety of reasons for their failure, but what unites them was their original vision: to showcase the grand prospects of African futures. However, these unfinished developments can have a detrimental impact on surrounding neighborhoods and lead to urban deserts that lack essential amenities. It may therefore seem obvious to view them as symbols of state failure and mismanagement, but what if they could symbolize opportunity, inspiration, and hope for the future? What if we transformed them into Afro-utopian symbols of spatial justice and models of community engagement?

Utilizing photographs and the technique of photogrammetry, Limbo Accra scans and creates an interactive digital archive of these structures across the African continent. The research and documentation has already taken place in Ghana, Nigeria, Senegal, and Sierra Leone, with the plan being to expand it to East, South, and North Africa and further grow the archive by inviting a range of practitioners to collaborate. The archive's ambition is to revitalize these structures and make visible their innate potential, particularly in light of the lack of public spaces in many African cities. Rather than top-down visions of how these voided spaces can be utilized, Limbo Accra envisions their sustainable, redistributive, and community-led development. Since 2018, the studio has produced a series of activations and public installations in liminal spaces across Accra—a first stepping stone for reappropriating these deserted structures and making them useful to society again.

Text:
Limbo Accra

Seit 2021 baut Limbo Accra ein Archiv verlassener Gebäude auf dem afrikanischen Kontinent auf, um zu ihrer Wiederaneignung und Umnutzung für gesellschaftlich nützliche Zwecke anzuregen. Die beiden Bilder zeigen zwei unfertige Gebäude in Diamniadio, einer Stadt nahe Dakar, 2023.

Since 2021, Limbo Accra has been compiling an archive of abandoned buildings on the African continent in order to stimulate their reappropriation and conversion for social purposes. Pictured here are two unfinished buildings in Diamniadio, a town close to Dakar, in 2023.

Es sollte das größte und schönste Gebäude des Landes werden, doch der Palast des senegalesischen Geschäftsmanns El Hadji Ndiouga Kébé in Touba ist seit den 1980er-Jahren unvollendet und leer.

It was supposed to be the largest and most beautiful building in the country, but the palace of Senegalese businessman El Hadji Ndiouga Kébé in Touba has remained unfinished and vacant since the 1980s.

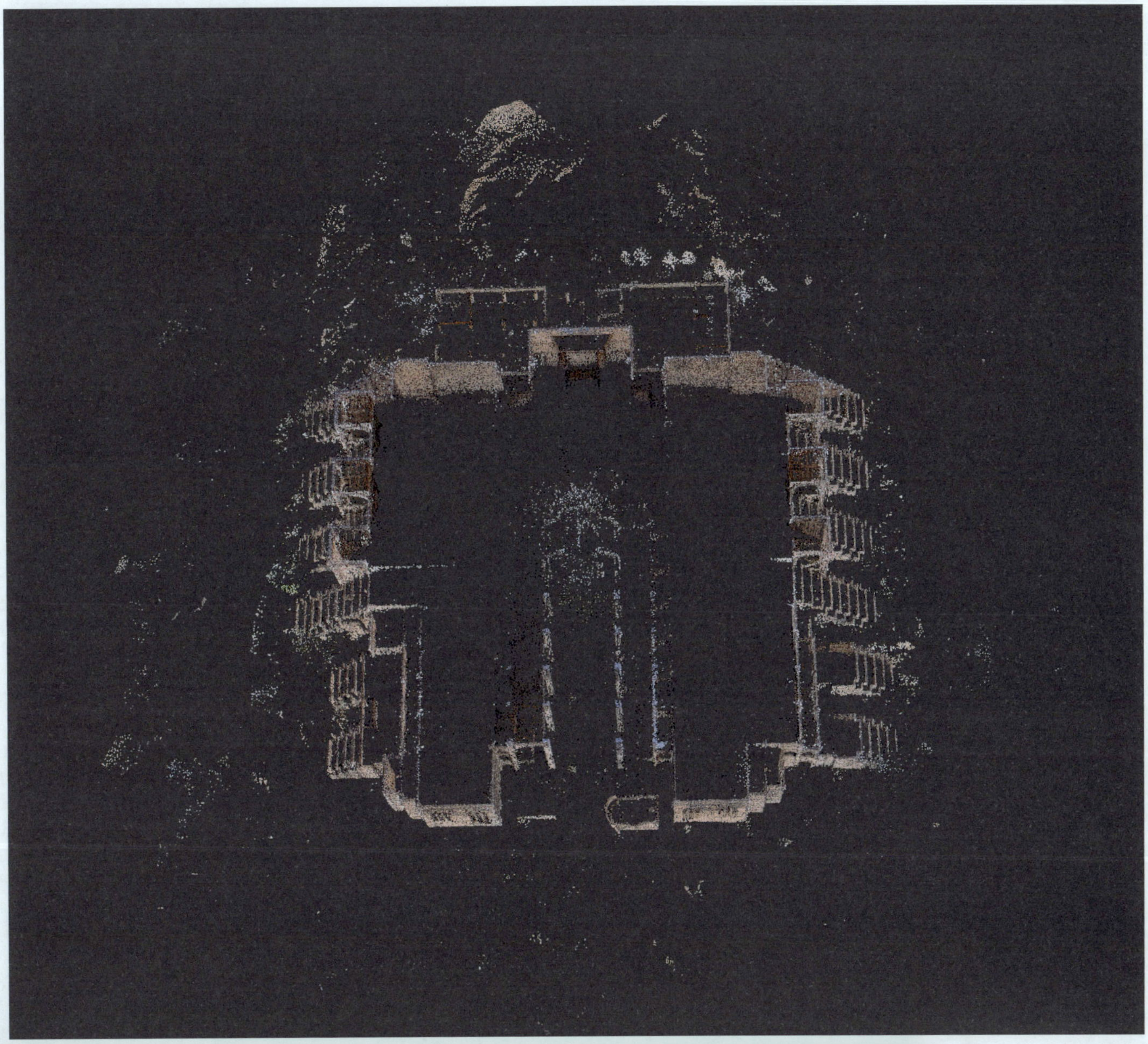

Mithilfe von Fotogrammetrie erstellte Limbo Accra eine Punktwolke des Gebäudes, die der dreidimensionalen digitalen Dokumentation der Struktur dient.

Limbo Accra used photogrammetry to produce a point cloud of the building, serving as a digital 3D record of the existing structure.

Manuel Chavajay

Tu industria, tu basura

DE

Seit mehr als zehn Jahren kommen Frauen der indigenen Tz'utujil-Gemeinschaft jeden Monat in der guatemaltekischen Kleinstadt San Pedro La Laguna zusammen, um das Ufer des angrenzenden Atitlán-Sees von Plastikmüll zu befreien. Der See ist seit jeher die Lebensgrundlage der Bewohner*innen der Region. Sein Fisch- und Krebsbestand schrumpft jedoch aufgrund jahrzehntelanger Verschmutzung durch Müll und Abwasser, zudem bedrohen Mikroplastik und Schadstoffe im Trinkwasser die Gesundheit von Menschen und Tieren.

2022 trugen die Aktivistinnen ihren Protest deshalb in die Hauptstadt Guatemala-Stadt. Gemeinsam mit dem Künstler Manuel Chavajay, der selbst der Gemeinschaft der Tz'utujil angehört, erarbeiteten sie die Performance *Tu industria, tu basura* (Eure Industrie, euer Müll), in der mehr als 100 der Frauen und zahlreiche weitere Vertreter*innen der Gemeinschaft in einer rituellen Prozession durch die Stadt zogen. Die Frauen balancierten auf ihren Köpfen Körbe aus Reet, anknüpfend an traditionelle Erntedank-Feiern der Maya, während die Männer volle Netze mit sich führten. Doch anstelle von Blumen, Früchten oder Fischen enthielten ihre Körbe und Netze Plastikmüll aus dem Atitlán See, den sie vor der Industriekammer und dem Parlamentsgebäude auskippten. Sie forderten, dass die Unternehmen Verantwortung für den Abfall übernehmen, den sie produzieren, und der Staat die Natur als Rechtssubjekt anerkennt und natürliche Lebensgrundlagen schützt.

Bei genauer Betrachtung ist in der auf Video dokumentierten Performance auch Manuel Chavajays Arbeit *Chakach / canasta 2* zu erkennen, für die er einen Teil eines handelsüblichen Plastikkorbs mit handgeflochtenem Reet zu einem Korb ergänzt hat. In der Arbeit kommt sowohl die Verdrängung traditioneller Techniken und Wissensbestände durch die kapitalistische Moderne als auch das Bewusstsein für die gleichzeitige Abhängigkeit indigener Gemeinschaften von einem extraktiven, ihre eigenen Lebensgrundlagen zerstörenden System zum Ausdruck.

2022
Protest-Aktion, Performance
Protest, performance
Video
Farbe, Ton
Color, sound
7 min
Dank an
Thanks to
Colectivo Tz'unun ya', Maíz de vida, Samuel Cumes Pop

EN

For over a decade, women from the Indigenous Tz'utujil community have gathered monthly in the Guatemalan town of San Pedro La Laguna to clear plastic waste from the shores of Lake Atitlán. The lake has long been essential to the livelihood of the region's residents. Its fish and crab populations have continuously diminished due to decades of trash and sewage pollution, while microplastics and pollutants in the drinking water threaten the health of people and animals.

In 2022, the activists staged a protest in the capital, Guatemala City, to express their concerns. Together with the artist Manuel Chavajay, who himself belongs to the Tz'utujil people, they developed the performance *Tu industria, tu basura* (Your Industry, Your Waste), in which over 100 of the women and other community representatives marched in a ritual procession through the city. The women balanced reed baskets on their heads, echoing traditional Mayan harvest celebrations, while men carried full nets. But instead of flowers and fruit or fish, their baskets and nets held trash and plastic waste from Lake Atitlán, which they demonstratively emptied before the Chamber of Industry and Congress buildings. They demanded that corporations take responsibility for the waste they produce and that the state recognize nature's juridic personhood and protect natural resources.

A close look at the video documenting their performance also reveals the presence of Manuel Chavajay's work *Chakach / canasta 2*, for which he mended an industrially produced plastic basket with hand-woven reeds. The work addresses the suppression of traditional practices and knowledge by capitalist modernity, while simultaneously articulating an awareness of the dependence of Indigenous communities on an extractive system that destroys their livelihoods.

Text:
Felix Hofmann

Manuel Chavajay, *Chakach / canasta 2,* 2022
Skulptur, Reet, Kunststoff
Sculpture, reeds, plastic
48 × 16 cm

Stills aus
Stills from
Manuel Chavajay
Tu industria, tu basura
2022
Video
Farbe, Ton
Color, sound
7 min

Sakiya

Sonic Faza3a

DE

Sakiya ist sowohl eine Akademie für experimentelle Wissensproduktion und -vermittlung als auch ein Bauernhof, dessen Bewirtschaftung auf lokalen landwirtschaftlichen Traditionen der Selbstversorgung und Permakultur beruht. Die Einrichtung befindet sich in Ein Qiniya, einem Dorf sieben Kilometer westlich von Ramallah. Wie bei den meisten Freiflächen und natürlichen Ressourcen im Westjordanland ist für die palästinensische Bevölkerung die Nutzung dieses Gebietes aufgrund von Auflagen der israelischen Zivil- und Sicherheitskontrolle massiv eingeschränkt. So ist es Palästinenser*innen oft untersagt, ihre Gärten einzuzäunen, damit diese für Sicherheitskräfte jederzeit zugänglich sind. Ebenso werden aus sicherheitspolitischen Erwägungen Vogelscheuchen, im Arabischen *faza3a* (فزاعة) genannt, regelmäßig von israelischen Soldat*innen entfernt, was ihnen eine politische Bedeutung verleiht.

Sakiyas *Sonic Faza3a* umgeht diese Beschränkungen, indem sie mit Klang arbeitet. Die akustischen Vogelscheuchen sollen einerseits Wildschweine fernhalten, um die Feldfrüchte zu schützen, andererseits die Tiere nach der Ernte gezielt anlocken, damit sie die Felder bei ihrer Suche nach Nahrung auf natürliche Weise umpflügen. Die fließenden Klänge stehen nicht für Abgrenzung, sondern für Durchlässigkeit, für eine Ethik des *Commoning*. Die Vogelscheuchen dienen nicht der Überwachung, sie flüstern stattdessen Worte des Schutzes und der Gastfreundschaft. Inspiriert von mythischen Kreaturen, die in der vorislamischen Spiritualität der Gegend verwurzelt sind, ist *Sonic Faza3a* ein Totem der Migration: des Kommens, Gehens und des Wiederkehrens.

Sonic Faza3a ist Teil eines umfassenderen Projekts zur Entwicklung ephemerer Infrastrukturen und folgt Sakiyas Vision, Beziehungen zur natürlichen Welt durch kollaborative künstlerische Projekte wiederherzustellen, die mit lokalen Praktiken und Wissen in einen harmonischen Dialog treten. In der vorliegenden Fassung sind die Vogelscheuchen als kelchförmige Wassergefäße aus Ton ausgebildet, die zwei Kompositionen abspielen. Diese stammen von den Künstlerinnen Jumana Emil Abboud und Bint Mbareh, die sich im Rahmen eines Artist-in-Residence-Programms intensiv mit dem Land beschäftigt haben, das Sakiya hütet. Jumana Emil Abbouds Komposition *She Inhabits our Roots and Futures from inside the Earth where She Dwells* handelt von Wassergeistern, die die Erde bewohnen. Bint Mbarehs Stück *Lentil Soup as an Antidote to Rampant Wildfires* verwebt Regen und andere Elemente zu einer spekulativen Zukunft, die sowohl von dystopischen als auch von hoffnungsvollen Vorstellungen durchdrungen ist.

2022
Sound installation
Keramik in Zusammenarbeit mit Nur Minawi, Palästina, und Mud Station, Schottland
Pottery in collaboration with Nur Minawi, Palestine, and Mud Station, Scotland
Sound in Zusammenarbeit mit
Sound in collaboration with
Jumana Emil Abboud, Bint Mbareh

EN

Sakiya is an academy for experimental knowledge production and sharing as well as a farm that builds on local agrarian traditions of self-sufficiency and permaculture. It is located in Ein Qiniya, a small agricultural village seven kilometers west of Ramallah. Like most of the West Bank's open spaces and natural resources, the area in which Sakiya operates is massively restricted for Palestinian use by Israeli civil and security control. For instance, Palestinians are often prohibited from building fences around their gardens, ensuring access for security forces at all times. In the same vein, Israeli soldiers regularly remove scarecrows, called *faza3a* (فزاعة) in Arabic, leading to these figures acquiring political meanings.

Sakiya's *Sonic Faza3a* circumvents these restrictions by working solely with sound. The acoustic scarecrows help local farmers protect their crops by deterring wild boar and, later, when it is time to till the soil, they attract the animals that naturally plow up the fields in search of food. The sounds are

fluid and permeable, challenging the binary of inside and outside, in favor of an ethics of commoning. Rather than monitor, the scarecrows whisper words of protection and hospitality. Inspired by mythical creatures rooted in the pre-Islamic spirituality of the area, *Sonic Faza3a* is a totem to migration: to coming, going, and returning.

Sonic Faza3a **is part of a larger ongoing project of imagining ephemeral infrastructures, following Sakiya's vision of reestablishing relationships with the natural world through artistic collaborations that communicate and harmonize with local practices and knowledge. In this iteration, the scarecrows manifest as germinating water vessels made of clay, playing two compositions recorded by artists Jumana Emil Abboud and Bint Mbareh, who, in a residency program, engaged closely with the land that Sakiya stewards. Jumana Emil Abboud created her composition, *She Inhabits our Roots and Futures from inside the Earth where She Dwells*, in search of water spirits. Bint Mbareh's composition, *Lentil Soup as an Antidote to Rampant Wildfires*, animates rain and other elements into a speculative future that is both dystopian and flooded with possibility.**

Text:
Sakiya

Sakiyas *Sonic Faza3a* ist eine Vogelscheuche, die allein mit Klang funktioniert. In der Ausstellung *The Great Repair* werden darüber zwei Kompositionen abgespielt: *She Inhabits our Roots and Futures from inside the Earth where She Dwells* von Jumana Emil Abboud und *Lentil Soup as an Antidote to Rampant Wildfires* von Bint Mbareh.

Sakiya's *Sonic Faza3a* is a scarecrow that works solely with sound. In the exhibition *The Great Repair*, it plays two compositions: *She Inhabits our Roots and Futures from inside the Earth where She Dwells* by Jumana Emil Abboud and *Lentil Soup as an Antidote to Rampant Wildfires* by Bint Mbareh.

Installationsansicht von *Sonic Faza3a* in der von Sakiya und Cooking Sections kuratierten Ausstellung *In the Eddy of the Stream* 2022 im Inverleith House des Royal Botanic Garden in Edinburgh

Installation view of *Sonic Faza3a* as part of the exhibition *In the Eddy of the Stream*, curated by Sakiya and Cooking Sections in 2022 at the Inverleith House of the Royal Botanic Garden of Edinburgh

Marjetica Potrč

The Rights of a River

2021
Serie von 10 Zeichnungen, Tusche auf Papier, jeweils
Series of 10 drawings, ink on paper, each
30 × 21 cm

The Time of Humans on the Soča River
2021
Wandarbeit
Wall drawing
280 × 380 cm

The Life of the Lachlan River
2022
Serie von 10 Zeichnungen, Tusche auf Papier, jeweils
Series of 10 drawings, ink on paper, each
30 × 21 cm

The Time on the Lachlan River
2022
Wandarbeit
Wall drawing
280 × 380 cm

Courtesy Marjetica Potrč & Galerie Nordenhake Berlin, Stockholm, Mexico City

DE

Die visuellen Essays von Marjetica Potrč – bestehend aus zwei ortsspezifischen Wandarbeiten und dazugehörigen Zeichnungen – erzählen die Geschichten zweier Flüsse in verschiedenen Teilen der Welt. *The Time of Humans on the Soča River* ist durch einen Volksentscheid in Potrčs Heimat Slowenien inspiriert. 2021 verhinderten Bürger*innen eine Änderung des Wassergesetzes, welches die Bebauung von geschützten Küstengebieten und Gewässerufern ausgeweitet und so Umwelt und Trinkwasser gefährdet hätte. *The Time on the Lachlan River* erzählt vom Kampf gegen die Erhöhung eines Staudamms in New South Wales, Australien, die dem flussabwärts gelegenen Land das Wasser zu entziehen droht. Die Arbeit ist in enger Zusammenarbeit mit Ray Woods entstanden, einem Ältesten der Wiradjuri, der das Land und Wasser in der Umgebung des Flusses hütet.

Beide Arbeiten sind ein Plädoyer für eine neue, gleichberechtigte Koexistenz des Menschen mit der natürlichen Welt, die die wechselseitige Abhängigkeit nicht nur anerkennt, sondern diese Beziehung auch gesetzlich untermauert. Sie fordern uns auf, Flüsse nicht länger als ausbeutbare Nutz- und Handelsobjekte zu betrachten. In Abkehr von diesem Anthropozentrismus plädieren sie vielmehr dafür, Flüsse als uns verwandte Subjekte mit eigener Handlungsmacht und Rechtsansprüchen anzuerkennen. Akzeptieren wir Flüsse und andere natürliche Ressourcen als Träger von Rechten, dann handeln wir nicht länger als ihre Nutzer*innen und Eigentümer*innen, sondern als ihre Hüter*innen und Pfleger*innen. Sie werden zu planetaren Gütern, die der gesamten lebenden Welt der Pflanzen, Tiere und Menschen zugutekommen.

EN

Marjetica Potrč's visual essays, accompanied by two site-specific wall drawings made from original diagrams, tell the stories of two rivers in different parts of the world. *The Time of Humans on the Soča River* was inspired by a referendum in Potrč's native Slovenia. In 2021, citizens prevented an amendment to the Water Act, which would have expanded construction on protected coastal areas and water banks and thus endangered the environment and drinking water. *The Time on the Lachlan River* chronicles the caretakers of a river in New South Wales, Australia, fighting the enlargement of a dam which threatens to deprive the land downstream of water. This second work was made in close collaboration with Ray Woods, a Wiradjuri elder who is one of the custodians of the river and the land along it.

Both works propose a new, egalitarian coexistence of humans with the natural world, whereby we not only understand and accept our interconnectedness but also consolidate this mutual relationship through law. They urge us to stop seeing rivers as objects for utilization, trade, and thus exploitation. Reversing this anthropocentrism, they suggest instead recognizing rivers as our kin, as subjects with their own agency and legal rights. If rivers and other natural resources are accepted as rights-bearing entities, then our role towards them shifts from user and owner to steward and guardian. They become planetary goods to be shared by the entire living world of plants, animals, and humans.

Text:
Nazlı Tümerdem

THE CONSTITUTION

FIVE YEARS AGO,
THE SLOVENIAN CONSTITUTION PROCLAIMED
THE RIGHT TO WATER,
MAKING ACCESS TO DRINKABLE WATER
A FUNDAMENTAL RIGHT FOR ALL.

THE RIGHT TO USE WATER.

IT IS MINE.

A REFERENDUM

FIVE YEARS LATER,
A REFERENDUM IS CALLED,
AFTER WATER IS TAKEN CAPTIVE
BY CAPITAL FOR PRIVATE ENTREPRENEURS.

WE THE PEOPLE
NEED WATER ON OUR SIDE.

IT'S ONLY COMMON SENSE:
WHEN WATER IS MISMANAGED,
THE COMMON GOOD BECOMES
THE COMMON MISFORTUNE.

RESOLUTION No. 1:
"WATER IS NEITHER LEFT NOR RIGHT!"

WE AGREE TO WORK TOGETHER.

WATER UNITES US ACROSS IDEOLOGICAL
DIVIDES.

THE RETURN OF COMMUNITY

RESOLUTION No. 2:
"WATER BELONGS TO NO ONE. IT IS
EVERYONE'S!"

WE ARE THE CARETAKERS
OF WHAT BELONGS TO YOU AND ME,
AND TO NATURE.

OURS IS A CULTURAL AUTHORITY
OVER THE COMMON LAND.

THE RETURN OF THE COMMONS

RESOLUTION No. 3:
"WATER IS OUR RIGHT. IT IS OUR DUTY TO
SAFEGUARD WATER FOR FUTURE GENERATIONS!"

WE LET GO OF THE OLD WAYS.

WE AGAIN DECOLONIZE OURSELVES,
THIS TIME FROM EXTRACTIVE CAPITALISM.

WHEN WE VOTED TO PROTECT WATER,
WE VOTED FOR A POST-IDEOLOGICAL FUTURE.

THE RETURN OF THE FUTURE

COEXISTENCE

I DEPEND ON WATER.
IT KEEPS ME ALIVE.
IT KEEPS US ALIVE.

WHEN I GAVE MY VOTE TO WATER,
THE WATER TURNED INTO A RIVER,
A LIVING BEING LIKE YOU AND ME.

I KNOW:
I CANNOT OWN MY CHILDREN,
I CAN ONLY BE THEIR CARETAKER.
I CAN ONLY BE THE RIVER'S CARETAKER.

I ASK MYSELF:
"WHO AM I? A HUMAN BEING, IN ONENESS
WITH NATURE?"

IN THE ANTHROPOCENE ERA,
THE EARTH TELLS ME
I AM A FORCE OF NATURE.

WHEN I AM NATURE, WHO AM I?

I ONCE KEPT NATURE AT A DISTANCE,
I THOUGHT I COULD USE IT OR ABUSE IT.
AND NOW IT'S GETTING CLOSER AND
CLOSER TO ME,

SO CLOSE IT IS PART OF MY FAMILY.

I ASK MYSELF:
"WHO AM I? A RIVER, IN ONENESS WITH
PEOPLE?"

I AM THE SOČA RIVER,
A LIVING BEING LIKE YOU.
I, TOO, CARE FOR MY FAMILY.
BUT THE TIME I LIVE IN IS LONG.

WHEN YOU REMOVE THE BURDEN OF DAMS
THAT REGULATE MY FLOW,
AND OTHER FOLLIES OF YOUR ERA,
THEN I WILL RENEW MYSELF.

THIS IS MY RIGHT.
IT IS MY DUTY TO SAFEGUARD WATER
FOR FUTURE GENERATIONS.

A NEW AGREEMENT BETWEEN PEOPLE
AND NATURE

IN A COMMON HOUSEHOLD:

THE RIVER IS A LIVING BEING,
NO LONGER AN OBJECT,
NO LONGER THE PROPERTY OF HUMANS.

WE PEOPLE ARE CARETAKERS OF THE RIVERS,
WE ARE GUARDIANS OF THEIR RIGHTS.

WATER IS SHARED
WITH OTHER LIVING BEINGS,
WITH ANIMALS AND PLANTS, SOIL AND ROCKS,
PEOPLE AND LAND.

IT IS OURS.

THE RETURN OF COLLECTIVE OWNERSHIP

A COMMON LAW

WE TAKE THE STRUGGLE FOR
THE RIGHTS OF RIVERS TO HUMAN COURTS,
IN THE SPIRIT OF OUR PAGAN GRANDPARENTS
WHO LIVED IN ONENESS WITH NATURE.

IN COURT, PEOPLE AND NATURE STAND
TOGETHER FOR THE COMMON GOOD,
AND NOT AGAINST EACH OTHER,
TO SET A JUDICIAL PRECEDENT.

WE STAND AT THE BEGINNING OF OUR
RENEWED COMMON TIME.
WE SUCCEED OR FAIL TOGETHER.

Marjetica Potrč, *The Rights of a River*, 2021
Der zehnteilige visuelle Essay erzählt, wie es slowenischen Bürger*innen 2021 gelang, mit einem Referendum die Gewässer des Landes zu schützen.

The ten-part visual essay relates how Slovenian citizens successfully protected their country's waters through a referendum in 2021.

The Guardians announce the death of Winter
and
The Tree of Life
Together: The pagan grandparents, Caretakers
of the Natural religion,
still alive
in the Soča valley
in the 1970s,
On the precipice of late capitalism: We who leave behind the senseless exploitation of Nature,
When we meet at the end of our common time: What can we do for each other? We

Marjetica Potrč, *The Time of Humans on the Soča River*, 2021
Die Zeichnung erzählt von einer durch die Ausbeutung natürlicher Ressourcen verwundeten Welt und dem notwendigen Wandel, der die Menschen nicht mehr als Eigentümer*innen der Natur, sondern als deren Hüter*innen und Pfleger*innen sieht.

The drawing tells the story of a world marred by the exploitation of natural resources, highlighting humanity's urgent transformation from perceiving itself as the owner of nature to assuming the role of its caretaker.

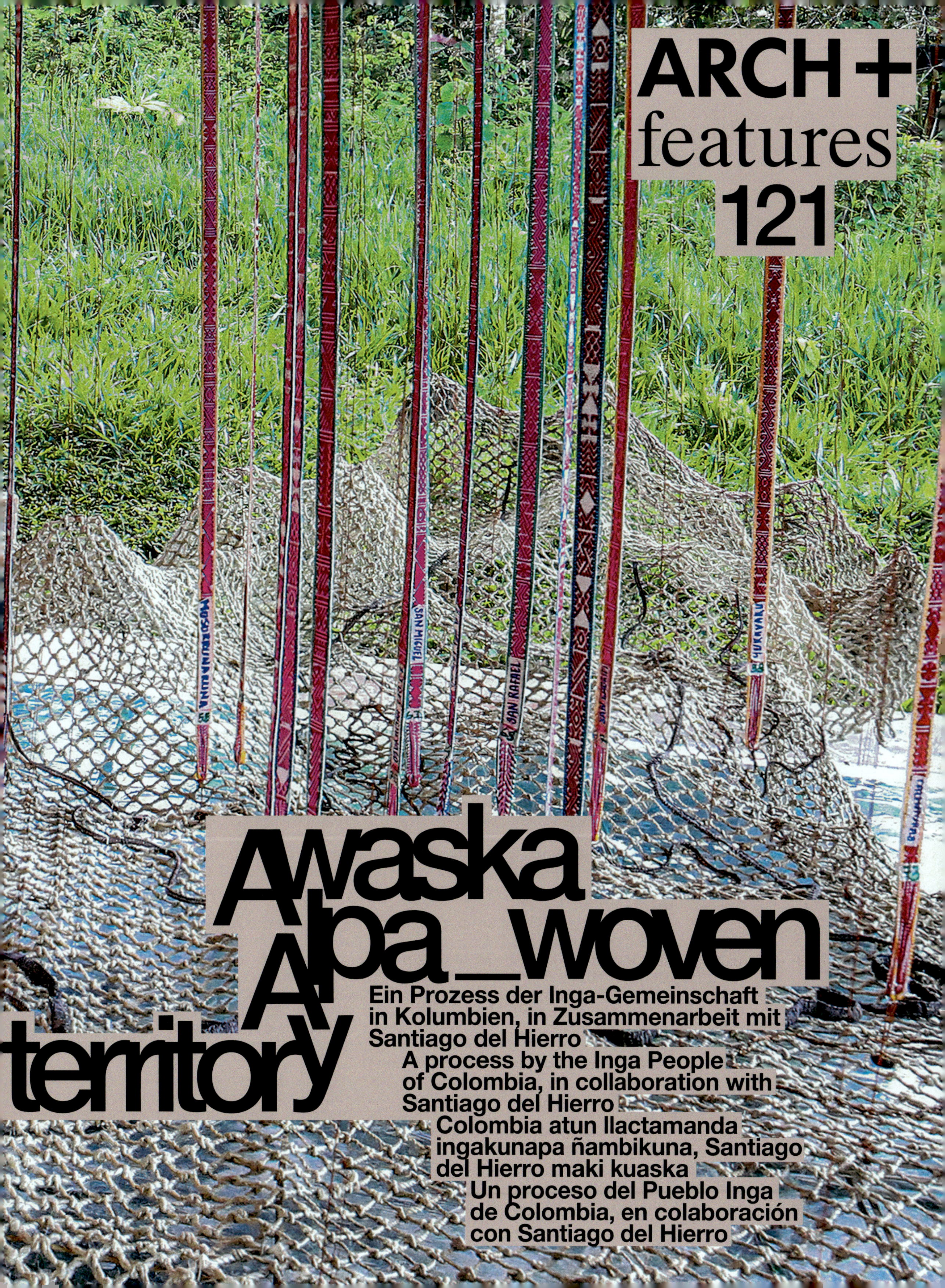

ARCH+ features 121

Awaska Alpa_woven territory

Ein Prozess der Inga-Gemeinschaft in Kolumbien, in Zusammenarbeit mit Santiago del Hierro

A process by the Inga People of Colombia, in collaboration with Santiago del Hierro

Colombia atun llactamanda ingakunapa ñambikuna, Santiago del Hierro maki kuaska

Un proceso del Pueblo Inga de Colombia, en colaboración con Santiago del Hierro

Awaska Alpa_woven territory

DE

Das Forschungsprojekt *Awaska Alpa_woven territory* setzt sich kritisch mit der Repräsentation des Inga-Territoriums im Anden-Amazonasgebiet Kolumbiens auseinander. Unter spanischer Kolonialherrschaft wurde das *resguardo* (Reservat) als eine Form des kollektiven Landbesitzes eingeführt, um die indigenen Völker zu „schützen", was de facto jedoch Eingrenzung und Kontrolle bedeutete. Bis heute ist dies die einzige vom Staat und von internationalen Organisationen verwendete Form der formellen Anerkennung von indigenen Gebieten. *Awaska Alpa* betrachtet die Formen der Organisation, der Bodennutzung und überlieferten sowie gegenwärtigen Verbindung der Inga zu ihren Lebensräumen genauer und erweitert so unser Verständnis von indigenem Territorium über seine rechtlich anerkannte Form hinaus.

Nachdem die verfassungsgebende Versammlung Kolumbiens 1991 die indigenen Reservate als vollständig autonome Gebietseinheiten mit eigenen Behörden, Teilhabe am Staatshaushalt und einer Selbstverwaltung ihrer Ressourcen anerkannt hatte, haben die Inga, wie viele andere indigene Gemeinschaften in Kolumbien, einen Prozess der kulturellen und territorialen Wiederaneignung angestoßen. Doch auch wenn die neue Verfassung nach Jahrhunderten der Gewalt und Missachtung einen historischen Wendepunkt für die Rechte der indigenen Bevölkerung in Kolumbien markierte, mangelt es immer noch an einem grundlegenden Verständnis für das tatsächliche Ausmaß der indigenen Gebiete und die komplexen Beziehungen zwischen indigenen Gemeinschaften und ihrem angestammten Land.

Neben den 36 Reservaten umfasst das Inga-Territorium 94 Selbstverwaltungseinheiten, die so genannten *cabildos*. Zusammen mit den Reservaten bilden sie ein komplexes Netzwerk sozialer, kultureller, biologischer und spiritueller Verbindungen zu den Wäldern, Bergen, Flüssen, Wegen, Städten und *chagras* (medizinisch-agrarökologische Stätten). Neben dem bewohnten Land betrachten die Inga auch die angrenzenden Landschaften, die von den „Ältesten durchwandert wurden", als Teil ihres Erbes. Das Inga-Territorium ist daher ein komplexes Beziehungsgeflecht, das sich der vereinfachten kartografischen Darstellung des Territoriums als eines rechtlich anerkannten Eigentums entzieht.

Für das Projekt *Awaska Alpa* sind Vertreter*innen der acht verschiedenen Inga-Gebiete aus dem Anden-Hochland, den Amazonaswäldern und mehr als 20 Städten im ganzen Land über mehrere Monate zusammengekommen, um gemeinsam eine 8 mal 6 Meter große textile Landschaft zu weben und so eine dreidimensionale Darstellung des Inga-Territoriums zu schaffen. Bunte *chumbe*-Gürtel markieren die Position der Inga-*cabildos*; Bananenblatt-Fasern kennzeichnen die Grenzen der Reservate; *iraka*-Palmfasern stellen Flüsse dar; *chakira*-Perlgeflechten stehen für Städte. All diese Elemente sind durch ein Netz aus *cabuya*-Pflanzenfasern miteinander verbunden, das eine inoffizielle, aber präzisere Topografie des Inga-Territoriums abbildet.

Awaska Alpa ist kein fertiges Objekt. Es ist vielmehr ein andauernder Prozess der Wiederentdeckung und der Bewusstwerdung, der eine territoriale Identität festigt, ohne die Anwesenheit anderer zu negieren. Es möchte ein Werkzeug zur Reparatur eines zerrütteten Territoriums werden, das jahrhundertelang unter Ausbeutung von Arbeitskraft, kultureller Enteignung und bewaffneten Konflikten litt und das noch immer mit der Gewalt zu kämpfen hat, die mit der aggressiven und oft illegalen Extraktion nicht-erneuerbarer Rohstoffe einhergeht.

EN

Awaska Alpa_woven territory is a research project that critically explores the representation of Inga territory in the Andean Amazon of Colombia. During colonial times, the Spanish crown established the Indigenous *resguardo* (reserve) as a form of collective land tenure to "protect," meaning to contain and control, Indigenous Peoples. Today, this is still the only form used by the state and international organizations to formally recognize Indigenous territory. By looking closely at Inga forms of organization, land occupation, and connectivity—both ancestral and contemporary—*Awaska Alpa* seeks to expand our understanding of Indigenous territory beyond what is acknowledged by national law.

Like many other Indigenous Peoples in Colombia, the Inga have been going through a process of cultural and territorial revindication ever since the Constituent Assembly of Colombia of 1991 recognized Indigenous reserves as fully autonomous territorial entities with their own authorities, self-administration of resources, and participation in national income. Although the new constitution marked a historical turning point for Indigenous rights in Colombia after centuries of violence and neglect, there is still no broader understanding of the real scale of Indigenous territories and the complex relations between Indigenous Peoples and their ancestral land.

In addition to 36 reserves, Inga territory also comprises 94 *cabildos* (community councils). Communities and reserves form an intricate network of social, cultural, biological, and spiritual connections to forests, mountains, rivers, pathways, cities, and *chagras* (medicinal agroecological sites). Beyond occupied land, the Inga People also consider the peripheral landscapes "walked by the elders" as part of their ancestral heritage. Inga territory is, therefore, a complex web of relations that defies its simplistic representation of territory as legally recognized property.

For the *Awaska Alpa* project, representatives of eight different Inga zones located in the Andean highlands, Amazonian forests, and more than 20 cities nationwide came together over several months to collectively weave an 8-by-6-meter fabric landscape composing a three-dimensional representation of Inga territory. Colorful *chumbe* belts mark the location of Inga *cabildos*, plantain leaf fibers mark the limits of reserves, *iraka* palm fibers represent rivers, and *chakira* beads stand for cities and towns. These elements are all interconnected by a mesh of *cabuya* fiber that forms a polygon of a less-official but more accurate Inga territory.

Awaska Alpa is not a finished object. It is an ongoing process of rediscovery and self-awareness that consolidates a territorial identity without negating the presence of others. It hopes to become a tool to repair a fragmented landscape that has fought for centuries with labor exploitation, cultural dispossession, as well as armed conflict, and that continues to struggle with the chronic violence often associated with illicit economies and nonrenewable resource extraction.

IN

Awaska Alpa_territorio tejido sug atun wachu tapurispa katichiska suma iuiaimandata imasami ingakunapa alpa Amazonía Andina Colombiapi kawariku. Iurakuna chaiamuskauramanda, paikuna kawachinkuna nukanchipurakunata sug piti alpa runakunata wakachingapa, runakunata charingapa, mana rurachukuna ima paikuna munaska nispa. Kunan punchakunapi, chi piti alpakunami kankuna kunan punchapi kaimanda iurakuna, sugnimanda iurakuna ningapakuna ari iukanguichimi alpa. Kaillamanda kawaspa imasami ingakunapa kausaii niralla paikunapa llactakunapi, paipurakunawa, achalakunapa iuiaikunawapas, Awaska Alpawa maskanakunchimi allichingapa sumaglla nukanchipa iachaikunata, ima nirallaskamanda runakunapa alpakuna, sug mailla tangachispa imasa iurakuna iuiai iukaskakunata.

Imasami sug runakuna kai atun Colombia llactapi iachaskakuna kispichirispa kausanga, chasallatatami ingakunapas iachaskakuna imasa paikunapa iuiaikuna, iachaikuna, kausaikunatapas kispichispa kausanga, imasami atun kilkaii 1991 pi niralla chasa, tukui runakunapa alpakuna kankunami tukui chi alpapi runakuna kausaskakunamanda sumaglla allichipa kausangapakuna, kikinkuna llalla churaspa, llactata allichispa, iurakunapa iuiaikunawapas parlaspa. Atun kilkii Colombiamanda allí kausaii runakunamanda rimagpipas, ajaii makanakuska watakunauramanda, sakii tukuskauramandapas, charami pisiku apachingapa achka ruraikuna, sutipa iachangapa imasami runakunapa alpakunapi niralla suma kausaii, paipurakunawa achalakunapa alpakunapipas.

Ingakuna llukankunami kimsa chunga sugta alpa pitikuna kausangapa paipurakunawa, chi ukuma tiami iskun chunga chusku *cabildo* wasikuna, awaskasina kausaikunata sulluchinkuna, paikunapa ruraikunawa, atun llallakunawa,

sachukukunawa, atun iakukunawa, ñambikunawa, chagrakunawa, chasa tukui ima paikunapa alpapi tiaskawapas. Kai ingakunapa alpakunapi, paikuna ninkunami achalakunapa ruku ñambikuna kankunasi iapa nimistidu, Chimandam ingakunapa alpa, mana kanchu sug piti alpalla, kami sug llacta kausadiru runakunapura, llallakunawa, uchulla wagkikunawa, tukuikunawa sugllapi, chasam ingakuna iuiankuna kagta alpa.

Kai atun wachu Awaska Alpa sutipi, tuparimuskakunami pusag piti alpamanda awadurkuna, chiri alpamandakuna, kunu alpamandakuna, iskai chunga awadur iurakunapa alpanigta tukui atun llacta Colombia sutipi kausaskakunapas tuparimuskakuna, sugllapi awangapa kikinkunapa alpa rigchasina atun awaipi, kai awai kidaskami chusku chunga palmu atun sugnimanda, kimsa chunga palmuwa sugsinama. Suma rigcha chumbikuna kawachinkunami maipi ingakunapa *cabildukuna* sallanakugta; anduchi ruradirupa waskakunawa kawachinakumi maipi piti alpakuna tukurinakuskata, iraka waskakunawa kawachinakumi maipi atun iakukuna rinakugta, maki watanakuna awaska mullukunawa kawachinakumi iurakunapa atun, uchulla kausadiru alpakunata. Tukui kai awaikuna kankunami sugllapi tupachiska sug atun *cabuya* waska suti awachiskawa, chasa kai awaikunapi kawarimi tukui ingakunapa alpa, mana kanchu iurakuna kawachinkuna chasa, kami imasami ingakuna rigsinkuna paikunapa alpata chasa.

Kai atun Awaska Alpa mana tukuchiska kanchu. Kami sug ñambi katichingapa kikin runakuna tarinakungapa, iuiarispa taringapa ima nirallagta ingakunapa alpa, mana sug runakunata sugma churaspalla. Munarimi kai awai aidachu ambiangapa ungug alpata kispichingapa iapa jiru kausaikuna apachiskamanda unai watakunauramandata, chara kunankama sinchillaspa kausaku jiru panga tarpuska kulkikuna challamunakugmanda, sisanakugmanda ima allí kausaipipa tiaskakunatapas.

ES

Awaska Alpa_territorio tejido es un proyecto de investigación que explora críticamente la representación del territorio Inga en la Amazonía Andina de Colombia. Durante la época colonial, la corona española estableció el resguardo indígena como una forma de tenencia colectiva de la tierra para "proteger", es decir, contener y controlar a los pueblos indígenas. Hoy en día, esta sigue siendo la única forma utilizada por el Estado y las organizaciones internacionales para reconocer formalmente al territorio indígena. Al observar de cerca las formas de organización, ocupación de la tierra y conectividad Inga, tanto ancestrales como contemporáneas, *Awaska Alpa* busca ampliar nuestra comprensión del territorio indígena más allá de lo reconocido por la ley nacional.

Como muchos otros Pueblos Indígenas en Colombia, el Pueblo Inga ha atravesado un proceso de reivindicación cultural y territorial desde que la Asamblea Constituyente colombiana de 1991 reconoció a los resguardos indígenas como entidades territoriales totalmente autónomas con autoridades propias, administración de sus recursos y participación en el presupuesto nacional. Aunque la nueva constitución marcó un punto de inflexión histórico para los derechos indígenas en Colombia después de siglos de violencia y abandono, aún queda mucho por hacer para tener una comprensión amplia de la escala real de los territorios indígenas y las complejas relaciones entre los pueblos y sus tierras ancestrales.

Además de 36 resguardos, el territorio Inga comprende 94 cabildos, formando una intrincada red de conexiones sociales, culturales, espirituales y biológicas con bosques, montañas, ríos, caminos, ciudades y chagras. Más allá del espacio ocupado por comunidades, el Pueblo Inga también considera los paisajes periféricos "caminados por los mayores" como parte de su patrimonio ancestral. El territorio Inga es, por lo tanto, una compleja red de relaciones que desafía una representación del territorio meramente como propiedad legalmente reconocida.

Para el proyecto *Awaska Alpa*, tejedores representantes de las ocho zonas del Pueblo Inga ubicadas en el altiplano andino, los bosques amazónicos y en más de 20 ciudades a nivel nacional se unieron durante varios meses para tejer colectivamente un paisaje tridimensional de 8 por 6 metros para representar su territorio. Coloridos *chumbes* marcan la ubicación de los cabildos Inga; cuerdas de látigo de plátano marcan los límites de las reservas, fibras de *iraka* representan los ríos; y los tejidos en *chakira* representan ciudades y pueblos. Estos elementos están todos interconectados por una malla de fibra de cabuya que propone un polígono del territorio Inga menos oficial pero más preciso.

La maqueta de *Awaska Alpa* no es un objeto terminado. Es un proceso permanente de redescubrimiento y autoreflexión que busca consolidar una identidad territorial sin negar la presencia de los demás. Espera convertirse en una herramienta para reparar un paisaje fragmentado que ha sufrido durante siglos con el conflicto armado, la explotación laboral y el despojo cultural, y que continúa luchando contra la violencia crónica asociada con las economías ilícitas y la extracción de recursos no renovables.

Ab April 2023 kamen Inga-Vertreter*innen aus ganz Kolumbien über mehrere Monate zusammen, um gemeinsam ein dreidimensionales Modell ihres Gebiets zu weben. Während des Eröffnungsworkshops, der in dem Versammlungsraum Muskui Wasi (Haus der Träume) in Mocoa, Putumayo, stattfand, einigten sich Weber*innen und Forscher*innen darauf, wie Materialien und Techniken aus verschiedenen Inga-Regionen integriert werden können.

Auf dem Bild unten weist Taita Hernando Chindoy, Oberhaupt der indigenen Inga-Gemeinschaft in Kolumbien, auf die Herausforderungen hin, mit denen die Inga-Gebiete derzeit konfrontiert sind; oben betrachten John Jairo Jansasoy und Luzdary Santacruz auf einer Luftaufnahme das Gebiet ihrer Gemeinschaft in Aponte.

Starting in April 2023, Inga representatives from across Colombia collectively wove a three-dimensional cartography of their territory over several months. During the inaugural workshop, which took place at Muskui Wasi (House of Dreams), a meeting space in Mocoa, Putumayo, weavers and researchers agreed on how to integrate materials and techniques from different Inga regions.

In the picture below, Taita Hernando Chindoy, leader of the Inga People of Colombia, points out current challenges facing Inga territories. Above, John Jairo Jansasoy and Luzdary Santacruz examine their community in Aponte in an aerial photo.

2023 watapi tamia killauramanda, sug runa ingakuna Colombia llactamanda tiarinkuna sugllapi awangapa imasa kagta kinkinkunapa alpa kausadiruta. Kai awai kallarikura, rurariska Musku Wasi sutipi ("Casa de Sueños") Mocoasullu Putumayo Llactapi, awadurkuna tapudurkunawa rimanakuspa niskakuna imasami tukui sugnimanda ingakunapa awaikunata chaia suglla awai ruranga.

Uraladu, Taita Hernando Chindoy, Iacha Inga Colombia llactamanda, kawachimi ima nimistidukuna tiagta tukui ingakunapa alpanigta. Awanimanda rigchapi, John Jairo Jansasoy Luz Dary Santacruswa, kawanakuni sug rigchapi kikinkunapa Apontemanda alpata.

A partir de abril de 2023, representantes del pueblo Inga de Colombia se reunieron durante varios meses para tejer colectivamente una cartografía tridimensional de su territorio. Durante el taller inaugural, que se llevó a cabo en el espacio de encuentro Muskui Wasi ("Casa de Sueños") de Mocoa, Putumayo, tejedores e investigadores acordaron cómo integrar materiales y técnicas de diferentes regiones del pueblo Inga.

Abojo, Taita Hernando Chindoy, líder del Pueblo Inga de Colombia, señala los desafíos que enfrentan actualmente sus territorios. En la imagen superior, John Jairo Jansasoy y Luzdary Santacruz examinan su comunidad de Aponte en una fotografía aérea.

San José (Descanse)
SAN JOSÉ (DESCANSE)
Rigcharikuna
Aponte
INGA DE APONTE
Yunguillo
San Carlos
YUNGUILLO
Tandarido
Osococha
SAN JOAQUIN
San Joaquin
INGA DE SAN PEDRO
INGA DE CONDAGUA
Inga de Condagua
Mandiyaco
Suma Yuyay
San Antonio
MANDIYACO
INGA DE COLON
San Pedro
Colón
Inga Kamentsa de San Francisco
Ambiwaska
José Homero
Santiago
San Andrés
Inga
Inga Mocoa
Kamentsa
Musu Nambi Kausai
INGA KAMENTSA DE SAN FRANCISCO
RUMIÑAWI
INGA DE SAN MIGUEL
La Leona
San Miguel
Musurrunakuna
San Antonio del Fragua
San Rafael
Brisas
San Ga
SAN ANTONIO DEL FRAGUA
MUSURUNAKUNA
Musurunakuna
WASIPUNGO
Aukawasi
Rumiñawi
Bajo Chuspisacha
INGA DE SANTIAGO
INGA DE SAN ANDRÉS
NASA
Wasipungo
Tigre Playa
La Cristalina
Puerto Limon
Inga Pakai
Caucapapungu
La Floresta
La Española
PUERTO LIMON
LA FLORESTA
LA ESPAÑOLA
GUAYUYACO
Guayuyaco
Ingakunapa Iuiai
Nukanchipa Alpa
San José del Inchiyaco
Ambiwasi
Wasipanga
WASIPANGA
Playarica
Villa Catalina de Puerto Rosario
Alpamanga
ALPAMANGA
NUKANCHIPA ALPA AMUKUNAPA WASI
Chaluayaco
Nukanchipa Alpa Taita Kausadero
Saladilloyaco
BLASIAKU
Blasiaku
Alto Mango
NASA
San Miguel de La Castellana
SAN MIGUEL DE LA CASTELLANA
Musu Waira Sacha Nukanchipa
Cachiyako Andaqui
CHALUAYACO
AWA
Musu Iuiai
Alparumiyaco
Albania
ALBANIA
Sacha Wagra
Suma Iuiai
Puerto Caicedo
Selvas del Putumayo
Santana
Nukanchipa Iukaska
Puerto Asís
El Palmar
Nukanchipa Yuyay
KOFAN
San Fidel Kimsayako

Karte der *resguardos* (Reservate) und *cabildos* (Selbstverwaltungseinheiten) der Inga im Südwesten Kolumbiens und in 22 Städten im ganzen Land. Für den Workshop wurde eine große Version der Karte im Maßstab 1:25.000 auf Vinyl gedruckt.

Map of Inga *resguardos* (reserves) and *cabildos* (community councils) in southwestern Colombia and 22 cities across the country. For the workshop, a large 1:25,000 scale version of the map was printed on vinyl.

Ingakunapa alpakuna kausadirusina rigcha cabildukunawa uranimanda Colombia llactapi, iskai chunga iskai iurakunapa alpakunapi kausadur ingakunapapas tukui Colombia llactamanda. Kai ruraikunapipa, suskuriskami sug ingakunapa alpakunasina rigcha 1:25.000 uchullallachiska.

Mapa de resguardos y cabildos Inga en el suroeste de Colombia y en 22 ciudades de todo el país. Para el taller, se imprimió en lona una versión del mapa a escala 1:25.000.

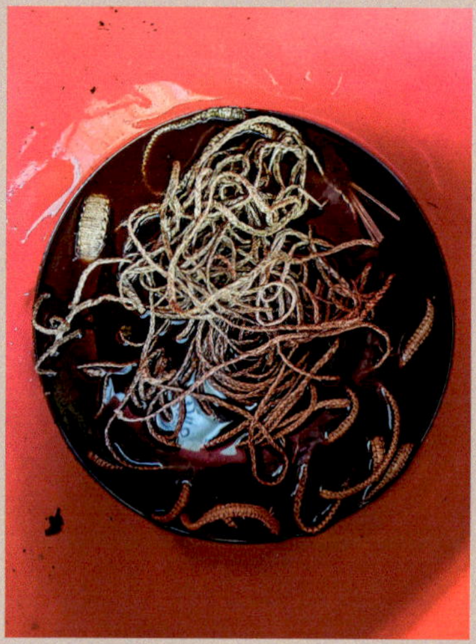

Auf dem Bild oben erklären Jhoni Huaca und Fanny Jamioy den Prozess des Webens von *iraka*-Fasern. In der Mitte werden nach einer traditionellen Technik *palmicha*-Fasern zu Schnüren gedreht und dann mit *kuriwaska*-Blättern und *tiñituru*-Lehm gefärbt. Das Bild unten zeigt Garn aus *cabuya*-Pflanzenfasern.

Above, Jhoni Huaca and Fanny Jamioy explain the process of weaving *iraka* fiber. In the middle, using a traditional technique, *palmicha* fiber is twisted into twine and then dyed with *kuriwaska* leaves and *tiñituru* mud. The image below shows *cabuya* fiber twine.

Awaladu, Jhoni Huaca Fanny Jamioywa rimankunami imasami ka iraka waskawa awai. Nispak ñugpamanda awai ruraikunata katichispa, palmicha waskata kaugchurimi, nispak tisnangapa tiñituru kuriwaska pangakunawa. Uraladu kawairimi cabuya waska, awangapa Ingakunapa alpakunata.

Arriba, Jhoni Huaca y Fanny Jamioy explican el proceso de tejido de la fibra de iraka. A continuación, siguiendo una técnica tradicional, la fibra de palmicha se tuerce en hilo y luego se tiñe con hojas de kuriwaska y barro de tiñituru. Abajo se aprecia la cabuya utilizada para tejer la malla topográfica.

Der Inga-Nationalkongress 2023 fand in Piamonte, Cauca, statt. Mehr als 450 Inga-Vertreter*innen nahmen an der Veranstaltung teil. Dort wurde die Karte genutzt, um die genaue Lage aller Gemeinden zu bestimmen und die Pfade der Vorfahr*innen zurückzuverfolgen.

The 2023 Inga National Congress took place in Piamonte, Cauca, with over 450 Inga representatives attending. The map was used during the event to pinpoint the precise location of all the Inga communities and identify their ancestral paths.

Ingakunapa atun rimanakui kunan watapi, apachiriskami Piamonte suti alpapi Caucaladubanda. Chaiskakunami chusku patsag pichka chunga runakuna tukuinimanda. Chiura ingakunapa alpakunsina rigchata aidaskami kawangapa maipi sutipa kausagtakuna runaku, chasallatata kawangapa ruku ñambikunatapas.

El Congreso Nacional del Pueblo Inga de 2023 se llevó a cabo en Piamonte, Cauca. Más de 450 representantes Inga asistieron al evento. En esta ocasión, se utilizó el mapa para confirmar la ubicación precisa de todas las comunidades e identificar rutas ancestrales.

Mit Garn aus *cabuya*-Pflanzenfasern webten Viviana Jacanamejoy, Marcelina Jamioy, Jean Mutumbajoy und Víctor Baltazar ein topografisches Netz.

Cabuya fiber twine was collectively woven into a topographic mesh by Viviana Jacanamejoy, Marcelina Jamioy, Jean Mutumbajoy, and Víctor Baltazar.

Cabuya Waska awariskami sugllapi rurangapa ima kangapa kaska ingakunapa alpakunasina rigcha, awaskakunami Viviana Jacanamejoy, Marcelina Jamioy, Jean Mutumbajoy Víctor Baltazarwa sugllapi.

La fibra de cabuya fue tejida colectivamente en una malla topográfica por Viviana Jacanamejoy, Marcelina Jamioy, Jean Mutumbajoy y Víctor Baltazar.

Ein Ritual der *armonización* (Harmonisierung) mit Materialien aller Weber*innen leitete den Aufbau des Modells ein.

The maquette's assembly started with an *armonización* (harmonization) ritual, where materials from all the weavers were brought together.

Kai ingakunapa alpa kausadiru ruraikuna kallariskami tukui awaikunata kusnichispa.

Un ritual de armonización con materiales de todas las tejedoras inició el montaje de la maqueta.

Chumbe-Gürtel, die von fünf Weber*innen aus den Andengebieten gefertigt wurden, dienten dazu, das Netz über der Karte aufzuhängen und die komplexe Topografie des Gebiets nachzubilden. Die in die *chumbe*-Gürtel eingewebten Symbole sind Teil des überlieferten Wissens der Inga, das anerkannt und geschützt werden muss.

Inga *chumbe* belts made by five weavers from the Andean territories were used to hang the mesh above the map and recreate the complex topography of the area. The symbols woven into *chumbe* belts are part of ancestral Inga knowledge which must be recognized and protected.

Churariskami pichka chiri awa sachukukunamanda awadurkunapa chumbikuna, chi chumbikunamanda warkuchiriskami cabuya waskawa awaskata, rurangapa imasa kai alpakuna kaskasina. Chumbimanda laburkuna kankunami ingakunapa iachaikuna, chikunata chaiami kawachinga, kispichingapas.

Se utilizaron chumbes inga hechos por cinco tejedoras de los territorios andinos para colgar la malla sobre el mapa y recrear la compleja topografía del área. Los símbolos tejidos en los chumbes son parte del conocimiento ancestral Inga que debe ser reconocido y protegido.

Aus *chakira*-Perlen gefertigte Muster stellen die Inga-Selbstverwaltungseinheiten (*cabildos*) in urbanen Kontexten dar.

Grids made with *chakira* beads were used to represent Inga community councils (*cabildos*) in urban contexts.

Chakirawa awaska maki watanakuna, kawachinkunami maipi calbildukuna tiagta atun puiblunigta.

Se tejieron manillas de chakira para representar los cabildos del pueblo Inga en el contexto de ciudades.

Auf das Netz aufgenähte *chakira*-Perlen zeigen Städte, während *iraka*-Palmfasern den Verlauf von Flüssen nachzeichnen.

Chakira beads were stitched on the mesh to represent towns, while *iraka* fibre twine was used to trace the courses of rivers.

Awariskami chakira mullukumawapas, apichingapa cabuya waskawa awaskapi, kawachingapa maipi aillukuna kausagtakuna, iraka waskawa rurariskami maipi iakukuna kalpanakuskapi.

Se cosieron tejidos de chakira a la malla para representar pueblos y se usó fibra de iraka para trazar los cursos de los ríos.

Im Juni 2023 wurde das Modell im *Muskui Wasi* ausgestellt, dort bietet sich den Besucher*innen eine inoffizielle, aber präzise Darstellung des Inga-Gebiets.

In June 2023, the maquette was presented in *Muskui Wasi*, providing visitors with a less official but more accurate representation of the Inga territory.

Watamanda sugta killapi, kai atun awai alpamanda, kawachiriskami Muskui wasipi, maikan munaskakunata kawangapa imami niraia ingakunapa kausadiru alpa.

En junio de 2023, la maqueta se presentó en Muskui Wasi, brindando a los visitantes una representación menos oficial pero más verídica del territorio del pueblo Inga.

Text
Inga-Gemeinschaft in Kolumbien, Santiago del Hierro
Inga People of Colombia, Santiago del Hierro
Ruradurkuna
Colombiamanda / aillu ingakuna Santiago del Hierrowa
Autoría
Pueblo Inga de Colombia y Santiago del Hierro

AWAI Indigene Gebietskörperschaft 2017–2023
AWAI Indigenous Territorial Entity 2017–2023
AWAI runakunapa alpa kausaii 2017–2023
Entidad Territorial Indígena AWAI 2017–2023

Gesetzlicher Vertreter
Legal representative
Ñugpanimanda iaia
Representante legal
Hernando Chindoy

Technischer Sekretär
Technical secretary
Iaiata aidadur
Secretario técnico
Freider Legarda

Gebietsberater*innen
Zonal advisors
Sumaglla rimadur alpanimansakuna
Consejeros zonales
Liliana Armero, Oscar Bastidas, Pablo Cuchalá, Héctor Fabián Garreta, Waira Jacanamijoy, Isidoro Jajoy, Pedro Jajoy, Irma Mojomboy

AWAI Indigene Gebietskörperschaft 2023–2027
AWAI Indigenous Territorial Entity 2023–2027
AWAI runakunapa alpa kausaii 2023–2027
Entidad Territorial Indígena AWAI 2023–2027

Gesetzlicher Vertreter
Legal representative
Ñugpanimanda iaia
Representante legal
Freider Legarda

Technischer Sekretär
Technical secretary
Iaiata aidadur
Secretario técnico
Gabriel Muyuy

Gebietsberater*innen
Zonal advisors
Sumaglla rimadur alpanimansakuna
Consejeros zonales
James Rafael Becerra, Diego Iván Cuaspa, Juan Domingo Cuatindioy, Waira Jacanamijoy, Antonio Jajoy, Miguel Candelo Mojana, María A. Ortega

Iacha spiritueller Führer
Iacha spiritual guide
Iacha ñambi kawachidur
Iacha orientador del proceso
Taita Luciano Mutumbajoy

Konzeptuelle und administrative Unterstützung
Conceptual and administrative support
Iuiaikunapi/kulki kawaii aidadur
Apoyo conceptual/administrativo
Cristina Rodríguez

Inga Mocoa Reservat
Inga Mocoa Reservation
Inga Mocoamanda Alpa
Resguardo Inga Mocoa

Gouverneurin
Governor
Ubirnadura
Gobernador
Agripina Garreta

Bürgermeister
Mayor
Atun Alkaldi
Alcalde Mayor
Carlos Porfirio Jacanamejoy

Akademischer Koordinator der Bildungseinrichtung IEB Inga Mocoa
Academic coordinator, IEB Inga Mocoa educational institution
Iachaikudiru IEB Inga Mocoamanda sumaglla allichidur
Coordinador académico IEB Inga Mocoa
Camilo Quiroga

Awaska Alpa
Gebietsrat
Territorial coordinating councilor
Sumaglla rimaspa alpata allichidur
Consejero coordinador de Territorio
Héctor Fabián Garreta

Gebietsratsbeauftragter
Delegated territorial coordinator
Sumaglla allichispa alpata almadur
Coordinador delegado de Territorio
Pablo Cuchalá

Konzept und Leitung
Concept and general direction
Iuiachidur ñugpama apachingapa
Concepto y dirección general
Santiago del Hierro

Logistische und politische Koordination
Logistical and political coordinator
Sumaglla ñambi apachidur, suma kausaipipa
Coordinadora logística y política
Liliana Armero

Team Muskui Wasi
Muskui Wasimanda almadurkuna
Equipo Muskui Wasi
Víctor Baltazar, Viviana Jacanamejoy, Jean Mutumbajoy, Felipe Pupo

Inga-Weber*innen
Inga weavers
Awadurkuna tukui ingakunapa alpanimandakuna
Tejedores zonales Pueblo Inga
María Gladys Bolaños, Sandra Chasoy, Sandra Patricia Chasoy, Juan Domingo Cuatindioy, Fanny Jamioy, Marcelina Jamioy, Mónica Marcela Muchavisoy, Nilson Peña, María Helena Tandioy

Regionale Inga-Verbindungspersonen
Inga regional liaisons
Tukui ingakunapa alpanimanda chaskikuna
Enlaces zonales Pueblo Inga:
Johanna Burbano Macias, Agustin Chasoy, Sandy Chindoy, Diego Iván Cuaspa, Jhoni Huaca, Andrés Jansasoy, Manuel Muyuy, María Alejandra Quiroga

Audiovisuelle Dokumentation
Audiovisual documentation
Kawangapa-ullangapa kilkadurkuna
Documentación audiovisual
Ñambi Rimai (Wilton Jajoy, Mayerly Trochez)

Beratung und Unterstützung
Consulting and support
Suma rimaspa aidadurkuna
Asesoría y apoyo
María Claudia Beltrán, Sorayda Chindoy, Lizeth Córdoba, John Jairo Jansasoy, Brita Lemmens, Kelly Mojomboy, Katerine Muchavisoy, Luzdary Santacruz, Karl von Oertzen

Übersetzung Inga–Spanisch
Translation Inga–Spanish
Sug rimaima kilkadur Español-ingama
Traducción Inga-Español
Manuel Muyuy

Gefördert von / Supported by
creative industries fund NL
GOETHE INSTITUT
NODO ALEMANIA

Impressum / Imprint

ARCH+ features

Diskursplattform von
A platform for discourse by
ARCH+ & SSS SIEDLE

Diese Publikation erscheint anlässlich der Ausstellung *The Great Repair* in der Akademie der Künste, Berlin / This publication is part of the exhibition *The Great Repair* at Akademie der Künste, Berlin.

Künstlerische Leitung / Artistic direction
Florian Hertweck, Christian Hiller, Markus Krieger, Alex Nehmer, Anh-Linh Ngo, Milica Topalović
Kuratorische Assistenz / Curatorial assistance
Marija Marić, Nazlı Tümerdem
Produktionsleitung / Production management
Felix Hofmann
Projektmanagement / Project management
Elke Doppelbauer
Kommunikation / Communications
Barbara Schindler
Geschäftsführung / Managing director
Arno Löbbecke
Team
Nora Dünser, Mirko Gatti, Daniel Kuhnert, Victor Lortie, Mona Rauch, Lea Scherer, Finn Steffens

Verlag / Publishers
ARCH+, Spector Books

Art Direction
Stan Hema, Berlin
Design
Sara Božić, André van Rueth,
Niki Moreira (Projektmanagement / Project management),
Daniel Vandré (Reinzeichnung / Final typesetting)

Übersetzung Inga–Spanisch / Translation Inga–Spanish
Manuel Muyuy
Übersetzung Spanisch–Englisch / Translation Spanish–English
Santiago del Hierro
Übersetzung Englisch–Deutsch / Translation English–German
Petra Gaines + Jeremy Gaines
Deutsches Lektorat / German copyediting
Kirsten Thietz
Englisches Lektorat / English copyediting
Jeremy Gaines
Spanisches Lektorat / Spanish copyediting
Rosa Joana García Latorre-Hoppstaedter
Satzkorrektur Deutsch / German proofreading
Sara Lusic-Alavanja
Satzkorrektur Englisch / English proofreading
James Copeland

Fotos / Photos
© Santiago del Hierro (sofern nicht anders benannt / unless otherwise stated)
© Brita Lemmens (S. / p. 15)
© Felipe Pupo (S. / p. 8 oben links / left above)
© Ñambi Rimai (Umschlag / cover, 5 links / left, 11 oben / above)

Lithografie / Prepress
max-color, Berlin
Druck / Printing
Medialis Offsetdruck GmbH, Berlin

Mit der Reihe ARCH+ features stellt ARCH+ in regelmäßiger Folge ausgewählte Positionen vor, die sich in besonderer Weise mit den gegenwärtigen Produktionsbedingungen von Architektur auseinandersetzen. ARCH+ features wird von Anh-Linh Ngo kuratiert und von Siedle als Initiativpartner langfristig ermöglicht. / With the ARCH+ features series, curated by Anh-Linh Ngo, ARCH+ regularly presents selected positions on the contemporary conditions of architectural production. The series is made possible by Siedle as the initiative partner.

Ein Projekt im Rahmen der Ausstellung / A project in conjunction with the exhibition

The Great Repair

14.10.2023–14.1.2024
Akademie der Künste, Berlin

Ein Projekt von / A project by
ARCH+ gGmbH

In Kooperation mit / In collaboration with
Akademie der Künste
ETH zürich | D ARCH
uni.lu | Faculty of Humanities, Education and Social Sciences | Arch MA UniLu

Eröffnungsprogramm in Kooperation mit / Opening program in collaboration with
Performing Architecture, Goethe Institut
FORWARD DANCE COMPANY von
LOFFT - DAS THEATER
Akademie der Künste, Berlin

Gefördert durch die / Funded by the German Federal Cultural Foundation
Kulturstiftung des Bundes

Gefördert von / Funded by the Federal Government Commissioner for Culture and the Media
Die Beauftragte der Bundesregierung für Kultur und Medien

Bildungsprogramm gefördert von / The educational program is funded by the Federal Agency for Civic Education
bpb: Bundeszentrale für politische Bildung

Weitere Förderer / Additional support from
Wüstenrot Stiftung
Hans Sauer Stiftung

Das Experimental Stipendienprogramm für junge Architekturforschende wird gefördert durch / The Experimental Scholarship Program for young architectural researchers is funded by
EXPERIMENTAL

SAN MIGUEL
SAN RAFAEL

DE

Aus marxistischer Sicht ist die Konzentration der Produktionsmittel einer der Hauptgründe für Ausbeutung und Entfremdung im Kapitalismus. Während die Entfremdung der Arbeitenden von den Produkten, die sie für den Profit anderer herstellen, offenkundig ist, folgt die Entfremdung der Verbraucher*innen aus dem mangelnden Wissen darüber, wie die Dinge, die sie benutzen, hergestellt, erhalten und repariert werden. In diesem System sind Waren austauschbare Güter, die für die Mülldeponie bestimmt sind. Um dieser Kommodifizierung und der daraus resultierenden ökologischen und sozialen Zerstörung entgegenzuwirken, müssen wir uns die Werkzeuge der Reparatur wieder aneignen. Mit Hilfe dieser Fertigkeiten, Techniken und Kenntnisse können wir unsere Beziehungen innerhalb der sozialen und natürlichen Umwelt neu gestalten und die Produktion wieder in die für ihre Reproduktion erforderlichen Zusammenhänge einbetten. Vor diesem Hintergrund hat der Architekt Yoshiharu Tsukamoto von Atelier Bow-Wow sein Credo formuliert: „Werkzeuge für alle!“

Text:
Daniel Kuhnert

Werkzeuge für alle

Tools to the People

EN

From a Marxist point of view, the concentration of the means of production is one of the main reasons for exploitation and alienation in capitalism. While the alienation of the workers from the products they produce for the profit of others is self-evident, the alienation of the consumer results from the lack of knowledge of how the things they use are constructed, maintained, and repaired. In this system, goods are replaceable commodities, destined for the landfill. To counter this commodification and the resulting ecological and social destructions, we need to reappropriate the tools of repair. With these crafts, techniques, and knowledge in hand, we can redesign our relationships within the social and natural environment and re-embed the production in the contexts needed for their reproduction. This is what architect Yoshiharu Tsukamoto from Atelier Bow-Wow meant when he formulated the slogan: "Tools to the People!"

Atelier Bow-Wow

Solar Garden

DE

Solar Garden ist ein als Wintergarten angelegter Verbindungsgang durch den Gräsergarten im ersten Obergeschoss der Akademie der Künste im Hanseatenweg, den Atelier Bow-Wow für *The Great Repair* entworfen hat. Seine Gestaltung reagiert auf verschiedene Gegebenheiten, angefangen bei der ungewöhnlichen Besucher*innenführung von *The Great Repair*, die das historische Gebäude selbst zum Thema der Ausstellung werden lässt. Eine Umleitung durch die Servicebereiche macht die Räume und Prozesse seiner Instandhaltung und Pflege sichtbar. Auch in den Ausstellungshallen wurde die übliche Besuchsroute umgekehrt, was eine neue Verbindung zwischen den Hallen 1 und 3 erforderte. Diese stellt der *Solar Garden* her, indem er Besucher*innen durch den sonst im Winter ungenutzten Außenraum im ersten Obergeschoss leitet.

Jeglicher Eingriff musste behutsam auf den Gräsergarten abgestimmt werden, der 1960 nach Plänen von Walter Rossow angelegt worden war, einem Landschaftsarchitekten, der beim Wiederaufbau der Berliner Grünanlagen nach dem Zweiten Weltkrieg eine Schlüsselrolle gespielt hatte und unter anderem auch für die Restaurierung des Tiergartens in unmittelbarer Nähe der Akademie der Künste verantwortlich gewesen war. Aufgrund der Auflagen des Denkmalschutzes, die eine Befestigung an der Fassade oder dem Dach verbieten, wurde eine freistehende Konstruktion gewählt.

Der Entwurf beruht, wie auch die gesamte Ausstellungsarchitektur, auf der Neuinterpretation vorhandener Elemente sowie der Wiederverwendung von Materialien, insbesondere einer großen Anzahl von Holzlatten aus einer früheren Ausstellung in der Akademie der Künste am Pariser Platz. Die Dimensionierung der Querschnitte von 2 × 4 Zentimeter bzw. 4 × 4 Zentimeter war ursprünglich für eine nicht-tragende Installation im Innenraum vorgesehen. Atelier Bow-Wow entwarf mit den dünnen Holzlatten eine tragende Konstruktion im Außenraum, die mit Unterstützung von Schlaich Bergermann Partner optimiert wurde. Um eine rein pragmatische Herangehensweise zu vermeiden, legten die Architekt*innen besonderen Wert auf gestalterische Aspekte, wie etwa die Knotenpunkte, die nicht nur statische Anforderungen erfüllen, sondern auch als räumliches Ornament dienen, das die Fügung des Materialverbunds sichtbar macht.

Darüber hinaus verweisen Atelier Bow-Wow mit eingebauten Sitzelementen, die aus den gleichen Kanthölzern konstruiert sind und über Sitzflächen aus geflochtenen Netzen verfügen, auf den *Rope Chair* des japanischen Designers Riki Watanabe, der den Stuhl vor dem Hintergrund der Materialknappheit nach dem Zweiten Weltkrieg entworfen hatte. Die Eindeckung des *Solar Garden* besteht aus Polycarbonatplatten, die von demontierten Gewächshäusern stammen. Insgesamt ist *Solar Garden* nach dem Prinzip *design for disassembly* konzipiert, um eine leichte Demontage und Wiederverwendung der Materialien nach dem Ende der Ausstellung zu ermöglichen.

2023
Tragwerksberatung
Structural engineering consultant
Stephan Arendt, Schlaich Bergermann Partner
Koordination und Umsetzung
Coordination and realization
Fachbereiche Ausstellungen und Infrastruktur der Akademie der Künste
Exhibitions and Infrastructure Departments, Akademie der Künste

EN

Solar Garden, designed by Atelier Bow-Wow for the exhibition *The Great Repair*, is a solarium passageway through the second-story courtyard garden of the Akademie der Künste's Hanseatenweg building. The structure's design responds to a number of local circumstances, beginning with *The Great Repair*'s unusual circulation route, which presents the historic edifice itself as a subject of the exhibition. A detour through the service areas makes processes and spaces of maintenance and care visible. In the exhibition halls, too, the

Der Außenbereich im ersten Obergeschoss der Akademie der Künste am Hanseatenweg von 1960 wurde vom Landschaftsarchitekten Walter Rossow entworfen. Bodenmuster aus Schieferfliesen und eingelassene Pflanzenbeete zeichnen den Garten aus.

The second story garden of the Akademie der Künste's Hanseatenweg building was designed by the landscape architect Walter Rossow and realized in 1960. It features a floor pattern comprised of slate tiles with embedded flowerbeds.

venue's usual circulation of visitors is inverted. This necessitates a new connection between halls 1 and 3, which *Solar Garden* ensures by leading guests through the courtyard garden, otherwise unused during winter.

Any intervention must cautiously approach the garden itself, which was created in 1960 according to plans by Walter Rossow, a landscape architect who played a key role in the restoration of Berlin's green spaces after the Second World War. Among many other commissions, he was also in charge of the reconstruction of Tiergarten park, in the immediate vicinity of the Akademie der Künste. Due to the building's heritage preservation requirements, which forbid attaching anything to the facade or roof, a freestanding structure was deployed.

The design of the structure, like the entire exhibition architecture, builds on reinterpreting existing elements as well as reusing materials, notably a mass of wooden slats from a previous exhibition at the Akademie der Künste's Pariser Platz location. The dimensioning of the cross-sections of 2 × 4 cm and 4 × 4 cm was originally intended for a non-load-bearing installation indoors. Atelier Bow-Wow reused the thin timbers to design a load-bearing structure outdoors, which was optimized with the consultancy of engineering firm Schlaich Bergermann Partner. To avoid a purely pragmatic approach, the architects placed particular emphasis on design aspects, such as the nodes, which not only fulfill structural requirements but also serve as spatial ornaments that make the material assembly visible.

In addition, Atelier Bow-Wow provides built-in seating elements, constructed from the same slats, with seats made of woven nets. The seating refers to the *Rope Chair* by Japanese designer Riki Watanabe, who designed the chair in the context of a material shortage after the Second World War. The cladding is made of polycarbonate sheets, which come from dismantled greenhouses. *Solar Garden* is designed for disassembly to ensure easy dismantling of the structure and repurposing of the materials after the exhibition ends.

Text:
Daniel Kuhnert,
Anh-Linh Ngo

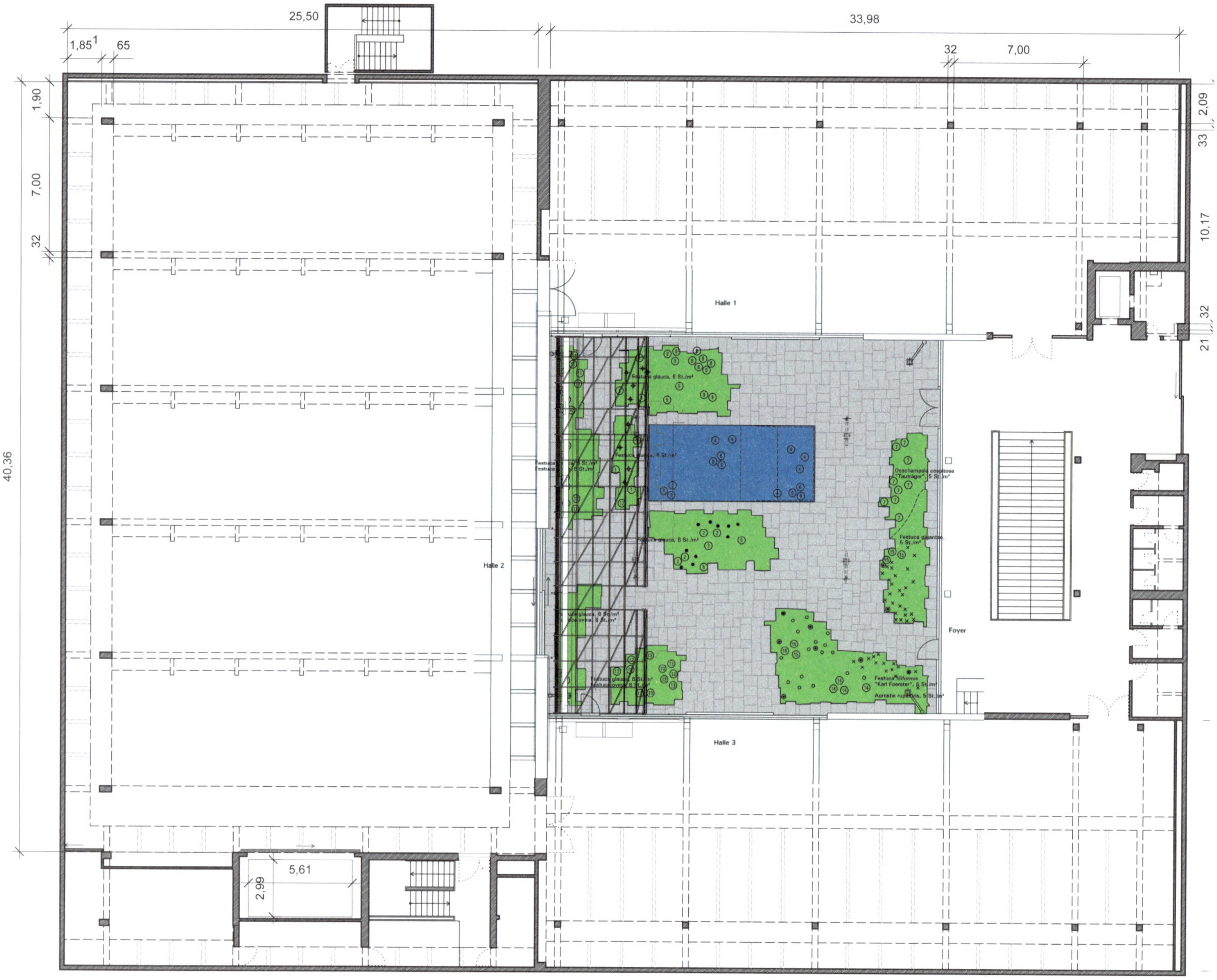
25,50
33,98
1,85
65
32
7,00
1,90
7,00
32
40,36
2,09
33
10,17
32
21
Halle 1
Halle 2
Halle 3
Foyer
5,61
2,99

1

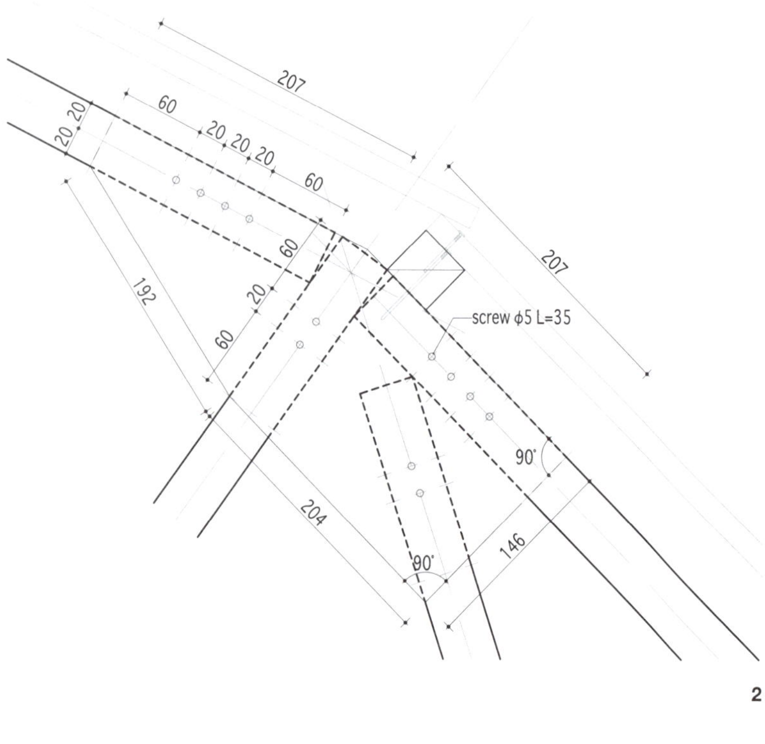
207
60
20 20
20 20 20
60
207
60
20
192
60
screw ϕ5 L=35
90˚
204
90˚
146

2

4

1
Solar Garden von Atelier Bow-Wow verbindet die Ausstellungshallen 1 und 3 während der Ausstellung *The Great Repair*.
Solar Garden by Atelier Bow-Wow connects exhibition halls 1 and 3 during the exhibition *The Great Repair*.
2
Detailansicht eines Knotenpunkts
Detail of the structural node
3
Da die Auflagen für das denkmalgeschützte Gebäude eine Befestigung an der Fassade oder dem Dach verbieten, hat Atelier Bow-Wow mit Beratung von Schlaich Bergermann Partner bei der Tragwerksplanung eine freistehende Konstruktion entwickelt.
Due to building's heritage preservation requirements, which forbid attaching anything to the facade or roof, Atelier Bow-Wow developed a freestanding structure with the support of structural engineering consultant Schlaich Bergermann Partner.
4
Hauptaugenmerk lag auf der Gestaltung der Knotenpunkte, die das Montagesystem von *Solar Garden* sichtbar machen.
Emphasis was placed on the design of the structural nodes, which give visibility to the *Solar Garden*'s assembly system.

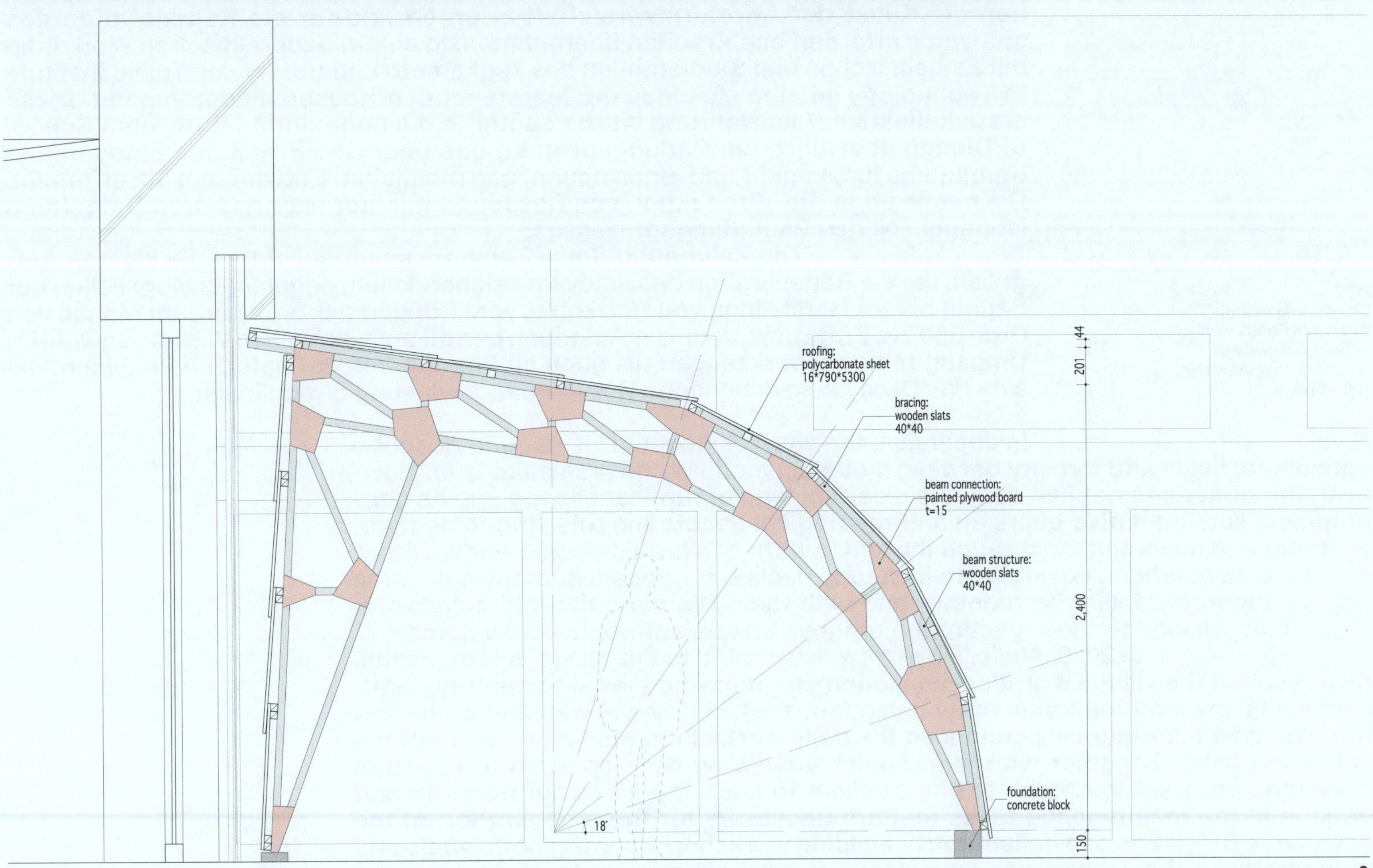

3

Atelier Bow-Wow, Tsukamoto Laboratory of the Tokyo Institute of Technology

Small Earth

2022
Bleistiftzeichnung, Druck auf Fensterfolie
Pencil drawing, print on window film
198 × 549 cm

DE

Im Japanischen wird der Begriff *satoyama* verwendet, um land- und forstwirtschaftliche Flächen zwischen Gebirgsausläufern und Flachland zu bezeichnen. Der Begriff beschreibt jedoch nicht nur eine bestimmte Landschaftsform und ihre geografische Lage, sondern umfasst auch eine anthropologische Bedeutung, indem er sich auf ihre Bewirtschaftung und Pflege durch die tatkräftige Arbeit einer bäuerlichen Gemeinschaft bezieht. Da die Landbevölkerung seit Jahrzehnten stetig abnimmt, verfallen in ganz Japan viele satoyama zusehends. Mit ihnen geht auch die jahrhundertealte Kultur der Instandhaltung und Reparatur verloren, die für die Regeneration dieser einzigartigen anthropogenen Ökosysteme unerlässlich ist.

2016 erhielt Atelier Bow-Wow eine Einladung in das Dorf Kamanuma, wo über die Jahre viele Häuser verlassen wurden, das Ackerland verwildert und mit Gestrüpp bewachsen und der Wald sich selbst überlassen ist. Yoshiki Hayashi war einer der wenigen, der die tägliche Arbeit für den Erhalt des satoyama unermüdlich fortführte. Gemeinsam mit ihm hat Atelier Bow-Wow ein Austauschprojekt zwischen Stadt und Land entwickelt, bei dem Stadtbewohner*innen die Kunst der Agroforstwirtschaft erlernen und für die Regeneration des satoyama erforderliche Arbeiten übernehmen. In einem baupraktischen Workshop mit Einheimischen und Studierenden des Tsukamoto Laboratory des Tokyo Institute of Technology setzten sie eines der leerstehenden Häuser wieder instand. Diese erste kollektive Bauerfahrung wurde später in die sogenannte Satoyama School of Design überführt, ein Bildungsprojekt, das über den Erhalt des satoyama in Kamanuma hinausgeht und einen neuen, ganzheitlichen Entwurfsansatz erforscht. Die nachhaltige (Re-)Produktion von Ressourcen in der unmittelbaren Umgebung ist dabei Teil des Gestaltungsprozesses.

Die Zeichnung *Small Earth* veranschaulicht all die kleinen Aufgaben, die die Regeneration des satoyama sicherstellen, angefangen vom Fällen der Bäume bis zur Herstellung von Holzkohle, vom Pflügen der Erde bis zum Mähen von Gras und zur Ernte usw. Jede der Aufgaben beruht auf wertvollem Wissen, sowohl im Umgang mit den Werkzeugen als auch im Verständnis der natürlichen Zyklen, die eine das Ökosystem schonende Ressourcengewinnung ermöglichen.

EN

In Japanese, the word “satoyama” is used to describe agricultural fields and forestry between mountain foothills and arable flat land. However, the term does not just describe a certain type of rural landscape and its geographical setting; it also bears an anthropological denotation referring to its management and maintenance through the active work of a farming community. Today, with rural populations having been in steady decline for decades, many satoyama across Japan are falling into decay, and with them the centuries-old cultures of repair that are vital to the regeneration of these unique anthropic ecosystems.

In 2016, Atelier Bow-Wow was invited to the village of Kamanuma. As a result of the village’s gradual abandonment, many houses stood empty, farmland lay fallow, and the forest grew untended. Yoshiki Hayashi was one of the few remaining who strenuously continued the daily work of maintenance that kept the satoyama alive. Together with him, Atelier Bow-Wow developed an urban–rural exchange program intended for city dwellers to learn the art of agroforestry and engage in the maintenance tasks that are necessary for the regeneration of the satoyama. By means of a collaborative building workshop involving both locals and students from the Tsukamoto Laboratory of the Tokyo Institute of Technology,

they repaired one of the vacant houses. This first collective building experience was later formalized in the so-called "Satoyama School of Design," a pedagogical project whose scope extends beyond the preservation of this satoyama, to explore a new holistic approach to design, one that integrates the (re)production of resources in one's immediate surroundings as part of the design process itself.

The drawing *Small Earth* presents all the little tasks necessary to maintain the satoyama and ensure its regeneration, from felling trees to making charcoal, from plowing the earth to mowing grass and harvesting. Each task requires invaluable know-how, in terms of both handling tools and understanding the natural life cycles that enable resource extraction in a manner that does not deplete the ecosystem.

Text:
Mirko Gatti

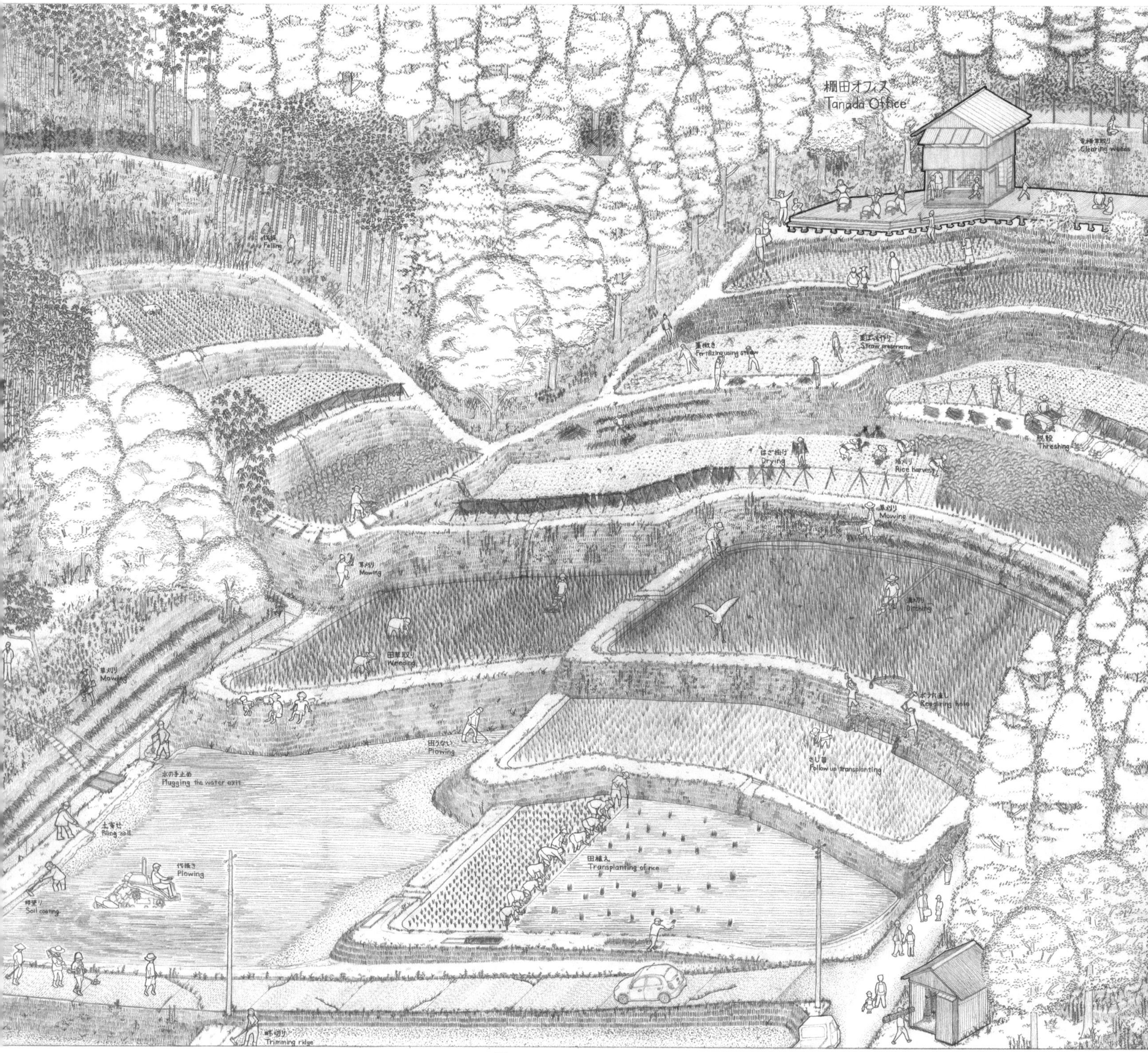
棚田オフィス
Tanada Office
Clearing weeds
Felling
Fertilizing using straw
Straw preservation
脱穀
Threshing
はざ掛け
Drying
稲刈り
Rice harvest
草刈り
Mowing
Ditching
Mowing
田草取り
Weeding
Mowing
田うない
Plowing
水の手止め
Plugging the water exit
Follow up transplanting
Piling soil
代掻き
Plowing
Soil coating
田植え
Transplanting of rice
Trimming ridge

Small Earth

Die Zeichnung *Small Earth* wurde von Studierenden des Tsukamoto Laboratory am Tokyo Institute of Technology kollektiv angefertigt. Sie zeigt all die kleinen reparativen Arbeiten, die im Laufe der Jahreszeiten zur Instandhaltung und Pflege des *satoyama* in Kamanuma anfallen.

***Small Earth* is a collective drawing realized by the students of the Tsukamoto Laboratory of the Tokyo Institute of Technology. It pictures the small repair works carried out throughout the seasons to maintain the satoyama in Kamanuma.**

Agnes Denes

Wheatfield – A Confrontation

Battery Park Landfill, Downtown Manhattan

DE

Mitten in New York City, auf einer Schuttdeponie nur zwei Blocks von der Wall Street und dem World Trade Center entfernt, legte die Künstlerin Agnes Denes im Mai 1982 ein 8.000 Quadratmeter großes Weizenfeld an. Während die Fotografien des fertigen Werks inzwischen berühmt geworden sind, zeigen die dokumentarischen Filmaufnahmen von Philip Delbourgo die monatelange mühsame und sorgfältige Arbeit, die sich hinter dem Projekt verbarg. Um die Brachfläche zu kultivieren, die damals 4,5 Milliarden US-Dollar wert war und seitdem der Luxusbebauung von Battery Park City gewichen ist, befreiten Denes und ihr Team das Gelände von Stein und Müll, verteilten 200 Lastwagenladungen frischen Mutterbodens und zogen von Hand 285 Furchen, bevor sie die Samen aussäten, bedeckten und ein Bewässerungssystem installierten. Über vier Monate pflegten sie das Feld, jäteten Unkraut, düngten, bekämpften Getreidebrand und Mehltau. Im August konnten sie schließlich 450 Kilogramm Weizen ernten.

Indem sie sich ein Stück städtischen Bodens für den Anbau eines Grundnahrungsmittels wiederaneignete, thematisierte Denes unsere Entfremdung von der natürlichen Welt und die Kommerzialisierung unserer Lebensgrundlagen. Die „Konfrontation", von der die Arbeit im Titel kündet, ist buchstäblich: Direkt gegenüber einem Zentrum des globalen Finanzkapitalismus ließ die Künstlerin ein dort als abstrakte Ware gehandeltes Gut Realität werden. Diese Kommodifizierung und die damit verbundene Verschärfung der ohnehin schon ungleichen Verteilung von Ressourcen und Wohlstand stand im Zentrum ihrer Kritik. Um ihrer Warenförmigkeit entgegenzuarbeiten, wurde die Ernte im Rahmen einer vom Minnesota Museum of Art organisierten Ausstellung mit dem Titel *The International Art Show for the End of World Hunger* in 28 Städten auf der ganzen Welt gezeigt. Dort wurden die Weizenkörner als Saat verschenkt – anknüpfend an die Tradition, Saatgut als Gemeingut zu teilen.

1982
5435_WHEATFIELD_R16MM
Dokumentarisches Filmmaterial von
Documentary film material by
Philip Delbourgo
16-mm-Film auf digitales Video übertragen, SW, ohne Ton
16mm film transferred to digital video, b/w, without sound
11 min
Courtesy Philip Delbourgo, New York

EN

In May of 1982, artist Agnes Denes planted an 8,000-square-meter wheatfield on a New York City landfill, just two blocks from Wall Street and the World Trade Center. While photographs of the finished work have since become famous, documentary footage shot by Philip Delbourgo reveals the months of arduous and attentive labor behind it. To cultivate this desolate land, which was worth 4.5 billion US dollars at the time and has since given way to the luxury developments of Battery Park City, Denes and her team cleared the site of rocks and garbage, brought in 200 truckloads of fresh topsoil, and dug 285 furrows by hand before sowing seeds, covering them over, and installing an irrigation system. They tended the field for four months, weeding, fertilizing, fighting against blight and mildew. In August, they harvested the crop, reaping over 450 kilograms of wheat.

By reappropriating a plot of urban land to produce an essential crop, Denes questioned our alienation from the natural world and the commercialization of our subsistence. The "confrontation," as stated in the work's title, is literal: Directly opposite a hub of global finance capitalism, Denes actualized one of the goods traded there as an abstract commodity. For her, this commodification was to be criticized particularly in light of the exacerbation of the already unequal distribution of resources and wealth. To symbolically counter this commodification, drawing on the tradition of seed commons, the harvested grain traveled to 28 cities around the world via an exhibition organized by the Minnesota Museum of Art titled *The International Art Show for the End of World Hunger*, in which the seeds were distributed to people for planting.

Text:
Daniel Kuhnert

Filmstills aus
Film stills from
Philip Delbourgo, *5435_WHEATFIELD_R16MM*
Dokumentarisches Filmmaterial zu
Documentary film material on
Agnes Denes, *Wheatfield – A Confrontation: Battery Park Landfill, Downtown Manhattan*
1982

Architecture of Territory, ETH Zürich

Power to the People

2022–2023
Modell
Model
50 × 490 × 370 cm

Basierend auf dem Forschungs- und Entwurfsstudio *Power to the People: Energy and Territory in the Rheinland* am Lehrstuhl für Architektur und Territorialplanung, ETH Zürich
Based on the design research studio *Power to the People: Energy and Territory in the Rheinland* at the Chair of Architecture and Territorial Planning, ETH Zürich
Lehrende, Juni–Dezember 2022
Teaching team, June–December 2022
Professor Milica Topalović, Jan Westerheide, Muriz Djurdjevic, Dorothee Hahn, Felix Hergert

Modellteam, April–September 2023
Model team, April–September 2023
Professor Milica Topalović, Jakob Walter, Jan Westerheide, Leslie Meyer
mit den studentischen Hilfskräften
with student assistants
Till Blaser, Amélie Lambert, Yufei Li
und den Studierenden
and students
Jérome Ammann, Ella Bacchetta, Filippo Biasca-Caroni, Charis Gersl, Nora Hauser, Martin Kohlberger, Elisa Nadas, Andela Pejic, Silvano Ursella
Fotos
Photos
Bas Princen

DE

Wem gehören die Energiequellen und wer bestimmt über die Energiewende? Wie können Menschen für Alternativen zur Abhängigkeit von fossilen Brennstoffen aktiv werden? Es gibt in Deutschland keinen besseren Ort, um diesen Fragen nachzugehen, als das Rheinische Revier, die Region um den Tagebau Hambach, die seit über einem Jahrhundert geprägt ist von extensivem Braunkohleabbau und dem Verlangen nach billiger Energie. In jüngerer Zeit hat sich die Region zu einem Austragungsort des globalen Klimakampfes entwickelt, gipfelnd Anfang 2023 in der Besetzung und Räumung des Weilers Lützerath.

Der multinationale Energiekonzern RWE (ehemals Rhein-Westfälische Elektrizitätswerke AG) wirkt in alle Lebensbereiche in der Region hinein, von den geologischen Strukturen bis hin zu den sozialen Realitäten. Auch wenn der Braunkohleabbau zugunsten von erneuerbaren Energien im Rahmen des von Deutschland angestrebten *Kohleausstieg 2030* auslaufen wird, kontrolliert RWE die Energiewende: Wind- und Solarparks werden einfach zu Kohlekraftwerken hinzugefügt, und zwar aus derselben Logik der Profitmaximierung, wie sie auch die Kohleförderung kennzeichnet. Fridays for Future, Alle Dörfer bleiben und andere Aktivist*innengruppen und Bürger*inneninitiativen kämpfen weiter in der Region, auch gegen das Greenwashing der Unternehmen, das dazu führt, dass das Kapital seine Kontrolle über den Boden vertieft und die sich wechselseitig bedingenden Krisen von Klimawandel, sozialer Spaltung, kultureller Auslöschung und ökologischer Zerstörung weiter vorantreibt. Sie fordern nicht nur einen sofortigen Ausstieg aus der Kohleförderung, sondern auch einen demokratisch kontrollierten und sozial gerechten Übergang zu erneuerbaren Energien.

Für das Projekt *Power to the People* haben Studierende des Lehrstuhls Architecture of Territory der ETH Zürich ein Modell der Region gebaut. Es erzählt Geschichten des Protests, die Möglichkeiten einer gerechten Energiewende sowie der sozialen und ökologischen Reparatur der Region aufzeigen.

Eine Welt, in der ökologische Energie demokratisch und kollektiv als Gemeingut verwaltet wird, ist möglich. Power to the people!

EN

Who owns energy sources and governs the energy transition? How can people mobilize for alternatives to fossil dependencies? There is no better place to ask these questions in Germany than the Rheinisches Revier, the region around the surface mine Tagebau Hambach, where the advancing coal mines and the desire for cheap energy have shaped the territory for over a century. The region has recently emerged as one of the battlegrounds of the global climate struggle, culminating in the occupation and eviction of the hamlet of Lützerath in early 2023.

The multinational energy corporation RWE (formerly the Rhein-Westfälische Elektrizitätswerke AG) governs all vital processes in the region, from geological structures to social realities and imaginaries, making it omnipresent in every aspect of life. Even as mining operations are being phased out in favor of renewable energy as part of Germany's intended *Kohleausstieg 2030*, RWE remains in control of energy transition: In this corporate landscape, wind and solar parks are simply added to coal-fired power plants, based on the unchanged rationale of increasing profits that characterizes the extraction of coal. Fridays for Future, Alle Dörfer bleiben, and other activist and citizen organizations continue their struggle across the region, contesting the corporate greenwashing which

deepens capital's control of the land as well as perpetuates the interconnected crises of climate change, social polarization, cultural erasure, and ecological exhaustion. They demand not just an immediate exit from coal but also a democratically controlled and socially just transition to renewable energy.

In the *Power to the People* project, presented in the form of a territorial model, students of the chair of Architecture of Territory at ETH Zürich have portrayed stories of struggle as opportunities for a just energy transition and the social and ecological repair of the land.

The world of ecological energy commons, democratically governed, can emerge. Power to the people!

Text:
Milica Topalović,
Jan Westerheide

Das Modell des Rheinischen Reviers, einer rund 5.000 Quadratkilometer umfassenden Bergbauregion mit fast 2,5 Millionen Einwohner*innen, enthält Miniaturszenen, die den Kampf für eine sozial-ökologische Reparatur der Region aufzeigen.

The model of the Rheinisches Revier, a 5,000 square kilometer coal mining region with a population of nearly 2.5 million residents, showcases miniature scenes illustrating stories of struggle for the social and ecological repair of the area.

HAMBACHER FORST VERTEIDIGEN
POLIZEI

Die Ausschnitte auf diesen Seiten stellen die Ereignisse um den Hambacher Forst sowie die Feuchtgebiete im Naturpark Schwalm-Nette und den auf ehemaligen Bergbauflächen errichteten Windpark Königshovener Höhe dar.

The scenes on these pages depict events related to the Hambach Forest, the wetlands in Schwalm-Nette Nature Park, and the new wind farm Königshovener Höhe built on former mining land.

Hans Hortig
mit
with
Tang Wei

In the Shadow of the Palms

Tracing Potential for Repair in the Plantationocene

DE

Ölpalmplantagen sind riesige Maschinerien, die Böden, Arbeitskraft und Kapital einsetzen, um Ressourcen für den globalen Markt zu gewinnen. Im Bundesstaat Johor in Malaysia sind drei Viertel der landwirtschaftlichen Flächen mit Ölpalm-Monokulturen bedeckt. Auch wenn sich Plantagensysteme in den letzten hundert Jahren von extraktiven kolonialen Apparaten zu nationalen Großunternehmen und Instrumenten der Entwicklungsplanung gewandelt haben, hat sich an ihren enormen räumlichen und ökologischen Folgen nichts geändert. Sie prägen auf verheerende Weise sozio-ökologische Räume in großem Maßstab, führen zu Bodenverarmung, Habitatverlust und einem steten Risiko ökologischen Zusammenbruchs. Aber die Plantagen Johors sind auch Orte des Widerstands und ein Nährboden für alternative Praktiken.

Das Projekt *In the Shadow of the Palms* untersucht solche wegweisenden Praktiken der Reparatur von Plantagenlandschaften. Es dokumentiert die Transformation einer Ölpalmenplantage in Ulu Tiram, Johor, in einen syntropischen Agroforst, der Waldbewirtschaftung mit Lebensmittelproduktion für den lokalen Markt verbindet. Seit 2020 bemüht sich ein Team aus singapurischen und malaysischen Unternehmer*innen eine 56 Hektar große Monokulturplantage durch die Einführung einheimischer Pflanzen und alternativer Anbaumethoden neu zu bewirtschaften. Die Hälfte des Areals soll als produktive Forstfläche genutzt werden, während der Rest zur Renaturierung und teilweise für Infrastruktur vorgesehen ist. Seit 2023 werden in den Agroforst auch Ölpalmen integriert, um mit pestizid- und düngerfreiem Anbau zu experimentieren. Das Vorhaben soll zeigen, wie ökologische Reparatur und Landwirtschaft zusammen funktionieren können.

2023
Video
Farbe, Ton
Color, sound
15 min
Zeichnungen, Druck auf Sandwichplatte und semitransparenten Vorhang
Drawings, print on sandwich panel and semi-transparent curtain
100 × 120 cm, 150 × 250 cm
Dank an
Thanks to
Milica Topalović, Karoline Kostka, Grace Baey, Klearjos Eduardo Papanicolaou

EN

Oil palm plantations are giant machineries that use land, labor, and capital to extract resources for the global market. In the Malaysian state Johor, three-quarters of agricultural land are covered by oil palm monocultures. Though these plantations have evolved from extractive colonial machineries into corporate entities and vehicles of national development, their enormous spatial and ecological consequences have remained unchanged. They shape socio-ecological spaces on a large scale and in devastating ways, leading to soil depletion, habitat loss, and a risk of ecological collapse. But Johor's oil palm plantations are also sites of resistance and seedbeds for alternative practices.

The project *In the Shadow of the Palms* explores a pioneering practice for repairing oil palm plantation landscapes. It documents the transformation of a 56-hectare plot of land in Ulu Tiram, Johor, into a syntropic agroforest that combines forestry with food production for the local market. Since 2020, a team of Singaporean and Malaysian entrepreneurs has been converting an oil palm monocultural plantation by introducing native crops and alternative agricultural practices. Half of the land will be turned into a productive forest, while the rest will be rewilded and partially occupied by infrastructure. Since 2023, oil palms have also been integrated within agroforestry systems to experiment with pesticide- and fertilizer-free farming methods. The project aims to demonstrate how ecological reparation and farming can work together.

Text:
Hans Hortig

Stills aus
Stills from
Hans Hortig, *In the Shadow of the Palms – Tracing Potential for Repair in the Plantationocene*, 2023
Der Film dokumentiert die Erfahrungen eines Teams aus singapurischen und malaysischen Unternehmer*innen, das sich seit 2020 um die Transformation einer 56 Hektar großen Ölpalmplantage in Ulu Tiram, Johor, bemüht.
The film documents the experiences of a team of Singaporean and Malaysian entrepreneurs that, since 2020, has been seeking to transform a 56-hectare oil palm plantation in Ulu Tiram, Johor.

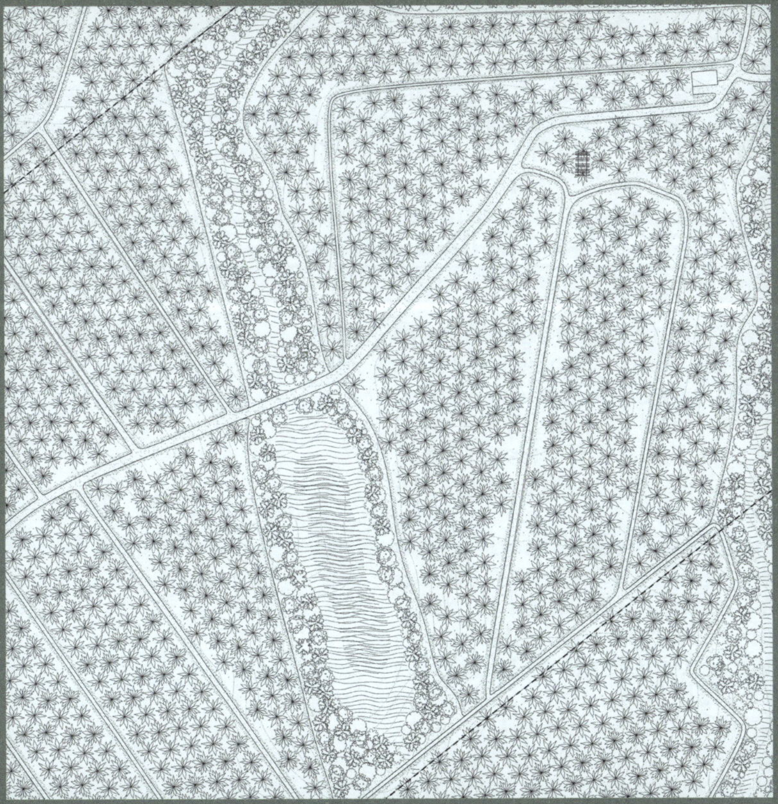

Die beiden Zeichnungen zeigen den Ausgangszustand der Ölpalmen-Monokultur vor Beginn des Projekts (links) und die geplante Umwandlung in einen syntropen Agroforst mit integrierten Ölpalmen (rechts).
The two drawings depict the initial state of the oil palm monoculture prior to the project's inception (left), and the envisioned transformation into a syntropic agro-forestry system with integrated oil palms (right).

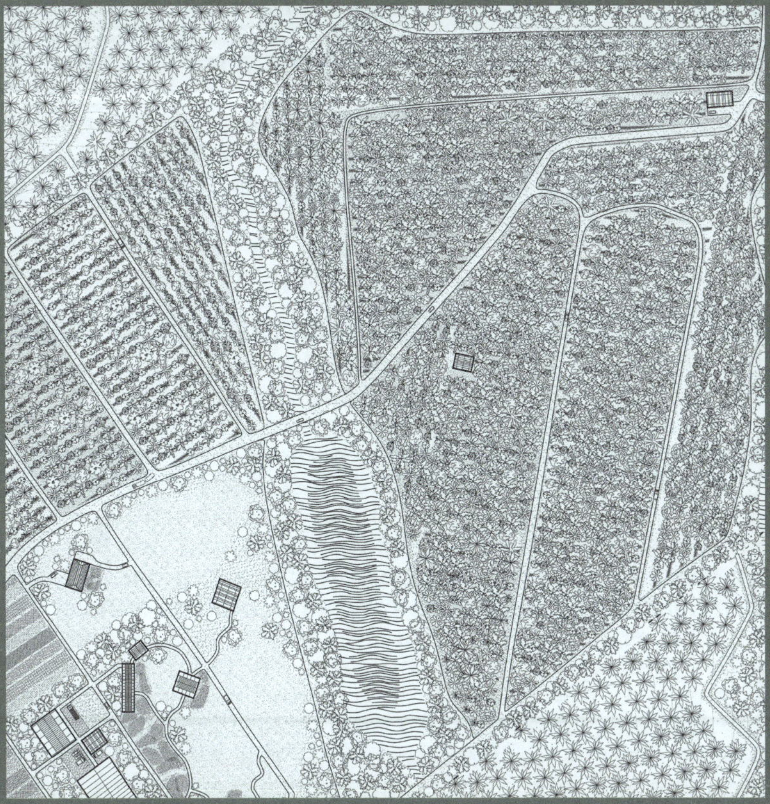

Paulo Tavares / autônoma

Auto-Demarcation

2019
In Kollaboration mit der Gemeinschaft der Xavante in Marãiwatsédé und der NGO OPAN
In collaboration with the Xavante of Marãiwatsédé and the NGO OPAN
Workshop-Team & Abbildungen
Workshop team & images
Ana Altberg, Magno Silvestre, Paulo Tavares
Digital video, 2023
Farbe, Ton
Color, sound
12 min
Erzählung von
Argument by
Paulo Tavares, Ana Altberg
Editiert von
Edited by
Maria Altberg

DE

Architektur und Planung spielen seit jeher bei der kolonialen Ausbeutung von Mensch und Natur eine entscheidende Rolle. Darauf verweist der Architekt Paulo Tavares in zahlreichen seiner Arbeiten. Wie die Werkzeuge der Architektur neu ausgerichtet werden können, um die Kämpfe für den Erhalt und die Reparatur der Erde zu unterstützen, ist Kern seiner Praxis. Ein Beispiel dafür ist das Projekt *Auto-Demarcation*, das er gemeinsam mit der von ihm gegründeten Architektur- und Advocacy-Plattform autônoma entwickelte.

Ursprünglich wurde Paulo Tavares / autônoma von der brasilianischen NGO Operação Amazônia Nativa (OPAN) beauftragt, Jugendlichen der indigenen Xavante-Gemeinschaft in Marãiwatsédé in Workshops Grundkenntnisse der Kartografie und Kartierungstechniken zu vermitteln. Ziel war es, ihnen Instrumente zur Umweltüberwachung an die Hand zu geben, damit sie ihr Territorium schützen können. Doch statt kartografische Methoden zu lehren, die ihre Wurzeln in einem kolonialen System der Inbesitznahme haben, beschloss das Projektteam, mit den Teilnehmer*innen gemeinsam zu überlegen, mit welchen anderen Methoden sie ihren Lebensraum schützen können. In den Gesprächen kristallisierte sich dabei ein zentrales Problem heraus: Eigentlich ist die brasilianische Regierung rechtlich verpflichtet, indigenes Land zu schützen und als solches zu kennzeichnen. Üblicherweise werden dazu große Hinweisschilder entlang der Grenzen der Territorien angebracht. Doch immer wieder werden indigene Landrechte durch illegale Eingriffe von Agrar-, Holz- und Bergbauunternehmen verletzt – geduldet und befördert durch den Staat. Am Territorium Marãiwatsédé der Xavante fehlte die gesetzlich vorgeschriebene Kennzeichnung gänzlich.

Im Workshop entstand deshalb die Idee, mit den Teilnehmenden Werkzeuge zu entwickeln, damit sie die fehlenden Schilder selbst gestalten, herstellen und montieren können. Benennung, Markierung und Abgrenzung – grundlegende Instrumente der Enteignung indigenen Lands – wurden dabei in autonome und kollaborative Werkzeuge der Selbstbestimmung und territorialen Reparatur verwandelt.

EN

Architecture and planning have always played a crucial role in the colonial exploitation of people and nature, as many works by the architect Paulo Tavares demonstrate. Tavares focuses his practice on exploring how architectural tools can be repurposed to support efforts to maintain and repair the Earth. One example of this approach is the project *Auto-Demarcation*, which was developed through autônoma, an architecture and advocacy platform founded by Tavares.

Originally, Paulo Tavares / autônoma was commissioned by the Brazilian nonprofit organization Operação Amazônia Nativa (OPAN) to teach young people from the Xavante community of Marãiwatsédé the fundamentals of cartography and mapping. The aim was to equip them with tools for environmental monitoring, empowering them to protect their territory. However, instead of teaching them cartographic methods, which have their roots in a colonial system of appropriation, the project team chose a collaborative approach. Together with the participants, they determined alternative methods the community could use to protect its habitat. During their conversations, a central concern emerged: By law, the Brazilian government is mandated to recognize and protect Indigenous land. To that end, it is supposed to demarcate Indigenous territories with prominent signs posted along their borders. Yet Indigenous land rights have been repeatedly violated as agricultural, timber, and mining corporations illegally encroach upon these areas, with the state often tolerating and even abetting these transgressions. In the Marãiwatsédé territory of the Xavante community, the legally mandated signs demarcating their land were absent altogether.

In Brasilien werden indigene Landrechte immer wieder durch illegale Eingriffe von Agrar-, Holz- und Bergbauunternehmen verletzt. Da am Territorium Marãiwatsédé der Xavante selbst die rechtlich vorgeschriebene Kennzeichnung fehlte, mangelte es der Gemeinschaft an grundlegenden Mitteln, ihre Rechte durchzusetzen. In Zusammenarbeit mit Paulo Tavares / autônoma suchte die Gemeinschaft deshalb nach Möglichkeiten, ihr Territorium eigenständig zu schützen.

In Brazil, Indigenous land rights have been repeatedly violated by agricultural, timber, and mining companies. The Xavante community in the Marãiwatsédé territory lacked even formal demarcation signs, leaving them without basic means to assert their rights. Therefore, in collaboration with Paulo Tavares / autônoma, the Xavante community sought autonomous ways to safeguard their territory.

The workshop thus led to the idea of providing the participants with the necessary tools to design, make, and erect the missing border signs themselves. Naming, marking, demarcating—fundamental elements in the process of expropriation of Indigenous spaces—were re-signified as autonomous and collaborative tools of self-determination and territorial repair.

Text:
Alex Nehmer

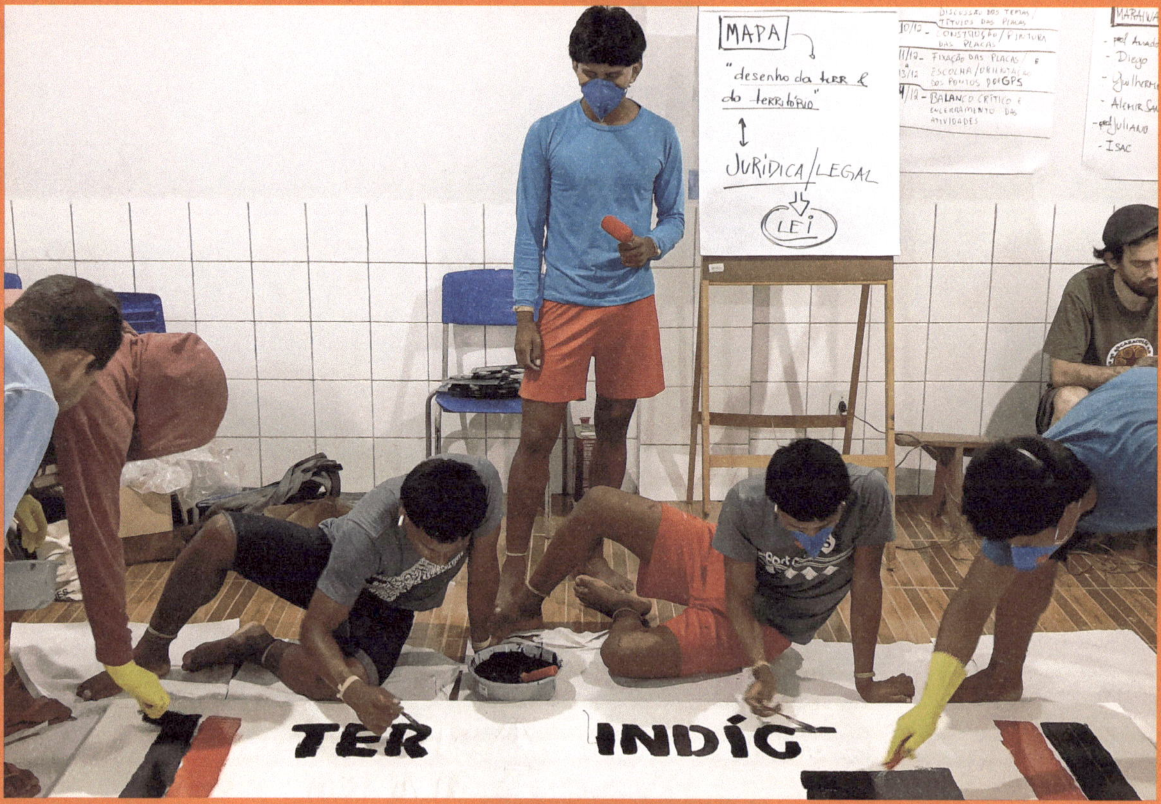
MAPA
JURIDICA/LEGAL
LEI
TER
INDÍG

INDIGENA

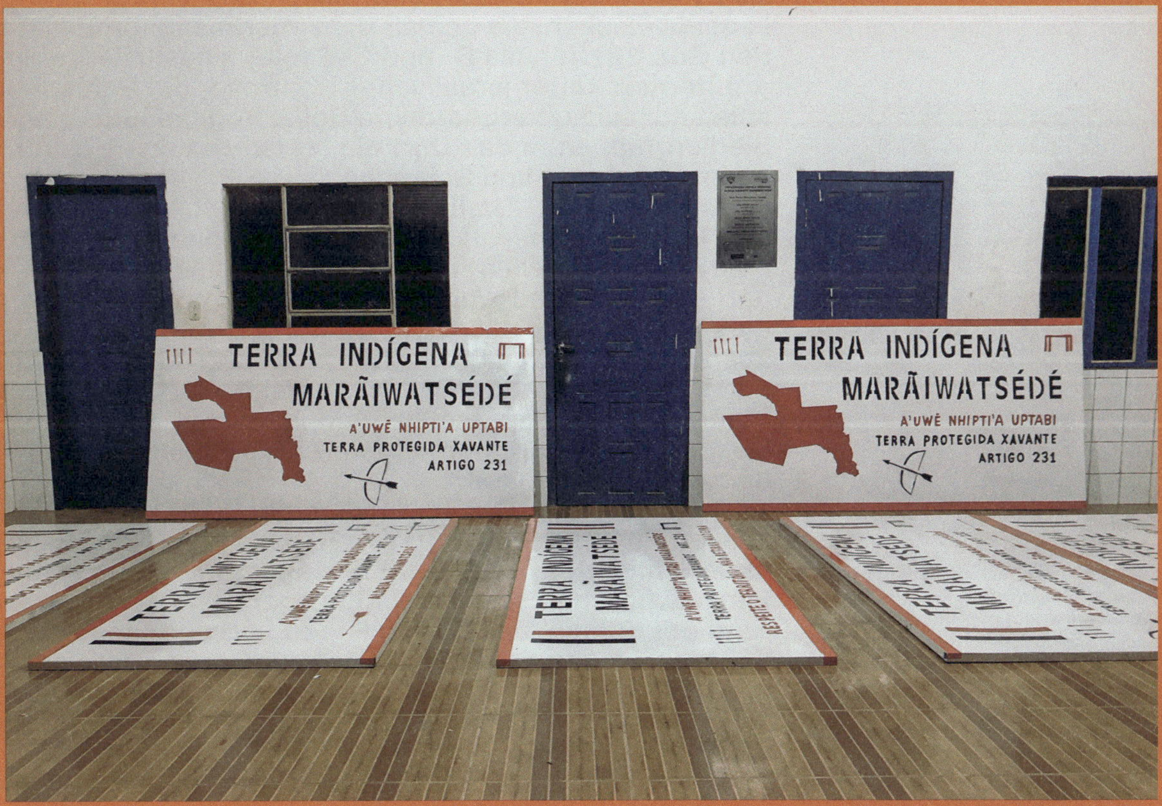

Inspiriert unter anderem von Paulo Freires *Pädagogik der Unterdrückten* entwickelte Paulo Tavares / autônoma eine Reihe kollaborativer Workshops. Darin gestalteten und errichteten die Jugendlichen der Xavante-Gemeinschaft neue Hinweisschilder, um ihre Landrechte zu behaupten.

Inspired by Paulo Freire's *Pedagogy of the Oppressed*, Paulo Tavares / autônoma developed a series of collaborative workshops. Through these workshops, Xavante youth designed and erected new demarcation signs to independently assert their land rights.

Takhayali

تخيّلي
Takhayali [imagine, feminine] Ein Qiniya!

DE

Das Dorf Ein Qiniya liegt nordwestlich von Ramallah im Westjordanland. Die Nähe zur teuersten palästinensischen Stadt hat ökologisch und sozial zerstörerische Urbanisierungsprozesse ausgelöst, die von Spekulation und Geldwäsche durch Immobiliengeschäfte dominiert werden: Vom Osten her wächst die Stadt rasch auf das Dorf zu; der Grund und Boden des Dorfes ist überwiegend im Besitz der Stadtbewohner*innen; etwa die Hälfte der Häuser liegt bereits innerhalb der Verwaltungsgrenze von Ramallah. Im westlichen Teil befindet sich die israelische Siedlung Dolev auf einem Stück Land, das in den 1970er-Jahren besetzt wurde. Ein Qiniya liegt auf Flächen, die gemäß dem Interimsabkommen über das Westjordanland und den Gazastreifen als B- und C-Gebiet klassifiziert sind, das heißt, es befindet sich größtenteils unter israelischer Kontrolle, die Palästinensische Autonomiebehörde spielt nur eine untergeordnete Rolle. Regelmäßig dringen die israelische Armee und Siedlergruppen in das Dorf ein, zerstören das Eigentum der Bewohner*innen und verbreiten Angst und Schrecken.

Da Ein Qiniya bisher über keinen Bebauungsplan verfügt, nahm das Projekt *Takhayali* (Arabisch: imaginieren, feminin) an, dass der Gemeinderat bald einen aufstellen muss. Üblicherweise werden dabei weder die ökologischen und sozioökonomischen Geschichten und Realitäten noch die Ansichten der Gemeinschaft berücksichtigt. Um den Bewohner*innen Gehör zu verschaffen, führte *Takhayali* eine ethnografische Forschung durch, die Interviews mit Bewohnerinnen und Aktivitäten in Ein Qiniya umfasste. Auf diesen Erkenntnissen aufbauend traf Mai Al-Battat sich anschließend jeweils über mehrere Stunden mit jeder ihrer 20 Gesprächspartnerinnen, um deren Vorstellungen von einem Masterplan in Zeichnungen zu übertragen.

Die Vorschläge der 20 befragten Frauen ähneln sich, doch nicht in allen Punkten. Manche wollen, dass Natur und Landwirtschaft erhalten bleiben, andere möchten, dass sich Ein Qiniya wie seine Umgebung städtisch entwickelt. Einige wünschen sich Produktionsgenossenschaften, eine Fabrik oder die Erweiterung der Schule, der Sportanlagen und des Einkaufszentrums. Die meisten legen Wert auf Zugang zu Einrichtungen der Grundversorgung wie Bäckerei, Lebensmittelgeschäft oder Kindertagesstätte. Alle betonen die Notwendigkeit eines medizinischen Zentrums oder einer Apotheke, von öffentlichen Verkehrsmitteln, Spielplätzen und Freiflächen. Vor dem Hintergrund, dass stromaufwärts eine erst kürzlich errichtete Kläranlage Ramallahs Abwässer in das Wadi al-Dilb (ein örtliches Flusstal) leitet, träumen zudem alle davon, dass das Wasser gereinigt und ein Abschnitt des Flussufers renaturiert und als öffentlicher Raum mit Badestellen, Kiosken oder einem Restaurant gestaltet wird.

Die Entwürfe wurden im September 2022 in Ein Qiniya ausgestellt, zusammen mit Aquarellporträts der Teilnehmerinnen, die die Künstlerin Yara Bamieh gemalt hat. Vertreter*innen des Gemeinderats waren anwesend, auch wenn nicht davon ausgegangen werden kann, dass sie Ideen des Projekts aufgreifen werden.

Warum Visionen entwerfen? Weil es ein Akt ist, der Sorgen in Wünsche übersetzt, der eine Wiederaneignung sozialräumlicher Narrative und Beziehungen ermöglicht, der Hoffnung gibt, Solidarität wiederaufleben lässt und Widerstand gestaltet.

2021–2022
Entstanden im Rahmen des Forschungsprojekts *Urbanization, Gender, and the Global South* mit Unterstützung des Social Sciences and Humanities Research Council of Canada, durchgeführt von UR°BANA in Zusammenarbeit mit Sakiya
Produced in conjunction with the research project *Urbanization, Gender, and the Global South* supported by the Social Sciences and Humanities Research Council of Canada, implemented by UR°BANA in partnership with Sakiya
Übertragung der Masterpläne in das Ausstellungsformat unter Mitarbeit von
Translation of the master plans into the exhibited format assisted by
Basel Nasr (alMasna'), Yara Bamieh
Aktivistischer Kurzfilm, Farbe, Ton
Advocacy short film, color, sound
5 min
von
by
alMasna' (The Animation Factory)

EN

Most of land in the village of Ein Qiniya in the West Bank is owned by Ramallites, and about half of the houses lie within the municipal boundaries of Ramallah—the most expensive Palestinian city—which is continuing to expand into Ein Qiniya from the east. Speculation and money laundering through real estate transactions dominate the ecologically and socially destructive urbanization patterns. On its western parts, the Israeli Dolev settlement sits on lands confiscated in the 1970s. Ein Qiniya is located on land classified as B and C areas under the Interim Agreement on the West Bank and Gaza Strip, meaning it is mostly under Israeli control with the Palestinian Authority playing a negligible role. The village is regularly raided by the Israeli army and settlers who vandalize properties and terrorize residents.

To date, there is no master plan for Ein Qiniya, which is why we assumed that the village council would soon be asked to prepare one. The regular procedures, however, neither take into account the ecological and socio-economic histories and realities, nor do they care for the opinions of the community. To make the inhabitants' voices heard, the project *Takhayali* (Arabic: imagine, feminine) conducted in-depth ethnographic research that included interviews and activities in Ein Qiniya. Based on these insights, Mai Al-Battat then met with 20 interlocutors, one at a time for several hours, to sketch imaginary master plans for the community.

The 20 proposals developed in *Takhayali* are similar and different. Some want rural nature and farming preserved, others see Ein Qiniya urbanizing akin to close-by neighborhoods. Some want productive cooperatives, a factory, to expand the school, sports facilities, or commercial centers. Most want access to basic amenities, e.g., a bakery, a grocery store, and infrastructure such as a nursery. What all *Takhayali* proposals desire is a medical center and/or a pharmacy, public transportation, playgrounds, and open spaces. Moreover, against the backdrop that a recently established upstream treatment plant of Ramallah dumps sewage into the Wadi al-Dilb (a local fluvial valley), they all imagine the water being cleaned and a stretch of the wadi being rehabilitated and designed as a social space with kiosks or a restaurant, and swimming areas.

These proposals were exhibited in Ein Qiniya in September 2022, together with watercolor illustrations of the contributors painted by artist Yara Bamieh. Representatives of the village council attended, but we cannot claim that any of this work will be considered.

Why imagine? Because it is an act that reconciles worries with desires, an act that reconstructs appropriated socio-spatial narratives and relationalities, an act that gives hope, repairs solidarity, and situates resistance.

Text:
Mai Al-Battat, Natasha Aruri, Sahar Qawasmi, Andreas Brück

Yara Bamieh, *Takhayali* [imagine, feminine] *Ein Qiniya!*, 2021
Serie von 20 Porträts, Aquarell auf Papier, je A5
Series of 20 portraits, watercolor on paper, each A5
Nach ausführlichen Interviews mit 20 in Ein Qiniya lebenden Frauen über ihre Visionen für das Dorf besuchte die Künstlerin Yara Bamieh sie, um sie zu porträtieren.
After extensive interviews with 20 women living in Ein Qiniya about their visions for the village, artist Yara Bamieh visited them to paint their portraits.

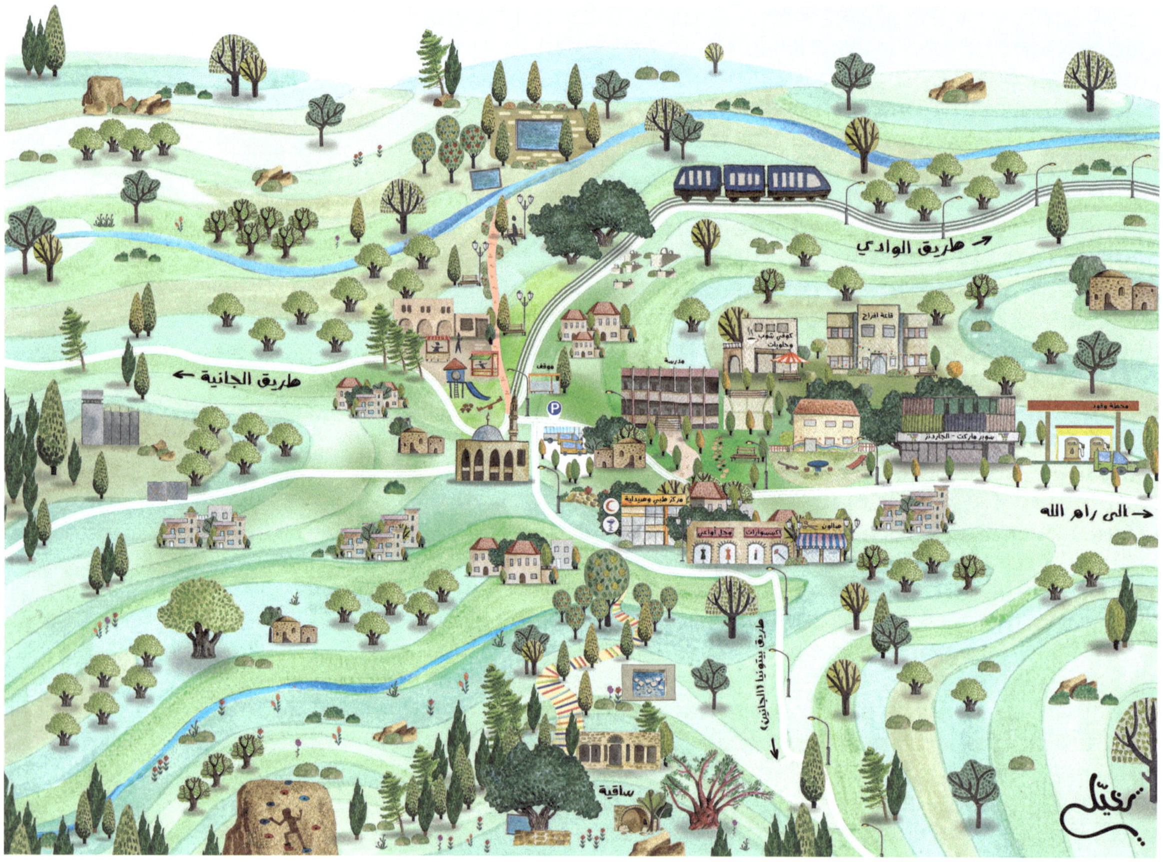

Mai Al-Battat mit Samah Yehya, Muntaha alKhatib, Razan Alqam, Farida (Um alQarawi), unterstützt von Basel Nasr und Yara Bamieh, *Takhayali* [imagine, feminine] *Ein Qiniya!,* 2022, Serie imaginärer Masterpläne für Ein Qiniya, Aquarell auf Papier, digital zusammengesetzt und bearbeitet, jeweils in A1 gedruckt

Mai Al-Battat with Samah Yehya, Muntaha alKhatib, Razan Alqam, Farida (Um alQarawi), supported by Basel Nasr and Yara Bamieh, *Takhayali* [imagine, feminine] *Ein Qiniya!,* 2022, series of imaginary master plans for Ein Qiniya, watercolor on paper, digitally assembled and processed, each printed on A1

Auf Grundlage der Gespräche wurden zwanzig Masterpläne ausgearbeitet, von denen hier vier zu sehen sind. Allen gemeinsam ist der Wunsch, trotz einer urbanisierten Zukunft die natürliche Landschaft des Wadi al-Dilb (ein örtliches Flusstal) zu erhalten und zu sanieren.

Building on the conversations, 20 master plans were created, of which a selection of four is presented here. Despite imagining an urbanized future, all master plans share a desire to preserve and rehabilitate the natural landscape of Wadi al-Dilb (a local fluvial valley).

Studio Anna Heringer

Dipdii Textiles

2012–fortlaufend
ongoing
Textildesign
Textile design
Veronika Lena, Anna Heringer
Konzept
Concept
Anna Heringer
Technisches Design
Technical design
Veronika Lena, Elke Burmeister-Haug
Partner in Bangladesch
Partner in Bangladesh
Dipshikha, Shanti Partnerschaft Bangladesh e.V.
gemeinsam mit Frauen aus dem Dorf Rudrapur und Umgebung
together with women from the village Rudrapur and surrounding

DE

Nach China ist Bangladesch der zweitgrößte Bekleidungsexporteur der Welt. Die globalisierte Textilindustrie ist nicht nur für immense Umweltverschmutzung und menschenunwürdige Arbeitsbedingungen verantwortlich, sondern hat auch lokale Ökonomien und – durch Abwanderung in die Produktionszentren – das soziale Gefüge zerstört. Um ein dezentrales Gegenmodell zu den ausbeuterischen globalen Lieferketten anzubieten, knüpft das Projekt Dipdii Textiles der Architektin Anna Heringer, der Designerin Veronika Lang und der gemeinnützigen Organisation Dipshikha an die Textiltradition und die weitverbreitete Alltagspraxis des Upcycling in Bangladesch an: Abgetragene Saris und Lungis werden zu mehrlagigen Decken vernäht. In der Werkstatt von Dipdii Textiles in Rudrapur werden aus diesen Stoffen neue Textilprodukte gefertigt.

Das Projekt bietet Frauen aus mehreren Dörfern im Norden Bangladeschs Arbeit und Einkommen, sodass sie nicht in die industriellen Zentren abwandern müssen; Lebens- und Produktionsbedingungen vor Ort werden so wieder gestärkt und das soziale Gefüge der Gemeinschaften bleibt intakt. Die Textilwerkstatt befindet sich im Obergeschoss einer von Heringer entworfenen Schule für Menschen mit Behinderung. Auch der Bau des Schul- und Werkstattgebäudes folgte Prinzipien der Nachhaltigkeit und der Stärkung lokaler Arbeit: Das Gebäude wurde aus lokal gewonnenem Lehm und Bambus errichtet und kann so zudem leicht repariert werden. Anders als frühere Projekte des Studios Anna Heringer, die unter deutscher Aufsicht standen, wurde die Baustelle von dem bangladeschischen Bauunternehmer Montu Ram Shaw zusammen mit einem Team im Dorf ansässiger Lehm- und Bambusarbeiter*innen selbst geleitet.

EN

Bangladesh is the world's second-largest exporter of clothing after China. The globalized textile industry is not only responsible for extreme pollution and inhumane working conditions but also has a detrimental impact on local economies and social structures through migration to industrial centers. In order to offer a decentralized counter-model to the exploitative nature of global supply chains, the project Dipdii Textiles by architect Anna Heringer, designer Veronika Lang, and Bangladeshi nongovernmental organization Dipshikha embraces the local textile culture and the everyday practice of upcycling in Bangladesh, where it is customary to sew worn-out saris and lungis into multilayered blankets. At the Dipdii Textiles workshop in the village of Rudrapur, these blankets are given a new lease on life by being reworked into clothing, tapestries, and pillowcases.

The project provides a livelihood for women in villages in northern Bangladesh, reducing the need to migrate to urban industrial hubs in pursuit of work. Consequently, local living and working conditions improve, and the social fabric of these communities remains intact. The textile workshop is situated on the top floor of a school for people with disabilities that Heringer designed. A testament to sustainability, the building was built with locally sourced mud and bamboo, ensuring ease of repair and supporting the local workforce. Unlike earlier projects by Studio Anna Heringer, which were built under German supervision, the construction of this building was managed by Bangladeshi developer Montu Ram Shaw together with a team of mud and bamboo workers from the village.

Text:
Alex Nehmer

Das Projekt bietet den Frauen des Dorfes eine Erwerbsgrundlage und vermindert somit den Zwang, zur Arbeitssuche in städtische Industriezentren abzuwandern.

The project provides a livelihood for women in the village, reducing the need for them to migrate to major industrial cities in search of work.

Symbolisch für die gewaltvollen Verhältnisse der globalisierten Textilproduktion steht hier ein Hemd, gefertigt aus einem Stoff mit Brandlöchern. Diese rühren von einem Straßenprotest in Bangladeschs Hauptstadt Dhaka her, den Anna Heringer miterlebte und der ihr den Anstoß für die Gründung des Projekts Dipdii Textiles gab.

A shirt made of fabric with burn holes symbolizes the violent conditions of globalized textile production. The fabric was damaged during a street protest in Bangladesh's capital Dhaka, which Anna Heringer witnessed, and which inspired her to found the Dipdii Textiles project.

Eine im Rahmen des Projekts entstandene Tapisserie (138 × 195 cm), bestickt mit einer Karte von Rudrapur.
A tapestry produced through the project (138 × 195 cm) features an embroidered map of Rudrapur.

Zwei Tapisserien, die eine bestickt mit einem Aufriss (103 × 200 cm), die andere mit dem Grundriss (120 × 190 cm) der von Anna Heringer entworfenen METI Handmade School, in der sich die Werkstatt von Dipdii Textiles befindet.

Two embroidered tapestries depict an elevation (103 × 200 cm) and a floor plan (120 × 190 cm) of the METI Handmade School. The building was designed by Anna Heringer and is home to the Dipdii Textiles workshop.

DE

Der Akt der Reparatur legt immer auch offen, was nicht repariert werden kann: Nie werden wir den ursprünglichen und unversehrten Zustand eines Körpers, Gegenstandes, Gebäudes und schon gar nicht unseres Planeten wiederherstellen können. Insofern beginnt Reparatur damit, die Unumkehrbarkeit der Zerstörung anzuerkennen. Wir können wiederaufbauen, ausbessern, heilen und instandsetzen, aber wir müssen uns eingestehen, dass all unsere Reparaturbemühungen die materiellen oder immateriellen Verletzungen nicht überdecken können. Dieses Kapitel versammelt Arbeiten, die die Narben sichtbar lassen und das Gedenken an Verschüttetes lebendig halten. Sie pflegen persönliche und kollektive Erinnerungen, die ausgelöscht zu werden drohen. In einem ko-kreativen Prozess entstehen mithilfe von Werkzeugen der Gestaltung und Raumforschung wachsende Archive, damit wir wieder aufbauen können, was zerstört wurde, dessen gedenken, was wir verloren haben, und in dem, was repariert wurde, neue Bedeutungen finden können.

Text:
Nazlı Tümerdem

Die Narben sichtbar lassen

Keep the Scars visible

EN

The act of repair always also reveals what cannot be repaired. One cannot return to an original and undamaged state of a body, object, or building, let alone the planet itself. In this sense, repair begins with acknowledging the irreversibility of destruction. We may rebuild, mend, heal, and overhaul, but we need to embrace the fact that all our efforts to repair will not obscure the material or immaterial wounds. This section brings together works and projects that span multiple temporalities and scales; they seek to keep the scars visible and recollections alive. They cherish our personal and collective memories which might otherwise be erased, co-create expanding archives through design and spatial research tools so that we can rebuild what was demolished, commemorate what we lost, and discover new meaning in what was repaired.

Center for Spatial Technologies

A City within a Building

The Mariupol Drama Theater

DE

Am 16. März 2022 bombardierte ein russisches Flugzeug das Akademische Dramatheater der Oblast Donezk in Mariupol, Ukraine, in dem zu diesem Zeitpunkt bis zu 2.000 Zivilist*innen Zuflucht gesucht hatten. Mehrere hundert Menschen wurden bei dem Luftangriff vermutlich getötet. Das zerstörte Theater wurde anschließend von russischen Streitkräften zuerst verhüllt und dann abgetragen, was ukrainisches Kulturerbe sowie Beweise für dieses Kriegsverbrechen unwiederbringlich vernichtete. Um das Ereignis gänzlich aus der Erinnerung zu tilgen, wurden Überlebende in dem von Russland besetzten Gebiet unter Druck gesetzt, Foto- und Videobeweise zu vernichten und dem ukrainischen Militär den Bombenangriff anzulasten.

Um dieser Geschichtsfälschung entgegenzuwirken, hat sich das Kiewer Forschungskollektiv Center for Spatial Technologies mit Forensis und Forensic Architecture zusammengeschlossen, um die Bombardierung des Theaters und seine vorherige Umwandlung in einen Schutzraum zu rekonstruieren. Dafür haben sie große Mengen an Fotos, Videos und Social-Media-Beiträgen gesammelt und mithilfe von Fotogrammetrie, digitalen Modellen und anderen räumlichen Analysemethoden untersucht. Zusätzlich führten sie lange Interviews mit Überlebenden und setzten dabei das von Forensic Architecture entwickelte Verfahren der sogenannten situierten Zeugenaussage ein, bei dem Zeug*innen sich durch ein digitales 3D-Modell eines Tatortes bewegen und sich so besser erinnern können. Aus diesem gemeinschaftlichen Rekonstruktionsprozess entstanden ein Film und ein wachsendes digitales Archiv. Dem Projekt gelang es nachzuweisen, dass zum Zeitpunkt des Luftangriffs keine ukrainischen Militärkräfte im Theater stationiert waren – womit das Argument der russischen Armee für die Bombardierung des Theaters und anderer ziviler Einrichtungen entkräftet war. Mehr noch zeichnet das Projekt ein detailliertes Bild des Lebens im Theater vor dem Angriff. Es zeigt eine Gemeinschaft von Menschen inmitten des Krieges, die Entscheidungen gemeinsam trafen, sich gegenseitig halfen und füreinander Sorge trugen. Zukünftig könnte diese Sammlung kollektiver Erinnerungen als Beweismittel vor internationalen Gerichten dienen – oder als Quelle für eine Rekonstruktion des Gebäudes.

2023
Video
Ton, Farbe
Color, sound
21 min

EN

On March 16, 2022, a Russian aircraft bombed the Donetsk Academic Regional Drama Theater in Mariupol, Ukraine, which was sheltering as many as 2,000 civilians at the time. Several hundred people were probably killed in the blast. Subsequently, Russian forces first concealed and then demolished the ruined theater, bulldozing Ukrainian cultural heritage as well as evidence of their war crime. They then further sought to erase the act from history by silencing survivors in the area under Russian occupation, putting them under pressure to delete photo and video evidence and to implicate the Ukrainian military in the bombing.

To counteract this attempted rewriting of history, Kyiv-based research collective Center for Spatial Technologies teamed up with Forensis and Forensic Architecture to reconstruct the bombing of the theater and its earlier transformation into a shelter. They compiled thousands of photos, videos, and social media posts, and analyzed them using spatial research tools including digital models and photogrammetry. This was augmented by dozens of hours of interviews with survivors, conducted by means of “situated testimony,” a technique developed by Forensic Architecture that facilitates recollection by allowing witnesses to move through a three-dimensional digital model of crime scenes. This collaborative process of reconstruction resulted in a film and a growing online archive. The project

was able to prove that there had been no Ukrainian military personnel stationed in the theater at the time of the air strike—a justification used by Russian forces for bombing the theater and other civilian structures. Moreover, the project paints a detailed picture of life in the theater in the days prior to the attack, showing a community of people in the middle of war who were engaged in mutual aid, care, and collaboration. In the future, this assemblage of collective memories could potentially serve as evidence in international courts—or as a source for the building's reconstruction.

Text:
Daniel Kuhnert

1

2

3

4

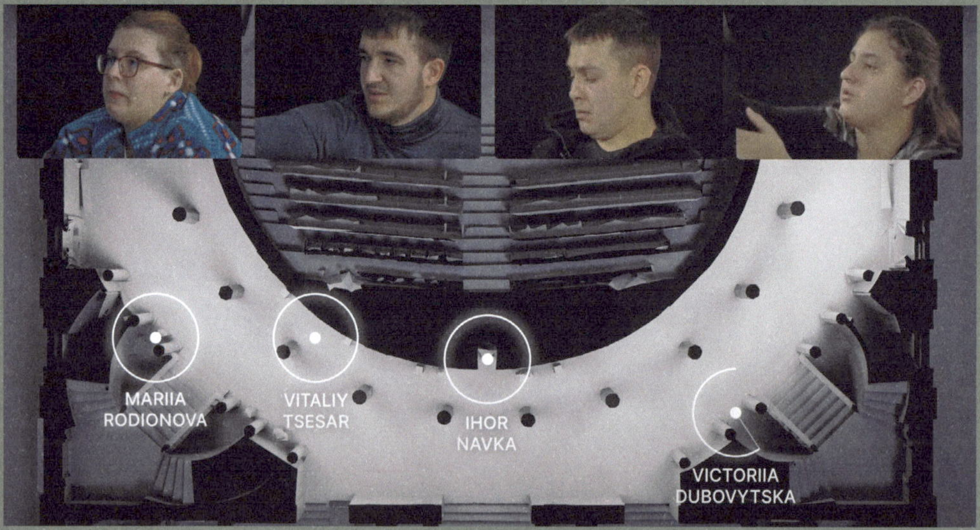

5

6

1
Die Videoreportage des Center for Spatial Technologies zeigt die Methoden, mit denen es den russischen Luftangriff am 16. März 2022 auf das Theater in Mariupol rekonstruiert hat.

The video by the Center for Spatial Technologies demonstrates how it reconstructed the Russian air strike on the theater in Mariupol that occurred on March 16, 2022.

2, 3
Ende 2022 wurde das Theater von den russischen Streitkräften abgerissen, um alle Beweise für das Kriegsverbrechen zu vernichten. Das Center for Spatial Technologies sammelte deshalb Tausende von Fotos, Videos und Social-Media-Posts und erstellte ein digitales 3D-Modell des Theaters, um ein kollektives forensisches Archiv zu schaffen.

In late 2022, the theater was destroyed by Russian military forces, effectively removing any remaining material evidence of the war crime. The Center for Spatial Technologies took action by gathering thousands of photos, videos, and social media posts into a collective forensic archive, which it used to generate a digital 3D model of the theater.

4, 5, 6
Vor dem Angriff hielten sich bis zu 2.000 Zivilist*innen im Theater auf. Mit einigen der Überlebenden führte das Team mithilfe des Verfahrens der sogenannten situierten Zeugenaussage Interviews. Während die Zeug*innen durch das 3D-Modell navigieren, liefern sie Informationen, die so räumlich zugeordnet und mit Fotos und Videos verknüpft werden können.

Prior to the strike, up to 2,000 civilians had taken shelter inside the theater. The team interviewed some of the survivors using a method called “situated testimony.” This involved witnesses sharing their accounts while navigating through the 3D model, allowing their information to be precisely linked to specific locations and cross-referenced with photos and videos.

7, 8, 9
Mit jedem Augenzeug*innenbericht wird das Modell detaillierter und wächst zu einer Ansammlung kollektiver Erinnerung heran.

With each witness recalling their experience of the event, the 3D model gains more and more detail, transforming into an amalgamation of collective memory.

10
Um das Theater präzise modellieren zu können, orientierte sich das Team auch an noch existierenden, fast baugleichen Theatern in der Ukraine. Das Theater in Poltawa, das dem in Mariupol am ähnlichsten ist, wurde fotogrammetrisch gescannt. So konnten selbst Details wie Vorhänge und Dekorationen rekonstruiert werden.

To create an accurate model of the theater, the team also used data from comparable existing theaters in Ukraine. The theater in Poltava, bearing the closest resemblance to the Mariupol theater, was photogrammetrically scanned. This scan enabled the reconstruction of even the most minor details, including stage curtains and ornamentation.

7

8

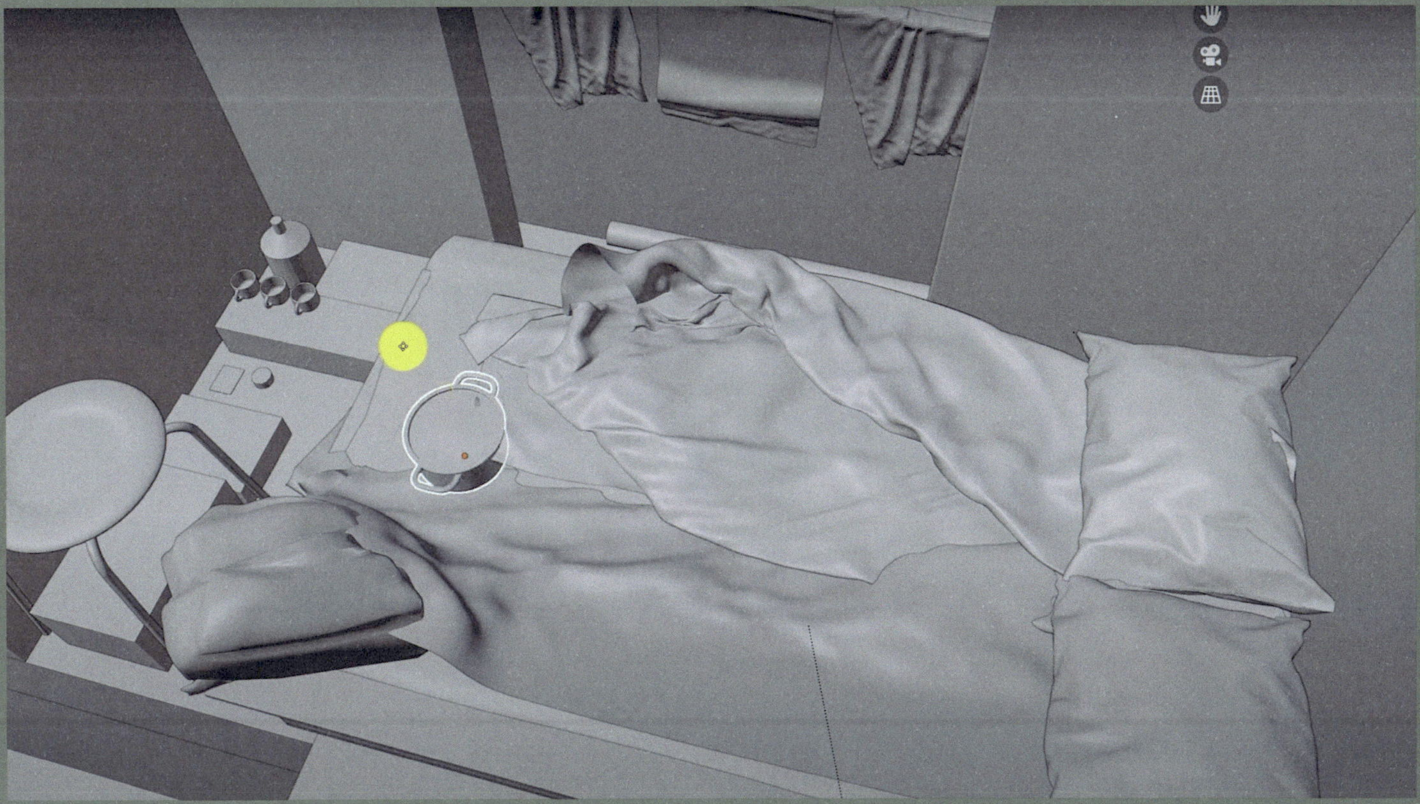

9

Mapping Ukraine

Building amidst Destruction

Mapping as a Tool for Repair

DE

Building amidst Destruction ist aus einer Zusammenarbeit zwischen dem Forschungsprojekt *Mapping Ukraine* (*MU*) der ETH Zürich und dem *Swiss Network with Ukraine* entstanden. Beide Initiativen eint der Wunsch, eine Brücke zwischen der vom Krieg geprägten gegenwärtigen Realität der Ukraine und einer möglichen nachhaltigen Zukunft für das Land zu schlagen. Beide verstehen Wiederaufbau als eine kollektive und dezentralisierte Aufgabe, ihre Arbeit vereint dabei sowohl kurz- und langfristige als auch lokale und globale Ansätze.

Mapping Ukraine entwickelt eine Online-Plattform, die die Auswirkungen von Russlands Krieg gegen die Ukraine dokumentiert. Hierfür wird die Vielzahl der vorhandenen Informationen aus Krisengebieten gebündelt, ihre Authentizität geprüft und frei zur Verfügung gestellt. Gleichzeitig bündelt das Projekt bereits laufende Wiederaufbauvorhaben. Verschiedene Datensätze werden kombiniert und zusammengeführt, um neue Informationen zu generieren, was eine ergebnis- und zweckoffene Nutzung ermöglicht und eine sowohl retrospektive als auch prospektive Auswertung von Ereignissen als Informationsquelle sowie als Forschungs- und Planungsinstrument erlaubt.

Das *Swiss Network with Ukraine* ist ein wachsendes Forum, das gegenwärtig 50 ukrainische und internationale in der Schweiz ansässige Expert*innen und Wissenschaftler*innen zusammenbringt, die die Ukraine seit der russischen Invasion aktiv unterstützen. Das Netzwerk besteht aus sieben Clustern, die sich jeweils mit unterschiedlichen Dimensionen des Wiederaufbaus befassen: IBA Ukraine, städtebauliche Rahmenplanung, Wohnungsbau, Sanierung und Materialbeschaffung, Kapazitätsaufbau und Bildung, Plattform für Kultur und gesellschaftlichen Zusammenhalt sowie Mapping Ukraine.

Der Ausstellungsbeitrag präsentiert mehrere Fallbeispiele des *Swiss Network with Ukraine* und eröffnet über die digitale Plattform *MU* sowie Videointerviews einen Einblick in die unterschiedlichen Perspektiven von Akteur*innen aus dem erweiterten Netzwerk des Projekts. Einige dieser Interviews werden im Herbst 2023 auch im Rahmen von *New Common* im ukrainischen Pavillon auf der Architekturbiennale in Venedig zu sehen sein. Gemeinsam veranschaulichen sie die Komplexität der Anstrengungen für den Wiederaufbau der Ukraine, die von kleinen Projekten bis zu übergreifenden Narrativen, von privaten bis zu öffentlichen Akteur*innen, von basisdemokratischen Initiativen bis zu zentralisierten Regierungsprojekten reichen.

2022–fortlaufend
ongoing
Installation
Mixed media

EN

Building amidst Destruction emerged from a collaboration between the ETH Zurich research project *Mapping Ukraine* (MU) and the *Swiss Network with Ukraine*. Both initiatives are united by a desire to build a bridge between Ukraine's current war-torn reality and its potentially sustainable future. Their work emphasizes reconstruction as a collective and decentralized effort and addresses both short and long-term as well as local and global approaches.

Mapping Ukraine is developing an online platform that documents the effects of Russia's war on Ukraine. It bundles the large amount of existing information from crisis areas, evaluates its authenticity, and makes it freely available. It also includes ongoing reconstruction projects. Combining and merging different sets of data to create new information allows for open-ended use in terms of results and purpose and permits retrospective and prospective assessment of events as a source of information and a research and planning tool.

The *Swiss Network with Ukraine* is a growing forum that currently unites some 50 Ukrainian and international experts and researchers residing in Switzerland, who have been actively supporting Ukraine since the Russian invasion. The network comprises seven clusters, each dealing with different aspects

and dimensions of reconstruction: IBA Ukraine, Master Planning, Housing, Rehabilitation and Materials Supply, Capacity Building and Education, Community and Cultural Platform, and Mapping Ukraine.

The contribution exhibits several case studies of the *Swiss Network with Ukraine* and offers insights into the collaborators' perspectives through the MU digital platform and video interviews with the extended network of actors. Some of these interviews will be featured in autumn 2023 in the project *New Common* in the Ukrainian Pavilion at the Architecture Biennale in Venice. Together, they illustrate the complexity of these undertakings, which range from small projects to overarching narratives, from private to public actors as well as from grassroots initiatives to centralized government efforts to rebuild Ukraine.

Text:
Jonathan Banz, Matthew Gordon, Gyler Mydyti, Nataliia Mysak, Basil Roth

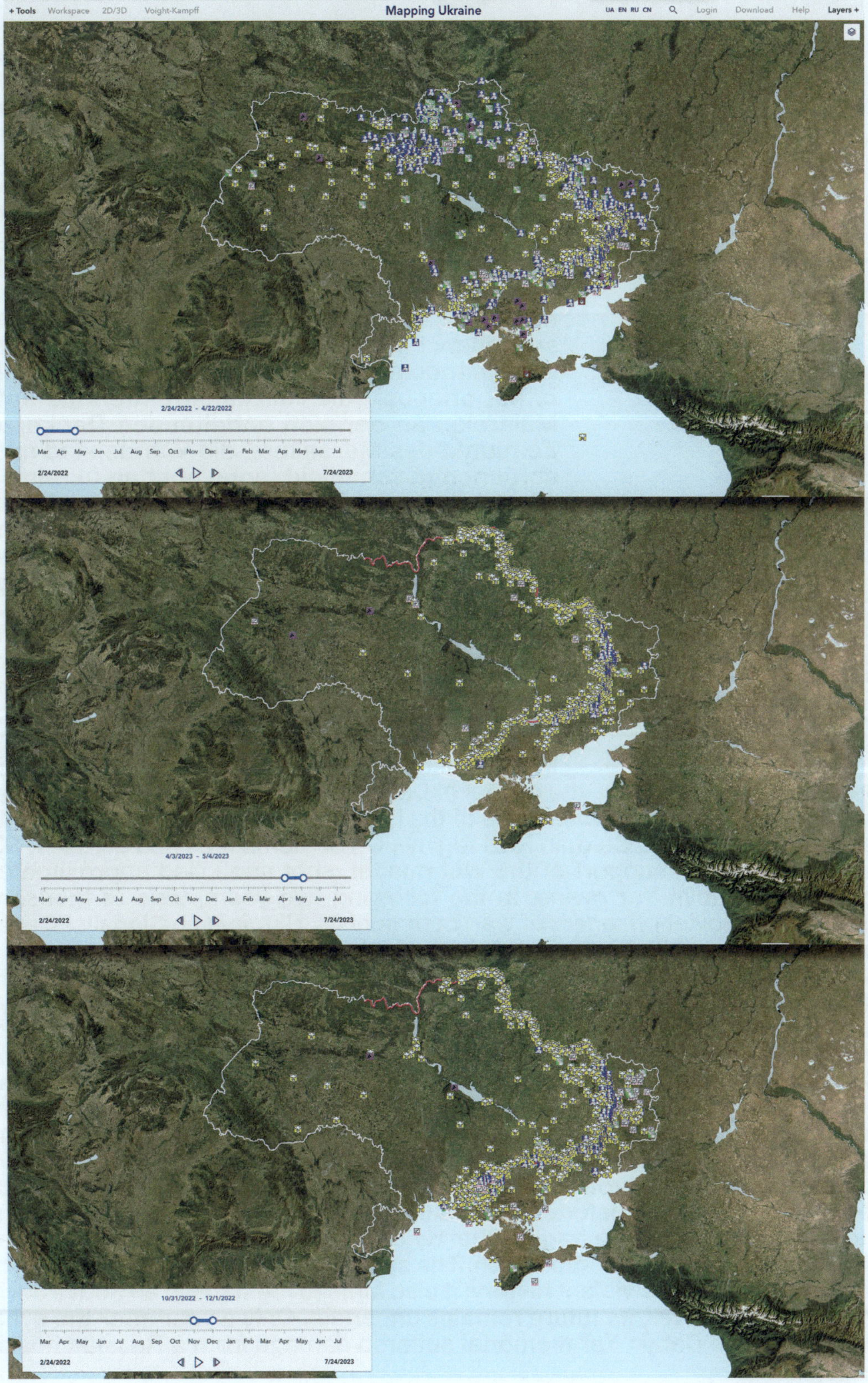

Eine Testversion der Plattform zeigt verschiedene Frontdaten zu drei verschiedenen Zeitpunkten während des Krieges.

A test version of the platform shows various frontline data at three different times during the war.

Manuel Herz Architects

Babyn Yar Synagogue

DE

Zwischen den Bäumen eines Parks im Nordwesten der ukrainischen Hauptstadt Kiew hat Manuel Herz eine Synagoge gebaut. Sie ist Teil einer Gedenkstätte, die den Ort eines der größten Massaker des Nazi-Regimes markiert. Am 29. und 30. September 1941 erschossen SS-Einsatzgruppen unter Mithilfe der Wehrmacht etwa 34.000 jüdische Menschen in der Schlucht von Babyn Jar. In den folgenden zwei Jahren wurden dort Zehntausende weitere Menschen aus antisemitischen, rassistischen, politischen und eugenischen Gründen ermordet.

Die Synagoge ist in ihrer Form und Gestaltung einem Siddur nachempfunden, einem Gebetsbuch, das in der religiösen Praxis des Judentums eine zentrale Rolle spielt. Und wie ein Buch lässt die Synagoge sich öffnen und schließen. Eine komplexe Mechanik ermöglicht es der Gemeinde, den Bau mithilfe einer handbetriebenen Kurbel in einem kollektiven Ritual zu transformieren. Geöffnet offenbart die Holzkonstruktion die aufwändige Bemalung im Inneren. Die Malereien an der sich entfaltenden Decke zeigen die Sternenkonstellation zum Zeitpunkt des Massakers, die Wände sind mit Ornamenten, Gebeten und Segenssprüchen geschmückt, angelehnt an ukrainische Holzsynagogen aus dem 16. bis 18. Jahrhundert. Das verwendete Holz stammt von über hundertjährigen Eichen aus der ganzen Ukraine und verbindet so symbolisch die Gegenwart mit der Zeit vor der Shoah. Zusammen mit der beweglichen Mechanik verleiht das Material der Synagoge eine Fragilität, die beständige Pflege und Auseinandersetzung mit dem Gebäude erfordert – wie auch das Gedenken selbst. Die Synagoge soll nicht nur an die gewaltvolle Geschichte des Ortes erinnern, sondern dort auch eine lebendige jüdische Präsenz wiederherstellen. Doch ihre Zukunft ist ungewiss. Nur ein Jahr nach ihrer Fertigstellung wurde die Gedenkstätte Babyn Jar im März 2022 bei einem russischen Raketenangriff beschädigt.

Auftraggeber
Client
Babyn Yar Holocaust Memorial Foundation
Projektteam
Project team
Manuel Herz, Maxim Gabai, Ben Olschner, Isabella Pagliuca, Angeliki Giannisi
Fertigstellung
Completion
April 2021

EN

Manuel Herz built a synagogue in between the trees of a park in northwestern Kyiv, the capital of Ukraine. It forms part of a memorial landscape commemorating the site where one of the largest massacres of the Second World War was carried out by the German Nazi regime. On September 29 and 30, 1941, SS deployment groups, with support of the Wehrmacht, shot and killed approximately 34,000 Jews in the Babyn Yar ravine. In the following two years, tens of thousands more Jews, Roma, Soviet prisoners of war, communists, Ukrainian nationalists, and patients from a nearby psychiatric hospital were murdered at that location.

The synagogue's shape and design are modeled on a siddur, a prayer book central to Jewish religious practices. Similar to a book, the synagogue can be opened and closed. A complex mechanism with a hand-operated crank allows the congregation to transform the building through a collective ritual. When opened, the wooden construction reveals intricate paintings inside. Paintings on the unfolding ceiling portray the constellation of stars on the night of the massacre, while the walls are adorned with ornaments, prayers, and blessings referencing Ukrainian wooden synagogues of the 16th to 18th century. The timber used comes from hundred-year-old oak trees, sourced from various locations across Ukraine, symbolically connecting the present to the time before the Shoah. The materiality and moving mechanics combine to lend the building a fragility that requires constant care and engagement, much like the act of commemoration itself. The synagogue's purpose extends beyond commemorating the site's violent history; it also aims to reestablish an active Jewish presence there. However, its future remains uncertain. Only a year after the synagogue's completion, the Babyn Yar memorial suffered damage from a Russian missile attack in March 2022.

Text:
Manuel Herz Architects

Die Synagoge von Babyn Jar wurde 2021 von Manuel Herz Architects als Teil der Gedenkstätte an der Schlucht von Babyn Jar im Nordwesten Kiews eröffnet und erinnert an den 1941 vom NS-Regime verübten Massenmord an 34.000 jüdischen Bürger*innen Kiews. Im März 2022 wurde die Gedenkstätte von einem russischen Raketenangriff getroffen.

The Babyn Yar synagogue, designed by Manuel Herz Architects and inaugurated in 2021, is situated within Babyn Yar memorial park, northwest of Kyiv. The site commemorates the massacre of 34,000 Jewish citizens, carried out under the Nazi regime in 1941. In March 2022, the memorial site was struck by a Russian missile attack.

Das Deckengemälde zeigt die Sternenkonstellation über Kiew in der Nacht des Massakers von 1941. Die dekorativen Elemente der Zeichnung nehmen Bezug auf die Ornamentik zerstörter Synagogen aus dem 16. bis 18. Jahrhundert auf dem Gebiet der heutigen Ukraine.

The ceiling painting depicts the constellation of stars over Kyiv during the night of the 1941 massacre. The mural incorporates decorative elements inspired by the ornamentation found in Ukrainian synagogues of the 16th to 18th centuries, many of which were destroyed.

Ausstellungsbeitrag
Exhibition contribution
The sky over Babyn Yar
2023
Installation, Holz
Installation, wood
Durchmesser
Diameter
3 m
Video
Farbe, ohne Ton
Color, without sound
4 min
Projektteam
Project team
Manuel Herz, Francesca Mautone
Mit Unterstützung der Schweizer Kulturstiftung Pro Helvetia
With support of the Swiss Arts Council Pro Helvetia

Die Synagoge in Form eines Buches lässt sich mittels eines handbetriebenen Mechanismus öffnen und schließen.

The book-shaped synagogue can be opened and closed using a hand-operated mechanism.

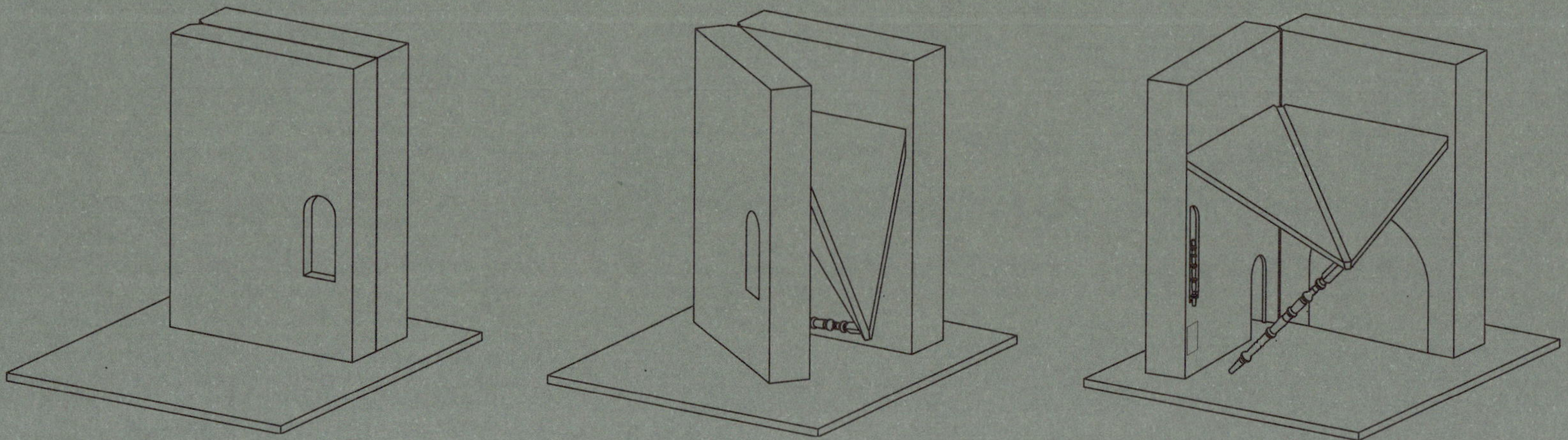

Unterhalb des Daches entfaltet sich die Bima – das Lesepult für die Tora – in den zentralen Gebetsraum, dessen Wände mit den wichtigsten Gebeten der jüdischen Liturgie geschmückt sind.

Beneath the roof, the bimah—the platform from which the Torah is read—leads into the central prayer room, whose walls are adorned with important prayers from the Jewish liturgy.

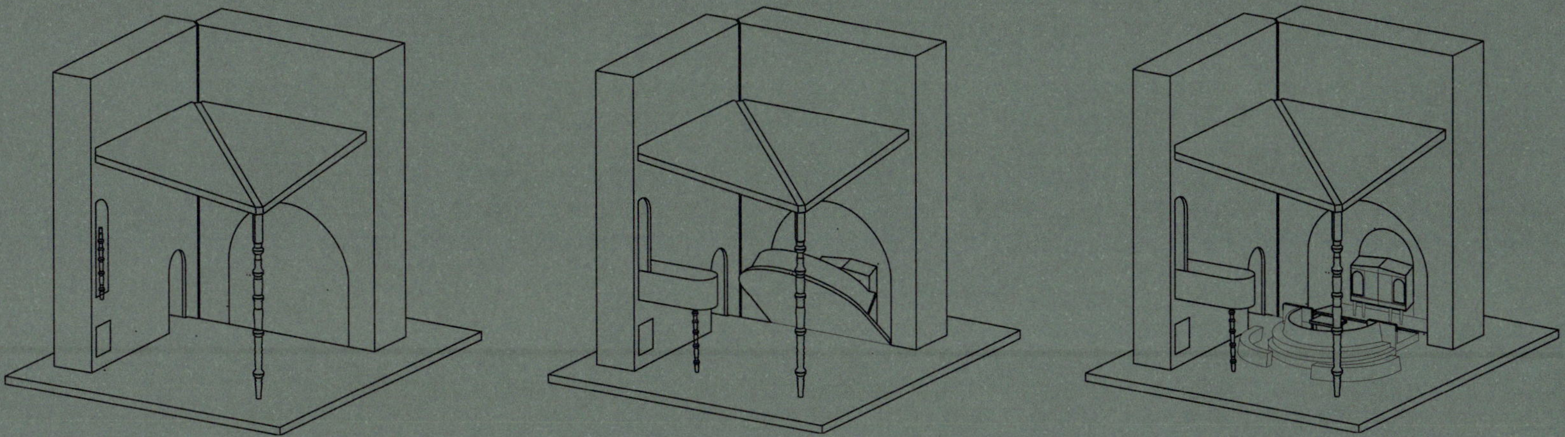

Bas Princen

Giotto's Fragments

DE

Die im 13. Jahrhundert errichtete Basilica di San Francesco in Assisi ist eines der prachtvollsten Bauwerke seiner Zeit. Die großen Freskenzyklen von Cimabue, aber vor allem die von Giotto (dessen Autorschaft nur durch stilkritische Argumente untermauert werden kann) in der Oberkirche, läuteten eine neue Ära der italienischen Malerei ein, die später in die Renaissance münden sollte.

Mehr als zwanzig Erdbeben hatten die Meisterwerke seit ihrer Entstehung überstanden, doch im Jahr 1997 brachten heftige Erschütterungen Teile der Basilika zum Einsturz. Mit zwei Gewölbekappen gingen Wandbilder Cimabues und Giottos zu Boden und zerbarsten in unzählige Einzelteile. Risse klafften in den Wänden, bemalter Verputz zerbrach, Kulturerbe von unschätzbarem Wert löste sich im wahrsten Sinne des Wortes in Staub auf. Es folgten Jahre der Rekonstruktion, in denen die rund 300.000 geborgenen Fragmente katalogisiert, anhand von Fotografien arrangiert und mithilfe von Computertechnik in ihre ursprüngliche Position wiedereingefügt wurden. Doch zehntausende der Bruchstücke ließen sich nicht zuordnen und werden bis heute im Depot aufbewahrt.

Den Künstler Bas Princen hatten diese Fragmente schon lange fasziniert. 2023 erhielt er im Rahmen von *The Great Repair* die Erlaubnis, sie zu fotografieren. Für ihn sind sie Objekte von unzweifelhafter Bedeutung, aber mit ungewisser Zukunft: Sie warten auf der „Baustelle der Utopie", wie Restaurator*innen und Geistliche sie genannt haben, darauf, in ihr Bild zurückzufinden. Die Fragmente sind mit der Aura Giottos und Cimabues aufgeladen, doch sie sind nicht mehr dem Inhalt der Meisterwerke unterworfen. Indem Princen die Fragmente zum Motiv seiner Fotografien macht, verleiht er ihnen als abstrakte Kunstwerke ein neues Eigenleben. Sie stehen für sich, aber auch für die irreparablen Narben, die Zerstörungen hinterlassen.

2023

EN

The Basilica of Saint Francis of Assisi, erected during the 13th century, stands as one of the most magnificent buildings of its time. The frescoes in its Upper Church by artists such as Cimabue and especially by Giotto (attributed through stylistic analysis only) heralded a new epoch in Italian painting, paving the way for the Renaissance.

In the centuries since their creation, these masterpieces survived more than twenty earthquakes. But violent tremors in 1997 brought sections of the basilica down. Two portions of the vaulting, adorned with frescoes by Cimabue and Giotto, plummeted to the ground, shattering into thousands of pieces. The walls filled with cracks, the painted plaster fractured, and a cultural legacy of inconceivable value disintegrated, literally turning into dust. Years of reconstruction efforts followed, during which some 300,000 salvaged shards were catalogued, reassembled based on photographs, and realigned with their original positions with the help of computer technology. Nevertheless, tens of thousands of fragments could not be matched and remain stored in repositories.

Long fascinated by these fragments, artist Bas Princen gained permission in 2023 to photograph them for *The Great Repair*. To Princen, they hold unquestionable significance yet an uncertain future, awaiting their return to their rightful place within the frescoes of this "utopian construction site," as conservators and clergy have described it. While Giotto and Cimabue's auras instill them with meaning, the fragments no longer adhere to the narrative confines of their original masterpieces. By photographing them, Princen lends them new independent lives as abstract works of art. These fragments are now representatives of themselves, but they also embody the indelible scars that destruction leaves behind.

Text:
Nora Dünser

Archive of Fragments (Basilica of Saint Francis of Assisi), 2023

Reconstructed Vaults (Basilica of Saint Francis of Assisi) (Detail), 2023

Reconstructed Vaults (Basilica of Saint Francis of Assisi), 2023

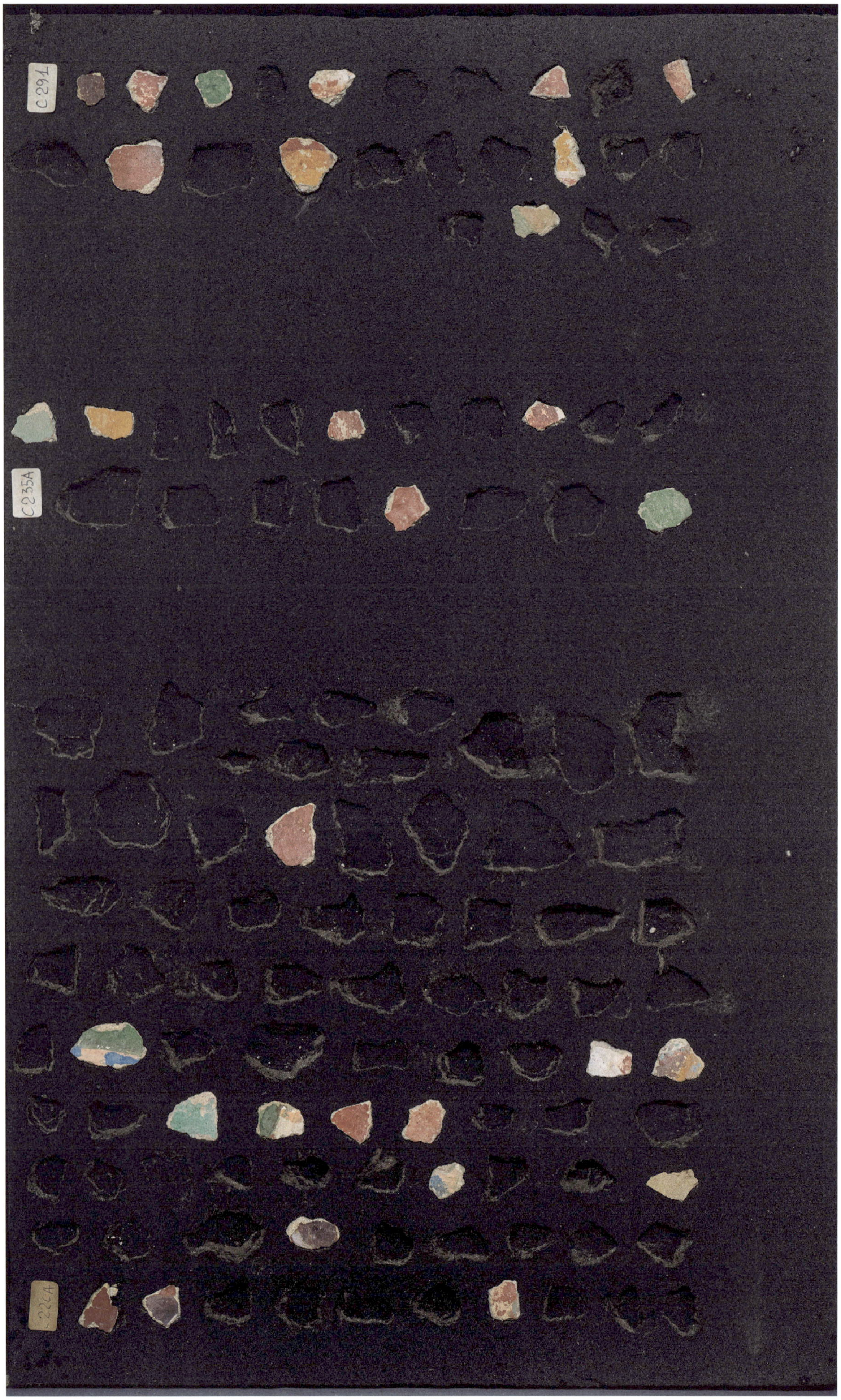

Giotto Fragment Box 530, 2023
Gerahmter Tintenstrahldruck
auf Reispapier
Framed inkjet print on rice paper
210 × 135 cm

Giotto Fragment Box 538, 2023
Gerahmter Tintenstrahldruck
auf Reispapier
Framed inkjet print on rice paper
210 × 135 cm

Giotto Fragment Box 543, 2023
Gerahmter Tintenstrahldruck
auf Reispapier
Framed inkjet print on rice paper
210 × 135 cm

Giotto Fragment Box 531, 2023
Gerahmter Tintenstrahldruck
auf Reispapier
Framed inkjet print on rice paper
210 × 135 cm

DE

Die Reparatur der Architektur sollte nicht zuerst bei ihren Objekten ansetzen, sondern bei ihren Subjekten – den Studierenden, Lehrenden, Arbeiter*innen – und deren Beziehung zur Disziplin. Das Büro, die Hochschule und die Baustelle – dort, wo die Bedingungen und die Handlungsmacht von Architekturarbeit und -wissen bestimmt und verhandelt werden – sind darum einige der wichtigsten Bereiche für eine Selbstreparatur der Disziplin. Gefragt sind Instrumente zur Stärkung und Organisierung von Architekturschaffenden in ihrem Kampf für gerechtere Arbeitsbedingungen, eine experimentelle Pädagogik, die Machthierarchien in der Lehre und tradierte Vorstellungen von Autorschaft hinterfragt, sowie Visionen für eine architektonische Praxis, die auf kollektiver Sorge und Solidarität aufbaut. Mit ihrem Blick über die Institutionen hinaus zeigen die Projekte in diesem Kapitel auch, wie Architekt*innen zunehmend das Selbstverständnis ihres Berufstands als Expert*innen, die immer mehr neu bauen, unterlaufen.

Text:
Marija Marić

praxis reparieren

Repair the Practice

EN

The repair of architecture needs to start not from its objects, but rather its subjects—students, teachers, workers—and their relationship to the discipline itself. The office, the school, and the construction site—where conditions and agencies of architectural labor and knowledge are shaped and negotiated—are some of the most important domains for disciplinary self-repair. What is needed are toolkits for empowering and organizing architectural workers in their struggle for fairer employment conditions, pedagogical experiments that challenge power hierarchies in education and complicate the notion of authorship, and visions for architectural practices that are built on notions of collective care and solidarity. Reaching beyond these institutions, the projects in this section also show how architects increasingly subvert the existing self-image of their profession as the experts in charge of building ever more.

Lacaton & Vassal

Place Léon Aucoc, Bordeaux

DE

1996 beauftragte die Gemeinde Bordeaux das Architekturbüro Lacaton & Vassal im Zuge ihres Programms der Stadtverschönerung den place Léon Aucoc neu zu gestalten. Das Büro begann mit einer Bestandsaufnahme der dreieckigen, von Bäumen und Sitzbänken gesäumten Fläche und der Befragung von Anwohner*innen. Der Platz wird auf zwei Seiten von Reihenhäusern einer Siedlung von 1913 und auf einer Seite von Doppelhäusern mit Gärten aus dem Jahr 1954 begrenzt, die der Staatlichen Eisenbahngesellschaft SNCF gehören und vorwiegend an ihre Mitarbeiter*innen vermietet werden.

Lacaton & Vassal sahen keinen akuten gestalterischen Handlungsbedarf, da der Ort für sie als solcher funktionierte. Einem Dorfplatz ähnlich treffen sich dort regelmäßig junge wie alte Anwohner*innen. Weder eine Modernisierung der Sitzgelegenheiten noch eine Änderung der Beleuchtung oder des Bodenbelags hätten nach Ansicht der Architekt*innen eine wirkliche Verbesserung dargestellt. Statt das zur Verfügung stehende Budget wie sonst üblich für die Umgestaltung des Platzes aufzuwenden, überzeugte das Büro die Kommune und Anwohner*innen, es in die Instandhaltung und Pflege des Vorhandenen zu investieren. Ihr „Verschönerungs"-Vorschlag beschränkte sich auf die regelmäßigere Reinigung des Platzes, eine Ausbesserung der wassergebundenen Wegedecke, die Verkehrsberuhigung durch eine Richtungsänderung der Straßen, sowie Maßnahmen zum Schutz der Sitzbänke unter den Lindenbäumen vor dem heruntertropfenden Honigtau. Wie in vielen anderen ihrer Projekte beweisen Lacaton & Vassal, dass es keine großen baulichen Eingriffe bedarf, um die Qualität eines Raums zu verbessern.

1996
Auftraggeber
Client
Ville de Bordeaux

EN

In 1996, the Bordeaux city council commissioned architecture firm Lacaton & Vassal to redesign Place Léon Aucoc as part of a city-wide beautification program. The firm began by evaluating the public square and conducting interviews with local residents. Shaped like a triangle and lined with trees and benches, the gravel-covered square is nestled between a townhouse estate dating back to 1913 and a row of duplex homes with gardens built in 1954. The latter is owned by the French National Railway SNCF and primarily rented to its employees.

Lacaton & Vassal concluded there was no need for a redesign since the site was already functioning well on its own terms. Resembling a village square, it serves as a popular gathering spot for residents of all ages. As the architects saw it, modernizing the benches, replacing the lamps, or altering the ground's material would serve little to improve the site. Instead of using the allocated budget to overhaul the square's design, the firm chose to invest in the maintenance and care of its existing elements. Their approach to its "beautification" focused on regular cleaning, spreading fresh gravel, calming traffic by changing the direction of the streets, and treating the linden trees to prevent sticky honeydew from dripping onto the benches. As in so many of their projects, Lacaton & Vassal demonstrate that grand architectural interventions are not always needed to enhance the quality of a space.

Text:
Nora Dünser

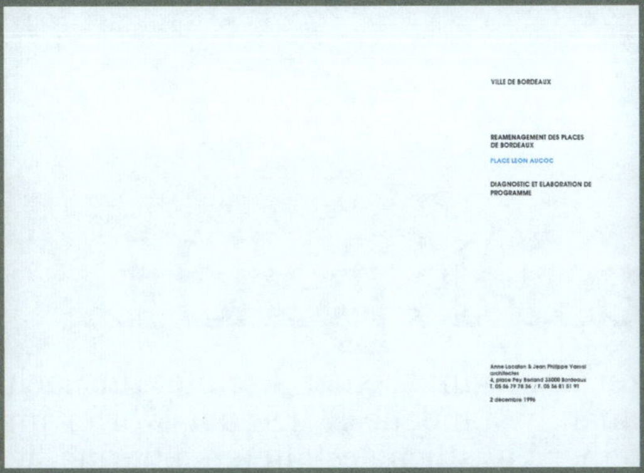

Im Zuge ihres Programms zur Stadtverschönerung beauftragte die Gemeinde Bordeaux 1996 Lacaton & Vassal mit der Umgestaltung des place Léon Aucoc. Nach einer ausgiebigen Bestandsaufnahme, die das Büro in einem 13-seitigen Bericht zusammenfasste, empfahl es, das vorgesehene Budget statt in bauliche Eingriffe in die regelmäßige Reinigung, Pflege und Instandhaltung des Platzes zu investieren.

In 1996, as part of its city-wide beautification program, the Bordeaux city council commissioned Lacaton & Vassal to redesign Place Léon Aucoc. After an extensive survey, which the office summarized in a 13-page report, it recommended devoting the available budget to the regular cleaning, maintenance, and repair of the square instead of structural interventions.

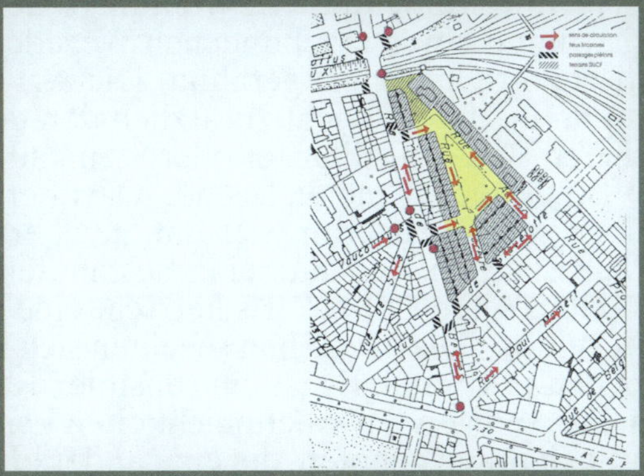

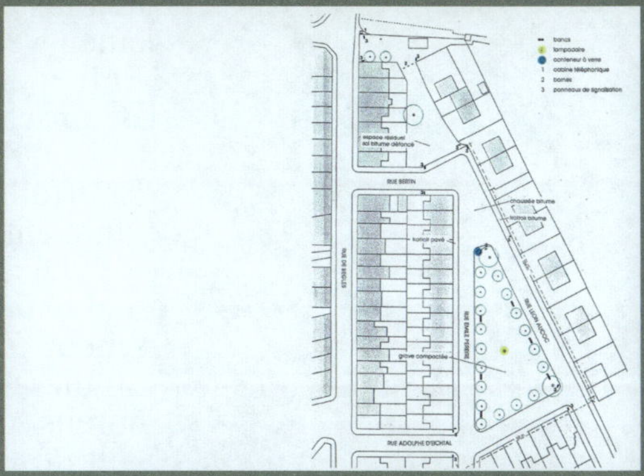

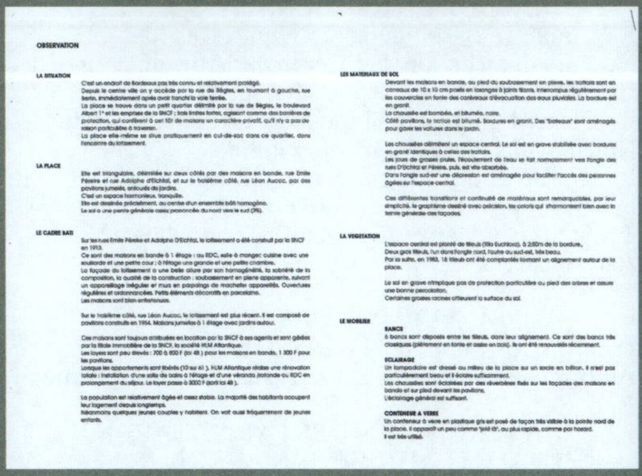

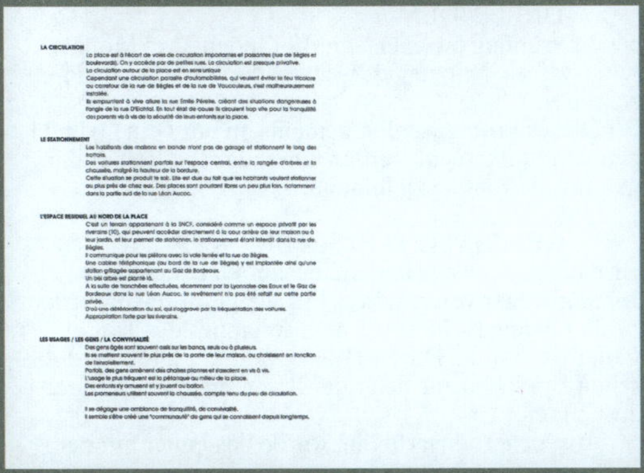

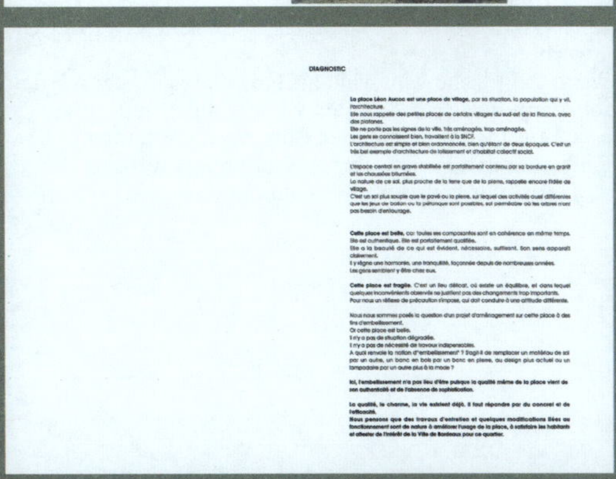

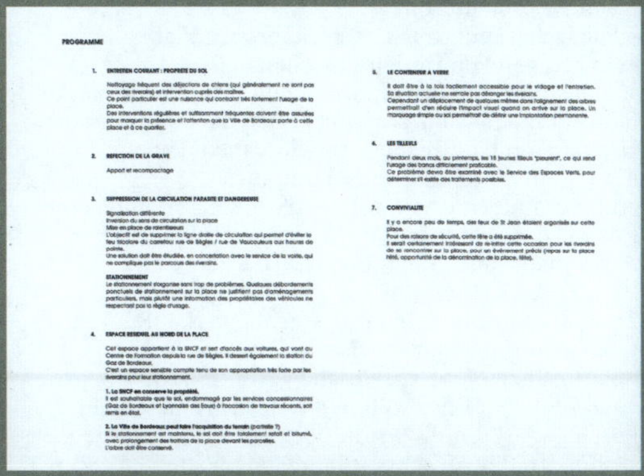

Schlussfolgerung aus Lacaton & Vassals Bericht

Der place Léon Aucoc ist seiner Lage, seiner Nutzer*innen und seiner Architektur nach ein Dorfplatz. Er erinnert uns an kleine, mit Platanen bestandene Plätze der Dörfer im Südwesten Frankreichs. Ihm fehlen die Merkmale einer künstlich gestalteten, übermäßig geplanten städtischen Umgebung. Die Leute kennen sich gut, viele arbeiten bei der SNCF. Die Architektur ist einfach und gut angeordnet, auch wenn sie aus zwei unterschiedlichen Epochen stammt. Es handelt sich um ein schönes Beispiel von Siedlungsarchitektur und sozialem, gemeinwohlorientiertem Wohnungsbau.

Der Platz mit der wassergebundenen Wegedecke wird durch die Graniteinfassung und die asphaltierte Straße perfekt gerahmt. Die Art des Bodenbelags, der der Erde mehr ähnelt als dem Stein, unterstreicht zusätzlich den dörflichen Charakter. Es handelt sich um einen weicheren Boden als Pflaster oder Stein, auf dem ganz verschiedene Aktivitäten wie Ball- oder Boulespielen möglich sind. Darüber hinaus macht der durchlässige Boden Baumscheiben zur Bewässerung der Bäume überflüssig.

Der Platz ist schön, weil alle seine Bestandteile in sich stimmig sind. Er ist authentisch. Er erfüllt bestens seinen Zweck. Es herrscht eine Harmonie, eine Ruhe, die sich über viele Jahre entwickelt hat. Die Menschen scheinen sich zu Hause zu fühlen.

Dieser Platz ist fragil. Es ist ein sensibler Raum, in dem ein Gleichgewicht herrscht und in dem die wenigen Unannehmlichkeiten keine größeren Eingriffe rechtfertigen. Uns scheint Zurückhaltung geboten, die eine andere Haltung erfordert. Wir haben uns gefragt, ob dieser Platz der Verschönerung wegen umgestaltet werden soll. Aber dieser Platz ist bereits schön. Es gibt keine Anzeichen von Verfall. Es besteht keine dringende Notwendigkeit für eine fundamentale Veränderung. Was soll „Verschönerung" heißen? Geht es darum, ein Bodenmaterial durch ein anderes zu ersetzen, eine Holzbank durch eine Steinbank in aktuellerem Design, oder eine Straßenlaterne durch eine andere, modischere?

Es gibt keinen Grund zur Verschönerung des Platzes, denn seine Qualität liegt in seiner Authentizität und Einfachheit. Qualität, Charme und Leben sind bereits vorhanden, eine Lösung muss daher einen praktischen Nutzen mit sich bringen. Wir sind der Meinung, dass es ausreicht, Instandhaltungsarbeiten und einige funktionale Veränderungen durchzuführen, um die Nutzung des Platzes zu verbessern, die Bewohner*innen zufriedenzustellen und die Fürsorge der Stadt Bordeaux für dieses Viertel zu bekunden.

Vorgeschlagenes Programm

1.
LAUFENDE INSTANDHALTUNG:
DEN BODEN SÄUBERN

Regelmäßige Beseitigung des Hundekots (der im Normalfall nicht von den Tieren der Anwohner*innen stammt) und Ansprache der Hundehalter*innen.

Dieser Punkt ist ein besonderes Ärgernis, das die Nutzung des Platzes stark einschränkt.

Die Instandhaltungsarbeiten müssen regelmäßig und häufig genug erfolgen, um die Präsenz und die Fürsorge der Stadt Bordeaux für diesen Platz und dieses Viertel zum Ausdruck zu bringen.

2.
AUSBESSERUNG DER WASSERGEBUNDENEN WEGEDECKE

Aufbringen von neuem Schotter und Nachverdichtung

3.
UNTERBINDEN DES PARASITÄREN UND GEFÄHRLICHEN VERKEHRS

- Neue Beschilderung
- Richtungsänderung des Verkehrs am Platz
- Anbringen von Bodenschwellen
- Ziel ist es, die Durchfahrt zu unterbinden, die es Autofahrer*innen bisher ermöglicht hat, die Ampel an der Kreuzung rue de Bègles / rue de Vaucouleurs während der Hauptverkehrszeiten zu umfahren.
- In Zusammenarbeit mit dem Straßenamt muss eine Lösung erarbeitet werden, die aber die Wege der Anwohner*innen nicht behindert.

PARKEN

Das Parken stellt kein großes Problem dar. Punktuelle Überschreitungen, wie z. B. das Parken auf dem Platz, rechtfertigen nicht, spezifische gestalterische Eingriffe vorzunehmen. Eher sollten die Besitzer*innen der falsch geparkten PKWs darüber informiert werden, dass sie die Straßenverkehrsordnung missachten.

4.
RESTFLÄCHE IM NORDEN DES PLATZES

Diese Fläche gehört der SNCF und dient als Zufahrt für Autos, die über die rue de Bègles zum Fortbildungszentrum wollen. Außerdem erschließt sie den Verteiler von Gaz de Bordeaux.

Es handelt sich in Anbetracht seiner starken Aneignung durch die Anwohner*innen zum Parken um einen wichtigen Raum.

1. SNCF bleibt Eigentümer
Es wäre wünschenswert, dass der Bodenbelag, den die Anbieter (Gaz de Bordeaux und Lyonnaise des Eaux) bei kürzlich erfolgten Arbeiten aufgerissen haben, wiederhergestellt würde.

2. Die Stadt Bordeaux kann das Grundstück (teilweise?) erwerben.
Wenn die Fläche weiterhin als Parkplatz genutzt werden soll, dann müsste der Boden vollständig erneuert und asphaltiert werden, und der Bürgersteig entlang des Platzes zu den Parkplätzen weitergeführt werden.

Der Baum muss erhalten bleiben.

5.
DER GLASCONTAINER

Er muss sowohl für die Leerung als auch für die Instandhaltung einfach zugänglich sein. Sein jetziger Standort scheint die Anwohner*innen nicht zu stören. Dennoch könnte eine Verschiebung um einige Meter in die Flucht der Bäume dafür sorgen, dass er beim Betreten des Platzes visuell nicht so stark hervorsticht. Eine simple Markierung auf dem Boden wäre hilfreich, um einen permanenten Stellplatz festzulegen.

6.
DIE LINDEN

Jeden Frühling „weinen" die 18 Linden zwei Monate lang, was die Nutzung der Bänke darunter stark einschränkt.

Dieses Problem sollte gemeinsam mit dem Grünflächenamt untersucht werden, um mögliche Behandlungen für die Bäume zu finden.

7.
GEMEINSCHAFTSLEBEN

Bis vor kurzem wurden auf diesem Platz noch jährlich Johannisfeuer veranstaltet [In ganz Frankreich werden rund um den 21. Juni zu Ehren Johannes des Täufers Feuer entzündet. Dieser Brauch fällt mit alten heidnischen Bräuchen zur Feier der Sommersonnenwende zusammen.]

Aus Sicherheitsgründen wurde das Feuer auf dem Platz unterbunden.

Es wäre interessant, dieses Fest wiederaufleben zu lassen, um den Anwohner*innen im Rahmen einer Veranstaltung eine Möglichkeit der Begegnung auf dem Platz zu geben (gemeinsames Essen auf dem Platz im Sommer, Event mit Wiedererkennungswert, Feier).

Conclusion from Lacaton & Vassal's rePort

Place Léon Aucoc acts as a village square – through its location, the people who frequent it, and its architecture. It evokes the atmosphere of small squares typically found in villages in the southwest of France with their characteristic sycamore trees. It does not bear the markers of an artificially designed, overly planned urban environment. The people know each other well, and many of them work for SNCF. The architecture is simple and well-organized, despite being built during two different time periods. It is a beautiful example of both residential architecture and social, collective housing.

The square, which is covered with compacted gravel, is perfectly framed by a granite border and the asphalt road. The ground's material is more akin to earth than stone, further accentuating the rural aesthetic. Its surface is softer than traditional pavement or stone, enabling different activities such as ball games or boules. Additionally, the permeable ground cover eliminates the need for tree grates.

The square is beautiful because of the coherence of all its elements when viewed together. It is authentic. It is perfectly appropriate. A sense of harmony and calm has developed over many years. People seem to feel at home here.

This place is fragile. It is a delicate space where equilibrium prevails, and a few minor inconveniences do not necessitate significant intervention. We believe it calls for a sensitive approach that prompts a shift in attitude. We asked ourselves whether the square should be remodeled for the purpose of beautification. But this square is already beautiful. There are no signs of decay. There is no need for a fundamental change. What does the term "beautification" refer to? Does it entail replacing one type of paving for another, updating a wooden bench with a more contemporary stone design, or substituting a conventional streetlamp with a more fashionable alternative?

There is no need for beautification here because the quality of the square stems from its authenticity and simplicity. Quality, charm, and vitality are already present. The solution must therefore be practical and efficient. We believe that carrying out maintenance works and implementing specific functional changes are appropriate to enhance the square's usability, fulfill the residents' needs, and demonstrate the City of Bordeaux's commitment to this neighborhood.

Text:
Lacaton & Vassal

ProPosed Program

1.
ONGOING MAINTENANCE:
CLEANING THE PAVEMENT

Regular removal of dog excrement (generally not attributable to residents' dogs) and addressing the dog owners directly.

This particular issue is a nuisance that greatly hampers the use of the square.

Consistent and frequent interventions are crucial to demonstrate the City of Bordeaux's presence and concern for this square and its neighborhood.

2.
REPAIR OF GRAVEL PAVING

Supply of fresh gravel and recompaction of the surface.

3.
ELIMINATION OF PARASITIC
AND HAZARDOUS TRAFFIC

- New traffic signage.
- Reversal of traffic direction around the square.
- Installation of speed bumps.
- The goal is to eliminate the direct route that allows drivers to bypass the traffic light at the intersection of rue de Bègles and rue de Vaucouleurs during rush hour.
- A solution must be found in collaboration with the road department that does not impede the daily travel of local residents.

PARKING

Parking is self-organized without major problems. Isolated violations like parking on the square do not justify specific design interventions. Rather, the owners of the improperly parked cars should be informed that they are in violation of the law.

4.
RESIDUAL SPACE NORTH OF
THE SQUARE

This space belongs to SNCF and is used for cars accessing the training center from rue de Bègles. It also provides access to the Gaz de Bordeaux gas distributor.

It is an important space given its heavy use by local residents for parking.

1. The SNCF retains ownership of it.
It would be desirable to restore the pavement that the gas and water providers excavated during their recent work there.
2. The City of Bordeaux can acquire (part of?) the land.
If parking is retained, it is recommended to resurface the entire area with asphalt and extend the sidewalk along the front of the parking lot.

It is crucial to ensure the preservation of the tree.

5.
GLASS RECYCLING CONTAINER

The glass recycling bin must be easily accessible for both emptying and maintenance. Although its current location does not seem to bother the residents, relocating it a few meters into alignment with the trees could help to reduce its visual prominence upon entering the square. Adding a distinct mark on the ground indicating the bin's designated spot would be beneficial.

6.
LINDEN TREES

Every spring, the 18 linden trees "weep" sap for two months, severely restricting the use of the benches underneath them.

This problem should be studied in collaboration with the parks department to find possible treatments for the trees.

7.
COMMUNITY LIFE

Until recently, bonfires for Fête de la Saint-Jean were held in this square. [Throughout France, bonfires are lit around June 21 to commemorate the birth of the Catholic Saint John the Baptist. It coincides with the old pagan rite of celebrating the summer solstice.—Ed.]

For safety reasons, this celebration was discontinued.

It would certainly be interesting to revive this practice to give residents an occasion to meet on the square in the context of a specific event (shared meal on the square in summer, namesake event for the square, party).

Interboro
mit
with
Center for Justice Innovation, Patterson Houses Neighborhood STAT Team, Richard A. Chance, Coco McPherson

Patterson Houses

Contested Maintenance

DE

Die Patterson Houses in der New Yorker Bronx bieten bezahlbare Sozialwohnungen für 4.460 Bewohner*innen. Eigentümer und Betreiber der 1950 erbauten Siedlung ist die New York City Housing Authority (NYCHA), die größte öffentliche Wohnungsbaugesellschaft der USA. Seit den Anfängen der staatlichen Wohnungsbauprogramme in den 1930er-Jahren setzten die US-Behörden in erster Linie auf den Bau moderner Hochhaustypologien, die vergleichsweise komfortablen, gepflegten und großzügigen Wohnraum boten. Doch Hochhaussiedlungen mit Aufzügen, Müllschluckern und Grünflächen sind mit einem hohen Wartungsaufwand verbunden. Seit die US-Bundesregierung in den frühen 1970er-Jahren die Mittel für den öffentlichen Wohnungsbau zugunsten privater Wohnbauförderung drastisch gekürzt hat, spart die NYCHA an der Instandhaltung. Selbst notwendige Reparaturen wurden immer wieder aufgeschoben, Rasenflächen eingezäunt oder asphaltiert.

Während auf der einen Seite die Instandhaltung der Wohnanlagen systematisch vernachlässigt wird, herrscht andererseits dort seit den 1990er-Jahren eine Strategie, die Ordnung durch Überwachung und Disziplinierung aufrechterhalten soll. Flutlichter, Überwachungskameras und Maschendrahtzäune sind seitdem allgegenwärtig. Dieser gefängnisartigen Umgebung stellt das gemeinnützige Center for Justice Innovation mit seinem Projekt Neighborhood Safety Initiatives einen anderen Ansatz öffentlicher Sicherheit entgegen, der auf die Stärkung der Gemeinschaft und die Handlungsmacht der Bewohner*innen setzt, ihr Wohnumfeld selbst zu gestalten und zu pflegen. Unter anderem wurden Gemeinschaftsflächen und Gärten angelegt, für die jeweils Anwohner*innen als *Stewards* Verantwortung tragen. Gemeinsam mit dem Center for Justice Innovation und den Bewohner*innen der Patterson Houses entwickelte das Planungs- und Architekturbüro Interboro mehrere Interventionen zur Erweiterung und Aufwertung der Gemeinschaftsflächen der Siedlung.

2023
Installation
Mixed media

EN

The Patterson Houses in the Bronx, New York, provide affordable housing for 4,460 residents. The development, which was built in 1950, is owned and operated by the New York City Housing Authority (NYCHA), the largest US public housing agency. Since the inception of federal housing programs in the 1930s, US housing authorities have primarily opted to construct modernist high-rise typologies that at the time embody comfortable, well-serviced, and spacious places to live, raise families, and build communities. However, high-rise developments with elevators, garbage chutes, and shared green spaces require a high level of maintenance. Following the federal government's decision in the early 1970s to drastically cut funding for public housing in favor of private housing subsidies, "low-maintenance" has been NYCHA's overriding dogma. Even basic repair work has been consistently deferred; lawns are fenced off or replaced by asphalt surfaces.

Since the 1990s, this low-maintenance approach has been overlaid with a landscape of policing designed to "maintain" and discipline—the strategy relies on ubiquitous floodlights, surveillance cameras, and chain-link fences. Neighborhood Safety Initiatives, a program of the nonprofit Center for Justice Innovation, has countered this carceral landscape with a different approach to public safety, focusing on strengthening the community as well as the residents' own agency in designing and maintaining their environment. Among other measures, community spaces and gardens were created, for each of which residents act as stewards. Together with the Center for Justice Innovation and the residents of Patterson, planning and architecture practice Interboro has co-designed several interventions to enhance the development's communal spaces.

Text:
Interboro

Materialien aus den Archiven der New York City Housing Authority (NYCHA) dokumentieren die Geschichte der Instandhaltung der Patterson Houses und die sich wandelnden Beziehungen zwischen der Wohnungsbehörde und den Mieter*innen. Ein Großteil der Archivaufnahmen zeigt Instandhaltungsarbeiten, die die NYCHA offiziell in Auftrag gegeben hat. Auf einer Reihe von Werbefotos aus dem Jahr 1959 sind beispielsweise uniformierte Reinigungskräfte zu sehen, die Aufzüge säubern, Wege kehren und Müll einsammeln.

Visual material from the archives of the New York City Housing Authority (NYCHA) documents the history of maintenance at the Patterson Houses and the shifting relations between the housing authority and the tenants. Most of the archival photographs celebrate officially sanctioned forms of maintenance. For example, a set of promotional images from 1959 depicts uniformed maintenance workers cleaning elevators, sweeping paths, and collecting trash.

Um den Bewohner*innen mehr Eigenverantwortung zu übertragen (und Wartungsarbeiten an sie zu delegieren), initiierte die NYCHA 1962 das Tenant Garden Program. Es sollte die Mieter*innen dazu animieren, kleine Gärten in der Siedlung anzulegen und zu pflegen, „als wüchsen sie im Hof eines kleinen Hauses", so das Handbuch zum jährlichen Blumengartenwettbewerb, der Teil des Programms war.

Hoping to instill a greater sense of agency (and outsource some maintenance work to tenants), NYCHA launched the Tenant Garden Program in 1962. The program encouraged residents to plant and maintain small gardens at their housing development "just as though they were growing in the yard of a small house," according to the Annual Flower Garden Competition Manual, which accompanied the program.

Angesichts zunehmenden Instandhaltungsbedarfs und sinkender finanzieller Mittel lagerte die NYCHA diese Arbeiten in den 1970er-Jahren immer weiter aus. 1973 wurden beispielsweise jugendliche Mitglieder der Black Spades, einer aktivistischen Community-Initiative und Straßengang, eingeladen, Freiwillige zusammenzutrommeln, um die Graffiti an den Patterson Houses zu übermalen.

In the 1970s, the NYCHA faced an increase in maintenance needs and a decrease in funding, which it sought to solve through outsourcing. For example, in 1973, it invited teenage members of the Black Spades, a community activist organization and street gang, to round up volunteers to paint over graffiti at the Patterson Houses.

Das Projekt Neighborhood Safety Initiatives setzt seit den 2010er-Jahren auf die Stärkung der Gemeinschaft und die Handlungsmacht der Bewohner*innen, ihr Wohnumfeld selbst zu pflegen. Vier Gärten sind über die Verschönerung hinaus zu wichtigen Orten geworden, an denen Informationen geteilt, die Community organisiert und Aktivismus betrieben wird.

Since the 2010s, the program Neighborhood Safety Initiatives has focused on strengthening the community and the residents' own agency in maintaining their environment. Four gardens have evolved into vital hubs for information, community engagement, and social activism, extending beyond their initial purpose of beautification.

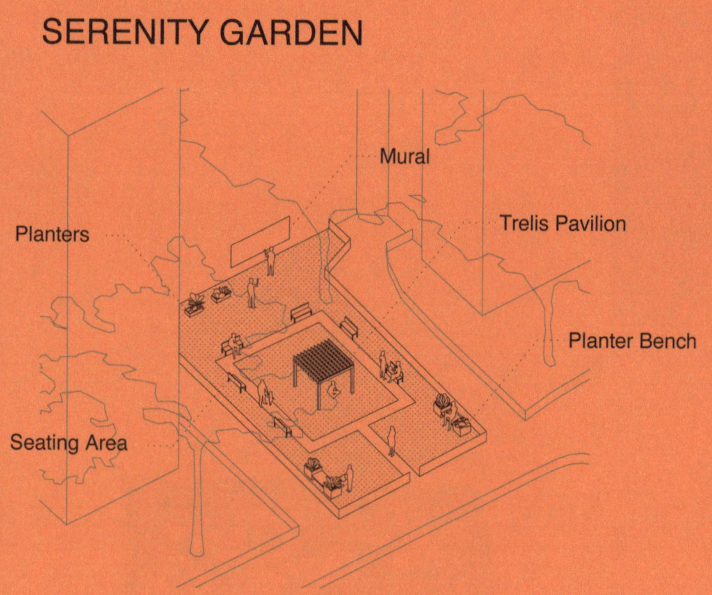

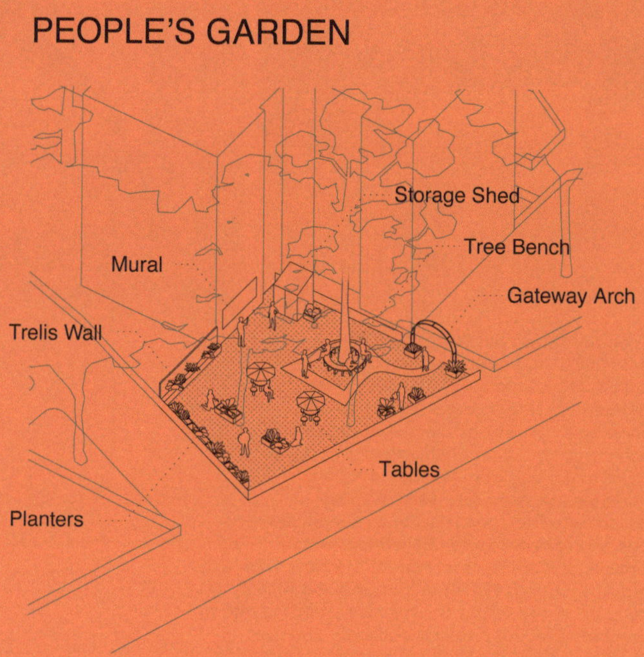

Towana Dunam, die seit 21 Jahren in der Siedlung wohnt, kümmert sich um den Serenity Garden, einen Ort der Ruhe, inneren Einkehr und des Gedenkens in einer Gegend mit hohem Drogenkonsum und viel Jugendgewalt.

Towana Dunam, a Patterson resident of 21 years, cares for the Serenity Garden. Situated in an area plagued by intravenous drug use and youth violence, this garden serves as a sanctuary of peace, contemplation, and remembrance.

Carmen Cheeseboro lebt seit 50 Jahren in den Patterson Houses und macht den People's Garden zu einem Ort, an dem Menschen jeden Alters zusammenkommen können, um zu kochen, zu feiern oder einfach nur um die Mittagspause hier zu verbringen.

Carmen Cheeseboro is a Patterson resident of 50 years. As the caretaker of the People's Garden, she has created a space that welcomes people of all ages to come together for cookouts, celebrations, or simply to have lunch.

OUR GARDEN

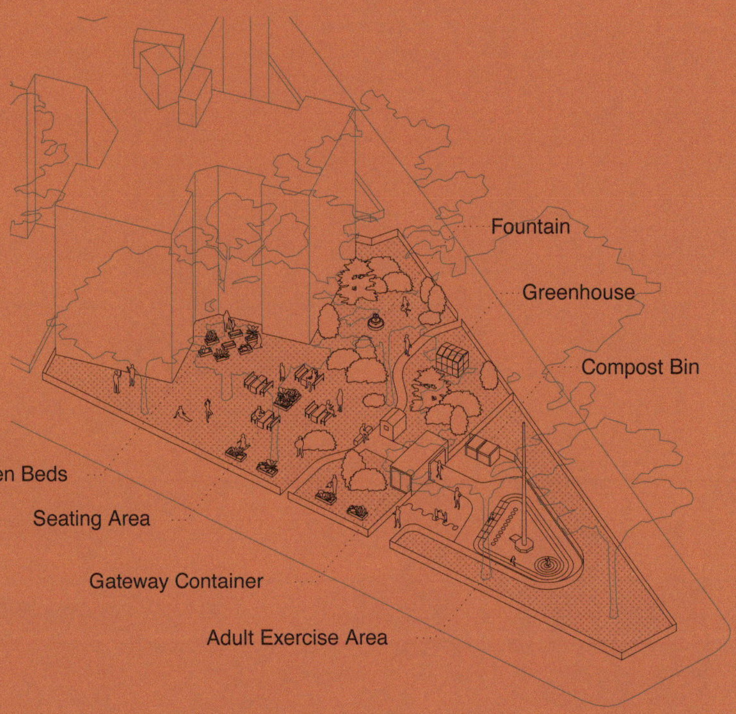

CHILDREN'S GARDEN

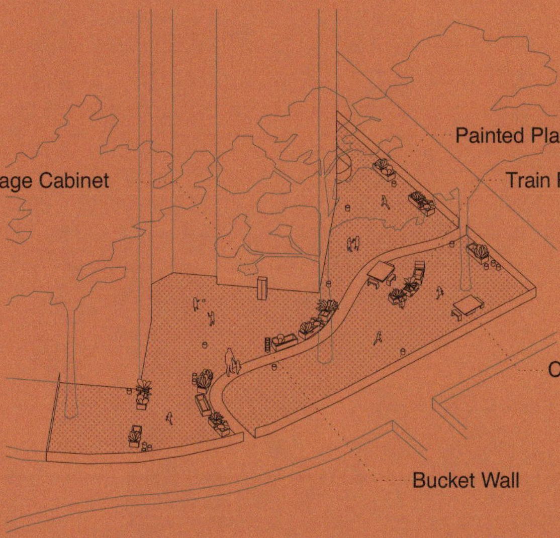

Tabitha Torres lebt schon ihr ganzes Leben in den Patterson Houses. Sie sorgt dafür, dass der Children's Garden sauber und sicher ist, damit jüngere Kinder dort ohne Bedenken spielen und an Bastelworkshops teilnehmen können.

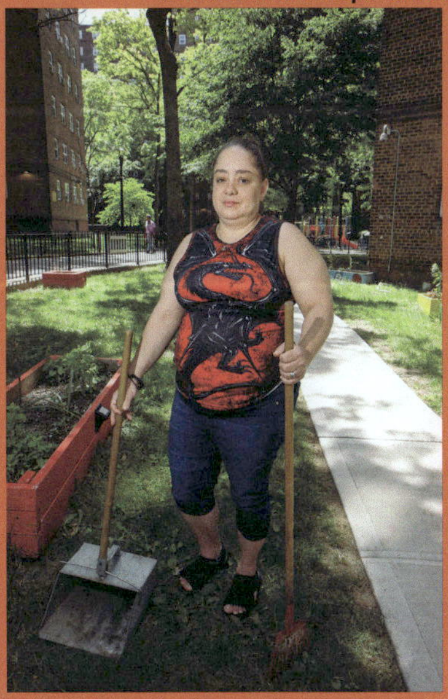

Tabitha Torres is a lifelong Patterson resident. She maintains a clean and safe environment where younger children can come together outdoors and participate in arts and crafts activities.

Eric Murray, der Our Garden betreut, wohnt seit 23 Jahren in der Siedlung. Er hatte bemerkt, wie Erwachsene aus der Community von der Polizei belästigt wurden, weil sie auf Geräten von Kinderspielplätzen trainierten. Daraufhin installierte Eric in seinem Garten eine Freiluft-Fitnessanlage, die von allen genutzt werden darf.

Eric Murray, steward of Our Garden, is a Patterson resident of 23 years. After noticing that adult neighbors were being hassled by the police for exercising on children's playground equipment, Eric set up a dedicated outdoor gym in his garden for the whole community to use.

Richard A. Chance, ***A Visual History of Contentious Maintenance at the Patterson Houses***, 2023
Digitale Zeichnung, Druck auf Fensterfolie
Digital drawing, print on window foil
180 × 600 cm
Das Bild illustriert die sich über die Zeit verändernden Instandhaltungspraktiken in den von der New York City Housing Authority erbauten Patterson Houses in der Bronx.
The mural is an illustrated timeline of changing maintenance practices at the New York City Housing Authority's Patterson Houses in the Bronx.

ZAS* (Zürcher Arbeitsgruppe für Städtebau)

Triemli Files

DE

Im Rahmen einer neuen Gesamtplanung für das öffentliche Stadtspital Triemli in Zürich wurde 2003 beschlossen, drei Hochhäuser aus dem Jahr 1969 abzureißen, die ursprünglich als Personalwohnhäuser gedient hatten. Anfang 2023 sollten die 15-stöckigen Betontürme rückgebaut werden, ohne dass klar war, wodurch sie ersetzt werden sollten. Doch seit dem Abrissbeschluss vor 20 Jahren beweisen vielfältige Zwischennutzungen das Potential der gut erhaltenen Struktur. Als ZAS* 2021 vom bevorstehenden Abbruch erfuhr, hinterfragte das rund 20-köpfige Kollektiv junger Architekt*innen im Austausch mit anderen Architekt*innen, Medien, Stadtverwaltung, Parlament und Bürger*innen die Gründe für den Abriss und entwickelte alternative Visionen für die Türme.

Angesichts des akuten Wohnungsmangels in Zürich bieten die drei Türme dringend benötigten Raum für unterschiedliche Nutzungen: In die Stadt ziehende Studierende fanden schnell ein Zuhause, ein Altersheim eine temporäre Ersatzunterkunft und Menschen aus der Ukraine Schutz nach ihrer Flucht vor dem Krieg. Aufbauend auf diesen Nutzungen rief ZAS* in Eigeninitiative einen spekulativen Ideenwettbewerb für die Zukunft der Triemli-Türme aus. Grundidee war, die 750 Zimmer als städtische Hotel-Infrastruktur zu verstehen: als öffentliches Angebot für Menschen in unterschiedlichen Lebenssituationen, für kurze oder längere Zeit. 45 Vorschläge für die Um- und Weiternutzung der Anlage wurden eingereicht und anschließend in einer öffentlichen Jurierung, einer Ausstellung und einem Online-Archiv präsentiert. Alle liefern Argumente gegen einen „Abbruch auf Vorrat". Inzwischen wurde der geplante Abriss vorerst aufgeschoben, eine zehnjährige Verlängerung der Zwischennutzung wird diskutiert. Die Aushandlung um die Zukunft der Triemli-Türme geht weiter.

2023
Installation
Mixed media
Mit Unterstützung der Schweizer Kulturstiftung Pro Helvetia
With support of the Swiss Arts Council Pro Helvetia

EN

In 2003, new general plans for Triemli Hospital, a public municipal hospital in Zurich, included demolishing three high-rise buildings from 1969, which previously served as staff housing. The 15-story concrete towers were supposed to be bulldozed in early 2023, although it was not clear what was to replace them. Since the decision to demolish the buildings was made 20 years ago, various interim uses have, however, proven the potential of the well-preserved structures. When ZAS* (Zurich Working Group for Urban Planning) learned of the buildings' impending demolition in 2021, the collective of around 20 young architects took an interest. They questioned why the demolition had been planned in the first place and developed alternative visions for the towers' reuse in dialogue with other architects, the media, the city administration, the cantonal legislature, and citizens.

In light of the acute housing shortage in Zurich, the three towers provide urgently needed space for a variety of uses: easy-access housing for university students new to the city, a temporary location for a retirement home, and shelter for people fleeing the war in Ukraine. Building on these uses, ZAS* took the initiative to launch a speculative competition focused on the future of the Triemli towers. The underlying idea was to understand the towers' 750 rooms as a municipal hotel infrastructure providing a public service for short or long periods of time for people in different circumstances. A total of 45 proposals for the transformation and adaptive reuse of the complex were submitted, publicly juried, and presented in an exhibition and online archive. The proposals all provide arguments against the idea of demolition for its own sake. For now, the demolition has been postponed, and a ten-year extension of the towers' interim use is under discussion. Negotiations about the future of the Triemli towers continue.

Text: ZAS*

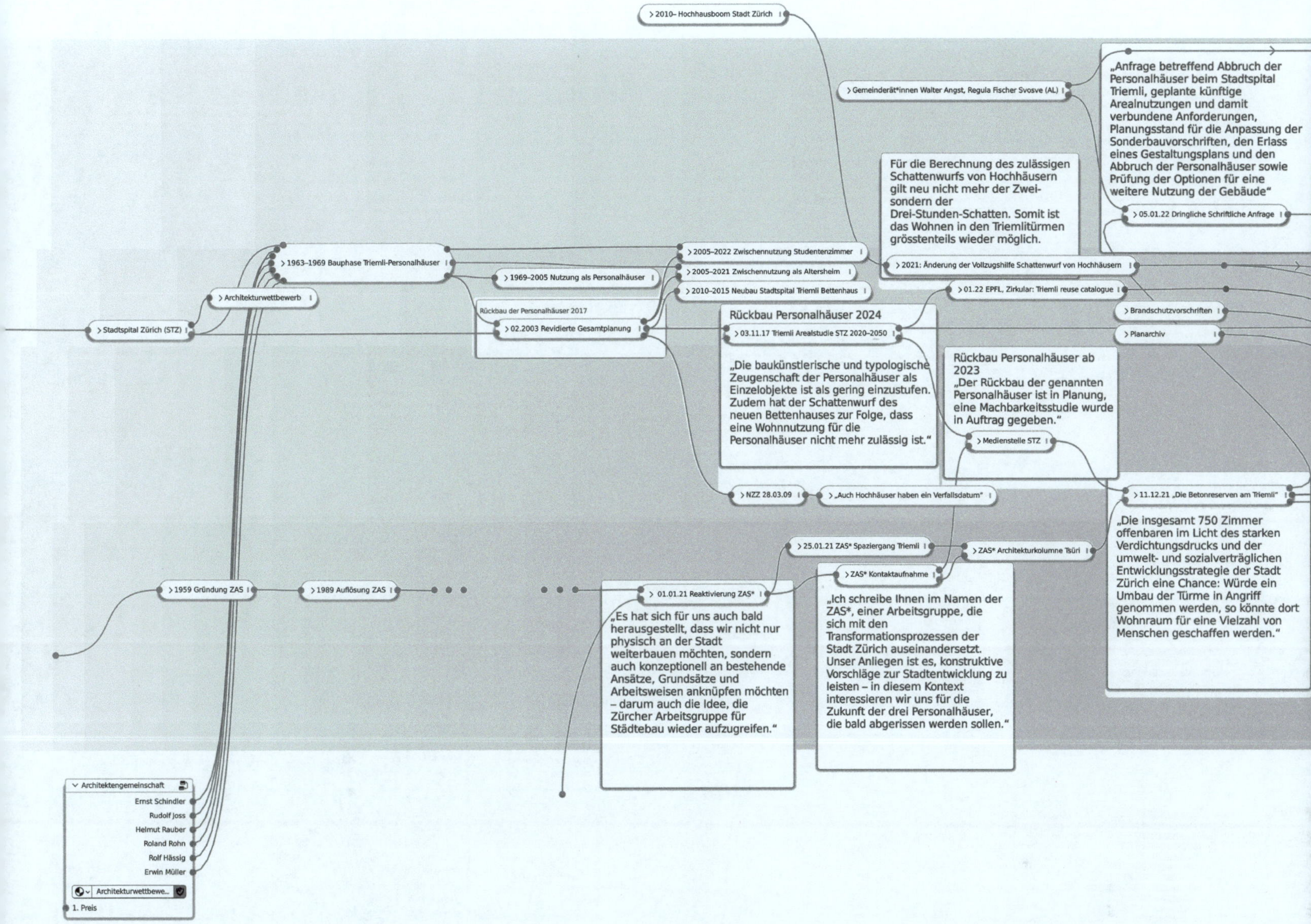

In den drei Hochhäusern von 1969 war ursprünglich das Personal des Zürcher Triemli-Spitals untergebracht. Nach einer neuen Gesamtplanung für das Krankenhaus war für Anfang 2023 der Abriss der Türme vorgesehen. Der Stadtrat argumentierte dabei unter anderem mit dem Schattenwurf eines neugebauten Bettenhauses auf die Türme, der deren Wohnnutzung unzulässig mache.

The three high-rises built in 1969 formerly served as accommodations for the staff of Zurich's Triemli Hospital. A new general plan for the hospital included demolishing the towers in early 2023. The city council argued, among other things, that the shadow cast onto the towers by a newly constructed ward would make their residential use inadmissible.

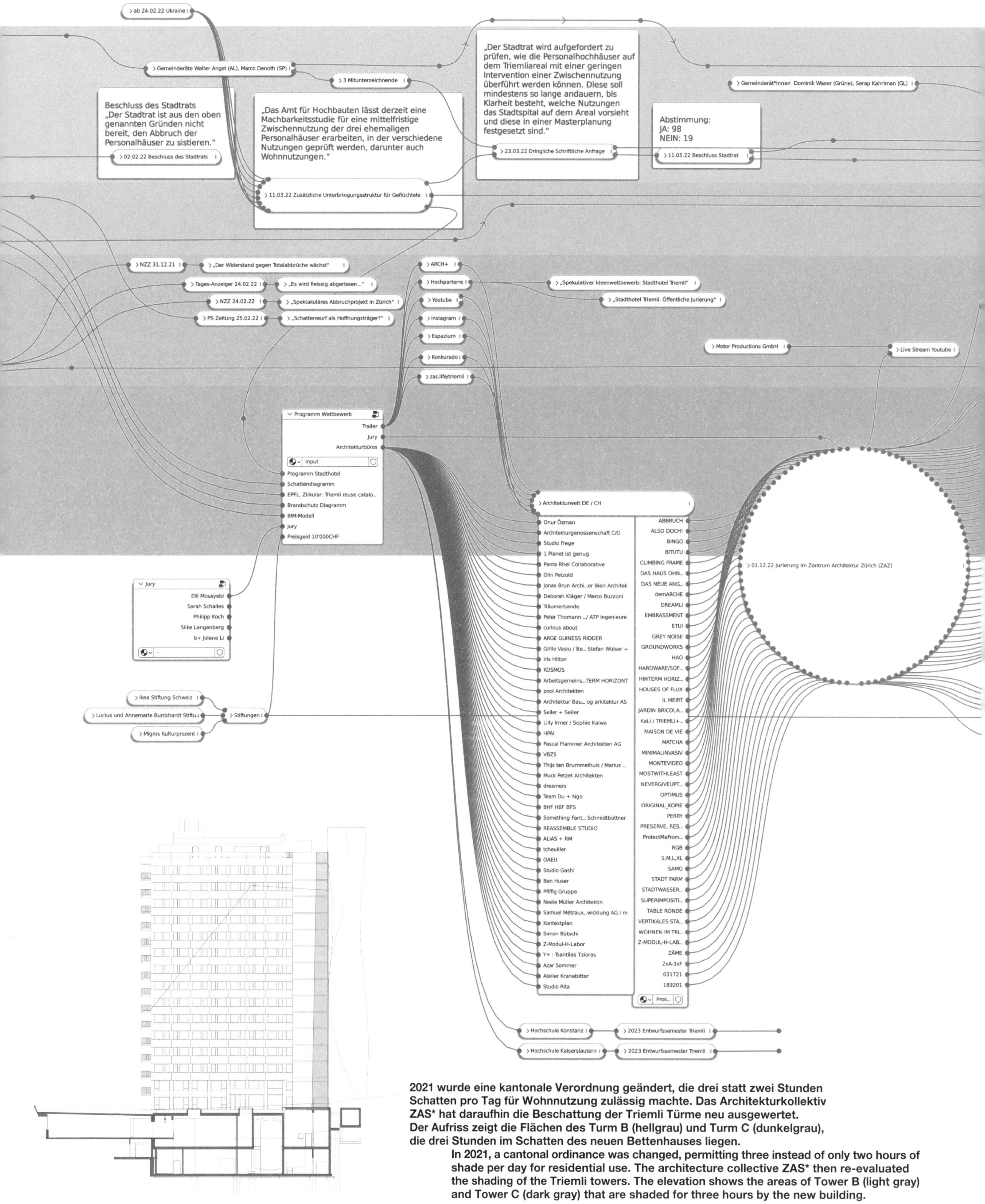

2021 wurde eine kantonale Verordnung geändert, die drei statt zwei Stunden Schatten pro Tag für Wohnnutzung zulässig machte. Das Architekturkollektiv ZAS* hat daraufhin die Beschattung der Triemli Türme neu ausgewertet. Der Aufriss zeigt die Flächen des Turm B (hellgrau) und Turm C (dunkelgrau), die drei Stunden im Schatten des neuen Bettenhauses liegen.

In 2021, a cantonal ordinance was changed, permitting three instead of only two hours of shade per day for residential use. The architecture collective ZAS* then re-evaluated the shading of the Triemli towers. The elevation shows the areas of Tower B (light gray) and Tower C (dark gray) that are shaded for three hours by the new building.

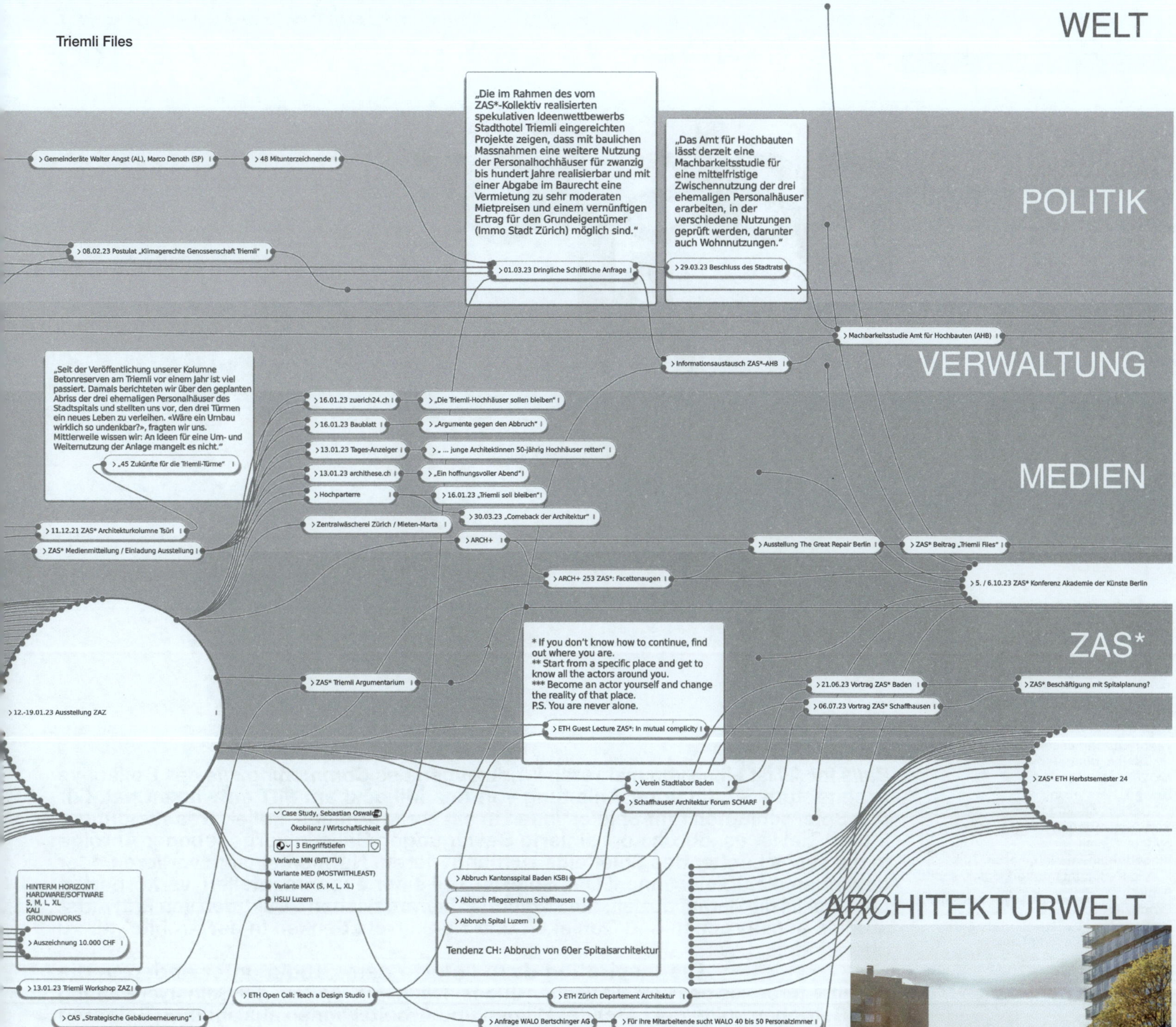

Der Abriss der Triemli-Türme konnte bislang verhindert werden. In der Morgensonne werfen die spiegelnden Fassadenpaneele des neuen Bettenhauses das Licht zurück auf die ehemaligen Personaltürme. Foto: Anne Morgenstern, 2023

So far, the demolition of the Triemli towers has been prevented. In the morning sun, the new ward's mirrored facade panels reflect light onto the tower formerly accommodating staff. Photo: Anne Morgenstern, 2023

Bis zur punktierten Linie im Diagramm werden die Türme zwei Stunden lang durch das Bettenhaus beschattet, bis zur durchgezogenen Linie drei Stunden lang. Nach der Berechnung von ZAS* haben 86 % der Fassaden weniger als 3 Stunden Schatten und könnten somit auch für Wohnzwecke genutzt werden.

Up to the dotted line in the diagram, the towers are shaded by the new ward for two hours, up to the solid line for three hours. According to calculations by ZAS*, 86 % of the facades have less than 3 hours of shade and could therefore also be used for residential purposes.

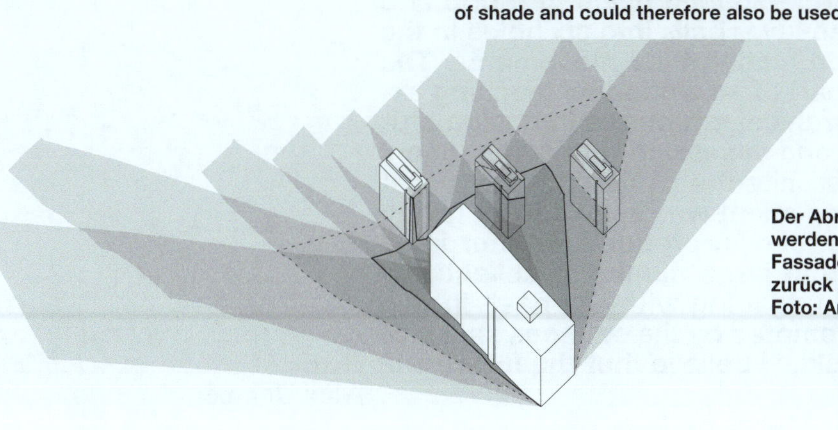

Collective Architecture Studio, Ana Miljački

Balls for All

2019
Textil, Durchmesser
Textile, diameter
ca. 200 cm
Design, Herstellung
Design, sewing
Stratton Coffman, Sarah Wagner, Sydney Cinalli
Videodokumentation, Farbe, Ton
Video documentation, color, sound
6 min
Produziert von
Produced by
Critical Broadcasting Lab
Gefilmt und editiert von
Shot and edited by
Jabari Canada
Dank an
Thanks to
Ous Abou Ras, Sloan Aulgur, Justin Brazier, Mara Jovanović, Angela Loescher-Montal, Luka Moreau, Pearl Willmer-Shiles, Calvin Zhong
2023
Produktion Ausstellungsbeitrag
Production exhibition contribution
Ana Miljački, Mara Jovanović, Jabari Canada

DE

Balls for All ist eines von mehreren Werkzeugen des *Commoning*, die das Collective Architecture Studio unter Anleitung von Ana Miljački am MIT entwickelt hat. Für das Spiel schlüpfen fünf Spieler*innen in ein kreisförmiges, kollektives Kleidungsstück. Ziel ist es, durch koordinierte Bewegungen Bälle in vorgegebener Abfolge in die sechs Löcher des Spielfelds zu manövrieren. Nur gemeinsam verlieren oder gewinnen die Spieler*innen. Das Spiel ist Teil einer experimentellen, verkörperten Lehrpraxis, die darauf abzielt, die traditionell hierarchischen Strukturen von Entwurfsstudios aufzubrechen und Geniekult und Konkurrenzdenken in der Architektur zu überwinden.

Die Inspiration dazu lieferte dem Studio unter anderem die Architekturpraxis des sozialistischen Jugoslawien. Ein System der Selbstverwaltung von Betrieben sollte dort Architekt*innen und Arbeiter*innen aus anderen Sektoren mehr Kontrolle über die Produktion geben. In kollektiver Autor*innenschaft entstanden in großem Maßstab preiswerte Wohnungen in Kollektiveigentum und Selbstverwaltung der Bewohner*innen. Die kritische Auseinandersetzung mit der Vergangenheit eröffnet hier neue Möglichkeitshorizonte für die Zukunft. „Angesichts der bedrohlichen Aussichten für unseren Planeten“, ist sich Ana Miljački sicher, „werden wir die Zukunft entweder kollektiv gestalten oder es wird keine Zukunft geben.“

EN

Balls for All is one of several *commoning devices* developed by the Collective Architecture Studio at MIT under the guidance of Ana Miljački. For this game, five players slip into a circle-shaped piece of fabric and wear it as a collective garment. Their goal is to maneuver balls into six holes in the playing field in a predetermined sequence by coordinating their movements. The players either win or lose together. *Balls for All* is part of an embodied teaching experiment that seeks to dismantle traditional hierarchical structures in design studios. It challenges architecture's cult of the genius and obsession with competition.

The studio was inspired by the architectural practice of socialist Yugoslavia, where a system of workers' self-management was established, giving architects and workers in other sectors more control over production. Affordable and collectively designed housing was produced in large numbers, collectively owned and self-managed by residents. Critically engaging with the past, in this respect, opens new possibilities for the future. “Prompted by the ominous shape of our planet's future prospects,” asserts Ana Miljački, “I believe that the future will be collective, or it won't be.”

Text:
Alex Nehmer

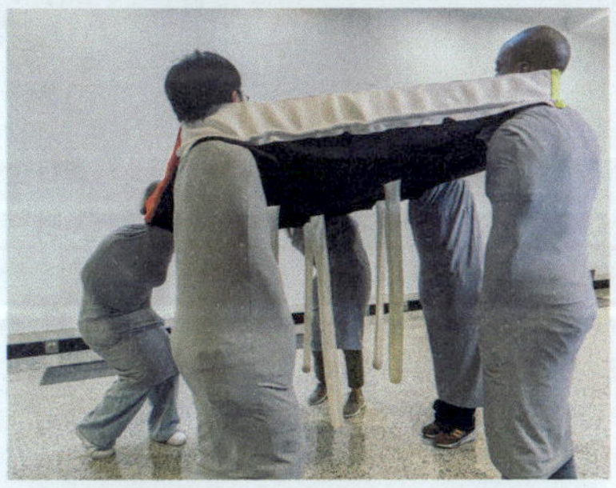

Stills aus einem Video, das *Balls for All* im Einsatz dokumentiert.

Stills from a video documenting *Balls for All* in use.

Realisiert von

Realized by

Ana Miljački, Mara Jovanović, Jabari Canada

für die Ausstellung

for the exhibition

The Great Repair, 2023

Das Spiel *Balls for All* wurde 2019 von Sydney Cinalli, Stratton Coffman und Sarah Wagner, Mitgliedern des Collective Architecture Studio, unter der Leitung von Ana Miljački am MIT produziert. Es wurde in Belgrad in der Galerie Kolektiv aktiviert.

Balls for All is a game produced in 2019 by Sydney Cinalli, Stratton Coffman, and Sarah Wagner, members of the Collective Architecture Studio at MIT led by Ana Miljački. It was activated in Belgrade at the gallery Kolektiv.

Zu den Studiomitgliedern gehörten

Studio participants included

Rodrigo Cesarman, Sydney Cinalli, Stratton Coffman, Boliang Du, Gabby Heffernan, Ben Hoyle, Eytan Levi, Catherine Lie, Yutan Sun, Marisa Waddle, Sarah Wagner, Ana Miljački

United Voices of the World – Section of Architectural Workers (UVW-SAW)

The Office

DE

Willkommen im Büro. Vielleicht sieht es ein bisschen aus wie deins. Du bist im Architektursektor beschäftigt; das Büro ist, wenn du Glück hast, 40 Stunden in der Woche dein Zuhause. Vielleicht gibt es in dem Büro, für das du arbeitest, teure ergonomische Stühle, vielleicht gibt es unbegrenzt Obst, vielleicht ist es seit 2019 eine Ecke deiner Wohnung, vielleicht wird dir das Abendessen bezahlt, wenn du länger als bis 22 Uhr arbeitest. Das Büro hält dich nachts wach; es ermüdet und entmutigt dich. Das ist seine Natur. Aber das ist auch das Material, aus dem wir ein neues Haus bauen werden, mit neuen Werkzeugen.

Unter der kalten Arbeitsbeleuchtung des Büros sitzen du und deine Kolleg*innen zwischen halb zugeschnittenen, blauen Schaumstoffblöcken und Mustern von Bodenbelägen, die niemals das Licht der Welt erblicken sollten. Ihr seid Sachbearbeiter*innen, Assistent*innen, Angebotskoordinator*innen, BIM-Manager*innen, Reinigungskräfte, Bauarbeiter*innen, Bauzeichner*innen, Dokumentenkontrolleur*innen, Modellbauer*innen, Planer*innen, Rezeptionist*innen, Bauleiter*innen, Techniker*innen, Visualisierer*innen und Architekt*innen. Zusammen könnt ihr auf jahrzehntelange Erfahrung zurückblicken. Einige von euch sind wahrscheinlich miteinander befreundet und einige von euch haben vielleicht schon überlegt, wie (anders) ihr zusammen ein Büro leiten würdet, wenn ihr bloß mit geerbtem Wohlstand gesegnet wärt. Der Trick des Büros besteht darin, das Geheimnis seines Fundaments zu verbergen: deine Arbeitskraft. Vielleicht hast du schon einmal danach gesucht, an deinem Schreibtisch, am Wasserspender, in den Toilettenpausen, die du damit verbracht hast, dank.lloyd.wright, zu reposten.

Willkommen in unserem Büro. Auch wenn es ein bisschen wie bei euch aussieht, lehnen wir es ab, dass wir an manchen Tagen erst morgens um 2 Uhr Feierabend machen sollen, oder dass es einen Gehaltsunterschied von 3.500 Euro zwischen dir und deinem weißen Kollegen gibt, oder dass Aufträge mit ausufernden Kohlenstoffbudgets angenommen werden. Die Gespräche vom Mittagessen darüber, wie wir Entlassungen verhindern oder die Chefetage zu sozialem Wohnungsbau bewegen, führen wir in unserem Büro weiter. Seit 2019 stärken wir uns gegenseitig und bündeln unsere kollektive Kraft in einer Gewerkschaft für Architekturarbeiter*innen – nicht nur Architekt*innen, sondern all jene, die für die Produktion von Architektur gebraucht werden – um ausbeuterische Institutionen von Grund auf neu zugestalten.

2023
Installation
Mixed media

EN

Welcome to *The Office*. Maybe it looks a little bit like yours. You are an architectural worker; *The Office* is your home for 40 hours a week, if you are lucky. Maybe *The Office* you work for has expensive ergonomic chairs, maybe there is unlimited fruit, maybe it has been the corner of your apartment since 2019, maybe they treat you to dinner if you work past ten p.m. *The Office* keeps you up at night; it leaves you tired and uninspired. This is its nature. However, this is also the material from which we will build a new house, with new tools.

Underneath *The Office's* white task lighting, between half-cut blocks of blue foam and samples for flooring that should never see the light of day, you and your fellow architectural workers sit. You are administrators, assistants, bid coordinators, BIM managers, cleaners, construction workers, draftsmen and women, document controllers, model makers, planners, receptionists, site inspectors, technicians, visualizers, and architects. You have decades of experience between you. Some of you are probably friends, some of you might have thought about how (differently) you would run a practice together if only you were born blessed with generational wealth. The great trick of *The Office* is hiding the secret of its foundation: your labor power. You might have looked for it in the past, at your desk, over the water cooler, on toilet breaks spent reposting from dank.lloyd.wright.

Welcome to *Our Office*. While it might look a bit like yours, in *Our Office*, we reject the idea that there are days when you clock out at two in the morning, that there is a 3,500 euros pay difference between you and your white male coworker, that we take on the project with the seemingly endless carbon budget. *Our Office* extends those lunchtime chats on how to fight the layoffs or how to sway the boss towards social housing. Since 2019, we have been empowering each other, consolidating our collective strength in a union of architectural workers—not only architects but all those necessary to produce architecture—to remodel exploitative institutions from the ground up.

Text:
United Voices of the World – Section of Architectural Workers

MEMBER'S GUIDE 2022

section of architectural workers

UNITED VOICES OF THE WORLD

WHY DO WE NEED A UNION?

The Workers' Inquiry: Architecture (WI:A) industry-wide surveys identified the main issues architectural workers face today:

overwork, pay, unstable employment, toxic office/studio culture, and ethics

Recognising that RIBA and ARB have little interest to address these issues, it was necessary to build a worker-led movement to fight poor working conditions. We joined the radical and grassroots trade union United Voices of the World (UVW), forming a new section for architectural workers in Sep 2019.

SHOULD YOU UNIONISE?

YES! We have to thank unions for some of our basic employment rights, but we need to unionise today to ensure those rights are met and improved!

anyone that goes to work and who cares about their pay and conditions needs a union.

You don't need to have a problem to join. Statistics show that workplaces that are unionised have higher than average working conditions, employees are paid better and are less likely to have issues in the future.

WHAT IS UVW-SAW?

UVW-SAW is a trade union of people working in the architectural sector.

we organise against the harmful impacts of architectural work on us as workers, but also on communities and the environment.

We organise around discriminatory & toxic working conditions directly as workers, not as a third party so that the demands we make and actions we take lead to lasting positive and inclusive change. As part of UVW, we learn from other branches that have historically been known to be unionisable.

WHO IS SAW FOR?

SAW is for anyone operating in the architecture industry who is not a boss.

architectural assistants, BIM/CAD technicians, cleaners, architects, interior designers, security guards, model makers, landscape architects, visualisers, students, educators, researchers, graphic designers, administrators, planners, IT staff, you!

Membership rates correspond to your monthly gross income from £3 - £10 per month. Those not eligible can still support SAW through the Solidarity Network.

HOW WE WORK

We organise. Organising means building the capacity within your own workplaces to take the collective action that will improve your working conditions and create the everlasting change you want.

it is our responsibility to share power, to listen to other voices, and to respect those without structural authority.

We operate in a democratic and non-hierarchical structure. We make decisions through consensus, through open dialogue and a voting system.

UVW-SAW STRUCTURE

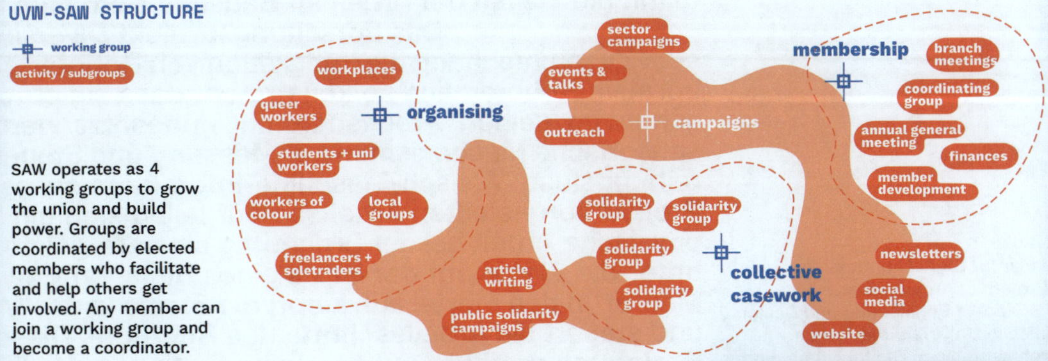

SAW operates as 4 working groups to grow the union and build power. Groups are coordinated by elected members who facilitate and help others get involved. Any member can join a working group and become a coordinator.

GET INVOLVED!

Your active participation will ensure we are all able to sustainably build collective power and change the sector.

HIGH PARTICIPATION IS A PREREQUISITE TO POWER

New members and solidarity members are always welcome, whatever your capacity, skills, or experience. Join an open branch meeting to find out more.

DON'T KNOW WHERE TO START?

How about start with step 1 and work your way up to 7! Or mix it up a bit, it's up to you. If you are unsure email saw.membership@uvwunion.org.uk

1. **Make some noise online @uvw_saw**
2. **Participate in branch meetings**
3. **Join as a member today!**
4. **Speak to your colleagues**
5. **Organize a workplace branch**
6. **Form a local/regional branch**
7. **Join the coordinating group**

UVW-SAW

JOIN TODAY!

Leitfaden für Mitglieder der Gewerkschaft United Voices of the World – Section of Architectural Workers (UVW-SAW), 2022

Member's guide issued by the Section of Architectural Workers of the trade union United Voices of the World (UVW-SAW), 2022

Lidia Atanasova,
Kathrin Dörfler

Diversifying Construction

DE

Die Trennung der Architektur vom Handwerk seit der Renaissance ging mit einer Privilegierung der geistigen gegenüber der körperlichen, der immateriellen gegenüber der materiellen Arbeit einher. „Die für den Bau verantwortlichen Personen wurden de facto degradiert und ihre Arbeit wurde nun mittels neuer Techniken des ‚Denkens, Zeichnens und Modellbaus' von einem anderen, sozial besser gestellten Berufsstand ferngesteuert",[1] so der Architekturtheoretiker Douglas Spencer. Wenn wir heute die Architekturpraxis mit ihren Ungleichheiten „reparieren" wollen, müssen wir uns vor allem mit dieser Arbeitsteilung in der Architektur auseinandersetzen.

Ein erster Schritt in diese Richtung wäre, jene Menschen wertzuschätzen und zu fördern, deren Kenntnisse und Fähigkeiten für die Errichtung und Erhaltung der Bausubstanz entscheidend sind. Die geringe Wertschätzung des Handwerklichen im Bausektor spiegelt sich in einer geringeren finanziellen Vergütung wider und macht das Berufsfeld für junge Menschen unattraktiv. Das hat zu einem Mangel an qualifizierten Arbeitskräften und einem Rückgang der Weitergabe grundlegenden handwerklichen Wissens geführt. Oft wird die Automatisierung als Lösung für diese Probleme angepriesen, doch die Erfahrung seit der Industrialisierung des Bauens hat gezeigt, dass der vollständige Ersatz menschlicher Arbeitskraft durch Maschinen nicht nur technisch unrealistisch ist, sondern auch die Gefahr des Deskilling sowie der Entfremdung der Beschäftigten im Bausektor birgt. Allerdings können wir die technologische Entwicklung nicht negieren und zu einer idealisierten handwerklichen Vergangenheit zurückkehren. Stattdessen gilt es, die heutigen Technologien für eine Emanzipation aller am Bau Beteiligten einzusetzen. So könnten technologische Fortschritte genutzt werden, um die Zusammenarbeit zwischen Menschen und Maschinen zu erleichtern und die Arbeitsbedingungen zu verbessern, damit die Vielfalt der Arbeit im Bausektor erhalten bleibt.

Das Forschungsprojekt *Diversifying Construction* erprobt in diesem Zusammenhang die Integration von Robotertechnologien auf Baustellen. Kollaborative Roboter sind so konstruiert, dass sie ergonomisch und sicher neben Menschen im selben Arbeitsbereich eingesetzt werden können. Sie verfügen über sensorische Mechanismen zur Messung und Steuerung der Kraftausübung, um eine reibungslose Mensch-Maschine-Interaktion zu gewährleisten. Bei dem in diesem Projekt vorgestellten Arbeitsablauf teilen sich ein Roboter und ein*e Maurer*in die physische Arbeit bei der Errichtung einer Ziegelsteinkonstruktion. Während der Roboter die Ziegel auf der Basis eines digitalen Entwurfsmodells platziert, bringt die Maurer*in den Mörtel auf, klopft die Steine in das Mörtelbett, reinigt die Mörtelfugen und steuert die Arbeitsschritte des Roboters. Diese kollaborative Mensch-Roboter-Beziehung profitiert auf der einen Seite von der Fähigkeit des Roboters, Aufgaben beliebig oft zu wiederholen, räumlich mit äußerster Präzision zu funktionieren und große Datenmengen verarbeiten zu können, und auf der anderen Seite von der Flexibilität, Geschicklichkeit und den Fertigkeiten des Menschen. Ein spezieller Kalkmörtel sorgt dafür, dass der Ziegelverbund und die Kraftübertragung konstant bleiben. Er bietet gleichzeitig die Möglichkeit, das Gebaute zu demontieren und die Ziegel wiederzuverwenden. Während der Demontage klopft die Maurer*in vorsichtig auf den Ziegelstein, um ihn zu lockern und Mörtelreste zu entfernen, während der Roboter ihn für die spätere Verwendung einsortiert.

Ziel des Projekts ist es, eine Diskussion über neue Formen der Zusammenarbeit im Bauhandwerk anzustoßen. Es fragt, wie eine sinnvolle Aufteilung der Aufgaben zwischen Mensch und Maschine aussehen und zur körperlichen Entlastung der auf dem Bau Beschäftigten beitragen kann. Gleichzeitig soll das Projekt eine kritische Reflexion im Hinblick auf die Perspektiven, Grenzen und Risiken in diesem sich fortwährend weiterentwickelnden Bereich anregen.

2022–2023
Professur für Digital Fabrication, Department of Architecture, TUM School of Engineering and Design, Technische Universität München
Professorship of Digital Fabrication, Department of Architecture, TUM School of Engineering and Design, Technical University of Munich
Konzept und Design
Concept and design
Lidia Atanasova, Kathrin Dörfler
Maurerin
Mason
Julia Ohlmeyer
3D Human Motion Capturing
Simon Schäfer, Stefan Leutenegger
Video und Schnitt
Video and editing
Moritz Heinrich
Video
Farbe, Ton
Color, sound
5 min

1

EN

Since the Renaissance, architecture has been distinguished from craft, privileging intellectual over physical labor, and immaterial over material labor. As architectural theorist Douglas Spencer argues, "Effectively deskilled, those responsible for construction found their labor remotely directed, through newly invented techniques of 'thinking, drawing and model-making,' by a professional class assuming superior status over them."[1] To "repair" the inequalities of architectural practice today, it is crucial to specifically address this division of labor within the sector.

A first step in this direction is to appreciate and empower those who possess essential expertise and skills critical for constructing and maintaining our built environment. The diminished status of craftsmanship within the construction industry is reflected in lower pay and lack of allure for the younger generation, resulting in a shortage of skilled labor and a decline in the transmission and preservation of invaluable craft knowledge. While automation is often promoted as the solution to these issues, industrialized construction has shown that wholly replacing human labor with machines is not only technically infeasible but also risks further deskilling and alienating construction workers. However, we cannot deny technological developments and regress to an idealized artisanal past. Instead, we must use today's technologies to emancipate all those involved in construction. Technological innovation can be used to foster collaboration between humans and machines, improving working conditions and preserving the multifaceted nuances of construction work.

In this context, the research project *Diversifying Construction* explores the integration of robotic technologies into construction sites. Collaborative robots are engineered to operate ergonomically and safely alongside humans within the same workspace. They are equipped with sensory mechanisms for measuring and controlling force to ensure a smooth human-machine interaction. The workflow presented in this project involves a mason and a collaborative robot sharing the physical labor required to construct a brick structure. While the robot places bricks based on a digital design model, the mason adds the mortar, taps the bricks into place, cleans the mortar joints, and triggers robot tasks. Together, they form a human–robot partnership leveraging the machine's capacity for repetitive tasks, spatial precision, and large-data processing, combined with the human's ingenuity, dexterity, and skills. A special lime mortar is used to maintain the brick bond and force transmission while enabling the dismantling of the structure and the reuse of the bricks. During disassembly, the mason gently taps the bricks to loosen them and clears residual mortar while the robot retrieves the bricks for future reuse.

This project aims to spark a discussion on new modes of collaboration in the fields of skilled and unskilled labor in the construction sector. It asks how human–robot collaboration could help sensibly distribute tasks and provide physical relief for construction workers. It also invites critical reflection on the prospects, limitations, and potential setbacks in this evolving landscape.

2

1 Douglas Spencer: „Arbeit, Produktion und der Zweck der Architektur", in: *ARCH+* 251: *Unternehmen Architektur* (März 2023), S. 26–33, hier S. 31
Douglas Spencer, "Arbeit, Produktion und der Zweck der Architektur," *ARCH+* 251, *Unternehmen Architektur* (March 2023): 26–33, here 31.

Text:
Lidia Atanasova,
Kathrin Dörfler

1
Während der Roboter die Ziegelsteine auf der Grundlage eines digitalen geometrischen 3D-Modells setzt, bringt die Maurer*in den Mörtel auf, schlägt die Ziegel in das Mörtelbett und reinigt die Fugen. Mensch und Roboter bilden so eine kollaborative Einheit, die von der Präzision des einen und der Flexibilität und Erfahrung des anderen profitiert.
The robot places the bricks according to the geometry of a digital 3D model, while the mason applies the mortar, taps the bricks into place, and cleans the joints. The human–robot collaboration leverages robotic precision combined with human ingenuity and experience.

2
Dieser Roboter, der an der TUM School of Engineering and Design der Technischen Universität München entwickelt und als Prototyp gebaut wurde, ist so programmiert, dass er auf der Baustelle mit Handwerker*innen zusammenarbeitet und sie bei der Ausführung der physischen Aufgaben unterstützt, die für den Bau einer Mauerwerksstruktur erforderlich sind.
This collaborative robot was designed and prototyped at the TUM School of Engineering and Design at the Technical University of Munich. It is programmed to work alongside construction workers on-site, supporting them with the physical tasks necessary to build a brick structure.

Charlotte
Malterre-Barthes

A Global Moratorium on New Construction

1) STOP BUILDING

2) HOUSE EVERYONE

3) CHANGE VALUE SYSTEMS

4) HALT EXTRACTION

5) REVOLUTIONIZE CONSTRUCTION

6) FIX THE OFFICE

7) REFORM THE SCHOOL

8) DON'T DIG

9) TAKE CARE

DE

A Global Moratorium on New Construction ist Ergebnis eines Forschungsprojekts, das die Architektin, Theoretikerin und Aktivistin Charlotte Malterre-Barthes 2020 an der Harvard GSD durchführte. Angesichts der ausbeuterischen Praktiken – sowohl in ökologischer als auch sozialer Hinsicht –, mit denen multinationale Unternehmen vor allem im Globalen Süden Material für die Bauindustrie gewinnen, regt Malterre-Barthes zu einem Gedankenspiel an: Was wäre, wenn das Bauen für eine gewisse Zeit gänzlich ausgesetzt würde und die Disziplin sich in dieser Zwangspause neu orientierte?

EN

A Global Moratorium on New Construction emerged from a research project by the architect, theorist, and activist Charlotte Malterre-Barthes at Harvard GSD in 2020. After identifying the ecologically and socially exploitative nature of how multinational corporations acquire materials for the construction industry, particularly in the Global South, she proposed a thought experiment: What if all construction were temporarily halted, allowing the discipline to reorient itself during this mandatory pause?

Never Build, Never Demolish?

DE

Dass Bauen nicht nur die Lösung, sondern auch die Ursache drängender Probleme darstellt, ist keine neue Erkenntnis. Schon während des mittlerweile legendären internationalen Architekturtheorie-Kongresses, zu dem der Dekan der Architekturfakultät Oswald Mathias Ungers 1967 an der TU Berlin geladen hatte, entrollten Studierende vor hunderten Zuhörer*innen das Transparent „Alle Häuser sind schön, hört auf zu bauen".[1] Wenige Jahre später stemmten sich Bewohner*innen der kaputten Mietskasernen in West-Berlin durch Instandbesetzungen gegen die Kahlschlagsanierung der Altbauquartiere, die neuen Infrastrukturbauten und funktional vom Rest der Stadt abgeschnittenen Wohnkomplexen weichen sollten.[2] Die Praxis der Instandbesetzung wurde im Zuge der Internationalen Bauausstellung 1984/87 legalisiert und löste ein neues Paradigma im Umgang mit der Stadt aus: die sogenannte „behutsame Stadterneuerung". Instandbesetzungen sind somit ein wichtiger Bezugspunkt der großen Reparatur, nicht zuletzt, weil sie in ihrem Widerstand gegenüber Abriss und mit der Reparatur des Bestands durch Selbsthilfe auch ein soziales und politisches Projekt waren.

Wie bereits der Planungsdirektor der IBA Berlin Hardt-Waltherr Hämer bei der behutsamen Stadterneuerung argumentierte der Wirtschaftswissenschaftler Daniel Fuhrhop in seinem von 2013 bis 2021 betriebenen Blog *Verbietet das Bauen*[3], dass Abriss für einen Entwickler finanziell nur interessant sei, wenn die Mieten oder Kaufpreise danach stiegen, Abriss also ein Instrument der Spekulation und Finanzialisierung sei. Zudem mache man sich etwas vor, wenn man alte Gebäude durch gut gedämmte Neubauten ersetze, erzeuge doch der gesamte Wohnungsneubau eines Jahres in Deutschland „ähnlich viele Treibhausgase wie die Nutzung sämtlicher 43 Millionen Altbauwohnungen".[4] In Frankreich regte kürzlich der Architekt Raphaël Ménard an zu prüfen, ob Neubau für den dringend erforderlichen bezahlbaren Wohnraum überhaupt notwendig sei oder ob nicht genügend Raum im Bestand zur Verfügung stehe, der sich adaptieren ließe.

1
Hartmut Frank: „Alle Häuser sind schön, hört auf zu bauen!", in: *Stadtbauwelt*, 74. Jg., Nr. 80 (1983), S. 343

2
Es soll nicht unerwähnt bleiben, dass auch konservative Intellektuelle die Zerstörung der Stadt monierten. So legte Wolf Jobst Siedler 1964 in seinem Buch *Die gemordete Stadt* eindrucksvoll dar, mit wie vielen Verlusten die Geschichte Westberlins verbunden ist. Im Jahr 2000 präsentierte der von Siedler beeinflusste damalige Senatsbaudirektor Hans Stimmann im Deutschen Pavillon der Architekturbiennale von Venedig Schwarzpläne, die das Projekt der Kritischen Rekonstruktion der Innenstadt von Berlin untermauern sollten. Besonders suggestiv war jene Karte, die den großflächigen Abriss zwischen 1953 und 1989 zeigte. Wie bei Siedler war auch hier die Aussage, dass die Moderne einen besonders ausgeprägten Zerstörungsfuror in sich trägt, was dann bei Stimmann allerdings dazu führte, die modernen Hinterlassenschaften zu beseitigen, um das Verlorene zumindest als Bild zurückzuholen. Philipp Oswalt hat das die doppelte Negation genannt, die Zerstörung mit einer Zerstörung und Rekonstruktion rückgängig zu machen.

3
Die Inhalte des Blogs flossen 2015 in das gleichnamige Buch und fünf Jahre später in eine erweiterte Neuauflage mit dem Untertitel *Streitschrift gegen Spekulation, Abriss und Flächenfraß*, München 2020. Wichtige Referenzen für Fuhrhop waren dabei Rudolf Schilling: *Rückbau und Wiedergutmachung* –

EN

The insight that building is not a solution but rather a cause of urgent problems in our world is not new. Already in 1967, during Oswald Mathias Ungers's storied *Architecture Theory* conference at Berlin's Technical University, architecture students unfurled a banner in front of hundreds of attendees that read: *Alle Häuser sind schön, hört auf zu bauen* (All buildings are beautiful; stop building more).[1] A few years later, residents of West Berlin's run-down apartment buildings resisted the slash-and-burn redevelopment of their historical neighborhoods by squatting and maintaining them instead of caving to authorities' plans to replace with new infrastructure and functionalist housing estates.[2] This practice of *Instandbesetzung* (a portmanteau of *Instandsetzung*, the German word for maintenance, and *Besetzung*, squatting) was legalized by Berlin's International Building Exhibition of 1984–87, colloquially referred to as IBA '87, catalyzing a new paradigm for approaching the city that became known as *Behutsame Stadterneuerung* (cautious urban renewal). The *Instandbesetzung* movement also serves as an important point of reference for *The Great Repair*, not least because its opposition to demolition and campaign for repairing the existing building stock according to principles of self-help made it an inherently social and political project.

Just as Hardt-Waltherr Hämer, planning director of IBA '87, advocated for sensitive urban renewal, so has economist Daniel Fuhrhop engaged the topic on the blog *Verbietet das Bauen* (Ban Building), which he ran from 2013 to 2021. Fuhrhop argues that demolition only becomes financially attractive for a developer when rents or sales prices increase afterward; in other words, demolition is fundamentally an instrument of financial speculation.[3] Furthermore, he asserts that it is a delusion to think that replacing old buildings with well-insulated new ones is, in terms of greenhouse-gas emissions, a net positive, since the combined

1
Hartmut Frank, "Alle Häuser sind schön, hört auf zu bauen!," *Bauwelt* 48 / *Stadtbauwelt* 80 (1983), 354–58.

2
It should not go unmentioned that conservative intellectuals also express regret over the destruction of cities. For example, in his 1964 book *Die gemordete Stadt* (The Murdered City), Wolf Jobst Siedler gave a powerful portrait of the losses associated with West Berlin's history. At the Venice Architecture Biennale in 2000, Berlin's Building Director Hans Stimmann, influenced by Siedler, presented figure-ground diagrams in the German Pavilion meant to undergird his project of a *Kritische Rekonstruktion* (critical reconstruction) of central Berlin. Especially suggestive was a map depicting the large-scale demolitions undertaken between 1953 and 1989. As with Siedler, Stimmann believed that modernism carries an inherent destructive impulse. He was therefore determined to remove the built legacy of modernism to recover what had been lost—at least as an image. German architecture theorist Philipp Oswalt has described this as a double negation: undoing destruction through further destruction and reconstruction.

3
The blog's content was incorporated into a book of the same name in 2015, and five years later into an expanded new addition

Was tun mit dem gebauten Kram?, Basel/Boston, 1987 und Günther Moewes: *Weder Hütten noch Paläste – Architektur und Ökologie in der Arbeitsgesellschaft. Eine Streitschrift*, Basel/Boston 1995

4 Daniel Fuhrhop: „Wissenschaft", www.daniel-fuhrhop.de (Stand: 6.6.2023)

5 Siehe *A Global Moratorium on New Construction*, stopconstruction.cargo.site (Stand: 6.6.2023)

6 Siehe www.bda-bund.de/2019/08/das-haus-der-erde_bda-position (Stand: 6.6.2023)

7 „Offener Brief an die Bauministerkonferenz", www.architects4future.de/portfolio/publikationen/offener-brief-an-die-bauministerkonferenz (Stand: 6.6.2023)

DE

Ähnlich wie die Studierenden 1967 unterstreicht Charlotte Malterre-Barthes in ihrem „Global Moratorium on New Construction" von 2021, dass Bauen heute ökologische und soziale Ungerechtigkeit erzeuge (und nicht löse), und fordert, die Zukunft mit dem zu gestalten, was vorhanden ist: ohne Abbruch alter Gebäude und ohne den Bau von neuen.[5]

Auch in Positionspapieren von Verbänden und Vereinen tauchen solche Vorstöße zunehmend auf, etwa in „Das Haus der Erde – Positionen für eine klimagerechte Architektur in Stadt und Land" vom Bund Deutscher Architektinnen und Architekten von 2019. Danach solle das Bauen „vermehrt ohne Neubau auskommen" und „dem Erhalt und dem materiellen wie konstruktiven Weiterbauen des Bestehenden" Priorität zukommen vor „dessen leichtfertigem Abriss".[6]

2022 forderte ein auf Initiative des Architekturhistorikers und Journalisten Alexander Stumm verfasster offener Brief an die Bundesministerin für Wohnen, Stadtentwicklung und Bauwesen Klara Geywitz (SPD) ein Moratorium auf Abriss. Eine Genehmigungspflicht für Gebäudeabrisse, die bislang nur in Berlin – und dort auch nur für Wohnungsbau – besteht, ist dabei die Hauptforderung. Genau mit dieser trat der Verein Architects 4 Future in seinen „Vorschlägen für eine Muster(um)bauordnung" bereits 2021 an die Bauminister*innen in Bund und Ländern heran: Der Abriss von Gebäuden solle immer einer Genehmigung bedürfen. Erteilt werden dürfe diese nur nach Nachweis, dass die Klimaneutralität eines Gebäudes durch Sanierung nicht zu erreichen sei oder wenn soziale Gründe dafür sprächen.[7]

Zahlreiche Stimmen wiederholen geradezu gebetsmühlenartig, dass Abriss, Versiegelung und Neubau nicht unsere Zukunft sein können. Diese seit langem geltenden Prämissen der Architektur und Stadtplanung müssen einer neuen Baukultur und neuen ökonomischen Bedingungen weichen, die extraktivistische Praktiken nicht länger gutheißen. Nur Reden allein wird nicht ausreichen. Nun liegt es an der Politik, auf die Forderungen auch in der Gesetzgebung einzugehen.

EN

annual construction of new buildings in Germany emits "an amount of greenhouse gases equivalent to all 43 million existing residential units."[4] In France, architect Raphaël Ménard recently proposed investigating whether new buildings are even necessary to meet our urgent need for affordable housing, or if there is enough space in the existing building stock to be adapted for the purpose.

The *Global Moratorium on New Construction*, an initiative launched by Charlotte Malterre-Barthes in 2021, echoes the students from 1967 by arguing that current building practices are a cause of ecological and social injustice and not a solution to it. Malterre-Barthes calls for architects to start designing for the reuse and care of the existing building stock rather than demolishing old buildings and constructing new ones.[5]

Proposals of this nature are also increasingly common in policy papers issued by associations and organizations, such as "Planet Home: Towards a Climate-Friendly Architecture in City and Country" published by the Association of German Architects (BDA) in 2019.[6] The paper argues that the discipline should increasingly "make do without new construction" and that "priority should be given to the preservation and development of existing [buildings] rather than their frivolous demolition."

In 2022, at the initiative of architecture historian and journalist Alexander Stumm, an open letter addressed to Klara Geywitz, Germany's Federal Minister for Housing, Urban Development, and Building, called for a moratorium on demolitions. One of its central demands was that building demolitions should require an official permit. This is currently only the case in Berlin, where the requirement only applies to residential buildings. This same demand was made in 2021 by the German-based association Architects for Future in their "Recommendations for a Model (Re)Building Code," addressed to all 17 responsible ministers at the German Federal and State levels. They argued along the same lines, adding that a demolition permit should only be granted in case of demonstrable social benefit or if the building cannot possibly achieve net-zero emissions through renovation.[7]

It has virtually become a mantra: voice after voice reiterating that demolition, soil sealing, and new construction cannot be our future. These age-old premises of architecture and urban planning must give way to a new culture of building and new economic conditions in which extractive practices are no longer tolerated. Merely discussing it will not suffice. The responsibility now lies with politicians to meet such demands with legislation.

with the subtitle *Streitschrift gegen Spekulation, Abriss und Flächenfraß* (Pamphlet against Speculation, Demolition, and the – Gobbling of Land) (Munich: oekom Verlag, 2020). Important references for Fuhrhop were Rudolf Schilling, *Rückbau und Wiedergutmachung: Was tun mit dem gebauten Kram?* (Deconstruction and Reparation: What to Do with the Built Stuff?) (Basel: Birkhäuser, 1987) and Günther Moewes, *Weder Hütten noch Paläste: Architektur und Ökologie in der Arbeitsgesellschaft. Eine Streitschrift* (Neither Huts nor Palaces: Architecture and Ecology in the Working Society. A Pamphlet) (Basel: Birkhäuser, 1995).

4 Daniel Fuhrhop, "Wissenschaft," accessed June 6, 2023, www.daniel-fuhrhop.de.

5 See *A Global Moratorium on New Construction*, accessed June 6, 2023, stopconstruction.cargo.site.

6 "Planet Home: Towards a Climate-Friendly Architecture in City and Country," *Association of German Architects*, May 28, 2020, accessed June 6, 2023, www.bda-bund.de/2020/05/planet-home/.

7 "Offener Brief an die Bauministerkonferenz," accessed June 6, 2023, www.architects4future.de/portfolio/publikationen/offener-brief-an-die-bauministerkonferenz.

Text:
Florian Hertweck

Alexander Stumm

Demolition Moratorium

DE

2022 initiierte der Architekturhistoriker und Journalist Alexander Stumm einen offenen Brief an die Bundesministerin für Wohnen, Stadtentwicklung und Bauwesen Klara Geywitz (SPD), der ein Moratorium auf den Abriss von Bestandsgebäuden forderte. Architects 4 Future, der Bund Deutscher Architektinnen und Architekten, der NABU-Bundesverband und zahlreiche weitere Institutionen und Expert*innen unterstützen die Initiative.

EN

In 2022 architecture historian and journalist Alexander Stumm initiated an open letter addressed to Klara Geywitz, Germany's Federal Minister for Housing, Urban Development, and Building, calling for a moratorium on demolitions. The push for new policies was supported by the German-based association Architects for Future, the Association of German Architects (BDA), the Nature and Biodiversity Conservation Union (NABU Bundesverband) of Germany, as well as numerous other institutions and experts.

DE

Ein Abriss-Moratorium:

+ aktiviert die großen Potenziale im Bestand und bereits versiegelter Flächen für die Schaffung der von Ihnen avisierten 400.000 neuen Wohnungen jährlich. Erhalt, Sanierung, energetische Verbesserung, aber auch Aufstockungen, Erweiterungen und die Anpassung an zukünftige Nutzungsanforderungen sind konstruktive Antworten auf die Wohnungsfrage.

+ nutzt den Gebäudebestand als wirksames Mittel gegen Energie- und Klimakrise. Es bewahrt und verwendet die im Material gespeicherte graue Energie. Außerdem vermindert es den Bedarf an energieintensiven und klimaschädlichen Baustoffen wie Beton und Stahl.

+ ist ein Schritt zur Kreislaufwirtschaft. Statt Abriss fördert es die Etablierung von Infrastrukturen für die Wiederverwendung von Bauteilen. In der zirkulären Stadt bedarf es schließlich keiner Deponie mehr.

+ verhindert Gentrifizierung und Verdrängung in Ballungsräumen, die mit Abriss und Neubau oftmals einhergehen, und begegnet so sozialen Spannungen.

+ ist ein Beitrag zur gesellschaftlichen und wirtschaftlichen Transformation. Es steht für die Wertschätzung von Pflege und Reparatur des Bestehenden in seinem ganzen baukulturellen und geschichtlichen Reichtum.

EN

A demolition moratorium:

+ activates the great potential in the existing stock and already sealed areas for the creation of the 400,000 new homes per year you have announced. Preservation, refurbishment, energy improvements, but also additions of new floors, extensions, and adaptation to future use requirements are constructive answers to the housing question.

+ uses the existing building stock as an effective means of combating the energy and climate crisis. It preserves and uses the gray energy stored in the material. It also reduces the need for energy-intensive and climate-damaging building materials such as concrete and steel.

+ is a step toward the circular economy. Instead of demolition, it promotes the establishment of infrastructures for the reuse of building components. In the circular city, after all, there is no longer any need for landfills.

+ prevents gentrification and displacement in metropolitan areas, which often accompany demolition and new construction, and thus counters social tensions.

+ is a contribution to social and economic transformation. It stands for the appreciation of the care and repair of the existing in all its architectural, cultural, and historical richness.

DE

Die sozialen und ökologischen Auswirkungen einer auf Wachstum, Bodenspekulation und Ressourcenraubbau ausgerichteten Raumproduktion sind verheerend: Landschaften sind zerstört und zersiedelt, Böden versiegelt, das Verkehrsaufkommen steigt kontinuierlich, Wohnraum ist für viele unerschwinglich geworden. Die Forderung nach noch mehr Neubau führt unter klimapolitischen Gesichtspunkten in die Sackgasse. Die Raumproduktion muss daher grundsätzlich neu gedacht werden. Sie muss Instrumente der Umverteilung von Raum entwickeln, dazu zählen: Bestehendes instand zu halten und zu pflegen, die Hinterlassenschaften von autogerechter Stadtgestaltung und Massenkonsumgesellschaft nachhaltig und sozial gerecht umzugestalten und bei notwendigem Um- und Neubau erneuerbare und lokal gewonnene Materialien einzusetzen.

Text:
Florian Hertweck

Reparatur Praktizieren

Practice Repair

EN

The social and ecological impacts of spatial production geared to growth, land speculation, and predatory exploitation of resources are devastating: Entire sections of land are destroyed and consumed by settlements, with a concomitant rise in traffic volume, while living space becomes increasingly unaffordable. From the viewpoint of climate policy, the call for even more new buildings leads us into a cul-de-sac. The production of space must therefore be fundamentally rethought. It must develop instruments for redistributing space, and these will include: maintaining and nurturing what already exists, redesigning the legacy of cities designed for cars and mass consumerism in a sustainable and socially just way, as well as using renewable and locally sourced materials where conversion work or new construction is necessary.

Material Cultures
Bildessay
Photo essay
Jess Gough

Cultivated Landscapes

2023
In Zusammenarbeit mit
In collaboration with
Bauhaus Earth & EXPERIMENTAL
Prototyp, verschiedene biobasierte Materialien, in 2 Teilen
Prototype, various biobased materials, in two parts
260 × 190 × 130 cm, 150 × 150 × 130 cm
Design und Konstruktion
Design and construction
Material Cultures, Bauhaus Earth
Gefördert von
Funded by
EXPERIMENTAL
als Teil des
as part of the
Bauhaus Earth Fellowship Program
Dank an
Thanks to
Buro Happold, Weichert Dachbau, Eileen Dorer Li, Michael Reindel, Gramitherm, Hiss Reet, Stadtforst Prenzlau, Holzindustrie Templin

3 Videos, Farbe, Ton
3 videos, color, sound
Extraction 7 min, *Timber* 5 min, *Straw* 7 min
Produktion
Production
Material Cultures
Schnitt
Editor
Ella Justine Frost
Redaktion
Script editor
Amica Dall
Sprecherin
Voice-over
Kate Handford
Sounddesign
Sound design
Mhamad Safa

DE

Wir, Material Cultures, sind eine gemeinnützige Organisation, die für einen grundlegenden Wandel der materiellen Kultur in der Baubranche eintritt. Mithilfe von Entwurf, Forschung und Bildung zeigen wir die positiven sozialen, ökologischen und wirtschaftlichen Auswirkungen eines regenerativen Ansatzes auf, der auf natürliche Materialien und emissionsarme Bautechniken setzt. Beim Entwerfen planen wir mit effizienten Bauweisen, pflanzlichen und mineralischen Baustoffen, die möglichst wenig verarbeitet sind, und zeitgemäßen Fertigungstechniken. Darüber hinaus erforschen wir, wie diese Ansätze skaliert werden können und – was entscheidend ist – wie sie mit einem allgemeinen Übergang zu einer regenerativen Bodenbewirtschaftung und Kreislaufwirtschaft zusammenhängen.

EN

Material Cultures is a nonprofit organization advocating materials reform in construction. Through design, research, and education, we seek to demonstrate the positive social, ecological, and economic impact of a regenerative approach that is based on natural materials and low embodied carbon construction technology. We design buildings that integrate plant-based materials and minimally processed minerals into efficient construction systems that have been adapted for contemporary fabrication. Alongside this, we carry out strategic research into how these processes and ideas can be applied on a large scale and, crucially, how they relate to a broader transition towards regenerative land management and a circular economy.

Das von Studio Abroad in Zusammenarbeit mit Material Cultures entworfene Block House wurde in Holzrahmenbauweise mit natürlichen Materialien wie lokal gewonnenem Holz, Hanfbetonblöcken und Holzfaserdämmung gebaut. Somerset, Großbritannien, 2021. Foto: Felix Koch

Designed by Studio Abroad in collaboration with Material Cultures, Block House is timber-framed house built using a natural material palette of locally sourced timber, hempcrete blocks, and wood-fiber insulation. Somerset, UK, 2021. Photo: Felix Koch

Boden
Land

Hafen von Anaklia, Georgien
Port of Anaklia, Georgia

DE

Wir Menschen haben Landschaften und Gewässer zerstört und ausgebeutet, um Baumaterialien zu gewinnen und zu verarbeiten. Die Folgen dessen treten immer deutlicher zutage, je weiter wir die Grenzen unserer Ökosysteme ausreizen. Um die Architektur zu transformieren, müssen wir ihren Umgang mit Boden überdenken.

EN

We have ruined and depleted the countryside and the waters by extracting and processing materials for construction. The consequences are becoming more evident as we keep pushing the limits of what our ecosystems can support. Our best hope for renewing architecture is to rethink its relationship to land.

Steinbruch auf Milos, Griechenland
Quarry on Milos, Greece

DE

Unsere derzeitigen Methoden der Bodenbewirtschaftung durch Forst-, Land- und Weidewirtschaft, Ressourcenabbau und -verarbeitung beuten lokale Ökosysteme aus. Monokultureller Anbau und industrielle Landwirtschaft sind in hohem Maße auf petrochemische Düngemittel und Pestizide angewiesen und zerstören damit Biodiversität und Bodengesundheit. Um die von uns benötigten Lebensmittel und Materialien zu gewinnen, ohne unser Ökosystem weiter zu schädigen, müssen wir uns fragen, was das Land und seine Hüter*innen brauchen, um zu gerechteren und regenerativen Strategien für Zugang, Nutzung und Verteilung von Land zu finden.

EN

Our current systems of land management exploit local ecosystems through forestry, agriculture, grazing, dredging, extraction, and manufacturing. Monoculture plantations and industrial agriculture rely heavily on petrochemical fertilizers and pesticides, violently exterminate biodiversity, and consequently degrade soil health. To grow the food and materials we need without damaging our ecosystems further, we must begin by asking what the land and its stewards need and then try and implement more equitable and regenerative approaches to land use, distribution, and access.

Recht auf Land
Access to land

Hafen von Dover, Großbritannien
Port of Dover, UK

DE

Der Zugang zu Land ist überlebenswichtig. Doch er ist gegenwärtig auf diejenigen beschränkt, die über Ressourcen verfügen, was in hohem Maße durch Machtverhältnisse und Ungleichheiten hinsichtlich Geschlecht, *Race* und Klasse bestimmt wird. Von den *Enclosure Acts* (Privatisierung von Allmenden) über die koloniale Expansion bis hin zum heutigen Landraub durch Konzerne hat die Aneignung von Land als Wirtschaftsgut über Jahrhunderte hinweg zur Vertreibung und Enteignung von Menschen und Gemeinschaften geführt. Der Verlust von Landrechten sowie die damit einhergehende globale Zunahme industrieller land- und forstwirtschaftlicher Praktiken haben die Resilienz jener Gemeinschaften, deren Existenzgrundlage einst mit der Bewirtschaftung von Land verzahnt war, unwiderruflich geschwächt.

EN

Access to land is key for survival, and it is currently limited to those who have access to resources, heavily determined by the intersection of gender, race, and class. From the Enclosure Acts (privatization of commons) to colonial expansion, and more recent land grabs by corporations, the appropriation of land as a commercial asset has displaced and dispossessed people and communities for centuries. The loss of access to and rights over land, and the attendant growth of industrial agriculture and forestry practices across the world, have irrevocably diminished the resilience of communities whose livelihoods were once intertwined with land management.

Regenerative Bodenbewirtschaftung
Regenerative land management

Niederwald in New Forest, Großbritannien
Coppiced woodland in New Forest, UK

DE

Regenerative Systeme der Bodenbewirtschaftung wie die Agroforstwirtschaft kommen sowohl der Gesundheit des Bodens als auch den Menschen und nichtmenschlichen Spezies zugute, die für ihr Überleben auf das Land angewiesen sind, da es ihnen Lebensraum, Nahrung und Rohstoffe bietet. Auch nachhaltige Nutzpflanzen wie etwa Hanf können zur Regeneration des Bodens beitragen und den Bedarf an Düngemitteln und Pestiziden verringern.

EN

Regenerative land management systems such as agroforestry allow for a range of different uses that benefit the land as well as the human and non-human species that depend on it for habitat, food, and materials. Sustainable crops such as hemp help to rehabilitate soil and reduce the need for fertilizers and pesticides.

Ziegelei H. G. Matthews Brickworks, Bellingdon, Großbritannien
H. G. Matthews Brickworks, Bellingdon, UK

Regeneratives Bauen
Regenerative construction

DE

Wir können nicht länger mit Materialien bauen, deren Produktion und weite Transportwege hohe Emissionen verursachen. Es wird immer deutlicher, dass wir auf Materialien mit weniger grauer Energie umsteigen müssen: biobasierte Materialien wie Holz, Hanf, Stroh oder Holzfasern, die aus Pflanzen gewonnen werden, die schnell nachwachsen und Kohlenstoff in unseren Gebäuden binden können. Nicht alle im Bausektor verwendeten biobasierten Materialien müssen dabei speziell für diesen Zweck angebaut und geerntet werden, vielmehr können es auch Nebenprodukte, Abfälle aus anderen Herstellungsprozessen oder recycelte Materialien sein.

EN

We cannot continue to build using materials that generate high levels of emissions through their production or by being shipped across great distances. It is increasingly clear that we need to use materials that are lower in embodied carbon: biobased materials such as timber, hemp, straw, or wood fiber, derived from plants which can regenerate sustainably and sequester carbon in our buildings. Not all biobased materials used in construction have to be grown and harvested specifically for that purpose; they can be byproducts, waste from other manufacturing processes, or recycled materials.

Zukünftige Beziehungen
Future relationships

Ehemaliger Steinbruch auf Lipari, Italien
Old quarry on Lipari, Italy

DE

Wir Menschen existieren in einem Netz von Beziehungen. Um unsere Bedürfnisse auf eine Weise zu befriedigen, die unsere Lebensgrundlagen repariert, heilt und erhält, können wir viel von dem Wissen und den Traditionen indigener Gemeinschaften lernen. Die Arbeit mit regenerativen Rohstoffen und das Bauen mit biobasierten Materialien erfordern einen neuen Umgang mit den Jahreszeiten und der Zeit, eine neue Form des Bauens, bei der wir uns nicht länger außerhalb der natürlichen Welt verorten und unseren Platz innerhalb der Ökosysteme erkennen.

EN

We exist within and among a network of relationships. In order to meet our needs in ways that repair, heal, and sustain our economies of life, we can learn a lot from Indigenous knowledge and traditions. Working with regenerative resources and biobased construction demands a different engagement with the seasons and time, a new way of building in which we stop thinking of ourselves as outside of the natural world and recognize our place within its ecosystems.

Text:
Material Cultures

Assemble

Methods of Assembly

DE

Das Entwurfsstudio des Architekturkollektivs Assemble an der EPFL in Lausanne setzt sich für eine nicht-extraktive Architekturproduktion ein, die bei der Rohstoffgewinnung ansetzt und eine beiderseitig vorteilhafte Beziehung zu lokalen Gemeinschaften im Blick hat. In den letzten zwei Jahren hat Assemble mit Studierenden und der Gemeinde Burtigny im Schweizer Kanton Waadt zusammengearbeitet, um Entwurfs- und Baukonzepte zu entwickeln, bei denen lokal verfügbare Materialien, Infrastrukturen und Arbeitskraft zum Einsatz kommen.

Im ersten Jahr des Studios lag der Schwerpunkt auf Holz als vielseitiger natürlicher Ressource. Im Rahmen von Feldstudien untersuchten die Teilnehmenden dabei sowohl den Wald als Ökosystem wie auch Holz als Ressource und Material. Sie besuchten Wälder, Sägewerke und Produktionsstätten und tauschten sich mit Wissenschaftler*innen, Forstverwalter*innen, Zimmerleuten und Ökolog*innen aus, um Möglichkeiten für Architekt*innen auszuloten, heute auf behutsame, intelligente und ressourcenschonende Weise mit Holz zu bauen. Die Studierenden analysierten Beispiele für Holzarchitekturen und entwickelten anschließend eigene Projekte, die sich die gemeindeeigenen Ressourcen wie selbst verwaltete Gärten, Forst und Ackerland zunutze machen. Im darauffolgenden Jahr entwarf das Studio Prototypen, um die Gemeinde in ihren Plänen für den Bau von Genossenschaftswohnungen aus nachhaltigen und lokal verfügbaren Materialien zu unterstützen.

Mit dieser Lehrpraxis trägt Assemble zu einer wachsenden Bewegung bei, die sich gegen Umweltzerstörung und zunehmende Ungleichheit wendet. In der Architektur erfordert dies ein radikales Umdenken in der Art und Weise, wie wir bauen, und insbesondere die Abkehr von den langen, undurchsichtigen Lieferketten des Bausektors. Denn diese verschleiern die Umweltschäden und ausbeuterischen Praktiken, die mit der Verwendung billiger Materialien einhergehen. Vielmehr gilt es, lokale Material- und Produktionsnetzwerke aufzubauen, die transparent, verantwortungsvoll und sozial gerecht sind.

2020–fortlaufend
ongoing
Master und Bachelor Entwurfsstudio an der EPFL in Lausanne
Master and Bachelor design studio at EPFL in Lausanne
Lehre
Teaching team
James Binning, Amy Perkins, Angela Schütz, Camille Sineau

EN

Assemble's design studio at EPFL in Lausanne advocates non-extractive practices in how architects utilize resources and encourages mutually beneficial relationships with local communities. For the past two years, Assemble has worked with students and the Municipality of Burtigny in the Swiss canton of Vaud to develop design and construction approaches that use local materials, infrastructure, and labor.

During the first year, the focus was on one of the most abundant and diverse natural resources—wood. Through field studies, the studio investigated both the forest as an ecosystem and timber as a resource and material. They visited forests, sawmills, and manufacturing sites, and consulted scientists, forest managers, carpenters, and ecologists to explore how architects can carefully, intelligently, and resourcefully practice timber construction today. Students studied examples of timber architecture and developed projects that draw on the municipality's own resources, including self-managed gardens, plantation forests, and farmland. During the subsequent term, the studio worked with the local community to design prototypes for the municipality's plans to build cooperative housing using sustainable and locally available materials.

Through this teaching practice, Assemble contributes to a growing movement countering systemic issues of environmental degradation and increasing inequity. This requires radically reframing how we build, specifically abandoning long, opaque supply chains that obscure the environmental impact and exploitative practices which underpin the use of cheap materials, in favor of local networks of materials and production that are more transparent, accountable, and redistributive.

Text:
Assemble

Baptiste Ansselin, Marine Freneat, Lan Nishiyama, Moises Sanchez, Justine Troillet, Manon Voide, *Rise of the Countryside*, Holzschnitt, 120 × 80 cm, aus der Serie *Future Scenarios*, entstanden im Rahmen des Entwurfsstudios von Assemble an der EPFL, Lausanne, 2022.

Das Entwurfsstudio von Assemble an der EPFL hat in Zusammenarbeit mit der Schweizer Gemeinde Burtigny verschiedene Entwurfs- und Bautechniken erforscht, die eine der wertvollsten lokalen Ressourcen nutzen: Holz. Dazu gehört auch der traditionelle Holzschnitt, der bei der Realisierung einer Serie von künstlerischen Drucken eingesetzt wurde, die Zukunftsszenarien für den ländlichen Raum der Schweiz zeigen.

Baptiste Ansselin, Marine Freneat, Lan Nishiyama, Moises Sanchez, Justine Troillet, Manon Voide, *Rise of the Countryside*, woodblock print, 120 × 80 cm, from the series *Future Scenarios*, produced as part of Assemble's design studio at EPFL, Lausanne, 2022.

Assemble's design studio at EPFL has been working with the municipality of Burtigny in Switzerland to explore various design and construction techniques that make use of one of the most valuable local resources: timber. Among these is traditional woodblock printing, which was employed in the realization of a series of prints depicting possible future scenarios for the Swiss countryside.

Nach Besuchen im Dorf Burtigny, wo sie mehr über die Gewinnung und Verarbeitung von Holz erfuhren, beschäftigten sich die Teilnehmenden mit verschiedenen Baumethoden und entwickelten architektonische Projekte, die die Ressourcen der Gemeinde nutzen.

After visiting the village of Burtigny and learning about the extraction, processing, and manufacturing of timber, studio participants looked at a variety of construction methods and developed architectural projects that draw on the municipality's own resources.

Über die Beschäftigung mit der Holzbauweise hinaus arbeitete das Studio zudem mit der Gemeinde zusammen, um neue Konzepte für den genossenschaftlichen Wohnungsbau zu entwickeln, die für einen ländlichen Kontext wie den von Burtigny geeignet sind.

Beyond its exploration of timber construction, the studio also worked with the local community to develop new concepts for cooperative housing that are suitable to a rural context like that of Burtigny.

Florian Hertweck,
Caroline Faber,
Marija Marić,
Céline Zimmer

Repairing a Commercial Zone

DE

Neben Aufstockungen und der Bebauung von Parkplatzflächen liegt das größte Potential, aber auch die größte Herausforderung einer Stadtreparatur, die keinen Abriss und Ersatzneubau, keine Versiegelung und keinen Neubau auf gewachsenem Boden mehr vorsieht, in der Transformation von Gewerbegebieten. Gewerbegebiete sind Hinterlassenschaften des funktionalen Planungsdogmas und der kapitalistischen Massenkonsumgesellschaft, trotzdem werden sie immer weiter (aus)gebaut. Ihre Lage folgt nicht einer bestimmten Planungsstrategie, sondern der Verfügbarkeit von billigem Land und einer autogerechten Anbindung. Der Versiegelungsgrad dieser monofunktionalen Zonen ist extrem hoch, da die Flächen um die *decorated sheds* soweit wie möglich als Parkflächen ausgewiesen werden – ein Raummodell, das Victor Gruen in den 1950er-Jahren für die amerikanische Shopping Mall entwickelt hat. Dabei werden die Stellplätze nur in wenigen Situationen im Jahr gänzlich genutzt.

Gewerbegebiete zielen auf regionale Konsument*innen, doch die offerierten Produkte werden entlang komplexer globaler Lieferketten bezogen. Damit sind Gewerbegebiete sowohl Mitverursacher als auch Leidtragende des Klimawandels: Sie emittieren direkt und indirekt große Mengen an Treibhausgasen, stehen aber auch unter enormem Stress durch vermehrt auftretende Hitzeinseln auf den durchgehend versiegelten Flächen, die das Versickern von Regen verhindern, was bei Starkregenereignissen zu Überflutungen führt. Sozialökonomisch sind sie ebenfalls problematisch: Der Großteil der Arbeitsplätze hier ist im Niedriglohnsektor angesiedelt. Gemeinden konkurrieren um die Grund- und Gewerbesteuereinnahmen, während die Profite international abgeschöpft werden. Vor diesem Hintergrund ist es erstaunlich, dass weltweit bislang noch kein einziges Gewerbegebiet vollständig zurückgebaut oder in ein durchmischtes Quartier umgebaut wurde. Im Gegenteil: Jeden Tag werden neue Gewerbegebiete ausgewiesen und bestehende vergrößert.

2020 schrieb Luxemburg einen internationalen Wettbewerb aus, für den interdisziplinäre Konsortien von Forscher*innen und Planer*innen Visionen und Konzepte entwickeln sollten, wie das Land mit dem europaweit höchsten ökologischen Fußabdruck pro Person dekarbonisiert und resilient gestaltet werden kann. Im Rahmen unseres Wettbewerbsbeitrags entwickelten wir Werkzeuge zur Umwandlung des größten Gewerbegebiets Luxemburgs, die auch auf andere Gewerbegebiete übertragbar sind. Die im Süden des Landes zwischen Luxemburg-Stadt und Esch-sur-Alzette gelegene Ortschaft Foetz zählt über 100 vorwiegend internationale Einkaufs- und Produktionsstätten mit insgesamt 6.200 PKW-Stellplätzen. Über 70 Prozent der Fläche sind versiegelt, wobei etwa ein Drittel auf Parkplätze entfällt. Jeden Tag strömen 60.000 PKWs in das Gewerbegebiet, die insgesamt 269.000 Reisekilometer zurücklegen und 55 Tonnen CO_2 ausstoßen.

Infolgedessen ist Foetz eine der größten Hitzeinseln der Region, der Temperaturunterschied zwischen dem Mikroklima des Gewerbegebiets und den umliegenden Feldern macht bis zu fünf Grad Celsius aus. Von den 100 Einkaufs- und Produktionsstätten sind nur 30 Unternehmen regional, die anderen sind Teil internationaler Ketten. Nur circa ein Drittel der Unternehmen gehört Branchen an, die als zukunftsträchtig gelten. Bei den restlichen Unternehmen ist die Zukunft ungewiss, bei vielen von ihnen steht das gegenwärtige Geschäftsmodell bereits erkennbar unter Druck.

Der Leitfaden zur Transformation des Gewerbegebiets ist in vier Zeithorizonte unterteilt, die sich in vier Modellen widerspiegeln. Er sieht eine kleinteilige, durchmischte Entwicklung der Randzonen der Parkplatzflächen sowie die Renaturierung der dazwischen liegenden Flächen vor.

2022
Universität Luxemburg
University of Luxembourg
4 Modelle
models
Acrylharz
Acrylic resin
Durchmesser
Diameter
120 cm
Modellbau
Modelmaking
Made by Mistake, Lukas Kropp, Liza Diekema

Vier Modelle, die von Florian Hertweck, Caroline Faber, Marija Marić und Céline Zimmer (Universität Luxemburg) für einen öffentlichen Wettbewerb realisiert wurden, zeigen einen Vorschlag für die schrittweise Umgestaltung eines typischen vorstädtischen Gewerbegebiets in der Nähe der Stadt Foetz im Süden Luxemburgs.

Four models realized for a public competition entry by Florian Hertweck, Caroline Faber, Marija Marić, and Céline Zimmer (University of Luxembourg), show a proposal for the progressive transformation of a typical suburban commercial zone near the town of Foetz, in southern Luxembourg.

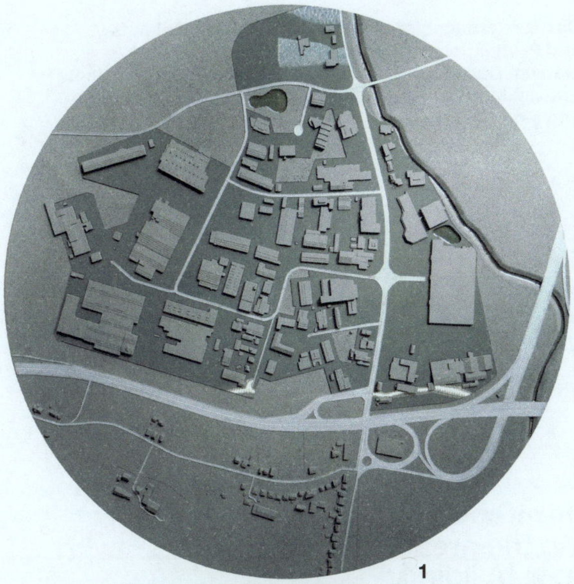

1

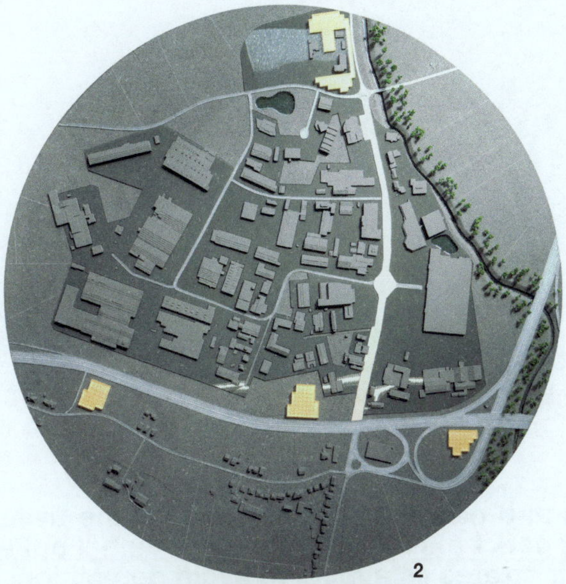

2

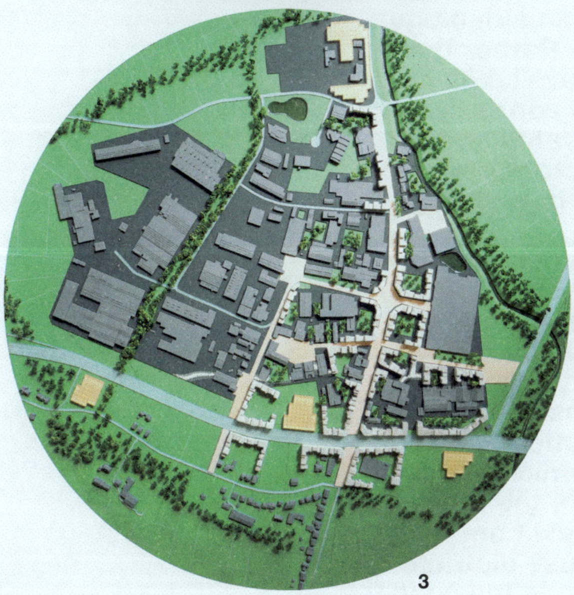

3

4

1
2021
Ist-Zustand
Current state

2
2025
Kurzfristige Maßnahmen, um die Nutzung der Zone durch PKWs zu reduzieren. Diese beinhalten den Bau wandelbarer Hochgaragen an strategischen Positionen, den Anschluss des Gebiets an den ÖNPV und die Transformation der Hauptstraße in einen *shared space* (für Busse, Fußgänger*innen und Radfahrer*innen).

Short-term measures to reduce car usage in the commercial zone. This includes building convertible parking garages at strategic spots, connecting the office park to public transit, and transforming the main road into a shared space for buses, pedestrians, and bicyclists.

3
2030
Kleinteilige Mischbebauung der Randzonen der Parkplätze bei gleichzeitiger Renaturierung der Zwischengebiete. Mindestens 70 Prozent sind dem Wohnungsbau vorbehalten, von dem 40 Prozent genossenschaftlich, 40 Prozent gefördert und 20 Prozent frei finanziert sind. Das Narrativ für das neue Gewerbe lautet Reparatur und Handwerk.

Small-scale mixed-use development of the parking lot peripheries with simultaneous renaturing of the areas in between. At least 70 percent of the redeveloped area is reserved for housing—of which 40 percent is cooperative housing, 40 percent subsidized housing, and 20 percent privately financed housing. The key principles for the new site are repair and craftsmanship.

4
2035
Das System wird auf das weitere Gebiet ausgeweitet, wodurch rund 10.000 Menschen hier leben könnten und 10 Hektar (circa ein Drittel der Parkplatzflächen) renaturiert würden. Das gesamte Areal bleibt autofrei.

The transformation measures are extended to the rest of the zone, creating accommodation for around 10,000 residents and renaturing 10 hectares (about one-third of the parking surface). The entire site is car-free.

Das Gewerbegebiet umfasst mehr als 100 Einkaufs- und Produktionsstätten mit insgesamt 6.200 Parkplätzen. Das Projekt sieht eine kleinteilige, durchmischte Entwicklung der Randzonen der Parkplatzflächen vor und eine Renaturierung der Zwischenräume.

The zone encompasses more than 100 shopping and production sites, with a total of 6,200 parking spaces. The project proposes a small-scale mixed-use development of the parking lots' peripheral zones, as well as renaturing the areas in between.

EN

Besides vertical extensions and parking lot conversions, the transformation of commercial zones and office parks offers the greatest potential but also the greatest challenge for urban repair strategies aiming to avoid demolition, new building, and soil sealing. Commercial zones are vestiges of functionalist planning ideology and consumer capitalism, yet their construction and growth persist. Rather than being strategically planned, their location is often determined by the availability of inexpensive land and easy automobile access. Such monofunctional zones often exhibit extensive soil sealing, with the areas surrounding their "decorated sheds" primarily serving as parking lots — a spatial concept pioneered by Victor Gruen in the 1950s for the United States shopping mall. These parking spaces, however, go largely unused, except for a few peak times per year.

Commercial zones and office parks cater to local consumers, but the products on offer are sourced through complex global supply chains. This positions commercial zones as both contributors to and victims of climate change. They emit large quantities of greenhouse gases, directly and indirectly. At the same time, these areas face significant challenges, as their sealed surfaces exacerbate the growing urban heat island effect, causing stormwater run-off issues during heavy rainfall. Commercial zones and office parks are also problematic in socioeconomic terms since they usually provide low-wage jobs. In turn, municipal governments compete for their property and revenue taxes while much of the profits flow to international firms. Given these drawbacks, it is striking how few commercial zones worldwide have been dismantled or converted into mixed-use districts. On the contrary, new commercial zones continue to be approved and existing ones are expanded at a steady pace.

In 2020, Luxembourg launched an international competition inviting interdisciplinary teams of researchers and planners to develop visions and concepts for decarbonizing the country, which has Europe's largest per capita ecological footprint, through resilient and sustainable design approaches. As part of our competition submission, we devised tools to redevelop Luxembourg's largest commercial zone, in ways that can be applied to other commercial zones.

Located in the south of Luxembourg between Luxembourg City and Esch-zur-Alzette, the commercial zone near the town of Foetz encompasses more than 100 shopping and production sites, most of them international companies, with a total of 6,200 parking spaces. This results in over 70 percent of the zone's surface area being paved or covered, with nearly a third occupied by parking lots alone. Every day, 60,000 cars flood into the commercial zone, traveling a total of 269,000 kilometers and emitting 55 tons of CO_2. As a result, Foetz is one of the region's largest heat islands, with a temperature difference of up to five degrees Celsius between the commercial zone's microclimate and the surrounding fields. Out of the 100 shopping and production facilities, only 30 belong to regional corporations; international chains own the rest. Only a third of the corporations can be considered "future-oriented" industries. For the remaining companies, the future looks uncertain, as many already face considerable challenges to their business models.

Our guidelines for transforming the commercial zone are structured in four phases, reflected in four corresponding models. We propose a small-scale mixed-use development of the parking lots' peripheral zones, as well as the renaturing of the areas in between.

Text:
Florian Hertweck

Christine Jiayi Chen,
Kristina Shatokhina,
Wilhelm Gardeleone

After Parking

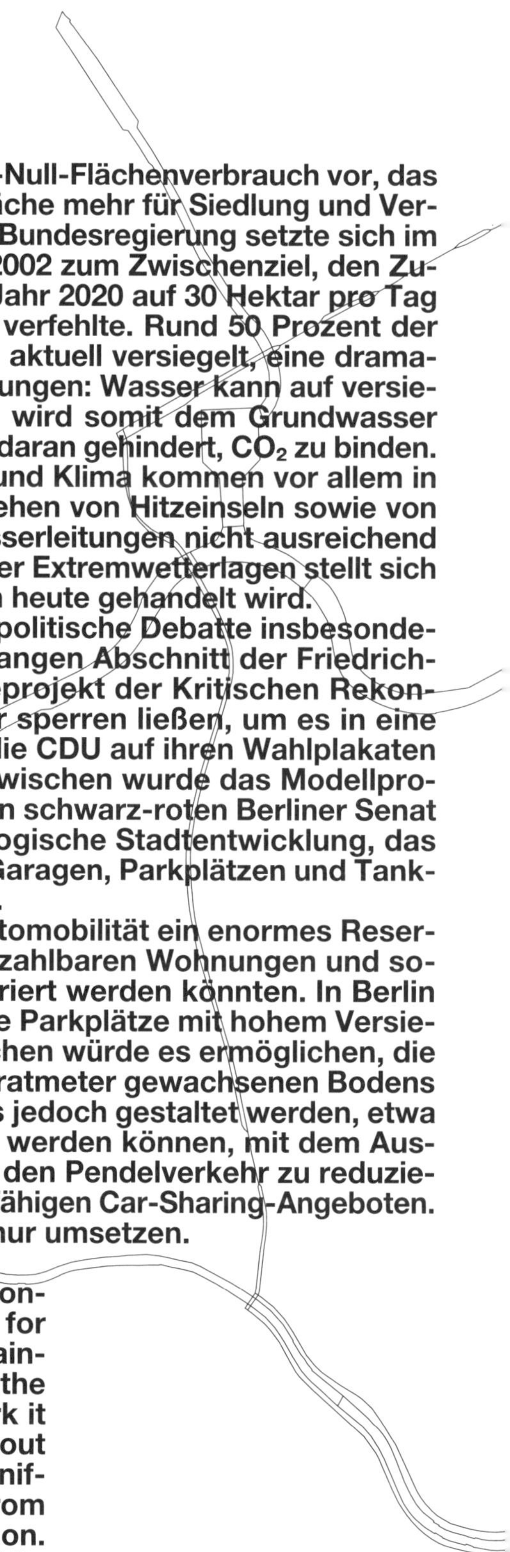

DE

Der European Green Deal sieht bis 2050 einen Netto-Null-Flächenverbrauch vor, das heißt, unter dem Strich darf in der EU keine neue Fläche mehr für Siedlung und Verkehr in Anspruch genommen werden. Die deutsche Bundesregierung setzte sich im Rahmen ihrer Nationalen Nachhaltigkeitsstrategie 2002 zum Zwischenziel, den Zuwachs der Siedlungs- und Verkehrsfläche bis zum Jahr 2020 auf 30 Hektar pro Tag zu reduzieren, was sie mit rund 55 Hektar deutlich verfehlte. Rund 50 Prozent der Siedlungs- und Verkehrsfläche in Deutschland sind aktuell versiegelt, eine dramatisch hohe Zahl, betrachtet man die Begleiterscheinungen: Wasser kann auf versiegelten Flächen nicht versickern, es verdampft und wird somit dem Grundwasser entzogen. Biodiversität wird zerstört und der Boden daran gehindert, CO_2 zu binden. Neben den verheerenden Auswirkungen auf Natur und Klima kommen vor allem in Städten noch zwei weitere Folgen hinzu: das Entstehen von Hitzeinseln sowie von Überschwemmungen bei Starkregen, da die Abwasserleitungen nicht ausreichend Wasser aufnehmen können. Angesichts zunehmender Extremwetterlagen stellt sich die Frage, warum bis 2050 gewartet und nicht schon heute gehandelt wird.

In Berlin entfachte sich 2023 die politische Debatte insbesondere an einer versiegelten Fläche: einem 500 Meter langen Abschnitt der Friedrichstraße. Als die Grünen ausgerechnet das Prestigeprojekt der Kritischen Rekonstruktion von Hans Stimmann für den Autoverkehr sperren ließen, um es in eine begrünte Fußgängerzone umzuwandeln, konterte die CDU auf ihren Wahlplakaten mit „Berlin ist für alle da. Auch für Autofahrer". Inzwischen wurde das Modellprojekt für eine entmotorisierte Straße unter dem neuen schwarz-roten Berliner Senat wieder beendet. Das Potential für eine sozial-ökologische Stadtentwicklung, das in den für Autos versiegelten Flächen wie Straßen, Garagen, Parkplätzen und Tankstellen steckt, wurde dabei komplett ausgeblendet.

Dabei würde Suffizienz in der Automobilität ein enormes Reservoir an Flächen freisetzen, die je nach Lage mit bezahlbaren Wohnungen und sozialen Infrastrukturen entwickelt oder auch renaturiert werden könnten. In Berlin entfallen allein 9,49 Quadratkilometer auf gruppierte Parkplätze mit hohem Versiegelungsgrad. Schon die Transformation dieser Flächen würde es ermöglichen, die Stadt nachzuverdichten, ohne einen weiteren Quadratmeter gewachsenen Bodens zu versiegeln. Dieser Transformationsprozess muss jedoch gestaltet werden, etwa mit Geschossparkhäusern, die optional umgenutzt werden können, mit dem Ausbau von Co-Working-Spaces in Wohngebieten, um den Pendelverkehr zu reduzieren, einer freien Nutzung des ÖNPV oder konkurrenzfähigen Car-Sharing-Angeboten. Sinnvolle Ideen gibt es zur Genüge, man muss sie nur umsetzen.

Unter der Leitung von
Under the supervision of
Florian Hertweck, Markus Miessen
Universität Luxemburg
University of Luxembourg
2023
Maßstäbliche Fotocollage,
Druck auf Fototapete
Photo collage, to scale,
print on photographic wallpaper
270 × 310 cm

EN

The European Green Deal stipulates net-zero land consumption by 2050, meaning essentially that no new land can be appropriated for settlement or transit from that point forward. As part of its 2002 National Sustainability Strategy, the German government set itself the interim goal of reducing the growth of settlement and transit areas to 30 hectares per day by 2020—a mark it failed to achieve by a wide margin, landing at around 55 hectares. Currently, about 50 percent of Germany's surface area for settlement and transit is sealed, a significant figure given the concerning side effects. Surface sealing prevents water from seeping into the ground; it evaporates instead, leading to groundwater depletion. This destroys biodiversity and prevents carbon absorption by the soil. Beyond its devastating repercussions for nature and the climate, surface sealing has two sig-

nificant implications for cities in particular: the formation of urban heat islands and an increased risk of flooding due to inadequate drainage by sewage pipes during heavy rainfall. Given the escalating frequency of extreme weather events, it seems questionable to delay action until 2050 rather than addressing the issue today.

In 2023, political discourse in Berlin centered around one sealed surface in particular: a 500-meter segment of Friedrichstraße, a prominent shopping street in the heart of the city. Targeting the prestige project of former city Building Director Hans Stimmann's "critical reconstruction" (*Kritische Rekonstruktion*) program, the Green Party closed the street to vehicle traffic, with the aim of converting it into a tree-lined pedestrian zone. The conservative Christian Democrats countered this initiative with election posters declaring *"Berlin ist für alle da. Auch für Autofahrer."* ("Berlin is for everyone. Drivers, too."). Under Berlin's subsequent governing coalition of Christian Democrats and Social Democrats, the model project for a car-free street was revoked. The potential for a more social and ecological approach to urban development by unsealing surfaces like streets, garages, parking lots, and gas stations was completely ignored.

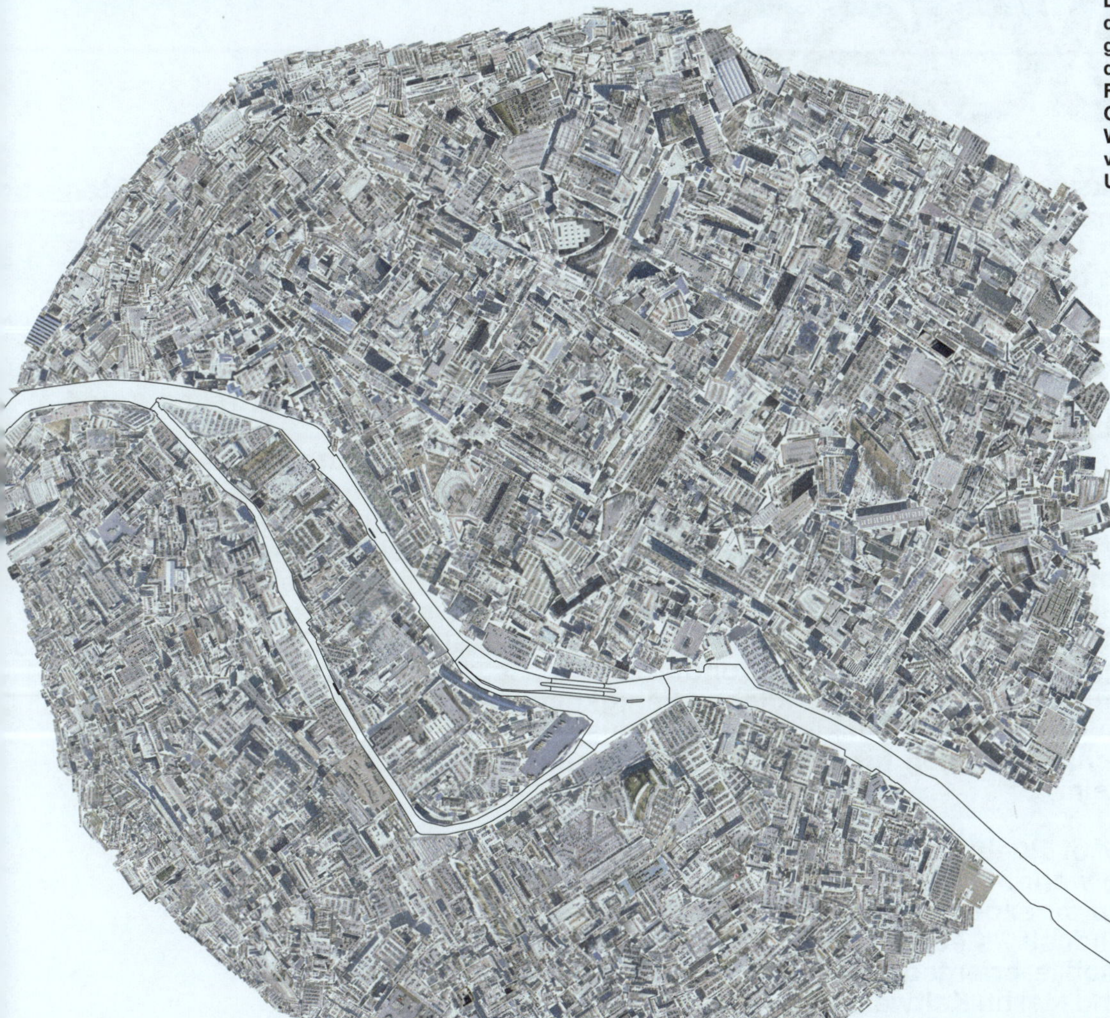

Die Collage *After Parking* verdeutlicht durch das maßstäbliche Zusammenlegen aller gruppierten Parkplätze in Berlin das Ausmaß der Versiegelung. Die resultierende Fläche umfasst 9,49 Quadratkilometer. Christine Jiayi Chen, Kristina Shatokhina und Wilhelm Gardeleone, unter der Leitung von Florian Hertweck und Markus Miessen, Universität Luxemburg, 2023

The collage *After Parking* illustrates the extent of soil sealing in Berlin by visualizing the city's grouped parking lots as if they were one contiguous surface in the city center. The resulting area covers 9.49 square kilometers. Christine Jiayi Chen, Kristina Shatokhina, and Wilhelm Gardeleone, under supervision of Florian Hertweck and Markus Miessen, University of Luxembourg, 2023

However, sufficiency-oriented mobility has the potential to unlock enormous reservoirs of surface area that could be utilized for affordable housing, social infrastructure, or renaturation. In Berlin, tightly sealed grouped parking lots amount to a total area of 9.49 square kilometers. By redeveloping these surfaces, the city could significantly increase densification without any further soil sealing. Such a process of transformation, however, requires careful planning, incorporating elements such as multilevel parking garages that can be adapted to other uses in the future, expanded coworking opportunities in residential areas to reduce commuting, free public transit, and competitive car-sharing services. There is no shortage of sensible ideas; all they need is someone to implement them.

Text:
Florian Hertweck

Folke Köbberling &
Martin Kaltwasser

Cars into Bicycles

2010
Video
Farbe, Ton
Color, sound
8 min

Cart
2013
Mobile Plastik
Mobile sculpture
Mixed media, 150 × 140 × 320 cm
Entstanden im Rahmen der Ausstellung *Zur Nachahmung empfohlen* (seit 2010)
Created in conjunction with the exhibition *Example to follow!* (since 2010)
unterstützt von
supported by
Arquetopia, Fundación para el Desarrollo

DE

Das Volkswagen Werk in der mexikanischen Stadt Puebla ist eines der größten des Konzerns weltweit. Seit 1967 laufen dort jährlich hunderttausende, hauptsächlich für den Export bestimmte Automobile vom Band. Wie lässt sich angesichts der wirtschaftlichen Übermacht der Automobilindustrie eine Alternative zur Autogesellschaft denken? Vor dem Hintergrund dieser Frage konzipierten Folke Köbberling und Martin Kaltwasser 2013 an der Universitario Bauhaus in Puebla den Workshop *Cars into …* Gemeinsam mit Architektur-, Kunst- und Designstudierenden entwarfen und konstruierten sie aus den Teilen eines schrottreifen Autos das funktionstüchtige dreirädrige Lastenfahrrad *Cart*.

Die kritische Auseinandersetzung mit der Autogesellschaft war ein zentrales Anliegen im Leben und Werk des 2022 verstorbenen Künstlers, Architekten und Aktivisten Martin Kaltwasser. Er organisierte gemeinsam mit seiner langjährigen künstlerischen Partnerin Folke Köbberling vielfältige performative und gestalterische Aktionen, die die autogerechte Stadt kritisierten und zur Wiederaneignung des urbanen Raums einluden. *Cart* ist Teil der Serie *Cars into Bicycles*, die die beiden 2008 begannen. Im Zentrum standen dabei nicht die Vorstellungen der Gestalter*innen, sondern Prozesse der Teilhabe. Die Beteiligten eigneten sich neben handwerklichen Fähigkeiten wie Metallbau und Schweißen auch ein kritisches Bewusstsein an, um aus den Instrumenten einer überholten Gesellschaft Visionen für eine neue, sozial und ökologisch gerechtere Welt zu entwickeln.

EN

The city of Puebla in Mexico is home to one of the largest Volkswagen factories in the world. Since 1967, hundreds of thousands of automobiles, most of them destined for export, have rolled off its assembly lines every year. Given the automotive industry's economic dominance, how can we imagine an alternative to the automobile-oriented society? Against the backdrop of this question, Folke Köbberling and Martin Kaltwasser developed the workshop *Cars into …* at Universitario Bauhaus in Puebla in 2013. Together with students of architecture, art, and design, they designed and constructed a three-wheeled cargo bicycle, *Cart*, using salvaged parts from a scrapped car.

Confronting and critiquing the automobile-oriented society was a central theme in the work of artist, architect, and activist Martin Kaltwasser, who died in 2022. Together with his longtime artistic partner Folke Köbberling, he organized performative and creative projects that challenged the car-centric design of cities and invited participants to reappropriate urban space. *Cart* belongs to the series *Cars into Bicycles*, which Köbberling and Kaltwasser began in 2008. Rather than placing the designers' ideas at the center of the creative process, they prioritized participatory processes. In addition to craft skills such as metal construction and welding, the participants also acquired a critical awareness for developing visions for a new, more socially and ecologically just world from the remains of an outdated society.

Text:
Christian Hiller,
Alex Nehmer

Cart ist ein funktionstüchtiges Lastenfahrrad, das als Teil der Serie *Cars into Bicycles* aus Autoteilen gebaut wurde. Es ist auch eine Hommage an die *triciclos de tamales*, die weit verbreiteten fahrbaren Verkaufsläden vieler Straßenhändler*innen in Mexiko.

Cart is a fully functional cargo bike created from salvaged car parts as part of the series *Cars into Bicycles*. It also pays homage to the *triciclos de tamales*, mobile retail shops widely used by street vendors in Mexico.

Die Serie *Cars into Bicycles* begann 2008 und wurde u. a. in Graz, Hamburg und Pueblo durchgeführt. 2010 fand die öffentliche Performance auf dem Parkplatz des Bergamot Station Arts Centers in Santa Monica, Kalifornien, statt, bei der ein Saab Turbo 900 in zwei funktionierende Fahrräder umgebaut wurde.

The performance series *Cars into Bicycles* began in 2008 and was enacted in various cities, including Graz, Hamburg, and Pueblo. In 2010, the public live performance took place in the parking lot of the Bergamot Station Arts Center in Santa Monica, California, where a Saab Turbo 900 was transformed into two fully functional bicycles.

Collective Works

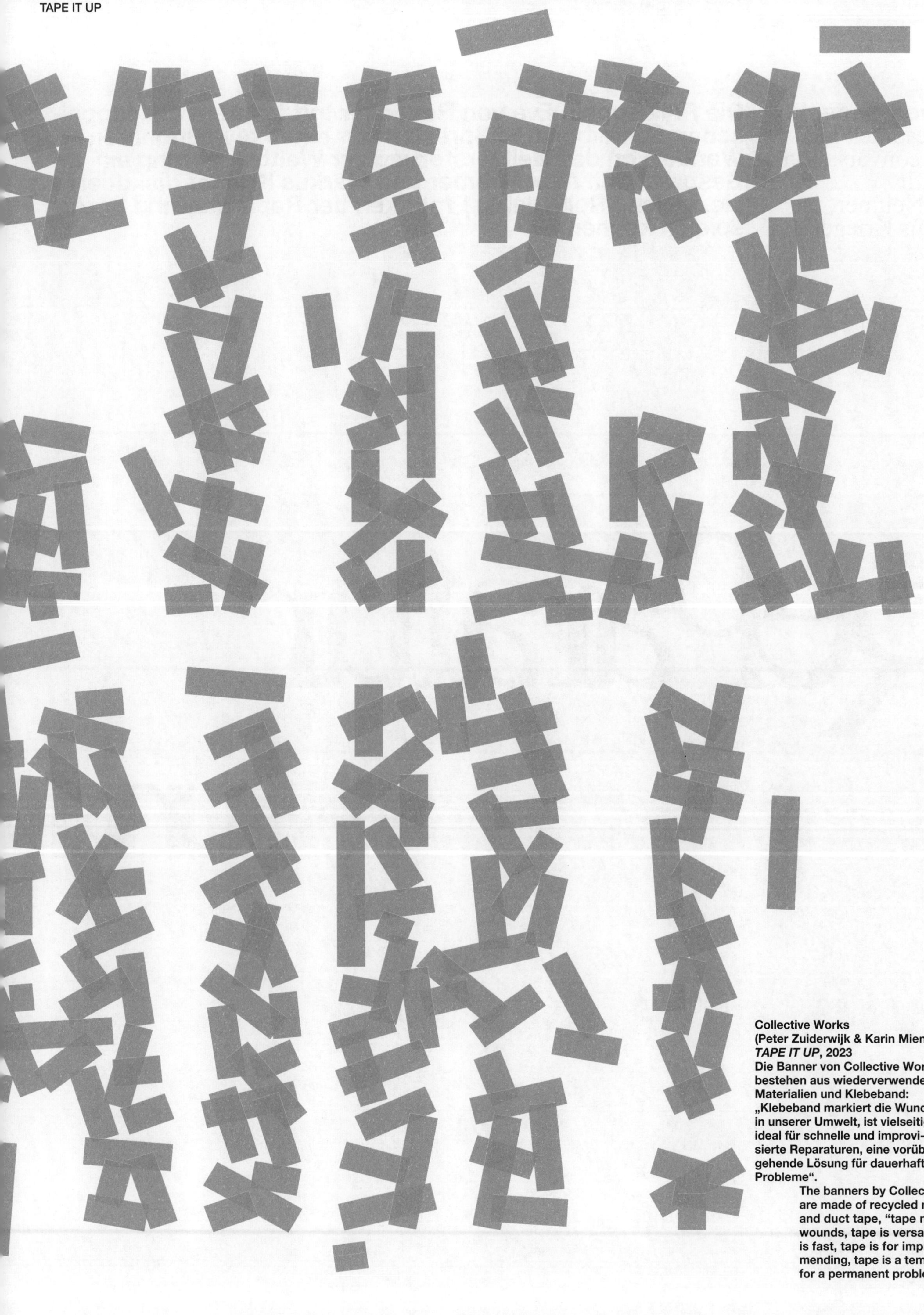

Collective Works
(Peter Zuiderwijk & Karin Mientjes),
***TAPE IT UP*, 2023**
Die Banner von Collective Works bestehen aus wiederverwendeten Materialien und Klebeband: „Klebeband markiert die Wunden in unserer Umwelt, ist vielseitig, ideal für schnelle und improvisierte Reparaturen, eine vorübergehende Lösung für dauerhafte Probleme“.

The banners by Collective Works are made of recycled materials and duct tape, “tape marks wounds, tape is versatile, tape is fast, tape is for improvised mending, tape is a temporary fix for a permanent problem.”

Eva von Redecker
im Gespräch mit
in conversation with
Alex Nehmer,
Markus Krieger

DE

Die Philosophin Eva von Redecker tritt in ihrem philosophischen Schreiben und Sprechen für einen revolutionären Wandel von der Weltzerstörung zur Weltbewahrung ein. Im Gespräch mit Alex Nehmer und Markus Krieger diskutiert sie, welche Rolle dabei Praktiken der Reparatur und Sorge spielen können.

Reparatur und

Repair and Revolution

EN

In her writing and public speaking, philosopher Eva von Redecker advocates for revolutionary change, from a destructive relationship with the world to one focused on preserving it. In conversation with Alex Nehmer and Markus Krieger, she discusses what role practices of repair and care can play in such a transformation.

DE

Alex Nehmer Beginnen wir mit einer Diagnose: Wie sind wir deiner Analyse nach zu dem Grad der Weltzerstörung gekommen, vor dem wir gegenwärtig stehen?

Eva von Redecker Die kapitalistische Ordnung hängt aus meiner Sicht wesentlich von der Entstehung der spezifischen modernen Form des Eigentums ab. Zwei Mechanismen sind dabei zentral, gewissermaßen zwei Schnitte durch das Gewebe des Lebendigen: Der eine und auch historisch erste Schnitt ist die Einhegung oder Vereigentümlichung. Die Welt ist nicht an sich schon Eigentum. Erst indem man etwas als Objekt definiert und eingrenzt, wird es überhaupt zum besitzbaren Objekt. Dazu braucht es Infrastrukturen, Rechtssysteme, Verwaltungsmaßnahmen, Zäune, Gewalt. Das bedeutet immer auch, Dinge aus Bezügen herauszureißen, aus den sozialen und vor allem ökologischen Bezügen, die sie überhaupt erst regenerieren und lebendig halten. Die moderne Form des Eigentums billigt Eigentümer*innen eine volle, willkürliche Verfügung zu, das heißt in rechtlicher Sprache: absolute Sachherrschaft. Das führt zu einer Entlebendigung. Denn wenn Dinge Eigentum sind, kann man sie behandeln, als wären sie tot. Und wenn man Dinge eine Weile behandelt, als wären sie tot, dann sind sie es irgendwann wirklich.

Der zweite Schnitt verläuft näher am Herzen des Kapitalismus: die Inwertsetzung von Dingen als Ware. Wenn der erste Schnitt etwas ausschneidet, schneidet der zweite es durch. In einen Teil, der verwertbare Ware ist, am Markt Profit einbringen kann. Und einen Teil, der als wertlos abgestoßen wird. Auch das ist ein wesentliches Merkmal des Rechtsbündels, das das moderne Eigentum ausmacht: das Recht zur Veräußerung. Das scheint uns heute selbstverständlich. Aber dass man etwas, das einem gehört, gleichzeitig jederzeit loswerden oder abstoßen kann, ist eine spezifische Regelung, ohne die wir nie eine profitable kapitalistische Wirtschaft hätten errichten können. Deswegen scheint es mir auch utopisch zu denken, dass man diese jetzt in Bahnen lenken könnte, indem man Externalitäten einpreist. Macht man das ernsthaft, bleibt kein Gewinn mehr übrig. Der entsteht, weil etwas abgeschnitten und für nichtig erklärt wird. Ein drastisches Beispiel dafür sind die Emissionen, die in jedem industriellen Fertigungsvorgang der letzten 250 Jahre freigesetzt wurden und derer man sich entledigen konnte, als hätte es sie nicht gegeben. Aus Sicht des planetaren Lebens gibt es sie jedoch weiter, und sie wirken zurück. Und das gilt für jede Warenproduktion: Immer gibt es Abfälle und Ausschuss, verwüstete Abbaugebiete, unfruchtbar gewordene Böden, Bauschutt, Körper, die nichts wert sein dürfen, damit andere Körper als fleißig verkäuflich werden. Durch die profitorientierte Produktion werden diese beiden Schnitte der Unterwerfung und Abspaltung ständig perpetuiert und führen zu den sozialen und ökologischen Zerstörungsdynamiken, deren Folgen heute immer deutlicher werden.

AN Oft können wir unsere Alltagsgegenstände und technischen Geräte heute nicht mehr reparieren. Siehst du da einen Widerspruch zu deiner Argumentation, dass das moderne Eigentum die volle Verfügungsgewalt über eine Sache bedeutet? Diese Verfügung über die Dinge scheinen wir nur noch in eine Richtung zu besitzen: Alles ist auf deren Verschleiß ausgerichtet. Darum zielt unser Projekt auch darauf, das Wissen und die Werkzeuge wiederzuerlangen, um Dinge reparieren zu können, aber sie auch so zu gestalten, dass sie reparierbar sind.

EvR Gerade weil es wie ein Widerspruch scheint – dass ich argumentiert habe, Eigentum heißt, alles mit einem Objekt machen zu können, und ihr sagt, gerade reparieren kann man es nicht –, passt das gut zusammen. Ihr verweist da treffsicher auf einen immanenten Widerspruch unserer Praxis, doch es ist leider relativ schwer, den zu politisieren. Der souveräne Eigentümer fühlt sich durch die Nicht-Reparierbarkeit offenbar viel weniger provoziert als durch eine Einschränkung der Verfügung, ein Tempolimit auf Straßen oder eine Instandhaltungspflicht wie beim Denkmalschutz. Der naheliegendste Anspruch ist immer, auch rücksichtslos agieren zu dürfen. Das hängt eng zusammen mit der Gewaltgeschichte, die die moderne Eigentumsform lostritt, insofern sie sich auf viel mehr als mittelgroße, gut handhabbare, vielleicht sogar selbst hergestellte Objekte bezieht. In den letzten Jahrhunderten wurden immer mehr Weltbestandteile zu Eigentum, von denen man sich kaum hätte vorstellen können, dass sie als abgrenzbare, übertragbare, missbrauchbare Objekte behandelt werden können: Land, Menschen, Arbeitskraft, Saatgut bis hin zur DNA.

Doch über Lebendiges besitzt man diese Verfügung in Wahrheit nie vollumfänglich. Das bleibt ein Phantasma, ich spreche von Phantombesitz. Es ist ein Anspruch, der immer schon ein Stück weit unterlaufen ist, sogar dort, wo er rechtlich garantiert ist. Trotzdem besteht der Wahn, sich der Verfügungsgewalt vergewissern zu wollen. Und wenn ich mich möglichst schnell vergewissern will, dass ich alles machen kann, dann ist die Zerstörung das ultimative Mittel. Die Reparatur hingegen ist erstens eine kompliziertere Praxis. Zweitens erfordert sie, sich einem Ding untertan zu machen, statt es zu beherrschen. Man muss dazu ein Ding verstehen lernen, Lösungen testen, abwarten und sich immer wieder korrigieren. Dafür ist heute aber meist gar keine Zeit, denn das Profitmotiv befeuert die Verwertung. Wer ein Produkt früher als die Konkurrenz auf den Markt bringt, mehr davon produziert, schneller verkauft, der gewinnt. Auch dadurch bekommt die Vollverfügung eine Schlagseite in Richtung Destruktion.

In meinen neueren Arbeiten versuche ich diese zeitliche Dimension stärker in den Blick zu nehmen. Warum verstehen wir Freiheit immer als das, was ich im Moment mit einer Sache machen kann? Wenn ich das vollkommen ausreize, liegt schnell alles in Scherben. Mehr Freiheit wäre doch, wenn ich etwas über längere Dauer machen kann. Ich nenne das Bleibefreiheit. Das wäre eine Perspektive, die sich mit der Langlebigkeit der Objekte, wie ihr das so schön nennt, verbünden könnte. Wenn man etwas repariert, dann repariert man es nie nur für sich selbst, denn es bleibt dadurch der Welt erhalten. Es könnte einen überleben und jemand anderem zukommen. Ein Stück weit macht man das womöglich gar für das Ding und nicht für sich. Das beschneidet unsere Souveränität als Eigentümer*innen, aber zugunsten von etwas, das im rechten Licht betrachtet viel freiheitsfördernder und verheißungsvoller ist.

AN Aus deiner Sicht braucht es als Antwort auf die zerstörerischen Verhältnisse der Gegenwart eine *Revolution für das Leben*, so auch der Titel eines deiner Bücher. Dem klassischen Bild von Revolution nach könnte man Revolution und Reparatur für Gegensätze halten. Reparatur erfordert, behutsam mit dem umzugehen, was schon da ist. Ein Ausgangspunkt unseres Projekts sind konkrete Alltagspraktiken, auch um zu zeigen, dass die Reparatur auch jetzt schon viel bedeutsamer ist, als sichtbar wird, wenn immer nur die Innovation und das Neue betont werden. Wir müssen weniger gänzlich neu schaffen, sondern können auf dem Vorhandenen aufbauen. Die Revolution hingegen bedeutet ihrem verbreiteten Verständnis nach den Bruch mit allem Alten. In deinem Denken scheint die Revolution der Reparatur jedoch viel näher.

EN

Alex Nehmer Let's start with a diagnosis. What is your analysis of how we have reached the level of destruction we see today?

Eva von Redecker As I see it, the capitalist world order is fundamentally dependent on the creation of specifically modern forms of property. Two mechanisms are central in this respect, two cuts, as it were, through the fabric of life. The first, historically speaking, is the cut of enclosure, or the establishment of property. The world is not property by default. Only when someone defines something as an object, and encloses it, does it become something that can be owned. This requires infrastructure, legal systems, administrative mechanisms, fences, and violence. And it also always involves tearing things away from their contexts, from their social and above all ecological contexts—which are responsible for regenerating them and keeping them alive in the first place. The modern form of property grants owners total, indiscriminate control and absolute possession in legal terms. This, in turn, removes it from the realm of the living. Because when things are property, you can treat them as if they're dead. And when you treat something as if it's dead for long enough, it eventually becomes truly dead.

The second cut runs closer to the heart of capitalism: the valorization of things as commodities. If the first cut serves to separate things from their contexts, the second slices them in two. One part becomes an exploitable commodity, which can generate profit on the market, and another part is thrown away, regarded as worthless. This is also an essential aspect of the legal bundle that constitutes modern property: the right to dispose of something. Today, we see this as self-evident. But the notion that we can offload or dispose of something that belongs to us is a specific arrangement. Without it, we could never have managed to set up a profitable capitalist economy. That's why it also strikes me as utopian to imagine that now, by pricing in externalities, we could succeed at reining in capitalism. If you were to do this seriously, no profit would be left. Profit is created because something is cut off and declared void. A drastic example is the emissions that have been released by every industrial manufacturing process of the past 250 years, emissions that producers are able to offload as if they didn't exist. From the perspective of planetary life, however, they certainly do continue to exist. They rebound off us. And this is true of every form of commodity production—there's always trash and construction waste, despoiled mining areas, land made barren, and bodies that are considered worthless so other bodies can be sold as hardworking. In the course of profit-oriented production, both of these cuts, the cuts of subjection and separation, are perpetuated over and over again, generating the dynamics of social and ecological destruction whose consequences are becoming ever more visible today.

AN It's often impossible for us today to repair our everyday objects and technical devices. Do you see a contradiction here to your argument that modern ownership means full power of disposal over a thing? Our disposal over things seems to run in only one direction: everything is oriented toward their exhaustion. That is why our project is aimed at reclaiming the knowledge and tools to be able to repair things—but also designing them so that they are repairable in the first place.

EvR Precisely because it seems as if there's a contradiction—that I have argued that ownership means being able to do anything with an object, and you are saying anything but repairing—these two things actually fit together. You are rightly pointing out a contradiction that's intrinsic to our practice but difficult to politicize. Sovereign owners, apparently, feel less frustrated by an item's non-repairability than by any limitations on their right to disposal: speed limits, for example, or maintenance obligations like those imposed by heritage protection laws. The overriding demand is always to be allowed to act heedlessly. This is closely related to the history of violence that the modern form of property unleashes—in that it applies to much more than only midsized objects, objects that are easily handled or possibly even made by their owners themselves. Over the past few centuries, more and more components of the world have been turned into property, components that people might have hardly imagined could one day become objects to be delimited, conveyed, or abused—whether we're talking about land, people, labor, seeds, or even DNA.

But in reality, when we enjoy disposal over living things, it's never complete or comprehensive. It remains phantasmagoric; I have called this "phantom possession." To a certain extent, the claim is always undermined, even when it's legally guaranteed. Nevertheless, this delusion remains, the wish to reassure yourself that you have full power of disposal. And when I want to reassure myself as quickly as possible that I can do whatever I want, destruction is the ultimate means of doing so. Repair, on the other hand, is a much more complicated practice. It requires you to subordinate yourself to something rather than dominate it. You need to learn to understand the thing, to test solutions, and to wait and correct yourself over and over again. But today there's often no time for this, because the profit motive fuels exploitation. Whoever can bring a product to the market faster than their competition, whoever can produce more and sell faster, will win. This is another factor that gives modern ownership a tendency toward destruction.

In my latest work, I focus more on this temporal dimension. Why do we always understand freedom as what we can do *at this very moment*? If I push that impulse to its absolute limits, everything will quickly fall to pieces. There would actually be more freedom in doing something over a longer period of time. I call this "the freedom to stay." This perspective could be allied with the longevity of objects, along the lines you describe in your project. When you repair something, you're never repairing it just for yourself; through the act of repair, you preserve it for the world. It can survive you and become useful for someone else. To some extent, you might even be doing the repair for the sake of the thing, and not for yourself. While this may curtail our sovereignty as owners, it does so in service of something that, regarded in the proper light, is much more promising and ultimately creates more freedom.

AN You have argued that, as an answer to today's destructive relationships with things, we need a "revolution for life," which is also the title of one of your books [*Revolution für das Leben*]. Going by the classic notion of revolution, revolution and repair could be considered opposites. Repair demands that you proceed cautiously with what's already there. For our project, everyday practices of repair are a key point of departure, with the idea of showing that repair is already much more prevalent than people realize when the focus is only on the new and the innovative. We don't always need to create something entirely new; instead, we can build on what already exists. Revolution, on the other hand—at least the way it's conventionally understood—means breaking with everything old. But in your thinking, revolution and repair seem much closer.

EvR We face such an enormous need for transformation that it would be downright absurd to disregard the most radical term for change that we have in our political vocabulary. The

EvR Wir stehen gegenwärtig vor einem so immensen Transformationsbedarf, dass es geradezu absurd wäre, den Maximalbegriff für Wandel auszuklammern, den wir in unserem politischen Vokabular haben. Dann ist die Frage, wie man ihn füllt. Ich verstehe Revolution tatsächlich viel weniger als Bruch und mehr als interstitiellen Wandel, also als Wandel, der über die und aus den Zwischenräumen des Alten heraus das Neue schafft. Damit ist man schon bei einem Bild der Reparatur, so wie ihr auch vorschlagt, sie zu verstehen, nicht als bloße Wiederherstellung des Alten, sondern als Umbau hin zum Besseren.

Tatsächlich scheint mir, dass auch die klassischen Ereignisrevolutionen, zum Beispiel die Französische Revolution, falsch verstanden sind als bloßer Bruch. Auch diese waren vielmehr Prozesse des sukzessiven Austauschs von dem, was ich Ankerpraktiken nenne. Etwa die Ersetzung feudaler Hörigkeit durch demokratische Selbstregierung – das betrifft ganz konkrete Verhaltensmuster, die jeweils paradigmatisch für eine Ordnung als Ganze stehen. Auch im gegenwärtigen historischen Moment brauchen wir weitreichende Wandlungen der basalsten Alltagspraktiken. Das kann gar nicht auf einen Schlag passieren. So funktioniert menschliches Handeln nicht. Nur lange, immer wieder nachgebesserte und reflektierte Bemühungen, oder auch freudige Experimente, können da Erfolg versprechen. Und tatsächlich halte ich solche revolutionären Prozesse in heutigen Protestformen wie etwa der Klimagerechtigkeitsbewegung oder feministischen Kämpfe auch schon für erkennbar.

Der nächste, vielleicht noch dramatischere Unterschied zu einer Hochphase des Nachdenkens über Revolution im 19. Jahrhundert ist, dass wir nicht nur Reichtum umzuverteilen haben. Es geht nicht nur darum, dass die Dinge jetzt endlich von denen, die sie herstellen, oder auch von denen, die sie reparieren, besessen werden. Sondern wir sind konfrontiert mit immensen Mengen von Undingen. Den abgespaltenen, abgestoßenen, zum Teil auch toxischen Dingen, die ich eben beschrieb. Nicht nur Ziegelbruch, den man einfach wegräumen könnte, sondern auch Asbest. Das macht weniger freudvolle, aber auch weniger auf einen Schlag zu erledigende Arbeiten zur Aufgabe der Revolution. Selbst wenn wir sofort aufhören, weiter toxische Dinge abzuspalten, sind diese nicht weg. Wir müssen Reparatur auch in die Zukunft als Entsorgung, Reinigung, Entgiftung fortsetzen.

Das heißt nicht, dass manche Dinge nicht ganz schnell gehen könnten! Ein sofortiges Moratorium für den Abbau fossiler Rohstoffe, die sofortige Vergesellschaftung von Amazon und RWE. Aber wir stehen an einem Punkt, wo die politische Macht, die es dazu bräuchte, so außer Reichweite ist, dass wir auch hier immer nur von langsamen Politisierungsprozessen ausgehen können.

Markus Krieger Deine Vorstellung von Revolution scheint weniger monolithisch zu sein, sondern sich aus unterschiedlichsten Praktiken zusammenzusetzen, die verschiedenste Bereiche unseres Lebens berühren. In der Konzeption unseres Projekts ist eine gewisse Spannung angelegt: Einerseits postulieren wir im Titel die große Reparatur, im Singular. Gleichzeitig sehen wir Pluralität als eine der Politiken der Reparaturgesellschaft, anknüpfend an die zapatistische Vision von einer Welt, in die viele Welten passen. Wie siehst du diese Spannung?

EvR *Great* kann auch heißen: an allen Ecken und Enden, überall. Euer Projekttitel ist ja auch eine Anspielung auf die Große Transformation nach Karl Polanyi. Polanyi beschreibt die letzten Jahrhunderte als Widerstreit zwischen Vermarktlichung, also dem Vordringen kapitalistischer Beziehungen in immer neue Bereiche, und dem Bemühen um sozialen Schutz. Er geht davon aus, dass in dem Moment, wo Boden, Arbeit und Geld selbst zu Waren werden, eine Erosion der Gesellschaft einsetzt. Diese Dinge halten es gewissermaßen nicht aus, einfach Marktgesetzen unterworfen zu werden. Deshalb braucht es die Gegenbewegung des sozialen Schutzes, der aber innerhalb der Marktgesellschaft sehr schwer zu realisieren ist. Nach Polanyi gibt es deshalb nur zwei stabile Ausgänge: entweder demokratischen Sozialismus als gelungene Selbstverteidigung der Gesellschaft oder die permanente Katastrophe, Faschismus. In Frankreich haben Pierre Charbonnier und Bruno Latour diese Idee aktualisiert und ausgeweitet. Gibt es so etwas wie die Selbstverteidigung der Natur? Gerade Latour dachte das aber sehr stark als bloßen Abwehrkampf, während auch bei Polanyi schon klar war, dass dieser Schutz im Bestehenden nicht möglich ist, sondern es eine neue sozialistische Vergesellschaftung braucht. Die Selbstverteidigung der Erde muss aktiv sein, oder sie ist aussichtslos.

Dazu gehört die Reparatur, die wir vornehmen müssen, aber es ist eben auch ein Akt der Selbstreparatur. Und die ist ja keine gezielte Arbeit, die planvoll etwas wiederherstellt. Deshalb spreche ich im ökologischen Bereich lieber von Regeneration – definiert als Zeit, in der sich etwas anstrengungslos wiederherstellt. Auch in einer Gesellschaft, in der wir uns der Reparatur verschreiben, sind wir verloren, wenn sich nicht zumindest Teile des natürlichen Ökosystems weiterhin einfach frei regenerieren. Im Sozialismus ist das Produkt der Arbeit des einen die Erfüllung des Bedürfnisses eines anderen. In Ökosystemen ist der Abfall des einen die Nahrung des anderen. Und es ist absolut zentral, sich klarzumachen, dass unsere gezielte Arbeit immer nur einen Teil unserer Bedürfnisse erfüllen kann. Der Rest ist Regeneration. Die Lungen müssen sich mit Sauerstoff füllen können, es muss ungiftiges Essen geben, man muss schlafen können. Nichts davon ist im kapitalistischen Anthropozän selbstverständlich. Sich einfach erholen zu können, scheint in der Gegenwart schon ein utopisches Versprechen. Vielleicht findet auch genau hier der Übergang von der Reparatur zur Regeneration statt, manchmal braucht die Reparatur nichts als Zeit. Und das ist ein großer Segen. Das ist die Welt, die wir gewinnen können, wenn wir mit dem Zerstören aufhören. Eine Aufgabe der großen Reparatur wird es dann umgekehrt auch sein, bestimmte Selbstregeneration der Natur zu unterstützen und weiter zu ermöglichen.

MK Verwandte Ansätze entstehen gerade auch in der Architektur. Die Non-Profit-Organisation Material Cultures etwa sucht nach Wegen, die Bauwirtschaft mit lokaler land- und forstwirtschaftlicher Produktion zu verbinden und gesamte Gebäude aus regenerativen Materialien zu fertigen. Zum Beispiel schlagen sie vor, Hanf als Rohmaterial für Dämmstoffe zu verwenden, das in Fruchtfolge mit anderen Pflanzen und ohne Pestizide angebaut werden kann, was den Böden, aber auch Insekten und Vögeln zugutekommt und gleichzeitig eine skalierbare Kohlenstoffsenke darstellt. Das ist eines von mehreren Beispielen aus unserer Ausstellung für transformative Bewegungen innerhalb der Architektur. Ein anderes sind die Forderungen nach Moratorien auf Neubau oder Abriss. Wo siehst du Potenziale, aber auch Grenzen dabei, eine Disziplin wie die Architektur, die gerade in ihrer industrialisierten Form in vielfältiger Weise als Instrument der Weltzerstörung wirkte, aus ihrem Inneren heraus zu verändern?

EvR Dass solche Vorstöße immer korrumpiert werden oder und einseitig bleiben können, ist klar. Dann kommt es darauf an, wirklich egalitär und rezeptiv die Akteur*innen mit anderem

question is how to fill it with meaning. I understand revolution less as a break and more as an interstitial change, a change that creates the new *through and out of* the in-between spaces of the old. This leads us to an image of repair along the lines you have suggested, not as a simple restoration of the old but as rebuilding towards something better.

It seems that even the classical historical revolutions, such as the French Revolution, are misunderstood as simple breaks. In fact, these were processes of successive replacements. The replacement of feudal bondage, for example, with democratic self-government, has to do with very concrete patterns of behavior which I call "anchor practices," each of which stands paradigmatically for an order as a whole. In today's historical moment, too, we need far-reaching transformations of the most basic everyday practices. This cannot happen in one fell swoop. Human behavior doesn't work that way. Only slow, reflective efforts, repeated and improved again and again—even joyful experiments—can lead to success. And I think we can already recognize certain processes that are genuinely revolutionary along these lines, for instance in contemporary forms of protest such as the climate justice movement or in feminist struggles.

The next difference from the heyday of 19th-century revolutions—maybe even a more dramatic difference—is that today the focus cannot only be on redistributing wealth. The central issue is not only ensuring that things are finally owned by the people who manufacture or repair them. Instead, we're confronted with an enormous mass of non-things—the split-off, discarded, sometimes toxic things I described earlier. Not simply broken bricks you can sweep away, but things like asbestos. This makes the work of revolution less joyful, but it also means there is less that can be done all at once. Even if we immediately stop splitting off toxic materials, they won't simply go away. We have to continue the act of repair into the future in the form of waste disposal, cleaning, and detoxification.

This doesn't mean that some things couldn't happen quite quickly. There could be an immediate moratorium on fossil fuel production. Amazon or RWE could immediately be brought into public ownership. But we're at a point where the political power necessary for this appears to be so far out of reach that the best we can hope for here as well is a slow process of politicization.

Markus Krieger Your idea of revolution seems to be less monolithic and more comprised of a wide variety of practices that affect the most diverse aspects of our lives. There's a certain tension built into our project's conception: While its title postulates ***the*** Great Repair, at the same time we view the politics of a repair society as grounded in plurality, inspired by the Zapatista vision of a "world where many worlds can fit." How do you see this tension?

EvR "Great" can also mean reaching into all nooks and crannies, everywhere. The title of your project is also a play on Karl Polanyi's *The Great Transformation*. Polanyi describes the last few centuries as a conflict between marketization—the penetration of capitalist relations into ever more areas—and efforts to establish forms of social protection. He presumes that the moment land, labor, and money become commodities, society begins to erode. In a sense, these things cannot stand simply being subjugated to market laws. That's why a counter-movement of social protection is necessary, although it is difficult to realize within a market society. According to Polanyi, therefore, only two stable outcomes are possible: either democratic socialism—a successful form of social self-protection—or permanent catastrophe in the form of fascism. In France, this idea has been brought up to date and expanded by Pierre Charbonnier and Bruno Latour. Does nature have its own form of self-protection? Latour, in particular, conceived this as a simple defensive struggle, whereas for Polanyi, it was already clear that such protection is not possible in the existing social order—it requires a new socialist order. The self-protection of the Earth is either active, or there is no hope.

This is the repair we have to undertake, but it's also an act of self-repair. And this is not a systematic form of labor that restores something in a planned way. That's why when I discuss ecology, I prefer to talk about "regeneration"—defined as the time in which something restores itself, without effort. Even in a society in which we dedicate ourselves to repair, we will be lost if at least certain parts of the natural ecosystem do not continue freely regenerating themselves. In socialism, the product of one person's labor fulfills the needs of someone else. In ecosystems, one organism's waste serves as another organism's nourishment. So it's absolutely essential to emphasize that our purposeful labor can only fulfill a portion of our needs. The rest is regeneration. Lungs must be able to fill themselves with oxygen. There must be non-poisonous food to eat. You need to be able to go to sleep. In the capitalist Anthropocene, none of this can be taken for granted. At the moment, simply being able to rest seems like a utopian promise. Perhaps this is precisely where the transition from repair to regeneration occurs; sometimes repair needs nothing but time. And that is a great blessing. That is the world we could achieve if we stopped destroying it. One task of the Great Repair will be to support certain self-regeneration processes in nature and to continue facilitating them.

MK Such approaches are currently emerging in architecture. For example, the nonprofit organization Material Cultures is looking for ways to connect the construction industry with local agriculture and forestry to promote the use of regenerative materials in building. Something they recommend is using hemp as a raw material for insulation. It can be grown in rotation with other crops and without pesticides, which helps the soil, alongside insects and birds, while also creating a scalable carbon sink. This is one of various examples from our exhibition on transformative movements within architecture. Others include demands for moratoria on new construction and demolition. Where do you see potential—or limits—in trying to change a discipline like architecture from within, which, in its industrialized form, has served prolifically as a major instrument of global destruction?

EvR It's clear that such efforts can always be corrupted or remain one-sided. It's important, therefore, to be truly egalitarian and receptive when actors with other forms of knowledge and longer experiences of oppression speak—not only to let them speak but to do what they say. Nevertheless, what strikes me first in the approaches you describe is not the inherent limits, but more the utopian aspects. To call for a moratorium on new construction from the perspective of architects seems radical to me. Even if this is only meant as a provocation, you have to ask yourself: What does this mean for architecture? Another way to characterize a moratorium on new construction would be to describe it as a vision of a "no-dig" construction industry. The term "no dig" is so concrete, yet it's astonishingly transferrable. The imperative can also be applied to the fossil fuel industry, as a demand for an end to extractivism with the slogan "leave it in the ground." The term originally comes from agriculture, where it describes cultivation methods that deliberately avoid plowing the soil, because recent research into soil biology

Wissen und längeren Unterdrückungserfahrungen nicht nur sprechen zu lassen, sondern auch umzusetzen, was sie sagen. Dennoch fallen mir da nicht als erstes die Grenzen auf, sondern eher das Utopische daran. Ausgerechnet aus Perspektive der Architekt*innen ein Moratorium auf Neubau zu fordern, erscheint mir radikal. Selbst wenn das nur als Provokation gemeint ist, muss man sich ja fragen: Was heißt das für die Architektur? Eine andere Art, das Neubaumoratorium auf den Punkt zu bringen, wäre, es als Vision für eine No-dig-Baubranche zu beschreiben. Die Chiffre *no dig* ist so konkret, dass es erstaunt, wie übertragbar sie dennoch ist. Dieser Imperativ lässt sich auf die fossile Energieversorgung übertragen, als Forderung nach einem Ende des Extraktivismus unter dem Slogan *Leave it in the ground*. Ursprünglich kommt der Begriff aber aus der Landwirtschaft und beschreibt dort Anbaumethoden, die bewusst auf das Pflügen des Bodens verzichten. Denn die neuesten Forschungen zur Bodenbiologie zeigen, dass das tiefe Umschichten äußerst schädlich für die Fruchtbarkeit und Lebendigkeit des Bodens ist. Zudem wird dabei Kohlenstoff freigesetzt, den die Pflanzen der Atmosphäre entzogen und im Boden gespeichert haben. Ich wohne auf dem Land in Brandenburg und hadere mit diesem Ansatz auch bei meinem eigenen Kartoffelbeet noch, weil er allem landwirtschaftlichen Wissen, mit dem ich aufgewachsen bin, widerspricht.

Für mich wäre das ein Beispiel für Ankerpraktiken, die sich nach und nach wandeln. In der Wissenschaftspraxis wirkt ein neues Paradigma zunächst auch wie ein kruder Versuch. Erst nach und nach zeigt sich, dass es doch ein Modell für viel mehr sein kann und sich darauf eine ganze neue Theorie des Feldes bauen lässt. Deshalb tut sich für mich von diesem kleinen Manifestbruchstück aus erstmal ein weiter Horizont auf.

AN Du schreibst auch in *Revolution für das Leben* von deinem Aufwachsen und Leben auf dem Land. In einer Szene aber schilderst du, wie du durch die Straßen einer fremden Stadt ziehst. Du zeichnest darin ein Bild von schnurgeraden Linien, ausdruckslosen Fassaden, versiegelten Bürotürmen, Betonplatte an Zementputz, beschreibst deine „Zementverzweiflung" und das Gefühl, dass diese Welt nicht für uns gemacht ist. Da schwingt vieles mit: die Stadt, die nach Kapitalinteressen statt nach menschlichen Bedürfnissen gestaltet ist, die ökologisch katastrophalen Auswirkungen ihrer Bauweisen. Aber man könnte darin auch lesen, dass du die Stadt an sich für unwirtlich und lebensfeindlich hältst. In der Szene sucht dein Blick nach der Himmelsrichtung und dem Wetter, dem Boden unter dem Asphalt – man könnte meinen, einem Außen jenseits der Stadt.

Ich musste beim Lesen an das Dorf in Bayern denken, in dem ich aufgewachsen bin und in dem meine Eltern heute noch wohnen. Rund herum liegt Maisfeld an Maisfeld, im Wald reiht sich Nadelbaum an Nadelbaum, sonst wächst höchstens noch Moos und mal ein Farn, es ist dunkel und still. Beim Spazierengehen dort beschleicht mich manchmal ein ähnliches Gefühl der Unwirtlichkeit. An anderen Stellen in deinem Buch beschreibst du auch deutlicher, dass das Land denselben Verwertungsinteressen unterworfen ist wie die Stadt und es dieses Außen nicht mehr gibt. Wie können wir die Gemeinsamkeiten und dadurch auch gemeinsamen Kämpfe dieser Räume stärken?

EvR Es ist ein guter Hinweis, dass man diese Verzweiflung auf dem Land genauso spüren kann. Vielleicht herrscht in dieser Hinsicht noch größere Ignoranz, nach dem Motto: Ist doch grün, also schön. Trotzdem verschlechtert sich die Bewohnbarkeit von Städten gerade objektiv durch ineinandergreifende Prozesse, die alle auf unterschiedliche Weise Resultat der Sachherrschaft sind: sowohl Gentrifizierung und Verdrängung als auch Zunahme von Hitze und Feinstaub, die Effekte der Pandemie und der Verlust öffentlicher Räume. Viele mittelständische Stadtbewohner*innen suchen deshalb Alternativen, die aber tatsächlich nicht existieren. Das idyllische Grün da draußen, in das alle wollen, ist selber fragil und prekär. Treiber der Verödung und Uniformierung der Landschaft ist jedoch die Stadt als Wirtschafts- und Konsumzentrum.

Der Historiker Kenneth Pomeranz hat dazu den Begriff des Phantomackers geprägt. Er beschreibt damit, dass der wirtschaftliche Aufschwung Westeuropas im 19. Jahrhundert überhaupt erst durch koloniale Expansion ermöglicht wurde, aber auch die Aufteilung der europäischen Räume im Inneren in Hinterland und Metropolen, in denen sich der Reichtum konzentriert. Die Phantomäcker, also die Flächen, die es braucht, um das gute Leben in den Städten zu reproduzieren, liegen woanders – von den Maisfeldern, die den Biodiesel liefern, bis hin zu den argentinischen Ranches auf abgeholzten Regenwäldern, wo die Steaks produziert werden, die in der Stadt verzehrt werden. Man darf sich nicht vormachen, dass unter dem Pflaster der fruchtbare Boden zu finden wäre, wie ich das in dieser Buchstelle beschwöre, und dass damit schon die Entfremdung aufgehoben wäre. Die Stadt könnte idyllisch sein, und trotzdem ist sie ein Ort der Verwüstung, denn sie kolonisiert große Bereiche des Landes. Das zu überwinden, war schon Thema in Marx' Nachdenken über die metabolische Kluft, den Riss zwischen Mensch und Natur, den der Kapitalismus verursacht. Aber in der marxistischen Sicht ist das noch viel zu optimistisch verstanden als ein Auseinanderfallen von zwei Hälften, die es nur wieder zusammenzubringen gilt. Inzwischen haben wir verödete Böden, toxische Substanzen, unlebbare Klimabedingungen. Eine einfache Überwindung der Entfremdung ist nicht in Sicht, sondern wieder nur mit ganz viel Reparatur zu erreichen.

MK Ein Beitrag unserer Ausstellung setzt sich mit dem Gebiet um Lützerath auseinander. Architekturstudierende der ETH Zürich bauen dafür ein Modell, das die Infrastrukturen fossiler Extraktion, aber auch den Widerstand dagegen untersucht. Dabei haben sie unter anderem herausgearbeitet, dass der Energiekonzern RWE durch Landeigentum und als Anteilseigener an Stadtwerken großen Einfluss auf die Ausgestaltung der Energiewende vor Ort nehmen konnte, beispielsweise durch Errichtung von Windparks auf konzerneigenen postextraktiven Flächen oder durch die Versorgung der neugebauten umgesiedelten Dörfer mit erneuerbarer Wärme. Die Menschen dort bleiben so entfremdet von diesen essentiellen Infrastrukturen, kaum in der Lage, über diese mitbestimmen zu können. Wie gehen wir auch im größeren Maßstab der Energiewende damit um, dass die für jede Vorstellung einer postfossilen Welt benötigten Dinge zwar nun bisweilen gebaut werden, diese aber weiter privatisiert sind und der kapitalistischen Sachherrschaft unterliegen?

EvR Das Dramatische ist, dass bislang nur das Abgestoßene, die Müllseite dieser Dinge, vergesellschaftet wird. Das störende Summen und die verstellte Aussicht, wenn ein Windrad vor dem eigenen Garten steht, das bekommen die Leute quasi umverteilt. Aber die Gewinne landen bei den großen Konzernen. Dass RWE in die Erneuerbaren investiert, überrascht nicht. Denn RWE kann eben investieren, weil das Kapital so konzentriert ist und privat darüber verfügt wird. Meiner Meinung nach ist es trotzdem besser, wenn sie darin investieren als in etwas anderes, aber eigentlich

has demonstrated that turning the soil too deeply is extremely harmful for its fertility and longevity. Additionally, it releases carbon that plants have removed from the atmosphere and stored in the ground. I live in the Brandenburg countryside, and I'm still struggling with this approach when it comes to my own little potato patch, because it contradicts all the agricultural knowledge I grew up with.

This is an example of the sorts of "anchor practices" that are slowly changing. In scientific practice, a new paradigm looks initially like a crude experiment. Only gradually does it prove that it can be a model for much more, and that whole new theories and fields can be built on top of it. That's why, for me, this little snippet of a manifesto opens up a wide horizon.

AN In *Revolution für das Leben* [Revolution for Life], you also write about growing up and living in the countryside. In one scene, however, you describe wandering through an unfamiliar city. The picture you paint is one of dead-straight lines, vacant facades, sealed-up office towers, concrete slabs and cement plaster. You describe your "despair of cement" and a feeling that this world isn't made for us. This resonates with a lot of different notions: That the city is designed according to the interests of capital rather than human needs. That the effects of its construction are ecologically catastrophic. But someone might also read in it that you see the city as inhospitable, as hostile to life. In this scene, your gaze searches for the sky, for the weather, for the soil under the asphalt. Someone might assume you're seeking something outside, beyond the city.

As I was reading this, I thought about the village in Bavaria where I grew up and where my parents still live. Around it, there are fields and fields of corn. In the forests, there are rows and rows of conifers; otherwise there's at most some ferns and mosses; it's very quiet and dark. On walks there, I also sometimes experience a creeping feeling of inhospitality. In other passages of your book, you describe more clearly that the countryside is subject to the same exploitation processes as the city, and that there is no longer any such thing as an "outside." How can we strengthen the commonalities between these two spaces, and therefore also the shared struggle?

EvR It's a good point, that you can also experience the same sort of despair in the countryside. Maybe there is still a greater lack of awareness in this respect, based on the idea that "if it's green, it's good." At the same time, the livability of cities is objectively getting worse, and this has to do with interlocking processes that, in various ways, stem from capitalist domination—be it gentrification and displacement, the increase of heat and air pollution, or the effects of the pandemic and the loss of public space. Because of this, many middle-class residents of cities are seeking alternatives, yet there are no real alternatives. The idyllic countryside into which everyone wants to escape is itself fragile and precarious. However, the driver of the landscape's desolation and uniformity is the city, as an economic center and a center of consumption.

The historian Kenneth Pomeranz has coined the term "phantom acres" for this. He describes how Western Europe's economic boom in the 19th century was made possible in the first place by colonial expansion, but also by dividing European space itself into hinterlands and metropoles, with wealth concentrated in the latter. Phantom acres are the areas needed to reproduce the good life in the cities, but they lie elsewhere—from the cornfields that produce biodiesel to the Argentinean ranches on former rainforests, where steaks are produced that get consumed in the cities. We cannot delude ourselves that merely lifting up the pavement to reveal the fertile soil underneath, as I imagine in this passage of the book, will be enough to overcome the alienation. The city could very well be idyllic and *still* be a place of devastation because it colonizes large swathes of the countryside. Overcoming this was already the subject of Marx's writing on the metabolic rift, the rift between humankind and nature caused by capitalism. But the Marxist perspective is still too optimistic on this, seeing it as a separation of two halves that only need to be reunited. Meanwhile, we have degraded soil, toxic substances, and unlivable climate conditions. A simple solution for overcoming the alienation is not on the horizon; again, it can only be achieved through a huge effort of repair.

MK One contribution to our exhibition addresses the Lützerath area in the German state of North Rhine–Westphalia, where a village was forcibly displaced in 2023 to make room for an open-pit coal mine. Architecture students at ETH Zürich built a model to study the infrastructure of fossil extraction, but also the resistance that took place there. One thing they discovered was that the energy company RWE, by owning land and being a shareholder in municipal utilities, could exert considerable influence on the shape of the local energy transition, for example by building wind farms on company-owned, post-extractive areas, or by providing renewable energy to the new buildings of the relocated villagers. The people there thus remain entirely alienated from these essential infrastructures, and are hardly in a position to have any say over them. How do we address the fact that, at the larger scale of the transition to renewable energy, the things necessary for any vision of a post-fossil future are being built now, yet remain in private hands, subject to the same logic of capitalist domination?

EvR The dramatic thing is that, so far, only the discarded and devalued side of these things, the rubbish, is socialized. The disruptive whirring and obstructed views when you have a wind turbine in your backyard—these are redistributed among the people, so to speak. But the earnings go to the major firms. It's no surprise that RWE is investing in renewable energy. RWE is able to invest because capital is so concentrated, and it's privately controlled. It's better if they invest in renewable energy, of course, as opposed to something else, but these processes of transformation should be steered at a political level.

A friend who works in politics asked me recently, somewhat despondently, what to do about rural resistance to wind turbines, because the transition to renewable energy urgently needs to happen. I suggested actually *giving* people wind turbines. Give free electricity to anyone who can see them from their homes. The fact that these new infrastructures are being implemented according to capitalist logic, even where it would be possible and make more sense to run them cooperatively, is only further testament to the fundamental alienation in the world in which we live.

In general, however, I try to avoid lamenting green capitalism. Naturally, it's not going to save the world. But the current state of affairs is much worse; we don't even have a capitalism that pretends to be green. Instead, we live in a state of total innovation suspension, as if our culture has reached the limits of its creativity. Oil companies would rather invest in disinformation campaigns than in renewable energy. Globally, dynamics of green colonialism are on the rise, for instance with land grabs for carbon offsetting. The international climate justice movement, especially Indigenous activists, are the leading analysts when it comes to these processes, and

müssten diese Transformationsprozesse politisch gesteuert werden.

Eine Freundin, die in der Politik arbeitet, hat mich vor kurzem verzweifelt gefragt, was man denn gegen den Widerstand der Landbevölkerung gegen Windräder tun könne, denn die Energiewende müsse nun mal kommen. Meine Antwort: Schenkt den Leuten doch die Windräder. Alle, die das Ding von ihrem Haus aus sehen, bekommen umsonst Strom. Dass die neuen Infrastrukturen nach der Logik des Kapitals umgesetzt werden, selbst da, wo es möglich wäre, sie genossenschaftlich zu gestalten, zeigt nur wieder die Grundentfremdung in der Welt, in der wir leben.

Generell neige ich aber kaum zu dem Lamento gegen den grünen Kapitalismus. Dass er die Welt nicht retten wird, ist vollkommen klar. Der gegenwärtige Zustand ist jedoch viel schlimmer: Wir haben nicht mal einen Kapitalismus, der so tut, als wäre er grün. Vielmehr herrscht eine komplette Innovationsstarre. Als wäre eine Kultur am Limit ihrer Kreativität angekommen. Ölfirmen investieren lieber weiter in Desinformationskampagnen als in erneuerbare Energien. Global gibt es natürlich Dynamiken eines grünen Kolonialismus wie Landnahmen für Kohlenstoffausgleich. Die internationale Klimagerechtigkeitsbewegung und darin besonders indigene Aktivist*innen sind die maßgeblichen Analyst*innen dieser Vorgänge und mobilisieren völlig zu Recht dagegen. Aber hier haben wir nicht mal die Landnahme für Windkraft, die es bräuchte, um zumindest einen Teil des Problems zu lösen.

AN In der Right-to-Repair-Bewegung wird das (Wieder-)Erlangen der Fähigkeiten zur Reparatur auch als eine Form der Ermächtigung und Wiederaneignung der Welt verstanden. Unser Projekt widmet sich der Wiederaneignung vor allem auch als einem Mittel des Widerstands gegen die Enteignungen durch den Kolonialismus. Du sprichst hingegen statt von Wiederaneignung von Weltwiederannahme. Was bedeutet das für dich?

EvR Für mich hängt viel davon ab, dass wir in Zukunft die Dynamik der Sachherrschaft im Kern des Eigentums hinter uns lassen. Man kann natürlich den Eigentumsbegriff so fassen, dass damit nicht absolute Verfügung gemeint ist. In vielen Formen der Wiederaneignung ist das auch schon der Fall. Revolutionäres Handeln kann darin bestehen, regenerativ erzeugte Energie allen und zuerst den Ärmeren zukommen zu lassen. Man könnte sagen, die Menschen sollen sich den Wind, der um ihr Haus weht, und das surrende Windrad neben ihrem Garten wiederaneignen.

Trotzdem spreche ich lieber von Weltwiederannahme, weil das der Tatsache besser Rechnung trägt, dass wir nicht einfach nur neu aufzuteilen haben, was es an Reichtümern und Vermögen gibt. Sondern dass Reparaturarbeit ansteht und dass wir uns speziell den Dingen, die diesen beiden Schnitten zum Opfer gefallen sind, also dem Unterworfenen und dem Abgespaltenen, zuwenden müssen. Das betrifft die schon beschriebenen destruktiven und giftigen Hinterlassenschaften, erfordert aber auch ein großes Maß an Sorgearbeit zwischen Menschen und die Bewältigung der Traumata, die diese tiefgreifenden historischen Brüche und die Gewalt der Sachherrschaftskatastrophe verursacht haben. Auch dafür gilt es, uns der abgespaltenen Teile, sowohl unserer persönlichen wie auch der gesellschaftlichen, anzunehmen. Dann können wir andere Beziehungen zueinander schaffen, nicht länger als isolierte, ausgebeutete Individuen, sondern verbunden, solidarisch leben, aber auch zu einem neuen Weltverhältnis finden, in dem wir uns als Teil der Welt verstehen und aufhören, ihrer Herr werden zu wollen.

AN Du zitierst in deinem Buch das Gedicht *Atlas* der englischen Dichterin U. A. Fanthorpe. Darin vollzieht sich ein Perspektivwechsel: Man denkt zunächst, es spräche eine Person, die einer anderen für ihre Fürsorge dankt, doch allmählich wird klar, dass es aus Perspektive eines Hauses geschrieben ist, das Akte seiner Instandhaltung würdigt. In deiner Deutung beschreibt das, was es heißt, „wenn Sorge und Solidarität den Umweg über die Dinge der Welt nehmen". Wie stehen für dich die Sorge für die materielle Welt und die Sorge unter Menschen miteinander in Beziehung?

EvR Die erste Zeile des Gedichts lautet: „There is a kind of love called maintenance" – es gibt eine Art der Liebe, die Instandhaltung heißt. Das scheint mir eine schöne Ergänzung der feministischen Debatten um Sorgearbeit, die bisweilen leerlaufen in einer Aufwertung der Sorge, als wäre nur das, was Frauen direkt mit ihren Körpern machen, Reproduktionsarbeit. Doch niemand kann versorgt werden, wenn es nicht auch ein Bett und ein Dach darüber gibt. Und auch bei der Herstellung der Betten und der Dächer wird es darauf ankommen, dass diese bedürfnis- statt profitorientiert gestaltet sind. Wir müssen die Sorgelogik nicht nur aufwerten und ihre Vergeschlechtlichung überwinden, sondern sie ausweiten auf alle möglichen anderen Tätigkeitsfelder, die gesamte Produktion. Und dafür ist der Begriff der Maintenance so passend, weil einem erstmal tropfende Wasserleitungen vor Augen stehen und nicht nur weinende Kinder. Wenn das den Kern zukünftiger Arbeit ausmacht, wenn sie Welt wahrend statt Waren produzierend ist, gibt ihr das auch eine gewisse Würde zurück, weil sie eindeutig sinnvolle Arbeit ist. Obwohl das prometheische Schaffen aus dem Nichts zurückgenommen ist in der Instandhaltungsarbeit.

MK Die Ausgabe, für die dieses Interview entsteht, erscheint als Katalog zu unserer Ausstellung. Du hast in Bezug auf die Energiewende davon gesprochen, dass wir mit der Kreativität am Ende zu sein scheinen. Welche Rolle können aus deiner Sicht ästhetische oder künstlerische Praktiken in einer Revolution für das Leben spielen?

EvR Entgegen dem Hang zur desillusionierten Lesart von Kreativität als Komplizin des Neoliberalismus habe ich nach wie vor ein positives Verhältnis zum Begriff der Kreativität. Alles kann vereinnahmt werden. Aber je stärker wir ernst machen damit, dass die wichtigsten und sinnvollsten Tätigkeiten der Gegenwart Reparatur sind und bescheidene, dienende Formen der Kreativität erfordern, umso größer ist der Bedarf an Kontexten, in denen wild und weitreichend experimentiert werden kann, in denen gerade das Ekstatische und das Destruktive, auch das Megalomanische, seinen Ort finden kann. Dafür scheint mir die Kunst sehr viel besser geeignet als die Wirtschaft. Solange die Wirtschaft so wahnwitzig und todesgetrieben ist, wie sie ist, glaube ich andererseits aber auch, dass in der künstlerischen Praxis Zwischenräume der Sinnstiftung liegen, die rar sind. Sie kann andere Arten der Arbeit modellieren. Und sie kann zusammen mit anderen, politischen Praktiken zu einer Vorwegnahme oder Sehnsuchtsschürung beitragen, nach einer Welt, in der wir pflegen, statt beherrschen und zerstören, teilen, statt verwerten, regenerieren, statt uns selbst und die Natur erschöpfen.

are quite justifiably mobilizing against them. Yet here we don't even face the land grabs for wind power that would be needed to solve at least part of the problem.

AN In the right-to-repair movement, acquiring the skills needed to repair, or reacquiring them, is also understood as a form of empowerment, of reappropriating the world. Our project is devoted to reappropriation also as a way of resisting colonial dispossession. Instead of reappropriation, you speak of *re-adopting* the world. What does this mean for you?

EvR For me, a great deal depends on leaving behind the dynamic of absolute dominion that lies at the heart of ownership. It could very well be possible in the future to structure the concept of property such that it does not entail full power of disposal. In many forms of reappropriation, this is already the case. Revolutionary action might consist in making regeneratively produced energy available to everyone, and first of all to the poor. You could say that people should reappropriate the wind that blows around their houses, and reappropriate the whirring wind turbines in their backyards.

Nevertheless, I prefer to speak of readopting the world because it better reflects the circumstance that our task is not only to redistribute existing wealth and assets; rather, what we are facing is repair work. We need to attend especially to those things that have fallen victim to those two cuts—the cuts of subjection and separation. This applies to the destructive and toxic legacies we discussed earlier, but it also demands a considerable amount of care work between people, the work of overcoming the trauma caused by the deep historical ruptures and violence stemming from the catastrophe of capitalist domination. In this process, too, we need to adopt and nurture the split-off parts, both at an individual and societal level. Then we can create new relationships with each other, no longer living as isolated, exploited individuals, but leading shared, connected lives in solidarity—while seeking a new relationship to the world, one in which we understand ourselves as part of the world and stop trying to become its master.

AN In your book, you quote the poem "Atlas" by the English poet U. A. Fanthorpe. In her poem, there's a reversal of perspective. Initially, you think the speaker is a person thanking another person for their care. But gradually, it becomes clear that the poem is written from the perspective of a house, honoring acts of its maintenance. In your interpretation, this describes what happens "when care and solidarity find their way through the things of the world." How do you see the relationship between care for the material world and care for fellow humans?

EvR The first line of the poem reads: "There is a kind of love called maintenance." To me, this seems like a beautiful complement to feminist discussions about care work, which can sometimes reach an impasse in the valorization of care by only considering actions performed directly by women with their bodies as reproductive labor. But nobody can be cared for if there isn't already a bed, and a roof over that. And it will matter if the manufacture of these beds and roofs is designed to serve needs rather than oriented toward profit. We not only need to valorize care work and overcome its gendering; we also need to extend the logic of care into all possible fields of activity, across the entire realm of production. And for this, the concept of maintenance is very fitting, because it makes you imagine leaking water pipes and not just crying babies. If the essential aspect of our labor for the future is that it's world-preserving rather than commodity-producing, this also gives it back a certain dignity, because it's clearly meaningful work. Even though Promethean creation from nothingness takes a back seat in maintenance work.

MK The issue in which this interview will appear also functions as the catalog to our exhibition. Discussing the energy transition earlier, you mentioned that we seem to have reached the end of our creativity. What role, in your opinion, can aesthetic or artistic practices play in a "revolution for life"?

EvR Contrary to the disillusioned reading of creativity as an accomplice of neoliberalism, I maintain a positive relationship with the concept of creativity. Anything, of course, can be coopted. But the more strongly we insist that the most important and meaningful activities of the present involve repair, and that this requires humble, caring forms of creativity, the greater becomes the need for contexts in which people can experiment wildly and broadly, in which the ecstatic and destructive, even the megalomaniacal can find a place. For such impulses, art seems better suited than the economy. But as long as the economy is as delirious and death-driven as it is, I also think that artistic practice opens up interstitial spaces for meaning that are otherwise rare. Art can model different forms of work. And together with other political practices, it can contribute to creating a longing for or anticipating a world where we nurture rather than dominate and destroy. A world where we share rather than exploit. A world where we seek to regenerate, rather than exhausting both ourselves and nature.

Sprache als Werkzeug der Reparatur

Language as a Tool of Repair

2023
In Kooperation mit
In cooperation with
Haus für Poesie
Video
Farbe, Ton
Color, sound
ca. 30 min
Mit Texten von
With texts by
Hinemoana Baker, Don Mee Choi, hn. lyonga, Tim Holland, Katharina Schultens
Produktion
Production
OFFscreen
Postproduktion
Postproduction
Tatjana Bergmeister, Anton Krebs

DE

Die Besucher*innen der Ausstellung *The Great Repair* werden mit einer Installation entlassen, die die Sprache als Instrument der Reparatur ins Zentrum rückt. Die Umkehrung der Besucher*innenführung, die im Servicebereich der Akademie der Künste am Hanseatenweg beginnt und beim großen Treppenaufgang im Foyer endet, eröffnet die Möglichkeit, die repräsentative Treppe als Sitztribüne umzunutzen, um am Ende des Rundgangs einen Ort der Sammlung anzubieten. Die Installation arbeitet mit der Fähigkeit der Lyrik, mit sprachlichen Mitteln Sachverhalte zu fokussieren und zu verdichten, aber zugleich auch zu öffnen und offenzulassen. In Kooperation mit dem Haus für Poesie werden eine Auswahl von Texten und Gedichten von Hinemoana Baker, Don Mee Choi, hn. lyonga, Tim Holland und Katharina Schultens präsentiert, die einen Nachklang der Themenstränge aus der Ausstellung erzeugen, ohne diese abzubilden oder zu interpretieren.

EN

The exhibition *The Great Repair* concludes with an installation that foregrounds language as an instrument of repair. The usual flow of visitors through the Akademie der Künste's Hanseatenweg location has been reversed—now starting in the building's service area and ending at the grand staircase in the foyer. This provides an opportunity to use the inviting staircase as a seating area, with the exhibition circuit culminating in a space for gathering. The installation itself harnesses poetry's capacity to condense and distill issues while leaving them open for interpretation. It features texts and poems by Hinemoana Baker, Don Mee Choi, hn. lyonga, Tim Holland, and Katharina Schultens, selected in collaboration with the Haus für Poesie. These works engage with thematic elements from the exhibition without attempting to directly depict or interpret them.

Text: Anh-Linh Ngo

Katharina Schultens

Anleitung für eine provisorische Salbe

DE

euer Raum sei wie folgt: es wurzeln Kronen
im Himmel, Stieglitze gebe es, ihre
Rufe habet auswendig parat

Füchse sollen flattern, schwarze Gelege
mögen Eulen bitte in der Scheune platzieren
und Feldmäuse in Mineralwollwänden nisten

dann trapst auf dünnem Holz, schlaft
unter schmalen Federn, bereitet einen Teig
der Blasen wirft und vermehrt ihn leise

sagt einmal, wo wir waren, zweimal
wo wir sind, sagt nicht, ob wir bleiben, wie viel
Wind wir haben, sagt immer von neuem

wo die Lücken sind

Instructions for a Makeshift Balm

EN

set up your room as follows: crowns
shall find their roots in the sky, let there be
goldfinches, you shall learn their cries by heart

and you shall have fluttering foxes, black
clutches of eggs placed by owls, and voles
shall make their homes in rock wool walls

then you may tiptoe on flimsy timber
and sleep in feathers, and make a dough
that blisters and begins to grow

tell us once where we were, twice
where we are now, don't tell us we're to stay
or where the wind will blow, but, if you may

tell us where to go

Assemble
ist ein in Architektur, Design und Kunst tätiges Kollektiv, das sich 2010 für ein Selbstbauprojekt zusammenschloss. Zu ihren vielfältigen und preisgekrönten Projekten zählen Atelier Luma in Arles (2023, mit BC Architects), Goldsmiths Centre for Contemporary Art (2018) und Yard House (2014), beide in London. Seit 2020 unterrichtet Assemble an der EPFL in Lausanne.
is a collective working across architecture, design, and art founded in 2010 in the context of a self-building project. Among their multifaceted and award-winning projects are Atelier Luma in Arles (2023, with BC Architects), as well as the Goldsmiths Centre for Contemporary Art (2018) and Yard House (2014) in London. Since 2020, Assemble has been teaching at EPFL in Lausanne.

Lidia Atanasova
(* 1988) ist wissenschaftliche Mitarbeiterin am Lehrstuhl für Digital Fabrication der TU München. In ihrer Promotion forscht sie zur Mensch-Roboter-Kollaboration im Bauwesen, insbesondere zu Montageprozessen durch Mensch-Roboter-Teams.
(b. 1988) is a research associate at the Chair for Digital Fabrication at the Technical University of Munich. Her doctoral research is centered on human–robot collaboration in the field of construction, with a focus on processes of cooperative assembly by human–robot teams.

Atelier Bow-Wow
wurde 1992 von Yoshiharu Tsukamoto und Momoyo Kaijima in Tokio gegründet, 2015 wurde Yoichi Tamai Partner. Das Architekturbüro hat weltweit Projekte realisiert, an zahllosen Ausstellungen teilgenommen und mehrere Bücher veröffentlicht, darunter *Made in Tokyo* (2001), *Graphic Anatomy* (2007), *Behaviorology* (2010) und *Architectural Ethnography* (2017).
was founded in Tokyo by Yoshiharu Tsukamoto and Momoyo Kaijima in 1992. Yoichi Tamai joined as partner in 2015. The firm has realized buildings across the world, taken part in numerous exhibitions, and published several books, including *Made in Tokyo* (2001), *Graphic Anatomy* (2007), *Behaviorology* (2010), and *Architectural Ethnography* (2017).

Kader Attia
(* 1970) ist Künstler und erforscht in seiner Arbeit die weitreichenden Auswirkungen der westlichen Kulturhegemonie und des Kolonialismus. Dabei spielen die Konzepte der Verletzung und Reparatur eine zentrale Rolle. 2022 kuratierte Attia die Berlin Biennale.
(b. 1970) is an artist whose work explores the wide-ranging effects of Western cultural hegemony and colonialism. Central to his inquiry are the concepts of injury and repair. Attia curated the 2022 Berlin Biennale.

Awaska Alpa Projekt
Awaska Alpa project
Mehr als 50 Mitglieder der Inga-Gemeinschaft in Kolumbien arbeiteten am dreidimensionalen Kartierungsprojekt *Awaska Alpa* mit. 14 Weber*innen aus verschiedenen Teilen des Inga-Gebiets waren für die Herstellung der Textilien zuständig und 8 Inga-Vertreter*innen stellten sicher, dass die kartografischen Elemente korrekt und auf dem neuesten Stand waren. Die Unterstützung durch den Rechtsvertreter, den Technischen Sekretär und die Berater der AWAI, der nationalen Organisation der Inga in Kolumbien, war für die Zusammenstellung der Web- und Forschungsteams von entscheidender Bedeutung. Vertreter*innen der Cabildo Inga de Mocoa stellten ihren Raum für das Modell zur Verfügung. Viele weitere Personen unterstützten das Projekt durch ihre Forschung, audiovisuelle Dokumentation, Zeichnungen, Übersetzungen und Logistik. Taita Luciano Mutumbajoys spirituelle Begleitung in Schlüsselmomenten des Prozesses war von besonderem Wert.
started in 2023, is a three-dimensional collaborative cartography project by more than fifty members from the Inga People of Colombia. Fourteen weavers from different parts of the Inga territory were in charge of elaborating fabrics. Eight Inga representatives were in charge of cartographic data. Support from the legal representative, the technical secretary, and counsellors of AWAI, the national organization representing the Inga People in Colombia, was crucial to the recruitment of the weaving and research teams. Representatives of the Cabildo Inga de Mocoa generously hosted the model at their communal space. Many more people supported the project through research, audiovisual documentation, drawings, translation, and logistics. Especially important was Taita Luciano Mutumbajoy's spiritual guidance in key moments of the process.

Jonathan Banz
studierte Architektur an der ETH Zürich. 2015 bis 2019 war er an der ETH Teil einer Forschungsgruppe von Karin Sander und kollaborierte im Bereich digitale Raumforschung mit Andreas Wiesers Lehrstuhl für Geosensorik und Ingenieurgeodäsie (GSEG), an dem er seit 2022 wissenschaftlicher Mitarbeiter ist. Mit Wieser und Basil Roth initiierte er im selben Jahr das Projekt Mapping Ukraine.
studied architecture at ETH Zürich, where, between 2015 and 2019, he was a member of a research group led by Karin Sander. He collaborated with Andreas Wieser's Chair of Geosensors and Engineering Geodesy (GSEG), where he has been serving as a research associate since 2022. Along with Wieser and Basil Roth, he initiated the project *Mapping Ukraine* in 2022.

Brenne Architekten
ist ein seit 40 Jahren erfolgreich tätiges Architekturbüro in Berlin mit dem Schwerpunkt Bauen im Bestand. Neben Industrie-, Verwaltungs- und Wohnungsbau ist das Team auf Schlösser, Theater und Ikonen der Moderne spezialisiert, von denen mehrere international ausgezeichnet und als UNESCO-Weltkulturerbe anerkannt wurden.
has been a successful architectural practice in Berlin for 40 years, with a particular expertise in building conversion. In addition to industrial, administrative, and residential construction, the multi-professional team also specializes in castles, theaters, and modernist icons, several of which have won international awards and been recognized as UNESCO World Heritage Sites.

Winfried Brenne
(* 1942) absolvierte sein Architekturstudium in Wuppertal und an der TU Berlin. Er leitete ab 1977 gemeinsam mit Helge Pitz die Architekturwerkstatt Pitz-Brenne, bevor er 1990 das Büro Winfried Brenne Architekten gründete. 2002 entstand mit Franz Jaschke die Brenne Architekten GmbH, der seit 2018 auch Fabian Brenne angehört. Brenne ist seit 2006 Mitglied der Akademie der Künste Berlin.
(b. 1942) studied architecture in Wuppertal and at the Technical University of Berlin. Together with Helge Pitz, he ran the Architekturwerkstatt Pitz-Brenne, established in 1977, before founding the firm Winfried Brenne Architekten in 1990. In 2002, Brenne Architekten GmbH was founded with Franz Jaschke, of which Fabian Brenne has been a member since 2018. Brenne has been a member of the Akademie der Künste Berlin since 2006.

Matthias Brenner
(* 1994) ist Doktorand an der ETH Zürich, wo er die Anwendung digitaler Fertigungstechnologien zur Reparatur komplexer High-Tech-Fassadenkomponenten erforscht. Dabei kooperiert er mit dem Advanced Manufacturing Lab der ETH und wird vom Nationalen Forschungsschwerpunkt (NFS) Digitale Fabrikation der ETH unterstützt.
(b. 1994) is a doctoral candidate at ETH Zürich, where he investigates the application of digital fabrication technologies for the repair of complex high-tech facade components. In this framework he cooperates with the Advanced Manufacturing Lab of ETH and is supported by the National Centre of Competence in Research (NCCR) Digital Fabrication at ETH.

Center for Spatial Technologies
ist ein interdisziplinäres Forschungszentrum in Kiew, das auf räumliche Analysen, Visualisierungstechniken und 3D-Modellierung spezialisiert ist. Seit Anfang 2022 liegt der Fokus auf der Analyse der zivilen Verluste durch die russische Invasion der Ukraine.
is a Kyiv-based cross-disciplinary research center specializing in spatial analysis, visualization techniques, and 3D modeling. From the beginning of 2022, CST has focused on analyzing civilian damage caused by the Russian invasion of Ukraine.

Manuel Chavajay
(* 1982) ist Künstler und Mitglied der indigenen Tz'utujil-Gemeinschaft in Guatemala. Zeitgenössische Kunst begreift er als Ort der Heilung. Seine Arbeit bezieht sich auf Praktiken und die Spiritualität, die mit der Kosmovision der Maya verbunden wird: eine tiefe Verbundenheit mit der Natur, dem Leben und der Energie, die in den Dingen liegt.
(b. 1982) is an artist and member of the indigenous Tz'utujil community. He understands contemporary art as a place of healing. His work draws on practices and spirituality associated with the Mayan cosmovision: a deep connection with nature, life, and the energy that lies within things.

Christine Jiayi Chen, Kristina Shatokhina, Wilhelm Gardeleone
studieren Architektur an der Universität Luxemburg. Unter der Leitung von Florian Hertweck und Markus Miessen erarbeiteten sie 2023 das Projekt *After Parking*, das in der Ausstellung *The Great Repair* gezeigt wird.
are studying architecture at the University of Luxembourg. Under the direction of Florian Hertweck and Markus Miessen, they developed the project *After Parking* in 2023, which is shown in the exhibition *The Great Repair*.

Collective Architecture Studio
ist ein laufendes pädagogisches Experiment. Das von Ana Miljački geleitete Entwurfsstudio am MIT befasst sich mit Fragen der kollektiven Urheberschaft, des kollektiven Eigentums und Lebens. 2019 und 2023 war Belgrad, das jugoslawische Architekturerbe und sein zeitgenössischer postsozialistischer Kontext Thema, 2022 arbeitete das Studio mit der Dudley Street Neighborhood Initiative in Boston zusammen.
has been an ongoing pedagogical experiment. The graduate design studio led by Ana Miljački at MIT is dedicated to exploring and experimenting with issues of collective authorship, collective ownership, and collective life. In 2019 and 2023, the studio focused on Belgrade, its Yugoslavian architectural heritage, and its contemporary post-socialist context; in 2022 it worked with the Dudley Street Neighborhood Initiative in Boston.

Collective Works
ist eine von Karin Mientjes und Peter Zuiderwijk in Den Haag gegründete kollaborative Arbeitsstruktur, für die die aktive Auseinandersetzung mit dem räumlichen und sozialen Kontext Teil der Gestaltungspraxis ist. Ihre Arbeit umfasst u. a. aktivistische Kampagnen, räumliche Interventionen zum Communitybuilding, partizipatives Design und forschungsbasierte Publikationen. Sie sind Teil des transdisziplinären Netzwerks ConstructLab.
is a collaborative work structure founded by Karin Mientjes and Peter Zuiderwijk, for whom active engagement with the spatial and social context is part of the design practice. Their work includes activist campaigns, spatial interventions for community building, participatory design, and research-based publications. They are part of the transdisciplinary network Constructlab.

Agnes Denes
(* 1931) ist Künstlerin und lebt in New York. Sie gilt als Pionierin der Ökologischen Kunst und arbeitet in verschiedensten Medien – von Poesie über philosophische Schriften bis hin zu Zeichnung, Skulptur und Land Art. Ihre Werke befinden sich in Sammlungen weltweit, darunter im MoMA und Metropolitan Museum of Art in New York.
(b. 1931) is an artist based in New York. She is widely recognized as one of the pioneers of ecological art and works in a wide range of media—from poetry and philosophical writings to drawings, sculptures, and land art. Her works are part of the permanent collections of galleries worldwide, including those of MoMA and of the Metropolitan Museum of Art in New York.

Kathrin Dörfler
(* 1983) ist Tenure-Track-Professorin für Digitale Fertigung am Department für Architektur der TU München. Sie studierte Architektur an der TU Wien und promovierte an der ETH Zürich. Ihre Forschung konzentriert sich auf kollaborative Fertigungsprozesse, Vor-Ort-Robotik und additive Fertigung an der Schnittstelle von Architektur und Bauwesen. Dabei legt sie besonderen Wert auf die Entwicklung hybrider, interaktiver Mensch-Maschine-Prozesse als Alternative zu vollautomatisierten Abläufen.
(b. 1983) is a tenure-track professor of digital fabrication within the Department of Architecture at the Technical University of Munich. She studied architecture at TU Vienna and holds a PhD from ETH Zürich. Her research focuses on collaborative fabrication processes, on-site robotics, and additive manufacturing at the intersection of architecture and construction. She is dedicated to forging an alternative path beyond the vision of fully automated design and construction towards hybrid, mutually augmented human–machine processes.

Edit
ist ein 2018 in London gegründetes feministisches Designkollektiv, das sich mit Hierarchien in der gebauten Umwelt auseinandersetzt. Design wird als Vehikel zur Förderung von Gleichberechtigung verstanden, was sich im Entwurfsprozess wie im gestalteten Objekt bemerkbar macht.
is a feminist design collective founded in London in 2018, which works to address prejudices and hierarchies in the built environment. Edit understands design to be a vehicle for promoting equality, which should be present in the design process as well as the designed object.

Caroline Faber
(* 1993) studierte Architektur an der TU Wien und ist Doktorandin an der Universität Luxemburg, wo sie mit Fokus auf Luxemburg und die Großregion zu historischen sowie zeitgenössischen Transformationsprozessen ländlicher Räume forscht.
(b.1993) studied architecture at the Technical University in Vienna and is currently doing her PhD at the University of Luxembourg. Her research focuses on historical and contemporary transformation processes of rural areas with a focus on Luxembourg and the Greater Region.

Fuminori Nousaku Architects
ist ein 2010 in Japan gegründetes Büro, dessen Praxis Architektur, Kunst, Installationen, Sanierungen und Publikationstätigkeiten umfasst. Für Forschungsprojekte über Architektur, Stadt und Ökosysteme kollaboriert das Büro auch mit universitären Einrichtungen. In ihrer Architektur denken sie Solarenergie, Bodenregeneration, die Verwendung biologisch abbaubarer Materialien, und Materialkreisläufe von der Produktion bis zur Entsorgung mit.
is a firm founded in 2010 in Japan, whose activities include architectural design, artwork, installation, renovation, and writing. To conduct research on architecture, cities, and ecosystems they collaborate with university laboratories. Their architectural designs focus on solar energy, soil regeneration, biodegradable materials, and material cycles from production to disposal.

Akshar Gajjar
(* 1998) ist Architekt und Stadtplaner und derzeit wissenschaftlicher Mitarbeiter am Labor THEMA des Instituts für Architektur der EPFL in Lausanne. Er forscht an der Schnittstelle von Architektur, Urbanismus, Ökologie und Queer Studies und konzentriert sich dabei auf postindustrielle Ruinen, um deren Potenzial für ein artenübergreifendes Über- und Zusammenleben zu untersuchen.
(b. 1998) is an architect and urban designer. He is currently a scientific assistant at the research laboratory THEMA within the Architecture Faculty of EPFL Lausanne. His research transects architecture, urbanism, ecology, and queer studies—focusing on postindustrial ruins for their potential of multispecies collaborative survival.

Matthew Gordon
ist Designer und Bautechnologe. Er studierte Architektur und absolvierte das Programm Master in Robotics and Advanced Construction am IaaC in Barcelona. Sein Forschungsgebiet sind Rückbau- und Kreislaufkonzepte.
is a designer and construction technologist, originally trained in architecture and holding a Masters in Robotics and Advanced Construction from IaaC, Barcelona. His research centers on deconstruction and circular concepts.

Jess Gough
(* 1989) ist autodidaktische Filmfotografin und lebt in London. Sie wurde für den FOAM Paul Huf Award 2020 nominiert und hat an einer Reihe von Langzeitaufträgen für Zeitschriften gearbeitet.
(b. 1989) is a self-taught film photographer based in London. She was nominated for the 2020 FOAM Paul Huf Award and has worked on a number of long-form commissions for magazines.

Franziska Gödicke
(* 1998) studierte Architektur an der Bauhaus-Universität Weimar und der Università Iuav di Venezia. 2021 bis 2023 war sie für ARCH+ tätig, seit 2022 ist sie Teil von b+ in Berlin. Sie ist Co-Kuratorin des Deutschen Pavillons der Architekturbiennale 2023 in Venedig.
(b. 1998) studied architecture at the Bauhaus-Universität Weimar and Università Iuav di Venezia. From 2021 to 2023 she worked at ARCH+, and since 2022 she has been part of b+ in Berlin. She is co-curator of the German Pavilion at the 2023 Venice Architecture Biennale.

Jana Hainbach
(b. 1990) ist Restauratorin für Wandmalerei und Architekturoberflächen spezialisiert auf Architektur des 20. Jahrhundert. Als wissenschaftliche Mitarbeiterin am Lehrstuhl für Restaurierung, Kunsttechnologie und Konservierungswissenschaft von Thomas Danzl an der TU München forscht sie zur Materialität und Farbigkeit der *Siedlungen der Berliner Moderne*.
(b. 1990) is a restorer of wall paintings and architectural surfaces specialising in 20th century architecture. As a research assistant at Thomas Danzl's Chair of Restoration, Art Technology, and Conservation Science at the Technical University in Munich, she is conducting research on the materiality and colorfulness of Berlin Modernism housing projects.

Anna Heringer
ist Architektin und Honorarprofessorin des UNESCO Lehrstuhls für Lehmbau, Baukulturen und nachhaltige Entwicklung. Seit 1997 ist sie in verschiedene soziale Projekte in Bangladesch involviert, insbesondere die METI-Schule, die 2005 in Rudrapur fertiggestellt und 2007 mit dem Aga Khan Award for Architecture ausgezeichnet wurde. Studio Anna Heringer realisierte weitere Projekte in Asien, Afrika und Europa.
is an architect and honorary professor at the UNESCO Chair of Earthen Architecture, Building Cultures, and Sustainable Development. Since 1997, she has been actively involved in various social projects in Bangladesh, most notably in the METI School, which was completed in 2005 in Rudrapur and received the Aga Khan Award for Architecture in 2007. Over the years, Studio Anna Heringer has realized further projects in Asia, Africa, and Europe.

Florian Hertweck
(* 1975) ist Architekt und Stadtforscher. Seit 2016 ist er ordentlicher Professor an der Universität Luxemburg, wo er den Masterstudiengang Architektur leitet, und Partner im Studio Hertweck Architecture Urbanism. Er ist Autor zahlreicher Publikationen und gab zuletzt *Architektur auf gemeinsamem Boden – Positionen und Modelle zur Bodenfrage* (2020) heraus. Er ist Co-Kurator von *The Great Repair*.
(b. 1975) is an architect and urban researcher. He has been a full professor at the University of Luxembourg since 2016, where he directs the master's program in architecture, and a partner at Studio Hertweck Architecture Urbanism. He is the author of numerous books and the editor of *Architektur auf gemeinsamem Boden: Positionen und Modelle zur Bodenfrage* (2020). He is a co-curator of *The Great Repair*.

Manuel Herz Architects
ist ein Büro in Basel und vorwiegend in Europa und Afrika tätig. Sie realisierten u. a. die Synagoge Mainz, das Wohnhaus Ballet Mécanique in Zürich, einen sozialen Wohnungsbau in Lyon und ein Krankenhaus in Tambacounda, Senegal. Manuel Herz kuratierte und gestaltete den Pavillon der Länder der Westsahara auf der Architekturbiennale 2016 in Venedig.
is an architectural practice based in Basel and operating across Europe and Africa. Realized projects include the Synagogue of Mainz, the apartment building Ballet Mécanique in Zurich, a social housing complex in Lyon, and a hospital for Tambacounda, Senegal. In 2016, Herz curated and designed the National Pavilion of Western Sahara at the 2016 Venice Architecture Biennale.

Christian Hiller
(* 1975) ist Medienwissenschaftler, Redakteur und Kurator. Er leitete Ausstellungs-, Veranstaltungs-, Publikations- und Forschungsprojekte, u. a. für die Stiftung Bauhaus Dessau und das Haus der Kulturen der Welt. Mit ARCH+ kuratierte er u. a. *projekt bauhaus* (2015–2019), *An Atlas of Commoning* (2018) und *Cohabitation* (2021). Er ist Co-Kurator von *The Great Repair* und des Deutschen Pavillons der Architekturbiennale 2023 in Venedig.
(b. 1975) is a media scholar, editor, and curator. He has managed exhibitions, event series, publications, and research projects for institutions such as the Stiftung Bauhaus Dessau, the Haus der Kulturen der Welt in Berlin. With ARCH+, he has curated projects including *projekt bauhaus* (2015–2019), *An Atlas of Commoning* (2018), and *Cohabitation* (2021). He is a co-curator of *The Great Repair* and of the German Pavilion at the 2023 Venice Architecture Biennale.

Felix Hofmann
(* 1992) studierte Geografie in Erlangen und Architektur in Stuttgart. Für ARCH+ ist er als Redakteur und Ausstellungsproduzent tätig. In diesem Rahmen war er 2020–2022 am Projekt *Cohabitation* beteiligt und arbeitet derzeit an der Ausstellung *The Great Repair*.
(b. 1992) studied geography in Erlangen and architecture in Stuttgart. He is an editor and production manager of exhibitions at ARCH+. In this context, he was involved in the 2020–2022 project *Cohabitation* and is currently working on the exhibition *The Great Repair*.

Hans Hortig
(* 1984) ist Landschaftsarchitekt und Forscher, und hat Research und Design Studios am Future Cities Laboratory in Singapur und an der ETH Zürich unterrichtet. Er ist Co-Kurator der Vortragsreihe *Sessions on Territory* und hat an mehreren Ausstellungen teilgenommen, darunter die Rotterdam Biennale, Shenzhen Biennale, und am S AM in Basel.
(b. 1984) is a landscape architect and researcher. He has taught research and design studios at the Future Cities Laboratory in Singapore and ETH Zürich. He is a co-curator of the lecture series *Sessions on Territory*, and has contributed to several exhibitions, including the Rotterdam Biennale, Shenzhen Biennale, and at S AM in Basel.

Interboro
ist ein Architektur-, Planungs- und Forschungsbüro in Brooklyn und Detroit, das 2002 von Tobias Armborst, Georgeen Theodore und Daniel D'Oca gegründet wurde. 2017 erschien ihr Buch *The Arsenal of Exclusion & Inclusion*. In den letzten Jahren arbeitete Interboro mit den Bewohner*innen der Patterson Houses zusammen. Am Projekt *Contested Maintenance* waren u. a. Caleb Mitchell, Joe Giambri und Ebony Payne beteiligt.
is a Brooklyn- and Detroit-based architecture, planning, and research firm founded in 2002 by Tobias Armborst, Georgeen Theodore, and Daniel D'Oca. Interboro's book *The Arsenal of Exclusion & Inclusion* was published in 2017. Interboro has been working with the residents of the Patterson Houses for the last few years. The *Contested Maintenance* project was developed with Caleb Mitchell, Joe Giambri, Ebony Payne, and others.

Martin Kaltwasser
(1965–2022) war Künstler, Architekt und Professor für Plastik an der TU Dortmund. In seiner künstlerischen Praxis verband er kritische Recherchen mit prozessorientierten, objekthaften, räumlichen Umsetzungen, und thematisierte dabei Fragen von Öffentlichkeit, Mobilität, Raumaneignung, Raumregimen, Ressourcen und Nachhaltigkeit.
(1965–2022) was an artist, architect and a professor for sculpture at the Technical University of Dortmund. In his work he combined critical research with process-oriented, object-like, spatial implementation and thereby addressed questions of publicity, mobility, appropriation of space, spatial regimes, resources, and sustainability.

Kleine Reinigungs- und Dienstleistungsgesellschaft
ist ein 1990 in Berlin gegründetes Unternehmen, das tägliche Unterhaltsreinigung sowie Veranstaltungsbetreuung und diverse Sonderleistungen wie Fassadenreinigung und Denkmalpflege anbietet. Neben den beiden Standorten der Akademie der Künste betreut Kleine Gebäude aus den Bereichen Bildung, Gastronomie, Handwerk, Industrie, Kultur, Medizin, Politik und Verwaltung.
was founded in Berlin in 1990 and offers daily maintenance cleaning as well as event support and various special services such as facade cleaning and monument maintenance. In addition to the two locations of the Akademie der Künste, the company also looks after buildings in the fields of education, gastronomy, crafts, industry, culture, health, politics, and administration.

Bettina Knaup
ist freie Kuratorin und Autorin und lebt in Berlin. Sie hat zahlreiche internationale Festivals, Ausstellungen und Projekte (co-)kuratiert, darunter *performance platform. body affects* (Sophiensaele, Berlin, 2012) und *re.act.feminism* (verschiedene europäische Stationen, 2008–2013; Manifesta 14 in Pristina, 2022). Auf der Grundlage ihrer Promotion *performing (as) waste* an der University of Roehampton in London entwickelt sie derzeit ein kollaboratives Projekt, das sich mit Müll-Infrastrukturen beschäftigt.
is a freelance curator and writer, based in Berlin. She has (co-)curated numerous international festivals, exhibitions and projects, including *performance platform. body affects* (Sophiensaele, Berlin, 2012) and *re.act.feminism* (touring in Europe from 2008 to 2013; Manifesta 14 in Pristina, 2022). Based on her PhD dissertation at the University of Roehampton in London, *performing (as) waste*, she is currently preparing a collaborative artistic project engaging with waste infrastructures.

Folke Köbberling
(* 1969) ist Künstlerin und Professorin an der TU Braunschweig, wo sie das Institut für Architekturbezogene Kunst leitet. In ihren Arbeiten formuliert sie Formen des Widerstands gegen die Auswüchse der neoliberalen Wirtschaftsordnung wie Konsumzwang, die Zerstörung der Städte, Landschaften, öffentlichen Räume, Ressourcen und Menschen. Dafür nutzt sie gefundene Materialien, die sie ortsbezogen transformiert und installiert.
(b. 1969) is an artist and a professor at the Technical University of Braunschweig where she directs the institute for architecture-related art. In her works, she formulates forms of resistance against the excesses of the neoliberal economic order, such as compulsive consumption and destruction of cities, landscapes, public spaces, resources and people. For this she uses found materials, which she transforms and installs on a site-specific basis.

Markus Krieger
(* 1993) ist ARCH+ Redakteur und Co-Kurator des Ausstellungs- und Publikationsprojekts *The Great Repair*. 2020 schloss er sein Studium am Architekturdepartement der ETH Zürich mit Auszeichnung ab.
(* 1993) is an editor at ARCH+ and a co-curator of the exhibition and publication project *The Great Repair*. In 2020, he graduated with honors from the Department of Architecture at ETH Zürich.

Lacaton & Vassal
wurde 1987 von Anne Lacaton und Jean-Philippe Vassal gegründet und 2021 mit dem Pritzker-Preis ausgezeichnet. Schlüsselprojekte sind u. a. der Umbau des Palais de Tokyo in Paris (2012), der Neubau der ENSA Nantes (2009) und der soziale Wohnungsbau der Cité Manifeste in Mulhouse (2005).
was founded by Anne Lacaton und Jean-Philippe Vassal in 1987 and was awarded the Pritzker Prize in 2021. Key projects include the conversation of Palais de Tokyo in Paris (2012), the new ENSA Nantes (2009), and the social housing estate Cité Manifeste in Mulhouse (2005).

Mierle Laderman Ukeles
(* 1939) begründete 1969 die Maintenance Art. Seit 1977 ist sie ehrenamtlich Artist-in-Residence des NYC Department of Sanitation und Percent for Art Artist (ab 1989) von Fresh Kills, der einst größten städtischen Mülldeponie der Welt, die heute zu einem öffentlichen Park in der Größe dreier Central Parks umgewandelt wird. Laderman Ukeles arbeitet international. Ihre multidisziplinären Werke, die die Grenzen von Arbeit und Performance, System und Geist sprengen, offenbaren fließende Verbindungen zwischen Feminismus, Fürsorge, Arbeit, Arbeiter*innen, der Stadt, der Umwelt und dem Planeten. Ihre Arbeiten befinden sich in den Sammlungen des Whitney, Guggenheim, Art Institute Chicago, Crystal Bridges, Wadsworth Atheneum, der Kunstsammlung Düsseldorf, Migros Zürich, des FRAC Lorraine Metz und Jewish Museum in New York. Sie wird von der Ronald Feldman Gallery, New York, vertreten.
(b. 1939) created Maintenance Art in 1969. Since 1977, she has continued as the unsalaried Artist-in-Residence of the NYC Department of Sanitation and Percent for Art Artist (since 1989) of Fresh Kills, once the largest municipal landfill in the world, being developed into a public park three times the size of Central Park. She works internationally; her multidisciplinary artwork, crashing boundaries between labor and performance, system and spirit, unveils flow connections between feminism, care, work, workers, the city, the environment, and the planet. Her works are in the permanent collections of the Whitney, Guggenheim, Art Institute of Chicago, Crystal Bridges, Wadsworth Atheneum, Kunstsammlung Dusseldorf, Migros Zurich, FRAC Lorraine Metz, and the Jewish Museum, NYC. She is represented by Ronald Feldman Gallery, NYC.

Silke Langenberg
(* 1974) ist Professorin für Konstruktionserbe und Denkmalpflege am Departement Architektur der ETH Zürich. Langenberg beschäftigt sich in Forschung und Lehre bereits seit Jahren mit dem Thema der Reparatur und Reparaturfähigkeit im Bauwesen. 2018 erschien ihre Publikation *Reparatur – Anstiftung zum Denken und Machen*, 2022 der Fortsetzungsband *Upgrade – Making Things Better*.
(b. 1974) is Professor of Construction Heritage and Preservation at the Department of Architecture at ETH Zürich. Langenberg's research and teaching have focused for many years on the topic of repair and reparability in construction. Her book *Reparatur: Anstiftung zum Denken und Machen* was published in 2018, followed by the sequel *Upgrade: Making Things Better* in 2022.

Limbo Accra
wurde 2018 von Dominique Petit-Frère und Emil Grip gegründet und ist ein interdisziplinäres Büro in Accra, das sich mit den Relikten unabgeschlossener Immobilienprojekte in Ghana und anderswo beschäftigt. Bekannt wurden sie mit der Aktivierung von Schwellenräumen in Accra, etwa der Adjiringanor Activation oder dem Freedom Skatepark, ihrem ersten realisierten Bauprojekt.
founded in 2018 by Dominique Petit-Frère and Emil Grip, is an interdisciplinary practice based in Accra, operating within the relics of incomplete property developments in Ghana and beyond. They became known through their activation of liminal spaces in Accra, such as the Adjiringanor Activation as well as their inaugural built project, Freedom Skatepark.

Charlotte Malterre-Barthes
ist Architektin, Stadtplanerin und Assistenzprofessorin für Architektur und Stadtplanung an der EPFL in Lausanne. Zuvor war sie Assistenzprofessorin an der Harvard Graduate School of Design. 2020 rief sie die Initiative „A Global Moratorium on New Construction" ins Leben. Sie ist Gründungsmitglied der aktivistischen Netzwerke Parity Group und Parity Front.
is an architect, urban designer, and Assistant Professor of Architectural and Urban Design at EPFL in Lausanne. She was previously an assistant professor at the Harvard Graduate School of Design. In 2020, she started the initiative "A Global Moratorium on New Construction." She is a founding member of the activist networks Parity Group and Parity Front.

Marija Marić
(* 1986) ist Architektin, Forscherin und Kuratorin. Sie ist Postdoctoral Research Associate im Masterstudiengang Architektur der Universität Luxemburg, wo sie auch unterrichtet. Marić ist Co-Kuratorin des Luxemburgischen Pavillons der Architekturbiennale 2023 in Venedig und Co-Autorin von *Staging the Moon – Resource Extraction Beyond Earth* (2023).
(b. 1986) is an architect, researcher, and curator. She works as a postdoctoral research associate at the Master in Architecture Programme, University of Luxembourg, where she also teaches. Marić is a co-curator of the Luxembourg Pavilion at the 2023 Venice Architecture Biennale and coauthor of *Staging the Moon: Resource Extraction Beyond Earth* (2023).

Material Cultures
wurde in London mit dem Ziel gegründet, Gestaltung, Materialforschung und strategisches Denken zu verbinden, um Fortschritte in Richtung einer Post-Carbon-Architektur zu machen. Material Cultures plant, führt Bau- und Sanierungsprojekte durch und arbeitet mit öffentlichen, privaten und non-profit Organisationen zusammen, die an der Entwicklung und Umsetzung einer regenerativen, CO_2-armen gebauten Umwelt interessiert sind.
was founded to bring together design, material research, and high-level strategic thinking to make meaningful progress towards a post-carbon built environment. The London-based office provides design services, undertakes hands-on construction and refurbishment projects, and works with public, private, and third sector organizations interested in developing and delivering a regenerative, low-carbon built environment.

Ana Miljački
ist Professorin für Architektur am MIT, leitet dessen SMArchS Programm und initiierte dort das Critical Broadcasting Lab. Sie war Co-Kuratorin des US-amerikanischen Pavillons *OfficeUS* der Architekturbiennale 2014 in Venedig und ist Autorin von *The Optimum Imperative – Czech Architecture for the Socialist Lifestyle, 1938–1968* (2017).
is Professor of Architecture at MIT, currently directs their SMArchS program, and launched the Critical Broadcasting Lab at MIT. She was co-curator of the US Pavilion *OfficeUS* for the 2014 Venice Architecture Biennale and is the author of *The Optimum Imperative: Czech Architecture for the Socialist Lifestyle, 1938–1968* (2017).

Marion Moutal
(* 1992) ist Architektin und wissenschaftliche Mitarbeiterin am Labor THEMA des Instituts für Architektur der EPFL in Lausanne. Zuvor arbeitete sie an der Beziehung zwischen Staudämmen und der Schweizer Alpenlandschaft und der Zukunft dieser Strukturen angesichts der Klimakrise.
(b. 1992) is an architect and scientific assistant at the research laboratory THEMA within the Institute of Architecture at EPFL in Lausanne. Prior to this, she has worked on the relation of dams to the Swiss alpine landscape, focusing on the engineering viewpoint of the future of these structures under the spectre of climate change.

Gyler Mydyti
ist eine im Kosovo geborene Architektin, Stadtplanerin und Forscherin, die derzeit als Senior Urban Designer bei KCAP in Zürich tätig ist. Ihr Spezialgebiet sind sozialräumliche Transformations- und Wiederaufbauprozesse in postsozialistischen und Nachkriegsgebieten, vor allem in den westlichen Balkanländern.
is a Kosovo-born architect, urban planner, and researcher who currently serves as the Senior Urban Designer at KCAP in Zurich. Her expertise lies in the socio-spatial transformation and reconstruction processes of post-socialist and post-war territories, primarily in the Western Balkan countries.

Nataliia Mysak
ist freie Architektin und Forscherin. Sie war Research Fellow an der TU Wien, Universität Malmö und ETH Zürich. Sie engagierte sich in städtischen Initiativen in Lviv, forschte am Lviv Center for Urban History und war Architektin bei Drozdov and Partners in Charkiw. Derzeit arbeitet sie mit dem Swiss Network with Ukraine zusammen.
is an independent architect and researcher. She is a former research fellow at the Technical University of Vienna, Malmö University, and ETH Zürich. She was engaged in urban initiatives in Lviv, worked as a researcher at the Center for Urban History (Lviv), and as an architect at Drozdov and Partners in Kharkiv. She is currently collaborating with the Swiss Network with Ukraine.

Alex Nehmer
(* 1989) ist Redakteurin von ARCH+. 2015 bis 2016 arbeitete sie für das Haus der Kulturen der Welt in Berlin an der Publikationsreihe zur Ausstellung *Wohnungsfrage*, 2019/20 lehrte sie im Studiengang Kultur der Metropole an der HafenCity Universität Hamburg. Sie ist Co-Kuratorin von *The Great Repair*.
(b. 1989) is an editor at ARCH+. From 2015 to 2016, she worked for the Haus der Kulturen der Welt in Berlin on the publication series for the exhibition *Wohnungsfrage*, and taught in the Metropolitan Culture program at HafenCity University Hamburg in 2019/20. She is a co-curator of *The Great Repair*.

Anh-Linh Ngo
(* 1974) ist Architekturtheoretiker, Kurator und Mitherausgeber von ARCH+. Er kuratiert mit ARCH+ regelmäßig Ausstellungs- und Forschungsprojekte wie *projekt bauhaus* (2015–2019), *Cohabitation* (2021) und *The Great Repair*. Er ist Mitglied des Kuratoriums der IBA 2027 StadtRegion Stuttgart und der Akademie Schloss Solitude sowie Beiratsmitglied des Goethe-Instituts. Seit 2022 ist er Mitglied der Akademie der Künste, Berlin. Er ist Co-Kurator des Deutschen Pavillons der Architekturbiennale 2023 in Venedig.
(b. 1974) is an architectural theorist, curator, and editor-in-chief of ARCH+. He regularly curates exhibitions and research projects with ARCH+, including *projekt bauhaus* (2015–2019), *Cohabitation* (2021), and *The Great Repair* (2023). He is currently a member of the board of trustees of IBA 2027 StadtRegion Stuttgart, the board of trustees of the Akademie Schloss Solitude, and the Goethe Institut's advisory council. Since 2022, he has been a member of the Akademie der Künste Berlin. He is a co-curator of the German Pavilion at the 2023 Venice Architecture Biennale.

Sarah Nichols
ist Assistenzprofessorin für Architektur an der EPFL in Lausanne und leitet dort das Labor Theory of Environment and Materials in Architecture (THEMA). Sie forscht zu ökologischen und politischen Verflechtungen im Bauwesen mit einem Fokus auf Baumaterialien. Derzeit arbeitet Nichols an dem Buch *Opération Béton – Constructing Concrete in Switzerland*, das auf ihrer, mit einer ETH-Medaille ausgezeichneten, Dissertation basiert.
is Assistant Professor of Architecture at EPFL in Lausanne, where she is also director of the Theory of Environment and Materials in Architecture lab (THEMA). Her scholarly work examines the environmental and political entanglements of construction, particularly through building materials. Nichols is currently working on the book *Opération Béton: Constructing Concrete in Switzerland* based on her dissertation, for which she was awarded the ETH Medal.

Zara Pfeifer
(* 1984) ist Künstlerin und beschäftigt sich mit sozialen Phänomenen großer Infrastrukturen. 2022 erschien ihr Buch *ICC Berlin* im Jovis Verlag. Pfeifer studierte Architektur an der Akademie der bildenden Künste Wien und Fotografie an der Friedl Kubelka Schule für künstlerische Fotografie in Wien. Sie lehrt an der TU Wien und TU Berlin.
(b. 1984) is an artist concerned with the social phenomena of large-scale infrastructure. In 2022, her book *ICC Berlin* was published by Jovis Verlag. Pfeifer studied architecture at the Academy of Fine Arts Vienna and photography at the Friedl Kubelka School for Artistic Photography in Vienna. She holds lecturing positions at the Technical University Vienna and the Technical University Berlin.

Marjetica Potrč

(* 1953) ist Künstlerin und Architektin und lebt in Ljubljana. In ihrer Arbeit beschäftigt sie sich damit, wie sich zeitgenössische architektonische Praktiken auf physische und soziale Infrastrukturen auswirken. Potrč nahm u. a. an den Skulptur Projekten Münster (1997), der Kunstbiennale von Venedig (1993, 2003, 2009), der Biennale von São Paulo (1996, 2006), der Yinchuan Biennale (2018) und der Biennale von Sydney (2022) teil.

(b. 1953) is an artist and architect based in Ljubljana. Her research investigates how contemporary architectural practices impact physical and social infrastructures. Potrč participated in exhibitions worldwide including Skulptur Projekte Münster (1997), the Venice Art Biennale (1993, 2003, 2009), the São Paulo Biennial (1996, 2006), the Yinchuan Biennial (2018), and the Biennale of Sydney (2022).

Bas Princen

(* 1975) ist Künstler und Fotograf. Er studierte Industriedesign an der Design Academy Eindhoven und Architektur am Berlage Institute in Rotterdam. Schwerpunkt seiner Arbeiten sind Stadtlandschaften im Wandel, wobei er mit den Mitteln der Fotografie die verschiedenen Formen, Auswirkungen und Wahrnehmungen der Veränderung des städtischen Raums festhält.

(b. 1975) is an artist and photographer. He studied industrial design at the Design Academy Eindhoven and architecture at the Berlage Institute in Rotterdam. Since then, his work has focused on urban landscapes in transition, using photography to examine the various forms, outcomes, and perceptions of changing urban spaces.

Basil Roth

arbeitete als Produktions- und Aufnahmeleiter für diverse Film- und Fernsehproduktionen, bevor er fünf Jahre als Koordinator und Geschäftsführer von Grassroots-NGOs tätig war, die Geflüchtete und Asylbewerber*innen in Griechenland unterstützte. Mit Andreas Wieser und Jonathan Banz initiierte er im Frühjahr 2022 das Projekt Mapping Ukraine an der ETH Zürich.

worked as a production and unit manager for film and TV productions, before he joined grass roots NGOs supporting refugees and asylum seekers in Greece as a Mission Coordinator and Managing Director for five years. Along with Andreas Wieser and Jonathan Banz, he initiated the Mapping Ukraine project at ETH Zürich in spring 2022.

Sakiya

ist Akademie, Residency, Research Hub und Bauernhof in Ein Qiniya, einem Dorf in den von Israel besetzten palästinensischen Gebieten. Durch die Verknüpfung lokaler Traditionen der Selbstversorgung mit zeitgenössischer Kunst und ökologischen Praktiken schafft Sakiya neue Narrative für die Beziehung zu Land, Wissensproduktion und Allmende.

is an academy, a residency program, research hub, and a farm located in Ein Qiniya, a village in Israeli-occupied Palestinian territory. By grafting local traditions of self-sufficiency onto contemporary art and ecological practices, Sakiya seeks to create new narratives around relationships to land, knowledge-production, and commoning.

Katharina Schultens

(* 1980) ist seit 2022 Leiterin des Haus für Poesie in Berlin. Seit 2004 veröffentlichte sie vier Lyrikbände sowie mehrere Essays. Ihre Arbeiten wurden vielfach ausgezeichnet. Ihr fünfter Lyrikband *Irrlichttiraden* erscheint demnächst bei kookbooks. Sie ist Mitglied der Akademie der Künste und lebt in Berlin.

(b. 1980) has been director of the Haus für Poesie in Berlin since 2022. Since 2004, she has published four volumes of poetry and several essays. Her work has won many awards. Her fifth volume of poetry, *Irrlichttiraden*, will soon be published by kookbooks. She is a member of the Akademie der Künste and lives in Berlin.

Alexander Stumm

ist wissenschaftlicher Mitarbeiter am Fachgebiet Architekturtheorie und Entwerfen der Universität Kassel und Dozent für Architekturgeschichte an der Vietnamese-German University in Ho-Chi-Minh-Stadt. Er ist Redakteur der *Bauwelt* und konzipiert Ausstellungen. 2017–2019 war er Redakteur der ARCH+, 2019–2021 lehrte an der TU Berlin, 2022–2023 war er Vertretungsprofessor für Architekturtheorie an der BTU Cottbus.

is a research associate at the Department of Architectural Theory and Design at the University of Kassel, and a lecturer in architectural history at the Vietnamese-German University in Ho Chi Minh City. He is an editor at *Bauwelt* and curates exhibitions. In 2017–2019 he was an editor at ARCH+, in 2019–2021 he taught at the Technical University of Berlin, and in 2022–2023 he was a substitute professor for architectural theory at BTU Cottbus.

Takhayali

ist eine Bürger*inneninitiative, die für die Beteiligung der Gemeinschaft an der Entscheidungsfindung in Fragen der Planung und Entwicklung in Palästina eintritt. Sie fordert die bestehenden Rahmenbedingungen und Akteur*innen heraus und schafft einen gemeinschaftlichen Raum des Widerstands gegen neoliberale und koloniale Politiken.

is a civic initiative that demands community participation in decision making on issues of planning and development in Palestine. It aspires to challenge existing frameworks and actors and provide a shared space of resistance against neoliberal and colonial policies.

Paulo Tavares

ist Architekt, Autor und Dozent. Er ist Autor mehrerer kritischer Bücher über das koloniale Erbe der Moderne, darunter *Des-Habitat* (2019) und *Lucio Costa era Racista?* (2022). 2023 kuratierte er mit Gabriela de Matos den Brasilianischen Pavillon der Architekturbiennale in Venedig, wofür ihnen der Goldene Löwe für den besten nationalen Beitrag verliehen wurde. In Brasilien leitet Tavares die Forschungs- und Interventionsplattform autônoma und unterrichtet an der Universität von Brasília.

is an architect, author and educator. He is the author of several books questioning the colonial legacies of modernity, most recently *Des-Habitat* (2019), and *Lucio Costa era Racista?* (2022). Together with Gabriela de Matos, he co-curated the Brazilian Pavilion of the 2023 Venice Architecture Biennale, for which they were awarded the Golden Lion for best national participation. In Brazil, Tavares leads the spatial advocacy agency autônoma and teaches at the University of Brasília.

Milica Topalović

ist außerordentliche Professorin für Architektur und Territorialplanung am Architekturdepartement der ETH Zürich. Mit der Forschungsgruppe Architecture of Territory führte sie weltweit eine Reihe von Territorialstudien in entlegenen Regionen, im ressourcenreichen Hinterland und in ländlichen Gegenden durch, um die Ansätze der Architektur in Bezug auf die Stadt, die Urbanisierung und das Urbane zu dezentrieren und ökologisieren. Sie ist Co-Kuratorin von *The Great Repair*.

is Associate Professor of Architecture and Territorial Planning at the Department of Architecture at ETH Zürich. With the Architecture of Territory group, she undertook a range of territorial studies around the world, in remote regions, resource hinterlands, and countrysides, in an effort to decenter and ecologize architects' approaches to the city, the urban, and urbanization. She is a co-curator of *The Great Repair*.

Nazlı Tümerdem

studierte Architektur an der Istanbul Technical University und der Istanbul Bilgi University. 2018 promovierte sie mit der Arbeit *Istanbul Walkabouts – A Critical Walking Study of Northern Istanbul*. In diesem Kontext entstand im öffentlichen Raum das performative Projekt *Istanbul Walkabouts*. Seit 2019 ist sie mit dem Bundes-Exzellenz-Stipendium der Schweizerischen Eidgenossenschaft Postdoktorandin am Lehrstuhl Architektur und Territorialplanung der ETH Zürich.

is an architect and researcher. She studied at Istanbul Technical University and Istanbul Bilgi University. In 2018, she completed her PhD entitled *Istanbul Walkabouts: A Critical Walking Study of Northern Istanbul*, in which conjunction she initiated the independent performance project *Istanbul Walkabouts*. In 2019, she joined the Chair of Architecture and Territorial Planning at ETH Zürich as a postdoctoral researcher and recipient of a Swiss Government Excellence Scholarship.

UVW-SAW

United Voices of the World – Section of Architectural Workers (UVW-SAW) ist eine 2019 gegründete Gewerkschaft von Architekturschaffenden in Großbritannien. SAW engagiert sich gegen die negativen Auswirkungen von Architekturarbeit auf Arbeiter*innen und Umwelt. Ihre Mitglieder organisieren sich gegen Überarbeitung, Unterbezahlung, prekäre Beschäftigungsverhältnisse, toxische Arbeitskulturen, Diskriminierung und unethische Praktiken.

United Voices of the World – Section of Architectural Workers (UVW-SAW) is a grassroots trade union for architectural workers in the UK founded in 2019. SAW collectively takes action and fights against the negative impacts of architectural work on workers, communities, and the environment. Its members organize both in their workplaces and across the sector around overwork, underpay, unstable employment, a toxic workplace, university culture, discrimination, and unethical practice.

Eva von Redecker

lebt als Philosophin und Autorin im ländlichen Brandenburg. Ihr jüngstes Buch, *Bleibefreiheit* (2023), nimmt sich angesichts der ökologischen Krise des Freiheitsbegriffs an und schlägt vor, diesen in Zukunft vermehrt zeitlich anstatt räumlich zu verstehen. Im September 2020 erschien *Revolution für das Leben*, das Kapitalismuskritik mit einer Philosophie neuer Protestformen verbindet. Sie ist seit April 2023 feste Kolumnistin des *Philosophie Magazin* und moderiert am Schauspiel Köln die Gesprächsreihe *Eva and The Apple*.

is a philosopher and author and lives in rural Brandenburg. Her most recent book, *Bleibefreiheit* (2023), takes on the concept of freedom in the face of the ecological crisis and suggests that in future it should be understood increasingly in temporal rather than spatial terms. In September 2020, *Revolution für das Leben* was published, which combines a critique of capitalism with a philosophy of new forms of protest. She has been a regular columnist for *Philosophie Magazin* since April 2023 and moderates the discussion series *Eva and The Apple* at Schauspiel Köln.

Tang Wei

(* 2000) studiert Architektur an der National University of Singapore. Ihr Forschungsinteresse sind periurbane Regionen Südostasiens und wie diese nachhaltig wachsen und entwickelt werden können. Aktuell arbeitet sie zum Ökotourismus in Indonesien.

(b. 2000) studied architecture at the National University of Singapore. Her research focuses on the sustainable growth and development of the peri-urban regions of Southeast Asia, currently she is working on ecotourism in Indonesia.

Jan Westerheide

(* 1991) ist Architekt sowie Forschungs- und Lehrassistent am Lehrstuhl für Architektur und Territorialplanung der ETH Zürich, wo er derzeit das Entwurfsstudio für Bachelor-Studierende leitet. Seine Forschungs- und Lehrschwerpunkte sind agrarökologische Transformationsprozesse, Fragen des Landbesitzes und der Arbeit in der Landwirtschaft sowie politische Potenziale zukünftiger Energielandschaften.

(b. 1991) is an architect and research and teaching assistant at the Chair of Architecture and Territorial Planning at ETH Zürich, where he is currently running the undergrad design studio. His research and teaching focuses on agroecological transformation processes, questions of land ownership and labour in agriculture and political potentials of future energy landscapes.

Michael Wolf

(1954–2019) war Fotograf und beschäftigte sich in seiner Arbeit vor allem mit dem Leben, der Architektur und Alltagskultur in Megastädten. Seine Werke wurden weltweit ausgestellt und befinden sich in zahlreichen Sammlungen. Er hat mehr als 40 Bücher veröffentlicht, darunter *Architecture of Density, Transparent City, Tokyo Compression, Hong Kong Inside Out, Informal Solutions und Sitting in China*.

(1954–2019) was a photographer whose work focused on life, architecture and vernacular culture in the mega cities. His work has been exhibited worldwide and resides in numerous permanent collections. He has published more than 40 books including *Architecture of Density, Transparent City, Tokyo Compression, Hong Kong Inside Out, Informal Solutions, and Sitting in China*.

ZAS*

steht für Zürcher Arbeitsgruppe für Städtebau und ist seit den späten 1950er-Jahren aktiv. Die Gruppe bezieht Position gegen offizielle Stadtplanung in Zürich und entwickelt transformative Gegenentwürfe. Mit Projekten wie dem Ideenwettbewerb für die Nachnutzung der Triemli-Türme hat ZAS* eine entscheidende Debatte über die Sinnhaftigkeit von Abriss- und Neubauprojekten angestoßen.

stands for Züricher Arbeitsgruppe für Städtebau (Zurich Working Group for Urban Planning). The group has been active since the late 1950s, marking opposition to official urban planning proposals in Zurich and providing transformative counter-proposals. With projects such as the ideas competition for the re-use of the Triemli Towers, ZAS* has initiated a decisive debate calling into question the demolition and redevelopment of existing buildings.

Céline Zimmer

(* 1994) studierte Architektur in Trier und Hamburg und promoviert derzeit an der Universität Luxemburg mit einer Arbeit über alternative Wohnmodelle, die sich von den Logiken des Immobilienmarkts und öffentlichen Wohnungsbaus befreit haben.

(b. 1994) studied architecture in Trier and Hamburg and is currently a PhD student at the University of Luxembourg. Her dissertation focuses on alternative housing models that have emancipated themselves from the logics of both market and public housing supply.

Cover: © Bas Princen
Umklapper / Inside cover flap: © ARCH+

19: Photo: Siegmann Horst. © Landesarchiv Berlin, F Rep. 290 (08) Nr. 0072210
20 (1): © Erb*innen von / Heirs of Werner Düttmann. Courtesy Akademie der Künste, Berlin, Werner-Düttmann-Archiv, Nr. 16, Foto 12/15. Photo: Rudolf Kessler
20 (2)(3): © Erb*innen von / Heirs of Werner Düttmann
20–21: © Holger Herschel

Mit dem Alltag beginnen
Begin with the Everyday

26, 27, 30, 31: © Mierle Laderman Ukeles. Courtesy Mierle Laderman Ukeles & Ronald Feldman Gallery, New York
29 oben / above: © Mierle Laderman Ukeles. Courtesy Mierle Laderman Ukeles & Ronald Feldman Gallery, New York. Photo: Marcia Bricker
29 unten / below: © Mierle Laderman Ukeles, Courtesy Mierle Laderman Ukeles & Ronald Feldman Gallery, New York. Photo: Vincent Russo
33–39: © Zara Pfeifer
41: © Edit Collective
43 (1): © Konstruktionserbe und Denkmalpflege, ETH Zürich, Nils Fischer
43 (2): © Konstruktionserbe und Denkmalpflege, ETH Zürich, Helia Jamshidi
43 (3): © Konstruktionserbe und Denkmalpflege, ETH Zürich, Defne Çetinkaya
43 (4): © Konstruktionserbe und Denkmalpflege, ETH Zürich, Eloïse Frey
43 (5): © Konstruktionserbe und Denkmalpflege, ETH Zürich, Nikolaus Berchtold
45–47: © Estate of Michael Wolf

Mit dem Bestand arbeiten
Work with the Existing

51: © Jana Hainbach
53: © Brenne Architekten
54 (l): © Arthur Rüegg, ETH Zürich, 1995
54 (r): © Winfried Brenne
55 (Photos oben / above): © Winfried Brenne
55 (Farbtonkarte / Color tone card): Aus / From: Bruno Taut, *Ein Wohnhaus*, Franckh'sche Verlags-Handlung W. Keller und Co., Stuttgart, 1927
57–59: © THEMA
61, 62 (1)(2): © Fosco Fosco-Oppenheim Vogt Architekten
62 (3): Photo: Matthias Brenner. © Clemens Estreicher, Matthias Brenner, Professur Langenberg, ETH Zürich
62 (4)(5): Photo: Clemens Estreicher. © Clemens Estreicher, Matthias Brenner, Professur Langenberg, ETH Zürich
63 (6)(7): © Matthias Brenner, Konstruktionserbe und Denkmalpflege, ETH Zürich
63 (8)(9)(10)(11): Zeichnung / Drawing: Clemens Estreicher. Supervision: Matthias Brenner. © Clemens Estreicher, Matthias Brenner, Professur Langenberg, ETH Zürich
65–71: Sofern nicht anders benannt / Unless otherwise stated: © Nousaku Tsuneyama
67 (3. Photo von oben / 3rd photo from above, 2. Photo unten / 2nd photo below), 69: © Junpei Suzuki
68 (2. Photo von oben / 2nd photo from above, Mitte / in the middle), 70, 71 (1. Photo oben / 1st image above, 3. Photo unten / 3rd photo below): © Ryogo Utatsu

Wissenswelten dekolonisieren
Decolonize Knowledge Worlds

75 (oben und unten / above and below): Aus dem persönlichen Archiv von Kader Attia / From Kader Attia's personal archive
75 (Mitte / in the middle), 76–77: © Kader Attia. © VG Bild-Kunst, Bonn 2023
79–83: © Bas Princen
85–87: © Emil Grip, Limbo Accra
89 (oben / above): © Manuel Chavajay
89 (unten / below): © Manuel Chavajay, Samuel Cumes
91: Photos: Shannon Tofts. © Royal Botanic Garden Edinburgh
93–95: © Marjetica Potrč. Courtesy Marjetica Potrč & Galerie Nordenhake Berlin, Stockholm, Mexico City
96–97: © Ñambi Rimai

Werkzeuge für alle
Tools to the People

101: Aus / From: *Bauwelt* 39 (1960), S. / p. 1139
102–103: © Atelier Bow-Wow
105–107: © Tsukamoto Lab, Tokyo Institute of Technology
109: Filmmaterial von / Filmed material of *Wheatfield – A Confrontation* von / by Agnes Denes. Courtesy Philip Delbourgo, New York
111–113: © Bas Princen
115: © Hans Hortig
117–119: © autônoma
121: © Yara Bamieh, Takhayali
122–123: © Samah Yehya, Muntaha alKhatib, Razan Alqam, Farida (Um alQarawi), Takhayali
125 (unten / below): Photo: unbekannt / unknown. © VG Bild-Kunst, Bonn 2023
125 (oben / above): © Stefano Mori. © VG Bild-Kunst, Bonn 2023
126–127: © Günter König. © VG Bild-Kunst, Bonn 2023

Die Narben sichtbar lassen
Keep the Scars Visible

131–135: © Center for Spatial Technologies
137: © Mapping Ukraine, ETH Zürich
139, 141 (oben / above): Photo: Iwan Baan. © Manuel Herz Architects
140, 140–141 (unten / below): © Manuel Herz Architects
143–149: © Bas Princen

Praxis reparieren
Repair the Practice

153: © Lacaton & Vassal
157 (oben und unten links / above and on the left below): © New York City Housing Authority. Courtesy La Guardia & Wagner Archives
157 (unten rechts / on the right below), 158–159 (oben / above): © Interboro
158–159 (unten / below): © Coco McPherson
160–161: © Richard A. Chance
163–165 (Zeichnungen / drawings): © ZAS*
163 (unten / below): Photo: Koehli Ernst, 1963. ETH-Bibliothek, Baugeschichtliches Archiv © CC BY-NC 4.0
165 (Photo): © Anne Morgenstern
167: Courtesy Ana Miljački, Critical Broadcasting Lab
169: © UVW-SAW
171 (Photos): © Moritz Heinrich
171 (Zeichnung / drawing): © Professorship of Digital Fabrication, Technical University of Munich
172: © Charlotte Malterre-Barthes

Reparatur praktizieren
Practice Repair

179: © Felix Koch
180–183: © Jess Gough
185: © Baptiste Ansselin, Lan Nishiyama, Manon Voide, Justine Troillet, Moises Sanchez, Marine Freneat
186 (oben / above): © Santiago Mancera, Nanda Nugraha, Théo Gaspar
186 (unten / below): © Anna Maerean, Joshua Adu Darko, Nathan Brichet, Merlin Dubois, Ilian Khan, Tatiana Goundiaeva
187: © Chiara Kempter, François Decurtins
189, 191 (2. und 4. Bild von oben / 2nd and 4th image from above): © University of Luxembourg: Florian Hertweck, Marija Marić / Aristaviva
191 (1. und 3. Bild von oben / 1st and 3rd image from above): © Florian Hertweck
192–193: © University of Luxembourg
195: © Folke Köbberling, Martin Kaltwasser. © VG Bild-Kunst, Bonn 2023

Epilog

196–197: © Collective Works

The Great Repair
Akademie der Künste, Berlin
14.10.2023 – 14.1.2024

Künstlerische Leitung / Artistic direction
ARCH+ (Christian Hiller, Markus Krieger, Alex Nehmer, Anh-Linh Ngo)
in Zusammenarbeit mit / in collaboration with
Florian Hertweck, Department für Geografie und Raumplanung, Universität Luxemburg / Department of Geography and Spatial Planning, University of Luxembourg, Milica Topalović, Department Architektur / Department of Architecture, ETH Zürich
Kuratorische Assistenz / Curatorial assistance
Marija Marić, Universität Luxemburg / University of Luxembourg), Nazlı Tümerdem (ETH Zürich)
Produktionsleitung / Production management
Felix Hofmann
Projektleitung / Project coordination
Christian Hiller
Projektmanagement / Project management
Elke Doppelbauer
Kommunikation / Communications
Barbara Schindler
Geschäftsführung / Managing director
Arno Löbbecke
Team
Nora Dünser, Mirko Gatti, Daniel Kuhnert, Victor Lortie, Mona Rauch, Lea Scherer, Finn Steffens

Projektumsetzung / Project realization
Akademie der Künste
Leitung / Direction
Johanna M. Keller
Projektkoordination / Project coordination
Meike Avner, Anja-Christin Remmert
Künstlerisch-technische Leitung / Exhibition design
Roswitha Kötz
Assistenz Koordination / Exhibition assistance
Mauve Weinzierl
Medienplanung / Media and lighting
Akademie der Künste
Medientechnik / Media technology
Act!worX
Leihverkehr / Registrars
Catherine Amé, Dalila Daut
Restauratorische Betreuung / Conservator
Jessica Schreiber
Holzwerkstatt / Woodwork
Paul Walter, Jörg Scheil
Papierwerkstatt / Paperwork and framing
Isabel Schlenther
Ausstellungsbau und Arthandling / Set up and art handling
mount berlin
Grafikproduktion und Montage / Graphic production and mounting
Villa Schmück Dich
KUNSTWELTEN – Kulturelle Vermittlung / Education program
Marion Neumann, Martina Krafczyk (Inklusionsbeauftragte / Inclusion officer), Miriam Papastefanou
Baukunstarchiv
Amrei Buchholz

Grafische Gestaltung / Graphic design
Stan Hema
Ausstellungsbanner / Exhibition banners
Collective Works (Karin Mientjes & Peter Zuiderwijk)
Tragwerksberatung / Structural engineering consultant
Schlaich Bergermann Partner
Key visuals
Bas Princen, Djenné Mosque, 2010
© Bas Princen
Webseite / Website
Selcuk C. Alan

Mit Unterstützung der Teams des Lehrstuhls für Architektur und Territorialplanung / Architecture of Territory, ETH Zürich, und des Lehrstuhls für Architektur, Universität Luxemburg / With the support of the teams of the Chair for Architecture and Territorial Planning / Architecture of Territory, ETH Zürich, and the Chair for Architecture, University of Luxembourg

Eröffnungsprogramm in Kooperation mit / Opening program in cooperation with
Performing Architecture, Goethe-Institut
FORWARD DANCE COMPANY von LOFFT – DAS THEATER
Alessandro Schiattarella

Workshopprogramm in Kooperation mit / Workshop program in cooperation with
KUNSTWELTEN
Haus der Materialisierung – Zentrum für klimaschonende Ressourcennutzung, Teil des Modellprojekts Haus der Statistik am Alexanderplatz, Berlin
NochMall – Das Gebrauchtwarenkaufhaus der BSR
S27 – Kunst und Bildung, Verein zur Förderung der Interkulturellen Jugendarbeit e. V.

Danksagung / Acknowledgement
Allen Autor*innen, Künstler*innen und Beteiligten danken wir sehr herzlich für ihren Beitrag zum Projekt. Darüber hinaus sind wir folgenden Personen und Institutionen für die Unterstützung des Projekts zu besonderem Dank verpflichtet / We would like to thank all authors, artists, and participants for their contribution to the project. In addition, we are especially indebted to the following individuals and institutions for their support of the project:
Akademie der Künste
Johanna M. Keller, Alexander Heymann, Johannes Odenthal
Atelier Bow-Wow
Momoyo Kaijima, Yoshiharu Tsukamoto, Saori Toyoshima
Bauhaus Earth
Matthias von Ballestrem, Philipp Misselwitz
Brenne Architekten
Winfried Brenne, Fabian Brenne, Jana Hainbach
FORWARD DANCE COMPANY von LOFFT – DAS THEATER
Gustavo Fijalkow
Alessandro Schiattarella
Goethe-Institut
Joachim Bernauer, Eva Schmitt
Haus für Poesie
Katharina Schultens
ifa – Institut für Auslandsbeziehungen
Schlaich Bergermann Partner
Mike Schlaich, Stephan Arendt

The Great Repair

ist ein Projekt der / is a project by
ARCH+ gGmbH

in Kooperation mit / in collaboration with
AKADEMIE DER KÜNSTE
ETH zürich | D ARCH
uni.lu | FACULTY OF HUMANITIES, EDUCATION AND SOCIAL SCIENCES

Gefördert durch die / Funded by the German Federal Cultural Foundation
KULTURSTIFTUNG DES BUNDES

Gefördert von / Funded by the Federal Government Commissioner for Culture and the Media
Die Beauftragte der Bundesregierung für Kultur und Medien

Das Workshopprogramm ist gefördert von / The Great Repair workshop program is funded by the Federal Agency for Civic Education
bpb: Bundeszentrale für politische Bildung

Weitere Förderer und Kooperationspartner / Additional support from
WÜSTENROT STIFTUNG
Hans Sauer Stiftung
PERFORMING ARCHITECTURE | GOETHE INSTITUT
FDC FORWARD DANCE COMPANY BY LOFFT
schweizer kulturstiftung prohelvetia
Kultur | lx Arts Council Luxembourg
GROSSHERZOGTUM LUXEMBURG Botschaft in Deutschland

Das Experimental Stipendienprogramm für junge Architekturforschende wird gefördert durch / The Experimental Scholarship Program for young architectural researchers is funded by
EXPERIMENTAL

PUBLIKATION / PUBLICATION
The Great Repair – Praktiken der Reparatur / A Catalog of Practices erscheint anlässlich der Ausstellung *The Great Repair* in der Akademie der Künste, Berlin / is published on the occasion of the exhibition *The Great Repair* at Akademie der Künste, Berlin.

ARCH+
Zeitschrift für Architektur und Urbanismus / Journal for Architecture and Urbanism
56. Jahrgang / September 2023

Herausgeber / Publishers
ARCH+ / Spector Books

Herausgeber ARCH+ / ARCH+ publishers
Nikolaus Kuhnert, Anh-Linh Ngo

Beirat / Advisory board
Arno Brandlhuber, Beatriz Colomina, Philipp Oswalt, Stephan Trüby, Georg Vrachliotis, Mark Wigley, Karin Wilhelm

Redaktionsleitung / Editor-in-chief
Anh-Linh Ngo* (V.i.S.d.P.)

Geschäftsführung / Managing director
Arno Löbbecke

Redaktion / Editorial team
Nora Dünser*, Mirko Gatti*, Christian Hiller*, Felix Hofmann*, Sascha Kellermann, Markus Krieger*, Victor Lortie, Melissa Makele, Alex Nehmer* (Projektleitung / project lead)

Gastredakteur*innen / Guest editors
Florian Hertweck, Milica Topalović

Gastredaktion / Guest editorial team
Santiago del Hierro, Marija Marić (Projektleitung Universität Luxemburg / project lead University of Luxembourg), Nazlı Tümerdem (Projektleitung / project lead ETH Zürich)

ETH Zürich D-ARCH
Lehrstuhl für Architektur und Territorialplanung / Chair for Architecture and Territorial Planning / Architecture of Territory

Universität Luxemburg / University of Luxembourg
Department für Geografie und Raumplanung / Department of Geography and Spatial Planning

CvD/Schlussredaktion / Managing editor
Nora Dünser*

Redaktionelle Mitarbeit / Editorial assistants
Daniel Kuhnert*, Finn Steffens*

Experimental-Stipendiatinnen / Experimental Scholarship
Mona Rauch*, Lea Scherer*

* Redaktionsgruppe dieser Ausgabe / Editorial team for this publication

Art direction
Stan Hema, Berlin

Design
Sara Božić, André van Rueth

Reinzeichnung / Final typesetting
Daniel Vandré

Projektmanagement Stan Hema / Project manager for Stan Hema
Niki Moreira

Deutsches Lektorat / German copyediting
Kirsten Thietz

Englisches Lektorat / English copyediting
Alisa Kotmair (S. / pp. 1–4, 18–21, 24–31, 40–55, 60–71, 78–83, 88–89, 116–119, 124–127, 138–149, 152–155, 162–167, 172–175, 188–195, 198–213)
Jeremy Gaines (S. / pp. 22–23, 32–39, 56–59, 72–77, 84–87, 90–95, ARCH+ features, 98–115, 120–123, 128–137, 150–151, 156–161, 168–171, 176–187)

Übersetzungen / Translations
GER–EN: Petra + Jeremy Gaines (S. / pp. 48–49, 176–177), Alisa Kotmair (S. / pp. 40–41), Rob Madole (S. / pp. 1–4, 18–21, 44–47, 50–55, 64–71, 88–89, 116–119, 124–127, 142–149, 152–153, 166–167, 172–175, 188–195, 198–208), Katharina Schultens (S. / pp. 209)
EN–GER: Petra + Jeremy Gaines (S. / pp. 22–23, 32–39, 56–59, 72–77, 84–87, 90–95, ARCH+ features, 98–115, 120–123, 128–137, 150–151, 156–161, 168–171, 176–187)
FR–EN: Victor Lortie (S. / pp. 154–155)

Satzkorrektur Deutsch / German proofreading
Sara Lusic-Alavanja

Satzkorrektur Englisch / English proofreading
James Copeland

Leitung Ausstellungs-/ Forschungsprojekte / Head of research and exhibition projects
Christian Hiller

Leitung Öffentlichkeitsarbeit/Marketing / Head of communications and marketing
Barbara Schindler

Organisation / Operations
Elke Doppelbauer

Leitung Veranstaltungsprogramm / Head of events
Sascha Kellermann

Verlagsassistenz / Publishing assistant
Friederike Kiko

Botschafter*innen / Ambassadors
Martin Luce, Christine Rüb

Lithografie / Prepress
maxcolor, Berlin

Druck / Printing
Medialis Offsetdruck GmbH, Berlin

Bildnachweis / Image credits
ARCH+ hat sich bis Produktionsschluss bemüht, alle Rechteinhaber ausfindig zu machen. Personen und Institutionen, die möglicherweise Rechte an verwendeten Abbildungen beanspruchen, werden gebeten, sich mit der Redaktion in Verbindung zu setzen. /
ARCH+ has made every effort to notify all copyright holders. Any person or institution wishing to make a copyright claim is requested to contact the editors.

ARCH+ features
Initiativpartner / Initiating partner

SSS SIEDLE

Anzeigen / Advertising
marketing@archplus.net
archplus.net/de/mediadaten
archplus.net/en/mediakit

ARCH+ Verlag GmbH
Friedrichstraße 23a
10969 Berlin
Tel +49 30 340 467 17
verlag@archplus.net
Geschäftsführung / Managing directors:
Nikolaus Kuhnert, Anh-Linh Ngo

ARCH+ gGmbH (nonprofit limited liability company)
ggmbh@archplus.net
Geschäftsführung / Managing director:
Arno Löbbecke

Spendenkonto / Donation account
GLS Bank
IBAN: DE47 4306 0967 1229 2768 01
BIC: GENODEM1GLS
archplus.net/nonprofit

Deutscher Vertrieb / National distribution
ARCH+ Leserservice
PressUp GmbH
Postfach 70 13 11
22013 Hamburg
archplus@pressup.de
Tel +49 40 386 666 355
Fax +49 40 386 666 299

Abonnement / Subscriptions (German issues only)
Regulär Inland € 85 / Ausland € 95
Förder Inland € 115 / Ausland € 135
Ermäßigt Inland € 62 / Ausland € 72
(für Studierende, Absolvent*innen)
Digital-Abo € 82
Digital-Upgrade € 20
archplus.net/abo

Einzelbestellung / Direct orders
vertrieb@archplus.net
archplus.net/shop

Internationaler Vertrieb / International distribution
Spector Books
Harkortstraße 10
04107 Leipzig
www.spectorbooks.com
Österreich / Austria:
GVA, Gemeinsame Verlagsauslieferung Göttingen GmbH & Co. KG, www.gva-verlage.de
Schweiz / Switzerland:
AVA Verlagsauslieferung AG, www.ava.ch
Frankreich, Belgien / France, Belgium:
Interart Paris, www.interart.fr
Großbritannien / UK:
Central Books Ltd, www.centralbooks.com
USA, Kanada, Zentral- und Südamerika, Afrika / USA, Canada, Central and South America, Africa:
ARTBOOK/D.A.P., www.artbook.com
Südkorea / South Korea:
The Book Society, www.thebooksociety.org
Japan:
twelvebooks, www.twelve-books.com
Australien, Neuseeland / Australia, New Zealand:
Perimeter Distribution, www.perimeterdistribution.com

ISBN 978-3-931435-80-6 (ARCH+)
ISBN 978-3-95905-788-2 (Spector Books)

Erstauflage / First edition: 2023
In Deutschland gedruckt / Printed in Germany